Dramas

*Available from the Simms Initiatives and the
University of South Carolina Press*

The Army Correspondence of
Colonel John Laurens, ed.

As Good as a Comedy
and Paddy McGann

Beauchampe

Border Beagles

Carl Werner, 2 vols.

The Cassique of Kiawah

Castle Dismal

Charlemont

The Charleston Book, ed.

Confession

Count Julian

The Damsel of Darien, 2 vols.

Dramas: Norman Maurice, Michael
Bonham, and Benedict Arnold

Egeria

Eutaw

The Forayers

The Geography of South Carolina

The Golden Christmas

Guy Rivers

Helen Halsey

Historical and Political Poems (*which
includes* Monody, The Vision of Cortes,
The Tri-Color, Donna Florida, and
Charleston and Her Satirists)

The History of South Carolina

Joscelyn

Katherine Walton

The Letters of
William Gilmore Simms, Vol. 1

The Letters of
William Gilmore Simms, Vol. 2

The Letters of
William Gilmore Simms, Vol. 3

The Letters of
William Gilmore Simms, Vol. 4

The Letters of
William Gilmore Simms, Vol. 5

The Letters of
William Gilmore Simms, Vol. 6 (exp. ed.)

The Life of Captain John Smith

The Life of the Chevalier Bayard

The Life of Francis Marion

The Lily and the Totem

Marie de Berniere

Martin Faber and
Other Tales, 2 vols.

Mellichampe

The Partisan

Pelayo, 2 vols.

Poems, Descriptive, Dramatic,
Legendary, and Contemplative, 2 vols.

The Remains of
Maynard Davis Richardson

Richard Hurdis

Sack and Destruction of
the City of Columbia

The Scout

Selections from the
Letters and Speeches of the
Hon. James H. Hammond, ed.

Simms's Poems Areytos

Social and Political Prose:
Slavery in America/Father Abbot

South Carolina in the
Revolutionary War

Southward Ho!

Stories and Tales

A Supplement to the Plays
of William Shakespeare

Vasconselos

Views and Reviews in
American Literature,
History and Fiction, 2 vols.

Voltmeier

War Poetry of the South

The Wigwam and the Cabin

Woodcraft

The Yemassee

Dramas

Norman Maurice, Michael Bonham,
and Benedict Arnold

William Gilmore Simms

Critical Introduction by Abigail Lundelius Smith
With a Biographical Overview by David Moltke-Hansen

The University of South Carolina Press

New material © 2016 University of South Carolina

Cloth original of *Norman Maurice* published by Walker and Richards, 1852
Board original of *Michael Bonham* published by Jno. R. Thompson, 1852
Serial original of *Benedict Arnold* published in the Richmond *Magnolia Weekly*, 1863
Paperback published by the University of South Carolina Press
Columbia, South Carolina 29208

www.sc.edu/uscpress

Manufactured in the United States of America

25 24 23 22 21 20 19 18 17 16
10 9 8 7 6 5 4 3 2 1

ISBN 978-1-61117-686-5 (pbk)

Published in cooperation with the Simms Initiatives, a project of the University of South Carolina Libraries with the generous support of the Watson-Brown Foundation, and with additional funding by the John Govan Simms Endowment.

William Gilmore Simms: A Biographical Overview

David Moltke-Hansen

Introduction

Harper's Weekly put it succinctly in its July 2, 1870, issue: "In the death of Mr. Simms, on the 11th of June, at Charleston, the country has lost one more of its time-honored band of authors, and the South the most consistent and devoted of her literary sons" (qtd. In Butterworth and Kibler 125–26). Indeed no mid-nineteenth-century writer and editor did more than William Gilmore Simms to frame white southern self-identity and nationalism, shape southern historical consciousness, or foster the South's participation and recognition in the broader American literary culture. No southern writer enjoyed more contemporary esteem and attention, at least after Edgar Allan Poe moved north. Among American romancers (or writers of prose epics), only New Yorker James Fenimore Cooper was as successful by the 1840s. In those same years, Simms was the South's most influential editor of cultural journals. He also was the region's most prolific cultural journalist and poet, publishing an average of one book review and one poem per week for forty-five years.

Before his death Simms saw his national reputation fall along with the Confederacy he had vigorously supported and with the slave regime that many in the North had come to despise. Nevertheless reprints of most of the twenty titles in the selected edition of his works, first published between 1853 and 1860, appeared up until World War I. Thereafter only *The Yemassee*, an early romance about an Indian war in South Carolina, continued in print. The tide began to turn in the 1950s, when five volumes of Simms's letters appeared and a growing number of his works were issued in new editions. Publication in 1992 of the first literary biography, by John C. Guilds, and establishment of the William Gilmore Simms Society and the *Simms Review* the next year at once reflected and fostered this revived interest. Yet not until the 2011 launch of the digital Simms edition of the South Caroliniana Library of the University of South Carolina did scholars of southern, American, and nineteenth-century culture have the prospect of ready access to all of Simms's separately published works. With the University of South Carolina Press's cooperation, readers also will have access to sixty works in paperback editions by the end of 2014. Simms himself never saw nearly so many of his works in print at one time.

Clearly the decline in the critical standing of, and historical attention to, Simms and his oeuvre in the century after his death has reversed in the years since. The last three decades of the twentieth century saw more published on Simms than the previous hundred years (Butterworth and Kibler 126–200; MLA International). The last decade of the twentieth and first decade of the twenty-first centuries saw more dissertations and theses on him (forty-one) than had appeared in all the years before. This is not to say that Simms is yet given the attention directed to some of his contemporaries. For the first decade of the twenty-first century, the Modern Language Association International Bibliography lists roughly four times as many scholarly publications on James Fenimore Cooper, more than ten times as many on Nathaniel Hawthorne, and sixteen times as many on Edgar Allan Poe. Not surprisingly, therefore, Simms is not yet included in most anthologies of American literature, although he is a subject or a source in an expanding and ever more diverse body of scholarship.

To prepare to read Simms, it is important to see his writings in multiple contexts. He rarely wrote about himself outside of his more personal poems and his letters (some fifteen hundred of the many thousands of which survive). Yet he systematically drew on his background, personal experience, and relationships in his work. He also shaped that work through a progressively developed poetics and philosophy of life, history, and art. He did so in the context of his very broad reading of both contemporary and earlier Western literature and in the midst of multiple professional engagements and responsibilities. The richness and variety of these writings and involvements make Simms a key figure for future understanding of the literary culture, issues, and networks in mid-nineteenth-century America.

Background

Simms's family history reflected the dynamics that fueled the spread southward and westward of the populations, plantation economy, and society of the South Atlantic states. Simms's ancestry also reflected the Scots-Irish and English roots of what became identified as southern culture by the 1830s, a generation after the end of most immigration to the region. Two of Simms's grandparents, William and Elisabeth Sims, were Scots-Irish and migrated to South Carolina from Ulster. One, John Singleton, was an American-born son of putatively English immigrants, who had come to South Carolina from Virginia. The fourth, Jane Miller, was daughter of two Scots-Irish and Irish descended people—John Miller, of North and then South Carolina, and Jane Ross. Ross's family also migrated to South Carolina from western Virginia, where members lived cheek by jowl with other Scots-Irish families, who migrated to the Carolinas (White, *Ross*). Simms's father and Uncle James migrated in 1808 from Charleston to Tennessee, then to Mississippi. This was after the bankruptcy of the elder William's business and the deaths of his wife and their other two sons. Following the last of these losses, the elder Simms's hair turned white in a week. To his anguished eyes, Charleston appeared "a place of tombs" (qtd. in Guilds 6, 12).

For the son, however, Charleston was home—so much so that he refused to leave his maternal grandmother and move to Mississippi when his uncle came to get him in 1816. Then the fifth largest and by far the wealthiest city, as well as one of the greatest ports, in America, Charleston was at the peak of its influence (Moltke-Hansen, "Expansion" 25-31; Rogers). Cotton culture on the sea islands to the south, begun in 1790, and rice culture in impounded lowcountry tidal marshes meant that the port was filled not only with sailors of many lands and languages, but also with enslaved people of many African and Creole cultures and speech ways (slaves continued to be imported legally in large numbers until 1808). This street life made vivid the transnational nature of plantation agriculture and the fact that the developing region's dramatically expanding borders "were not just geographic; they also were human, historical, and intellectual" (Moltke-Hansen, "Southern" 19).

Even more important for the future author, the expanding region's borders and nature were taking imaginative shape. The West of the senior William Gilmore Simms and the first Creek War in which he fought, the Revolutionary War of the young Simms's maternal grandfather, the backcountry of many related Scots-Irish settlers, all these became grist for a lonely, energetic boy, who spent as much time with books as he could (Simms, *Letters* 1:161). The possibilities of such settings, incidents, and characters were not confined to history alone. Simms reported that he "used to glow and shiver in turn over 'The Pilgrim's Progress,'" while "Moses' adventures in 'The Vicar of Wakefield' threw [him] into paroxysms of laughter" (Hayne 261-62). Sir Walter Scott's Border and medieval romances and James Fenimore Cooper's Leatherstocking tales also deeply colored his imagination (Simms, *Views* 1:248, and Moltke-Hansen, "Southern" 6-15). As affecting were the ghost stories and Revolutionary War tales of his grandmother and the verses sent, and tales told, by his father.

These diverse tales became reasons to explore—in books, but also on the ground. As a boy, Simms ranged through the city and along the banks of the Ashley River, which fed into Charleston Harbor. He did so in search of scenes of colonial and Revolutionary battles and incidents (*Letters* 1:lxii). He first heard his uncle's and father's many Irish and frontier stories when they visited in Charleston in 1816 and 1818, respectively. He heard more on his trips to Mississippi during the winter of 1824 through the spring of 1825 and again in 1826. The first trip took him through Georgia and Alabama, where he saw elements of the Creek and Cherokee nations. At the time, Simms later reported, he was a boy "cumbered with fragmentary materials of thought, . . . choked by the tangled vines of erroneous speculation, and haunted by passions, which, like so many wolves, lurked, in ready waiting, for their unsuspecting prey" (*Social* 6). When he first got to Mississippi, traveling partly by stage, partly by riverboat, and partly by horse, Simms learned that his father had just come back from "a trip of three hundred miles into the heart of the Indian country" (Trent 15). Later father and son "rode together on horseback to various settlements on the frontier of Alabama and Mississippi" (Guilds 10-11, 17-18). Simms recalled as well "having traveled 150 miles beyond the Mississippi" (Shillingsburg, "Literary Grist" 120). The next year he returned to the Southwest by ship. "During this [second] trip he carried a 'note book.'" There he jotted episodes, encounters, stories heard, characters seen, and descriptions of the landscapes unfolding around him. He also wrote "at least sixteen poems" (Kibler, "First"; Shillingsburg, "Literary Grist" 123).

Simms took a third western trip five years later, writing letters back to the newspaper that by then he was editing (*Letters* 1:10-38). Together these three trips provided materials for his writings over more than forty years. "The first . . . produced mainly short fiction; the second inspired much poetry; . . . the first and third . . . yielded three novels written in the 1830s" (Shillingsburg, "Literary Grist" 119). This was, in part, because of the trips' timing. Sixteen years after the first trip, Simms told students at the University of Alabama that in the interval their world had changed from a howling wilderness into a place of growing civilization (Simms, *Social* 5-6). Had he not gone when he did, he would have been too late to see the frontier. Later travels took him many other places and also provided much grist for his writing. Never again, however, did he experience the frontier firsthand. Furthermore, on these later trips Simms was a practiced professional writer, no longer that boy haunted by passions.

Personal Life

After the ten-year-old boy's momentous refusal to leave Charleston, his grandmother sent Simms for two years to the grammar school taught on the campus and by the faculty of the nearly moribund College of Charleston. By then he already was "versifying the events of the war [of 1812]," just concluded, publishing "doggerel" in the local papers, and learning to read in several languages (*Letters* 1:285). His trip west a decade later helped him decide to pursue both literature and a career in law, but back in Charleston—this despite his father's urging that he stay in Mississippi. Upon his return home, he began to read law and also launched a literary weekly, the *Album*, which ran for a year. He became engaged as well to Anna Malcolm Giles, daughter of a grocer and former state coroner.

A year later the young couple married. This was six months before Simms was admitted to the South Carolina bar, on his twenty-first birthday, not long before he was appointed as a city magistrate. Although living up the Ashley River in the more healthful, less expensive village of Summerville, Simms kept a law office in the city. Shortly after using his maternal inheritance to buy the *City Gazette* at the end of 1829 and moving down to Charleston Neck, just north of the city limits where he had lived as a boy, Simms lost both his father and his maternal grandmother. He also found himself attacked because of his Unionist stance in the Nullification crisis resulting from South Carolina's rejection of a federal tariff. Then, in early 1832, Simms's wife died. Soon after, he took his four-year-old daughter back to Summerville to live and determined to sell his newspaper and leave the state for a literary life in the North.

Fueling his ambition was the correspondence Simms had begun several years earlier with an accountant whom he had published in his *City Gazette* but not yet met—Scots immigrant James Lawson. At the time Lawson, seven years Simms's senior, edited a New York City newspaper and, in addition to writing plays and poetry, was a friend (and, later, informal literary agent) to a wide circle (McHaney, "An Early"). Simms's trip north in the summer of 1832 saw the two begin a lifelong friendship, cemented as they squired ladies about and interacted with Lawson's literary circle. In subsequent years Simms multiplied the number of his friendships, in both the North and the South, making them in some measure a replacement for the family that he had lost. Lawson remained the closest of his northern friends, while James Henry Hammond, a future governor and U.S. senator, became his closest friend in South Carolina.

Late in 1833, after his Summerville house burned, Simms wrote Lawson to say that he was enamored of "a certain fair one" (*Letters* 1:73). Seventeen-year-old Chevillette Eliza Roach was the daughter of "a literary-minded aristocrat of English descent" with two plantations on the banks of the Edisto River in Barnwell District (later County) (Guilds 70). The courtship was protracted, as Simms felt it necessary first to clear debts that friends had bought up on his behalf. He also was determined "to marry no woman" before he was "perfectly independent of her resources, and her friends" (*Letters* 1:78). Therefore he did not propose until the spring of 1836. The nuptials took place seven months later, and as a result, Simms came to call the four thousand acres of Woodlands Plantation, with its seventy slaves, home. It was twenty years, however, before he took over management of the plantation and, then, only in the wake of his father-in-law's final sickness and death. Five years after that, he lost his wife, the mother of fourteen of his fifteen children. Nine of the children Chevillette bore him had already died, devastating Simms repeatedly. Five were still living (three sons and two daughters), as was Simms's daughter by his first marriage, who helped raise the youngest of her siblings. Those remaining children—even Gilly, who fought in the Confederate army—all outlived their father. Gilly and a brother-in-law ran Woodlands after the war, when Simms, though dying of cancer, was earning what he could by writing again for publications in the North and editing one or another South Carolina newspaper.

Career

The trip north in 1832 did not result in Simms moving there. Except during the Civil War, however, he returned almost every year. This was because the contacts he made, and the exposure to literary culture that he enjoyed, helped him define his future as an author. Earlier he had written fiction and criticism as well as journalism, filling the pages of several short-lived cultural journals and his newspaper, but between the ages of nine and twenty-six Simms had focused his literary efforts primarily on poetry. Beginning with his first book of verse in 1825, he had published five small volumes in Charleston. A couple had received positive notice in New York, and in the fall of 1832, J. & J. Harper issued the sixth anonymously from there, *Atalantis: A Story of the Sea*. Coming back the following summer, Simms had in hand for the Harpers a gothic novella, *Martin Faber*, and after his return south, he also would send the manuscript of his first two-volume border romance, *Guy Rivers: A Tale of Georgia*.

The reception of these and the romances and short stories that followed quickly made Simms one of the nation's most successful fictionists. He continued to issue poetry as well—roughly a collection every three years over the thirty-seven years that he worked as a professional author. But this output was dwarfed by the fiction—on average a title every year (counting several serialized works but not counting the many revised editions). Then there were the two dozen separately published orations, histories, and biographies as well as edited collections of documents and dramas and a geography of South Carolina. Add to these the revised editions and the further printings and issues of his own works and it appears that Simms saw a title coming off the presses at the rate of one every three months or so. Making that figure all the more astounding is the fact that, during more than a dozen of those years (the early-to-mid 1840s, the late 1840s-to-early 1850s, and the mid-to-late 1860s), he also was editing a cultural journal or newspaper. Furthermore he contributed reams of reviews and poems, hundreds of op-ed pieces and columns, and dozens of short stories and public addresses, which were never collected and published in volume form.

His career mapped an arc. It ascended meteorically in the 1830s and peaked in the early-to-mid 1840s, before beginning to descend. One reason was the popularity of the historical fiction that Simms began to write. When he left behind the law, his first newspaper, and the Nullification controversy, as well as his sadness, historical fiction was all the rage. Sir Walter Scott had fueled the craze, beginning with the publication of his first Border romance in 1814. He died in September 1832. Seventeen years Simms's senior, James Fenimore Cooper, the closest America had to a Scott at the time, was at the peak of his reputation and success, having started publishing his romances in 1820. Thus the way had been prepared for a writer of Simms's historical imagination and preoccupations. Within five years of his first trip north, moreover, Lawson's (and now his) circle became loosely affiliated with a nationalistic and Democratic group, self-styled Young America, this after Young Italy and similar ethnic, nationalist, European, cultural and political movements (Moltke-Hansen, "Southern"). Edgar Allan Poe and other members gave Simms's first fictions positive, if not uncritical, attention.

By the end of the 1830s, paradoxically, Simms, like Cooper, found his success attracting unauthorized editions of his works because Britain and America did not have an international copyright agreement. Further, in the wake of the panic of 1837, Americans bought fewer books. Simms's response was to diversify his portfolio. He turned to biography and history, including his hugely successful *Life of Francis Marion* (1844). He also returned to the editor's chair, overseeing one and then another cultural journal. These were unlike the ones he had edited in the 1820s: they included contributions by numerous authors, not just those from Charleston, but from the region and also the North. The ambition motivating the journals was to connect and promote Charleston intellectually. Consequently the journals more closely resembled metropolitan quarterly reviews in their offerings.

The mid-1840s saw Simms involved in politics, even serving a term in the South Carolina legislature. By the middle of the Mexican-American War in 1847, he had concluded that the South needed to become an independent nation. Thereafter, although he maintained ties with many in the Young America circle, he no longer promoted his writings as fostering Americanism in literature (*Views*). Instead he increasingly emphasized the ways in which his three romance series — the colonial, the Revolutionary, and the border — were making tangible and meaningful the origins and development of the future southern nation and the sad but inevitable consequences for Native Americans (Watson, *From Nationalism*; compare Nakamura).

Sectional politics colored more and more of Simms's perceptions, speeches, and private communications. The rising tide of abolitionism had him aghast. It also fed his growing sense that his position in American letters was slipping. He returned to editing, and his poetry, which was more often explicitly about the South, became increasingly patriotic in tone. Although his first biographer, William Peterfield Trent, insisted that Simms's declining standing reflected the change in literary fashion from historical romances to realistic novels, Simms in fact wrote more and more as a social realist in the 1850s (Wimsatt, "Realism").

The Civil War consumed Simms. As he wrote Lawson, "Literature, especially poetry, is effectually overwhelmed by the drums, & the cavalry, and the shouting" (*Letters* 4:369–70). He did manage to editorialize often and to rework and finish things long on his desk, including poems, a novel, and a dramatic treatment of Benedict Arnold, the northern traitor in the Revolutionary War. Then, in the wake of the Confederacy's loss and the failure of his vision for the South, he found himself recording the loss in a new newspaper, dealing with the trauma in his poetry, and becoming more existential and psychological in his fictional treatments. Simms's old New York friends tried to help. He did edit and see through publication a volume of Confederate war poetry. Yet it is a measure of his reduced stature that the several new romances he published appeared only in serial form. In part this may have been because he was in a sense competing with himself. Publishers were beginning to reprint volumes out of the selected edition of his writings. Many of Simms's works were available in book form, just not new works.

Associations

As the *Letters* testify, Simms had complex, overlapping networks of friends and colleagues. As a boy and young man, he received the friendship, patronage, and commendation of a variety of well-placed people in Charleston, including Charles Rivers Carroll. It was Carroll with whom he read law, to whom he dedicated his first romance, and after whom he named a son. Both men were Unionists during the Nullification controversy. So were Hugh Swinton Legare (later U.S. attorney general) and the considerably older William Drayton, as well as lawyer and editor Richard Yeadon and Greenville, South Carolina, newspaper editor Benjamin Franklin Perry. Also considerably older was James Wright Simmons, who had joined with Simms to launch the *Southern Literary Gazette* in 1828, when Simms was twenty-two. Through him Simms had direct contact with such British literary figures as Leigh Hunt and Byron (Kibler, *Poetry* 15).

The next group of influential friends and collaborators that Simms acquired were members of the Lawson circle and included such figures as Edwin

Forrest, the Shakespearean actor, and Evert Duyckinck, who published several of Simms's volumes in Wiley and Putnam's series Library of American Books, which he edited. Among the many others were poets and editors William Cullen Bryant and Fitz-Greene Halleck. Simms also made nonliterary friends in New York and Philadelphia, such as John Jacob Bockee and William Hawkins Ferris, the cashier at the U.S. Treasury office in New York who, after the war, helped Simms, Henry Timrod (poet laureate of the Confederacy), and others.

As a Barnwell planter, Simms met a widening circle of South Carolina's leaders and literati. For instance his acquaintance with James Henry Hammond began in the late 1830s and deepened into a friendship in the early 1840s. It was in the early 1840s, too, when he again was editing cultural journals, that Simms became friends with many southern writers. He regarded several of them, including Virginians George Frederick Holmes, Edmund Ruffin, and Nathaniel Beverley Tucker as members, together with Hammond and himself, in a "sacred circle." Uniting the circle were members' devotion to the South and a shared sense of the marginal status and critical importance of the life of the mind in a largely rural and unintellectual region (Faust, *Sacred*). Others of Simms's wide connections in the region did not interact as much with each other, but Simms long corresponded with Maryland novelist and lawyer John Pendleton Kennedy, Irish-born Georgia poet Richard Henry Wilde, Alabama lawyer and writer Alexander Beaufort Meek, and Louisiana historian and assistant attorney general Charles Gayarré, among others. By the 1850s, when Simms once more returned to editing a cultural journal, many of the writers whom he recruited were members of a younger generation. Poets Paul Hamilton Hayne and Henry Timrod were two. Often they and a half dozen others of Simms's and their generations met in John Russell's Charleston Book Shop and adjourned to dinner at Simms's Smith Street home, "dubbed 'The Wigwam'" (*Letters* 1:cxxxvi). Shortly before his death fifteen or so years later, Simms wrote Hayne, "I am rapidly passing from the stage, where you young men are to succeed me" (*Letters* 5:287).

Thought

The welter of Simms's works disguises unities and dynamics of the thought underlying them. From early on Simms was convinced that art ennobles or transforms, as well as gives voice to individuals and societies; therefore it must be cultivated assiduously. Without the potential for high artistic attainment, he insisted, societies are not ready for the independence and regard of free peoples. This is where Simms the historian joined Simms the poet. Societies develop, he argued (using the stadialism of the Scottish historical school), from imitation through self-assertion to achievement and also from savagery through strife to settled agricultural communities and, ultimately, to a hierarchical civilization supporting a rich artistic life. It was the job of the artist to help envision the goal, inspire the pursuit, and inform the process. That process was at once progressive and dialectical. Order, without dynamism, stifled development, as did the obverse—the dominance by ungoverned impulses or uncontrolled license. This was true in the individual, but also in societies as a whole. War was necessary for civilization, but its success was measured in the securities of the home, the center of cultural production and reproduction.

Whether in the public or in the domestic arena, "the true governor, as [Thomas] Carlyle call[ed] him—the king man—" guided rather than impeded the forces of change and progress (Simms, "Guizot's" 122). There were few such men with the capacity to lead. The same was true of nations. Neither all people nor all peoples were equal in either capacity or attainment. That was why Native Americans were overrun and Africans had been enslaved by European peoples in the New World. Indeed, Simms argued, "slavery in all ages has been found the greatest and most admirable agent of Civilization," giving education and examples to less evolved peoples (*Letters* 3:174). The degree to which a people had evolved mattered. That was why, he held, Americans had won independence from the most powerful empire in the world. They had done so through their Revolution, led by an elite that felt correctly its time had come (Simms, "Ellet's" 328). By mid-1847 that also was Simms's judgment for the South: the region had evolved enough to become independent (*Letters* 2:332). The hope inspired and then failed him and the people he sought to lead.

While not all men could rise to the highest rank, they all had the same responsibility at home. There the father was patriarch, protector, and head, while the mother was nurturer, moral instructor, and heart. There, too, children's characters and minds were formed by age twelve ("Ellet's"). Children's upbringing was critical to citizenship, and it was through her sons and the support of her husband, father, and brothers that a woman shaped the public sphere. The culture and character instilled in the child expressed and informed not just the household, but the larger society—the people.

"The history of peoples and their embodiments in institutions, states, and artistic productions—these were the great subjects" in Simms's view (Moltke-Hansen, "Southern" 120). Yet "poets were the only class of philosophers who had recognized" this until his own day, when at last "we now read human histories. We now ask after the affections as well as the ceremonies of society" ("Ellet's" 319-20). Peoples or races—that is, ethnic groups—were not unchanging any more than were their politics and their cultures. They either advanced or were overrun by history. Further, new peoples emerged, and old identities were submerged. The Spanish conquistadors were the creation of centuries of conflict with the Moors: their motivation was the glory of conquest, not the routine of trade or the plow. On the other hand, the English settlements in North America reflected the impulse to transform the wilderness into verdant farms and build society (*Views* 64, 178-85; *Social* 8). The same impulse drove Americans westward in Simms's own day and gave Americans their Manifest Destiny.

To explore these facts of the South's settlement and its place in international conflicts, Simms wrote all together, between 1833 and 1863, two romances set in eighth-century Spain, two set during the Spanish exploration and conquest of the Americas and two during the later English colonization of South Carolina, seven set during the American Revolution, and—depending on how one counts—perhaps eight set on the borders of the nineteenth-century South. After the war he published one more Revolutionary romance and two more that, like it, were set beyond the boundaries of civilization. He also left two unfinished romances, also set beyond society's normal reach. These late works, however, no longer had as their framing justification the cultivation of the South's future and civilization.

White southerners had their independence foreclosed by the war. In his last works, therefore, Simms found himself exploring the psychological, philosophical, and historical impulses that led to the Confederacy's demise and what, in the aftermath, it meant to be a good man and to build for the future, however impoverished. On the first score, he argued that the impulse to idealism behind abolitionism ignored historical realities, becoming inhuman in its consequences. On the latter score, he affirmed responsibility for one's dependents and the virtues of stoicism, as well as a continued commitment to the beauty and truth of art and the impulses to the cultivated life and fields. Therefore, in the face of the burning of his Woodlands home and library in February 1865 — during Sherman's march and in the midst of desperate circumstances—he insisted that home, or the ideals and past characterizing its potential, still was at the center of true civilization, but only if elevated by art (*Sense* 8, 17). It was wrong to measure civilization by the getting, spending, and mad dashing, or material progress and utilitarianism, characteristic of both a capitalistic North and also many southerners. These traits he often had attacked even before the war, insisting that "the work of the Imagination, which is the Genius of a race, is only begun when its material progress is supposed to be complete" (*Poetry* 12).

Writings

Simms expressed many of his ideas most personally in letters and most cogently in essays, speeches, and occasional introductions to his books. But he illustrated them most fully in his fiction and poetry. By the time he arrived in New

York in 1832, he had formed many of the core ideals and beliefs that would shape his work. His application of them, however, modified his understanding over time. Growing as a writer and growing in knowledge and experience, he also grew as a thinker.

In his hierarchy of values, poetry came first. It was a prophetic calling as well as evocative of the deeply felt (or, sometimes, the fleeting) and thus testimony to the perdurance and transcendence of the beautiful and the human spirit. Yet, as Simms often ruefully reflected, prose spoke to many more people. That was a principal reason why he turned to writing prose epics or romances. He gave his most concerted consideration of poetry's value and roles in three lectures in Charleston in 1854. Over the prior three years he had given portions of them in Augusta, Georgia, Washington, D.C., and Richmond and Petersburg, Virginia. Entitled *Poetry and the Practical*, they did not see print until 1996, as Simms never found the time to expand them as he wanted. On the other hand, his last address on the same themes, *The Sense of the Beautiful*, was issued soon after he delivered it, also in Charleston.

Many of his important reviews have not yet been gathered, but Simms collected some in 1845–46, and *Views and Reviews in American Literature, History and Fiction* came out in 1846 and 1847 in two "series." Beginning with a consideration of "Americanism" in literature, the first series explored the themes and periods of American history for treatment by the novelist. Simms argued there, and in forewords to several of his romances, that fiction rendered the past more truthfully, interestingly, and tellingly than histories and biographies could because fiction—like poetry—required imagination to look beyond what is not known or expressed. The second series examined additional American writers and what distinguished them, for instance, in their humor.

Despite their early success, Simms's romances, novellas, and stories provoked mixed reviews. Poe eventually concluded that Simms had become "the best novelist which this country has, on the whole, produced" but also insisted that "he should never have written 'The Partisan,' nor 'The Yemassee.'" This was in a review of *Confession*. That novel, like the gothic *Martin Faber*, demonstrated, Poe contended, that Simms's "genius [did] not lie in the outward so much as in the inner world." Yet he nevertheless wrote of Simms's short-story collection *The Wigwam and the Cabin* that "in invention, in vigor, in movement, in the power of exciting interest, and in the artistical management of his themes, he has surpassed, we think, any of his countrymen." Other critics, especially in the genteel and Whiggish Knickerbocker circle, joined Poe in condemning what they considered to be the excessively graphic and vulgar qualities of many characters and scenes, and Simms's prolixity and sententiousness, in his romances (Butterworth and Kibler 64, 50).

The violent realism and earthiness of the romances did not result in realistic novels. Although Simms received early praise for his characterizations (particularly of women), he used the romance formula, with its stereotypic heroes and heroines, predictable themes, and conventional polarities. People were on quests or had lost their way or were fighting long odds or were carrying forward the banner of (and modeling) civilization or were mired in the slough of despond or were resisting all the claims of civilized society and behavior or were pursuing love interests. Deceitfulness, selfishness, and greed opposed honor, high-mindedness, and honesty against the backdrop of the South's development from the earliest days of Spanish exploration to the westward movement in Simms's own youth.

It was only gradually that Simms married the psychological acuity of some of his portraits of the interior struggles of his gothic characters and fiction to the historical romance. Helping him think through how to do so were the biographies he wrote in the mid-1840s, but also the incidents on which he focused particular fictions, such as the murder in *Beauchampe; or, The Kentucky Tragedy* (1842). However incomplete the blending of realism and romanticism or of stereotypical and socially individuated renderings through the 1840s, by the 1850s Simms fundamentally had made the transition to social realism in such works as *Woodcraft* and *The Cassique of Kiawah*. Indeed some scholars have considered *Woodcraft* the first realistic novel in America (Bakker; Wimsatt, "Realism").

In some sense disguising the transition is the fact that Simms also increasingly wrote as a humorist and, in so doing, often rendered his late narratives fabulistically, when not writing social comedy or stories of manners. This dimension of Simms's work was largely hidden, however, until the 1974 publication of *Stories and Tales*, volume 5 in the Centennial Simms edition. There, for the first time, readers had access in print to "Bald-Head Bill Bauldy." There, too, for the first time one could read together that story, "Legend of the Hunter's Camp," and "How Sharp Snaffles Got His Capital and Wife," which was published posthumously in *Harper's Magazine* in October 1870. These and other stories and tales made it clear that Simms was a fecund contributor to southern and American humor.

Humor let Simms take up issues that he could not otherwise address in print and still expect to be well received. He did so both during and after the war. The war also pushed Simms past the emerging fashion of social realism. Having destroyed the familiar, the preoccupation of much realistic fiction, the war made the liminal central (Shillingsburg, "Cub"). While his romances and tales had often explored life on the edge or in extreme circumstances, whether in war or on the frontier or on the verge of madness or in fanciful realms, it had done so against a backdrop of, and with the goal of affirming, social norms and development. In the war's wake that goal seemed absurd. Mythologized memories of a healthy past might nurture a sense of the beautiful but could not help one deal with the present. Thus Simms's conclusion, in a March 1869 letter to Paul Hamilton Hayne: "Let us bury the Past lest it buries us!" (*Letters* 5:214). Fifteen months later he lay dead in the 13 Society Street, Charleston, home of his oldest daughter, with the shell holes in the walls of the bedroom he had shared with several children.

Posthumous Reputation

The twenty years after Simms's death saw him often respectfully treated, first in obituaries, later in memoirs and columns, and also in literary dictionaries and encyclopedias. Yet Charles Richardson's 1887 *American Literature: 1607–1885* proved a harbinger of a shift: Simms, Richardson observed, was "more respected than read," having "won considerable note because he was so sectional" and then having "lost it because he was not sectional enough," although he showed "silly contempt for his Northern betters" (qtd. in Butterworth and Kibler 130). Five years later Trent's biography of Simms appeared. It was the first full-length, scholarly treatment. Its central thesis was that Simms's environment frustrated his abilities: the South was inimical to art and the life of the mind, and Charleston high society's hauteur marginalized Simms despite his talent and character. Trent's second thesis was that Simms's commitment to the romance and his romanticism meant that his works had become largely unreadable in an age of literary realism. Although Vernon Parrington and later scholars recognized Simms's impulses to realism, the two theses long shaped Simms criticism and, indeed, also helped frame study of antebellum southern literature and intellectual life (Parrington 119–30).

A Virginian born in 1862, Trent was a progressive who wanted a New South radically different from the old. He saw his pioneering study of Simms as an opportunity to criticize what the Civil War had made untenable. From his perspective the Old South was not the expanding and rapidly developing environment, with a deep history, that Simms portrayed, but a place where slavery stultified and stunted the growth and progress displayed by the North. Southern — especially South Carolinian — writers occasionally challenged Trent's agenda and conclusions, but those critiques had little impact. Not until after publication of the Simms letters in the 1950s did scholars begin to consider the author in the historical and contemporary contexts that he had rendered in his poetry and fiction. And not until after the centennial of his death did a growing number of scholars, having concluded that southern intellectual history was not an oxymoron, begin to study in detail the culture in which Simms participated and to which he contributed so voluminously and variously.

Some of these scholars also have had agendas: they have wanted to see Simms included in the American literary canon, for instance, or they have wanted to defend the heritage that in their view Trent, and so many others, inappropriately belittled or ignorantly dismissed. More fruitfully, other scholars have begun to reframe the understanding of nineteenth-century American intellectual life by stripping away preconceptions that characterized earlier evaluations of Simms and his contemporaries. They are closely examining the historical record and transatlantic and other contemporary contexts and developments in the process. Although the pursuit of canonical status in a post-canonical age seems quixotic at this point, the explosion of the canon is leading to more varied fare being offered and may, therefore, mean that Simms, once his work is widely available, will be more often anthologized as well as studied. Defensiveness about Simms and the antebellum South may warm the hearts of like-minded people, just as critics of the Old South have been encouraged by shared presuppositions and disdain. Yet dueling cultural ideologies do not advance comity and may only reinforce mutual incomprehensions. Continued, deep research in original sources and the theoretical reframing that Atlantic history, the history of the book, and other perspectives offer—these approaches promise most for further study of Simms, his works, and his world.

Works Cited

For amplified readings by and on Simms and on his world, go to http://simms.library.sc.edu/bibliography.php.

Bakker, Jan. "Simms on the Literary Frontier; or, So Long Miss Ravenel and Hello Captain Porgy: *Woodcraft* Is the First 'Realistic' Novel in America." In *William Gilmore Simms and the American Frontier,* edited by John Caldwell Guilds and Caroline Collins, 64-78. Athens: University of Georgia Press, 1997.

Butterworth, Keen, and James E. Kibler Jr. *William Gilmore Simms: A Definitive Guide.* Boston: G. K. Hall, 1980.

Faust, Drew Gilpin. *A Sacred Circle: The Dilemma of the Intellectual in the Old South, 1840-1860.* Baltimore: Johns Hopkins University Press, 1977.

Guilds, John C. *Simms: A Literary Life.* Fayetteville: University of Arkansas Press, 1992.

Hayne, Paul Hamilton. "Ante-Bellum Charleston." *Southern Bivouac* 1 (October 1885): 257-68.

Kibler, James E. "The First Simms Letters: 'Letters from the West' (1826)." *Southern Literary Journal* 19 (Spring 1987): 81-91.

———. *The Poetry of William Gilmore Simms: An Introduction and Bibliography.* Columbia: Southern Studies Program, University of South Carolina, 1979.

McHaney, Thomas L. "An Early 19th-Century Literary Agent: James Lawson of New York." *Publications of the Bibliographical Society of America* 64 (Spring 1970): 177–92.

Moltke-Hansen, David. "The Expansion of Intellectual Life: A Prospectus." In *Intellectual Life in Antebellum Charleston*, edited by Michael O'Brien and David Moltke-Hansen, 3–44. Knoxville: University of Tennessee Press, 1986.

———. "Southern Literary Horizons in Young America: Imaginative Development of a Regional Geography." *Studies in the Literary Imagination* 42, no. 1 (2009): 1–31.

Nakamura, Masahiro. *Visions of Order in William Gilmore Simms: Southern Conservatism and the Other American Romance*. Columbia: University of South Carolina Press, 2009.

Parrington, Vernon L. *The Romantic Revolution in America, 1800–1860*. Vol. 2 of *Main Currents in American Thought*. New York: Harcourt, Brace and Company, 1927.

Rogers, George C., Jr. *Charleston in the Age of the Pinckneys*. Columbia: University South Carolina Press, 1980.

Shillingsburg, Miriam J. "The Cub of the Panther: A New Frontier." In *William Gilmore Simms and the American Frontier*, edited by John Caldwell Guilds and Caroline Collins, 221–36. Athens: University of Georgia Press, 1997.

———. "Literary Grist: Simms's Trips to Mississippi." *Southern Quarterly* 41, no. 2 (2003): 119–34.

Simms, William Gilmore. *Atalantis: A Story of the Sea: In Three Parts*. New York: J. & J. Harper, 1832.

———. *Beauchampe; or, The Kentucky Tragedy*. 2 vols. Philadelphia: Lea and Blanchard, 1842.

———. *The Cassique of Kiawah: A Colonial Romance*. New York: Redfield, 1859.

———. *Confession; or, The Blind Heart. A Domestic Story*. 2 vols. Philadelphia: Lea and Blanchard, 1841.

———. "Ellet's 'Women of the Revolution.'" *Southern Quarterly Review*, n.s. 1 (July 1850): 314–54.

———. "Guizot's Democracy in France." *Southern Quarterly Review* 15, no.29 (1849): 114–65.

———. *Guy Rivers: A Tale of Georgia*. 2 vols. New York: Harper & Brothers, 1834.

———. *The Letters of William Gilmore Simms*. Edited by Mary C. Simms Oliphant, Alfred Taylor Odell, and T. C. Duncan. 6 vols. Columbia: University of South Carolina Press, 1952–82.

———. *The Life of Francis Marion*. New York: Henry G. Langley, 1844.

———. *Martin Faber, the Story of a Criminal; and Other Tales*. 2 vols. New York: Harper & Brothers, 1837.

———. *Poetry and the Practical*. Edited by James E. Kibler. Fayetteville: University of Arkansas Press, 1996.

———. *The Sense of the Beautiful: An Address . . . before the Charleston County Agricultural and Horticultural Association, May 3, 1870*. Charleston: Charleston County Agricultural and Horticultural Association, 1870.

---. *The Social Principle: The Source of National Permanence. An Oration, Delivered before the Erosophic Society of the University of Alabama . . . December 13, 1842*. Tuscaloosa: Erosophic Society, University of Alabama, 1843.

---. *Stories and Tales*. Vol. 5 of *The Writings of William Gilmore Simms*. Centennial edition; introductions, explanatory notes, and texts established by John Caldwell Guilds. Columbia: University of South Carolina Press, 1974.

---. *Views and Reviews in American Literature, History and Fiction*. 2 vols. New York: Wiley and Putnam, 1845 (1846).

---. *The Wigwam and the Cabin*. 2 vols. New York: Wiley and Putnam, 1845–46.

---. *Woodcraft, or Hawks about the Dovecote: A Story of the South, at the Close of the Revolution*. New York: Redfield, 1854.

Trent, William Peterfield. *William Gilmore Simms*. Boston: Houghton, Mifflin, 1892.

Wakelyn, Jon L. *The Politics of a Literary Man: William Gilmore Simms*. Westport, Conn.: Greenwood Press, 1973.

Watson, Charles S. *From Nationalism to Secessionism: The Changing Fiction of William Gilmore Simms*. Westport, Conn.: Greenwood Press, 1993.

White, William B., Jr. *The Ross-Chesnut-Sutton Family of South Carolina*. Franklin, N.C.: Privately printed, 2002.

Wimsatt, Mary Ann. "Realism and Romance in Simms's Midcentury Fiction." *Southern Literary Journal* 12, no. 2 (1980): 29–48.

Critical Introduction

DRAMAS

Abigail Lundelius Smith

On 8 April 1841, William Gilmore Simms confided in a letter to George Roberts, "My *penchant* is for another field very different from that in which I am more generally known to the public; and I will avail myself of the earliest leisure to send you a specimen of Dramatic Composition" (*Letters* 1: 244). Confident in his ability, yet hesitant of its appreciation, Simms continued, "If the compensation for such labors were at all encouraging, I should perhaps, contribute one or two Dramas annually" (*Letters* 1: 244). Three years later, he was no less assured of the possibility of success when writing to James Lawson: "I am more and more inclined to the conviction that I am to prove my fate in the drama" (*Letters* 1: 428). Such was not to be. Despite his commitment to his dramatic endeavors, evidenced in part by their regular mention within his correspondence, Simms never garnered critical acclaim as a playwright. And by November of 1847, Simms seems resigned to a far less illustrious fate for his plays. Writing to Lawson, Simms announced, rather dramatically, "I will make a volume of my Arnold, Michael Bonham, Locrine, Atalantis & adding this 'man of the people' [*Norman Maurice*], close my account with the Dramatic World in a single publication" (*Letters* 2: 369). As Edd Winfield Parks so succinctly notes, "The hoped-for glory never became a reality" (68).

The intervening years have done nothing to ameliorate the lackluster response to Simms's dramatic works. Writing about *Norman Maurice*, C. Hugh Holman says, "The effort to make a tragedy of the materials of contemporary life is admirable and daring; the effort to use the outmoded form of Shakespearean blank verse resulted in ... absurdities" (80). Regarding *Michael Bonham*, he is even less kind: "to the present day reader it seems largely fustian bombast" (80). Simms's earliest biographer, William P. Trent, notes that "when read in the closet the play [*Michael Bonham*] seems to be the work of a precocious youth of eighteen rather than of a practical writer and constant student and spectator of the drama" (216). Critic William Hoole agrees: "by few, if any, standards, could *Michael Bonham* be considered a first-rate drama.... When read today it is slow and dull" (257). And, in the most recent of discussions, Erma Richter acknowledges, albeit more diplomatically, that *Michael Bonham* "was a failure aesthetically and financially" (108). Simms's last play fares no better. In her concluding remarks about *Benedict Arnold*, Miriam Shillingsburg suggests that the work has been "largely overlooked because of the inaccessibility of the play" (287).

Given the lukewarm response of both contemporary and current critics, an obvious question arises: Why this collection? First, it behooves the careful reader and scholar to consider the fullness of Simms's canon. This is not to suggest that the entirety of any writer's body of work is equally meritorious; that seems a hardly defensible assertion. Still, where possible, providing the opportunity for scholarly exploration is both appropriate and worthwhile. Second, although most critics concur that Simms's dramas are artistically insipid, they nonetheless agree that the plays remain historically and theoretically interesting. Note the remarkable shift in critical tone when the critics consider the plays as other-than-plays. Hoole argues that *Michael Bonham*'s "chief appeal is the interesting way in which the author altered historical facts" (257). Richter suggests that *Michael Bonham* reveals "the author's ability to merge fact and fiction to promote a political agenda" (109). Shillingsburg ultimately argues that, in its two-part structure, *Benedict Arnold: The Traitor. A Drama in an Essay* "is the most specific and detailed of Simms's works on the relationship between history and art, for he has opportunity in the Drama to develop his artistic rendition; yet in the Essay he plays literary critic discussing the handicaps to his art of adhering to the history" ("Traitor" 289). In another essay, Shillingsburg more generously suggests, "in several ways Simms's play represents an interplay of history and art that remains of lasting interest" ("Treason" 83). Perhaps the final reason to consider Simms's drama comes from the playwright himself. Speaking of *Benedict Arnold*, Simms writes, "I probably see, quite as clearly as any other critic, the objections that may be urged against it" (*Benedict* 259). And yet, Simms offered it. That confidence, both in his dramas and in his audiences, deserves our attention. To that end, this edition offers readers the opportunity to explore the three long-form dramas completed by Simms. While other works within the Simms canon contain dramatic elements, particularly the poetry, these three are noteworthy for being fully-fledged, multi-act, book-length compositions ostensibly suitable and intended — at least in the case of *Norman Maurice* and *Michael Bonham* — for the stage.

Norman Maurice; or, The Man of the People. An American Drama

Published serially in the *Southern Literary Messenger* from April through August of 1851, *Norman Maurice* reappeared later that year in pamphlet form, published by John R. Thompson of Richmond. The following year, Walker and Richards of Charleston published it as *Norman Maurice; or, The Man of the Peo-*

ple. *An American Drama*. The 1852 publication included three additional one-act plays: "Caius Marius; An Historical Legend," "Bertram; An Italian Sketch," and "The Death of Cleopatra." This 1852 edition, reprinted by Lippincott, Grambo, & Co. in 1853, serves as the edition chosen for this collection.

Though enjoying numerous manifestations throughout the early 1850s, *Norman Maurice* made first mention four years earlier in a letter from Simms to James Lawson on 31 July 1847 (*Letters* 2: 341). By September of that year, Simms had finished the work. "I have been doing the tragedy. It is finished. Four acts have been sent to [prominent nineteenth-century actor, Edwin] Forrest,... I have drawn the hero with F. himself in my eye — a portrait which I hope will not displease him" (*Letters* 2: 350). Apparently, the portrait did not please. In a letter written the following month, Simms admitted to Lawson that Forrest "speaks of it as not being as 'carefully elaborated' as it should be." And while Simms granted that the "style is not greatly elevated above that of ordinary conversation," he suggested that "this moderation of tone was deliberately determined on, in consequence of my wish to make the piece strictly a *domestic drama*." Simms continued, "The style was just sufficiently elevated to make it meet the exactions of rhythm.... [I]t will be quite easy to raise the style where it is necessary, & throw in those extraneous passages of poetry, which I rather suppressed" (*Letters* 2: 356-57).

Not everyone found the play lacking in elevation. A review in the September 1851 edition of *The Literary World* praised Simms for his use of "blank verse" and suggested that he had "shown art and judgment." The review continued, "If [Simms] had given us nothing but prose,... the whole tone of the piece would have been let down ... with the aid of skilfully [sic] delivered verse — [he has offered] a happy medium between slow-footed prose and the remoter elegancies of pure fancy" (223). After reading *Norman Maurice* in 1852, fellow poet Thomas Holley Chivers offered this encouragement and advice to Simms: "I have received and read your Drama, and find it the best thing that *I* have ever seen of yours — in fact, I am now puzzled to know why you should ever have worn out your faculties in writing Novels.... You have shown in this Play that you are not unacquainted with the *true Dramatic Style*" (qtd. in *Letters* 3: 169).

Norman Maurice tells the story of a young man's rise to political stardom. Written in the wake of the 1820 Missouri Compromise, *Norman Maurice* explores the political implications of statehood in America's border regions. By the play's end, the title character is the newly elected Senator from Missouri, a "champion of the people" who promises to defend the Constitution as a "ligament of fix'd, unchanging value, / Maintained by strict construction, — neither warp'd, / By the ambitious demagogue or statesman, / Who, with the baits of station in their eyes, / Still sacrifice the State!" (117). Certainly, *Norman Maurice* is a defense of the rule of original constitutional intent in the face of changing political sentiment. In proper Simms fashion, however, the curtain rises not upon the plot political, but romantic. Maurice has wooed the heart of young Clarice, and nothing can convince her guardian aunt of his worthiness. Mrs. Jervas has another suitor in mind, Robert Warren, Maurice's "kinsman and enemy" (5). Explaining Warren's hatred for Maurice, Simms writes, "Warren hates his cousin Maurice for several reasons. He has always proved his superior — has *proved* him a coward — has pardoned him a wrong, is his rival in love, and these rouse his *passion* for a vindictive triumph over him who has always triumphed hitherto" (*Letters* 2: 369). Through an unexplained turn of events, Warren is in possession of documents that can devastate all of Maurice's aims. Though Maurice believes the papers destroyed, Warren reveals to Clarice that he maintains possession of the originals. The price of Warren's silence is Clarice's submission to his carnal desires. One fateful night, as Maurice wins nomination to the Senate, Clarice meets Warren in the woods where she stabs him and recovers the damning documents. Soon overcome by her act of violence, Clarice suffers a stroke. Maurice rushes to her side moments before her death, catching the ruinous papers as they "fall from her bosom" (125).

The intensity of Simms's drama is difficult to overstate. As one contemporary critic opines, "We unhesitatingly say that Mr. Simms' 'Norman Maurice' is one of the boldest literary ventures on record" (Hayne 242). Despite this lofty praise, the review concludes with a warning:

> There are so many ideas necessarily low and sordid, connected with the scenes through which Maurice, the lawyer and politician, *must* pass in his way to place and power, that no genius — not the genius of Shakspeare [sic] himself — could have *completely* harmonized them with the proprieties of High Art. Therefore, let the dramatist — bent upon writing tragedy — hereafter beware of contemporary *American* topics. (Hayne 254)

Ignoring this advice, Simms published *Michael Bonham* the following year.

Michael Bonham; or, The Fall of Bexar. A Tale of Texas

On 9 November 1843, in a letter to James Lawson, Simms made first mention of a new literary endeavor. Simms wrote "of a melodrama which I have been projecting as an experiment, for the Charleston Theatre — the scene in Texas — the subject the fall of the Alamo &c. — But of this, say nothing. 'I would not willingly be known'" (*Letters* 1: 387). Just over a week later, on November 15, Simms again wrote to Lawson, "I am preparing a melodrama ... founded upon the conquest of the Alamo by the Texans & the subsequent battle of San Jacinto.... I am writing it just to see if I can accomplish the action of a drama.... Say nothing on the subject" (*Letters* 1: 388). Obviously enamored of his fledgling project, Simms wrote — again to Lawson and again after the passing of a week — to explain his foray into the dramatic: "I have half done a melodrama — my only object to test my powers of dramatic situation. I make no attempt at fine writing. There is much bustle in the piece so far & will be more" (*Letters* 1: 391). The following month, Simms mentioned his play once again to Lawson. "It is in five acts and has a melancholy conclusion, though the hero triumphs &c. This almost makes it a Tragedy. In parts, indeed, it rises into the dignity of one.... But do not mutter this even in your garden" (*Letters* 1: 393-94). Simms's curious secretiveness about this play continued with its anonymous publication.

Like *Norman Maurice*, *Michael Bonham* was first published serially in the *Southern Literary Messenger*, from February to June of 1852, and again as a separate volume by John R. Thompson later that same year. Unlike its dramatic predecessor, however, this latter play was published both times without the benefit of Simms's name, authorship credited simply as "By a Southron." In her fine essay on the play, Erma Richter offers a political, rather than personal, motive for this decision: "In spite of Simms's statements to Lawson that his interest in composing *Michael Bonham* was purely to test his ability to write a drama, significant evidence points to a broader, more political intent" (101). Richter notes, particularly, that this was quite reasonable "for one desiring annexation of Texas to strengthen the political position of the South" (101) — namely, its inclusion as a slave-holding state. No wonder, then, that Simms expected *Michael Bonham* to "make a rumpus, be sure, if ever it reaches light upon the stage" (*Letters* 2: 23-24). It was a drama intended to create some drama.

Michael Bonham is the story of a young hero keen on infiltrating and undermining the Mexican stronghold at San Antonio, all while wooing the heart of the Governor's daughter and securing a place in the annals of Texas history. The play opens with the Texans encamped outside Bexar awaiting their next encounter with the Mexican military force. Eager to assess the enemy's strength, the Texan commander, Milam, sends Bonham on a reconnaissance mission inside the city walls. Bonham is no less eager to penetrate Bexar's defenses — it affords him the felicitous opportunity of seeing his beloved Olivia once again. The romantic and political plots collide during a Bal Masqué hosted by Bexar's Governor, Don Esteban. Arriving in disguise, Bonham must contend not only with Olivia's spurned suitor, Don Pedro, but also with the woman whose love he has rejected, Olivia's cousin, Maria. Furious at his refusal of her advances, Maria unmasks Bonham, revealing his true identity as a spy. Summoned by Bonham's bugle call, the awaiting Texans overwhelm the city. With the political story concluded, the marriage of Bonham and Olivia offers a fitting dénouement. Simms complicates this comic end, however, with the stabbing of Don Pedro in the antepenultimate scene, the attempted murder and subsequent suicide of Maria in the final scene, and the swooning of Olivia into a dead faint at the curtain's fall. No wonder, then, that Arthur Hobson Quinn describes *Michael Bonham* as a "vigorous if lurid melodrama" (501).

Michael Bonham did eventually see the light of stage at the New Charleston Theatre in March of 1855. Although appearing without its intended political polemic — Texas having been admitted as a state nearly ten years before in December of 1845 — the production, according to Simms, "was quite successful — greatly applauded, & played for 3 nights — which in our little city [of Charleston], is a great event — audiences rarely suffering for more than one" (*Letters* 3: 384). This reception might have surprised Simms. Three years earlier, when the *Southern Literary Messenger* serialized *Michael Bonham*, Simms seemed resigned to an unperformed play. In fact, he conceded in his introduction to the published edition, "The tale which follows, [sic] was originally prepared with a view toward performance. Subsequently, however, I have persuaded myself that it would read better as a story" (129). Part of the story's success must reside, as well, in its inclusion of a bit of local flavor. Although, as Hoole clarifies, there was "no 'Michael' Bonham," there was a South Carolinian Bonham "associated with the Texas Revolution ... James Butler Bonham, of Edgefield, South Carolina, who died in the Alamo" (258). The discrepancies in historical detail pose no threat to Simms, though. While Simms acknowledged that he had "taken some liberties with the historical facts," he insisted that "the history will suffer little from my freedoms, while ... the story gains by them" (129). Here, Simms provides an inkling of the theoretical framework defining his canon — an idea he would further explore in another drama, *Benedict Arnold*.

Benedict Arnold: The Traitor. A Drama in an Essay.

By May of 1863, with America deep into her civil hostilities, Simms was ready to present a drama not for the stage, but for the page. As the title indicates, the plot of *Benedict Arnold* details the events leading to the traitorous actions of the American Revolution's most infamous figure. Simms was not the first to attempt such a dramatic feat; as Shillingsburg summarizes, "Simms joined William Dunlap, James Fenimore Cooper, George Henry Calvert, and a score of amateurs who had attempted to use the Arnold-Andre conspiracy to surrender West Point to the British in 1780 in serious literature" ("Traitor" 273). Simms's treatment of this narrative is unique, however, in his exploration of the relationship between history and art. As with Simms's first two dramas, *Benedict Arnold* was published serially, this time by the *Magnolia Weekly* from May to

August of 1863. Given the timing of its appearance and its Richmond, Virginia publisher, *Benedict Arnold* appears not only as Simms's retrospective on the American Revolution but his contemporary look at America's second great civil conflict.

It is quite clear that Simms intended Arnold to be the hero of the drama. In his introductory comments, Simms says, "The deeds of the hero are as brilliant as his treason is utter and unqualified. Arnold was no imbecile in action. He was only so in morals. His courage was unquestionable; and he exposed himself personally in battle, as was the case with the valiant man in ancient warfare" (276-77). Despite this approbation, it is worth noting that Arnold neither opens nor closes the play which bears his name. In the opening scene, Arnold's commitment to the Crown is the subject of conversation although he is not present to make his own defense; at the conclusion, Arnold has fled the stage, this time unwilling to mount any defense. In fact, like Simms's previous dramas, *Benedict Arnold* focuses largely on intrigues of the heart.

Throughout the course of the drama, three distinct love plots swirl around Mrs. Margaret Arnold. The first, of course, is her relationship with her husband, Benedict. Of their relationship, Simms offers this explanation, "Margaret Shippen was a fashionable damsel of the time — a *belle*.... She married, as such persons usually do, not a lover, but an establishment!... As for the *heart*, the less we say about that ... the better!" (359). On the night of a *Bal Masque* hosted by the Arnolds, in a plot move borrowed from *Michael Bonham*, both John Andre, Arnold's fellow conspirator, and Randolph Peyton, a young man in service to Washington, reveal their undiminished love for Margaret. Although she holds them both at arm's length, it is nevertheless clear that her affections once favored them. Love does not ultimately favor Margaret, however. By the play's end, she has been cruelly abandoned by her husband, watched helplessly as Andre is captured and sentenced to hang, and swooned hopelessly over the dead body of Peyton.

The response to Simms's final dramatic creation was limited and dismissive. A critic of the *Charleston Evening News* noted that the play suffered due to Simms's "too great *nearness* to the period in which he writes" (qtd in Hoole 256). Simms himself acknowledges this dilemma in his prefatory comments to *Benedict Arnold*:

> All of the writers have been hampered, not by the barrenness of the subject, but the fear of violating the details of history. To be successful in this material, one must assert a certain degree of audacity — must be content with looking to the history for the main facts — the treason — the conspiracy — the detection and disgrace — but must boldly conceive for himself the

events, incidents, and situations.... I was baffled by the details of history. I had no sufficient freedom. There was too much known to suffer invention its privileges. I was stopt by stern barriers of fact. (285-86)

At one moment, historical fact impedes dramatic action; in the very next, artistic license offends history's sensibilities.

That Simms, ever the historian and always the artist, found himself caught between an unusual irreconcilability of these two demands is evidenced long before the publication of *Benedict Arnold*. In a letter dated 4 March 1853, Simms wrote to Henry Carey Baird to inquire about Mrs. Benedict Arnold:

Have you any thing in relation to the private life of Arnold while in Philadelphia? What was the christened name of his wife? Is there any thing in respect to her private history and character.... Were not all Mrs. Arnold's kindred loyalists & active as such. What were the names of uncles & aunts, — or is any thing known of them? Were they quakers [sic]; in other words, can I give her an uncle who is at once Quaker & Loyalist? (*Letters* 3: 226)

Over two years later, Simms was still in communication with Baird regarding the historicity of the Arnold saga. "[W]hat was Mrs. A's Christian name? And were her father & mother living then, either of them, and are there any descendants or connections now?... [I]s there any faith to be put in the alleged facts in a book about Arnold — a quasi historical fiction" (*Letters* 3: 407). Simms's line of questioning reveals his commitment to the facts. Over the course of two letters, in the space of a few lines, Simms asked eleven questions — most regarding Mrs. Arnold. And yet, Simms was not shy regarding his artistic intent. By the play's public appearance, Simms had christened Margaret Arnold with a Christian name and saddled her with a Loyalist Quaker uncle. Simms's justification for the artistic license of these decisions appears in the "essayical [sic] portions" (*Letters* 3: 7) of *Benedict Arnold* where he writes, "In this narrative, there is nothing improbable in the case, as reported by the dramatist. He does not really conflict with the Historian. He only knows *more* than the historian has been suffered to find in the written records" (430). Herein lies the most unique theoretical aspect of Simms's play — a willingness to grant freedom to the artist while remaining faithful to the demands of the historian.

Simms and his Dramatic Women

The general response to Simms's treatment of women is one of tempered praise. In an essay exploring the relationship between gender and secession in Simms, Patricia Okker writes, "As much as Simms portrayed women as exerting a powerful influence on the forces of history, his ambivalence about independent women tempers his celebration of women's historical power" (26). Ultimately, Okker argues that Simms's "idealization of women as willingly subordinate to men undercuts his otherwise fervent celebration of independence" (30). Debra Johanyak agrees, suggesting that while "Simms somewhat softened his views toward feministic behavior late in his career, for the most part he held to his theory of domestic purity dominated by masculine authority as the structural framework for the society he believed in and upheld" (588). Shillingsburg attempts to give Simms a bit more credit. "Simms's opinion of women was not merely representative of the received opinion of his day that women were inferior and that too much education and accomplishment was a dangerous thing. He did sometimes reflect such received opinion, but he also had a deep respect for the talented and able women he knew" ("Battered" 219).

In her essay, "Toward a Feminist Reading of Simms," Caroline Collins paints a far different picture:

> Simms's strong women serve as enacters and enablers, providing important keys to the survival of individuals and cultures, and to the survival of the social order. At the very least, his later romances achieve a tension between 'man-centered' and 'women-centered' narratives.... [indeed] are probably more 'woman-centered' than any other 'male-authored' works of literature in nineteenth century America. (6)

Collins sees Simms's women rejecting the notion of women as domestic dependents and embracing their role as active participants in not only their own destiny, but in the future of the world they inhabit. This freedom is not, however, without responsibility. Collins goes on to argue that Simms's female "characters' participation in their own undoing certainly evokes Shakespeare's notion of the tragic flaw, but also displays a desire for realism and a keen understanding of human psychology and behavior" (11). Not only is Simms willing to endow his women with freedom, he allows them a will of their own.

Looking at Simms's reimagining of Shakespearean characters, Charles S. Watson argues that Simms "expressed the Romantic view that Hamlet's will was defective. He stressed Hamlet's indecision and impulsive action as his principal traits, and ... argued that Shakespeare's message in *Hamlet* is that action is the chief end of existence" (21). If action is evidence of a robust will, the men of Simms's plays certainly seem to fit the bill. Simms's friend and protégé Paul Hamilton Hayne, in considering *Norman Maurice*, proposed that in "the hands of the author, an unpromising subject has been wrought into a work vivid in action" (254). Writing in 1869, James Davidson described both *Norman Maurice* and *Michael Bonham* as "vigorous productions" (525). As if to highlight Maurice's willingness to act, Simms places a particularly violent scene at the center of *Norman Maurice*. One evening, as Clarice and Maurice have just completed supper, Warren knocks on the door. During the lengthy exchange that follows, Maurice is violently active, as evidenced by the numerous stage directions: "*Laying his hand on Warren's shoulder*" (59); "*flinging him* [Warren] *away and rising*" (60); "*hurling the table over*" (61); "*Rushes upon him* [Warren] *and wrests the weapon from his hand*" (62); "*Takes Warren by the throat*" (62); "*Hurls him* [Warren] *out headlong*" (63). With every page, Maurice becomes more agitated and his reaction more pronounced.

In *Michael Bonham*, Simms clearly distinguishes between the man of words and the man of deeds. Don Esteban de Monteueros, the Governor of Bexar, first appears writing at a desk where his "sword lie[s] before him among papers" (163). Initially, it seems that Don Esteban might stand as the character who best unifies deed and word. In his opening speech, he says, "It is well done! It is written! The record is made. I may now take my rest.... The battle is over" (163). The letter in which Don Esteban lauds his efforts to Santa Ana, however, quickly reveals his passivity. He writes, "I have the honor to inform you of the complete defeat, — I may almost say, the total annihilation, of the Texian [*sic*] invading army.... This defeat, so utter and complete, is due entirely to the terror inspired by our arms!... Ours was a victory without a blow" (163-64). Within the Simms milieu, however, there is no victory without a blow.

Benedict Arnold also hears the call to action. In his opening soliloquy, he acknowledges, "The whole world sees my wrongs, yet I am silent! / The whole world know my claims, yet I ask nothing!"(328). Inaction will not always mark his course, however. By speech's end, he declares, "I cannot always be denied and baffled! / I feel it here!—a power and will to conquer, / Which will not be subdued;--yet, heart be still / While THOUGHT and subtlest WISDOM tutor will!" (328). And, of America's great traitor, Simms writes, "Arnold, as we see, has attained one of his objects, and that one of vital importance to all the rest. He has not suffered the grass to grow beneath the feet of his ambition" (406).

And yet, the men of Simms's dramas appear on the stage with words writ large and deeds largely unseen. At the close of the first act, Maurice promises to exact retribution on Warren: "But, let him dare / Once more to cross my path, and he shall feel / His serpent head grow flat beneath my heel" (32). Despite this explicitly Christological allusion, Maurice never crushes Warren's head – Clarice does. Michael Bonham's great action, rescuing Olivia and Maria from their captors, occurs prior to the play's beginning and Olivia tells the tale: "Señor, by that rancho — / That scene of strife and dread, I still remember, / Never to lose it — when the wild Camanché, / Smote me to earth, and 'neath his savage fury, / Hopeless, I shriek'd for succor, and — I found it! / Nor succor only! You came, you conquer'd" (173). Even Benedict Arnold, America's great traitor, is remarkably passive. Prior to his dastardly deed, Simms claims that "Arnold, like Macbeth, is one to falter in decision — to show himself quite capable of conceiving the crime, but to be infirm of purpose" (330). This lack of resolve haunts Arnold throughout the play. Just before his capture, he cries out, "It is not yet too late! The damned deed, / That blackens me forever; wife and child; / Friends, country, honor'd name and ancient valor; — / It is not beyond recall! I will recall it!" (449). And yet, he protests too much; by the soliloquy's end, Arnold has talked himself out of an honorable retreat and chosen cowardly flight

With astounding clarity and conviction, it is the *women* of these plays who act. Consider, once again, *Norman Maurice*. Upon learning that Warren remains in possession of the infernal documents, Clarice agrees to a clandestine meeting in a "thick wood" where, as the text makes clear, Warren anticipates the long-awaited fulfillment of his passionate desire for her (108). Clarice has plans of her own. Answering Warren's call, she enters the wood and exits the stage. The stage direction indicates a struggle and *"a moment after a cry of agony, and then a sound as of a falling body. Reënter Clarice with paper in her hand, and garments all bloody"* (111). Clarice exults, "He'll lie no more. / He wish'd for my embrace, and sure he had it! / Such close embrace, so sharp, so sudden, sweet, / It made him shriek and shrink with such a pleasure, / As men endure not twice" (112). In a rather shocking, and wholly unexpected reversal, Clarice's knife penetrates Warren. The victim has become the victor. Her act of violence is even more impressive when juxtaposed, in the very next scene, against Maurice's refusal to kill the man he has bested in a duel.

In *Michael Bonham* there are two women of action. The first is Ellen Harris. Disguised as a boy, Ellen has followed her husband to the Texas battlefield in order to reclaim his soul for heaven. Believing his wife unfaithful, Richard Harris murdered both the parson who witnessed their marriage and the brother who defended her honor. Upon learning of his error, he fled to Texas to die as honorable a death as possible. While all of Richard's actions occur prior to the opening of the play, Ellen spends the entirety of the play acting as "Billy" Harris. And, in their final scene, Ellen takes on her greatest role — that of intercessor. With his last breath, Richard beseeches Ellen, "Come closer — let me hear you; in my ears / Still tell me of forgiveness. Christ! Have mercy! / Look down upon me! Would that I had time / For pray'r; but no! I cannot" (248). Although calling on Christ for mercy, Richard looks to Ellen as the embodiment of that atonement. Ellen speaks absolution over Richard, saying, "Have mercy on him, Heaven! / Let not these murders hang about his soul, / Dragging it downwards" (248). Unwilling to let him die alone, she begs that God "take us both together" (249) and, in so doing, she pleads redemptive efficacy in her final act of sacrifice.

Also active, though not sacrificially, is Maria, Olivia's cousin who suffers an unrequited passion for Bonham. After hearing her pleas for his love, a love he has already given to Olivia, Bonham remarks, "Was ever so cruel a woman! Soul so proud, / And yet so passionate, was never seen! / ... ready with her life, / To prove her heart's devotion; not less ready, / That heart's devotion set at nought or wronged, / Avenging it with life!" (219). A truer portent was never spoken. When it becomes clear that Bonham's affections lie with Olivia, Maria wastes no time in enacting her revenge. She attempts to secure Bonham's love by threatening to reveal his identity. When he refuses, she exposes him to the Mexican authorities. After the Texans take Bexar and Bonham secures Olivia's hand, Maria attempts to murder her cousin at their wedding. Failing in that, she stabs herself declaring, "[Olivia] cannot love as I have done. This hand, / That smote its kindred heart, had, in your cause, / Borne weapon 'gainst a thousand foes" (269). Both in life and in death, Maria's love for Bonham is marked by action.

Finally, Margaret Arnold appears as the most complete of Simms's dramatic women. In an essay looking at this play, Miriam Shillingsburg writes, "Simms made Mrs. Arnold the traditional virtue personified — a dutiful wife, a loving mother, a noble woman, and an innocent victim" ("Benedict" 278). Shillingsburg goes on to argue, "This entire characterization of Mrs. Arnold is ... the product of the nineteenth-century veneration of womanhood" ("Benedict" 287). Shillingsburg's reading of Margaret as the stereotypically passive victim, however, fails to watch Margaret in her final moments on stage.

In the penultimate scene of *Benedict Arnold*, and for the first time in the entire play, Arnold and Washington are in the same scene — it is not, however, the Arnold we would expect. In hot pursuit of the traitorous Benedict, Washington and several of his officers enter the Arnold home. Hearing a shot outside, Washington turns to the door but Margaret "rushes into the room, and places herself between Washington and the entrance" (485). Their initial verbal parlay quickly escalates:

Washington.
... Let me go forward.

Margaret.
Only o'er my corse [*sic*]!

Washington. (*Seeks to put her aside.*)
Each moment lost.

> Margaret.
> (*Aside.*) Is a life-gain to Arnold! (*Struggling.*)
> Is this your manhood? To assault a woman? (487)

At no other time in this drama does Washington physically engage with another character. That Simms would have him do so with Mrs. Arnold is significant. She alone is his equal. Shillingsburg is correct when she argues that Washington "is the moral yardstick against which all characters must be measured, and, in all cases ... they are found wanting" ("Treason" 84). The men fall remarkably short — Benedict Arnold is a coward, Peyton Randolph is impetuous, and John Andre is a spy. Margaret, on the other hand, measures up to Washington. This moral fortitude allows Margaret to defend Arnold, intercede for Andre, and mourn over Peyton. Washington might be the iconic moral pillar, but with Margaret, Simms creates a character, a woman, who is far more real and far more good.

Further examination of the presence and power of the women within these dramas certainly seems worthwhile. Not only for their sake, but for the ways in which watching these women act on Simms's stage casts new light on Simms himself. As Collins suggests, "It seems unlikely, or at least contradictory, that someone who is not interested in women or who is interested in only keeping women down would create such a vast and intriguing array of strong, determined women" (7).

The Play's the Thing

This is, by no means, the fullness of what these three dramas offer. Numerous avenues of fruitful exploration remain — hospitality in *Norman Maurice* and *Benedict Arnold*; the way in which food imagery shapes the conversation in *Michael Bonham*; *Norman Maurice*'s similarities to *Paradise Lost*; the parallels between Shakespeare's *Macbeth* and *Benedict Arnold*; the role of masking and unmasking in *Michael Bonham* and *Benedict Arnold*. Herein lies the value of the *Simms Initiatives*, the digital collection of the author's work, headquartered at the University of South Carolina. It makes Simms's long overlooked plays more readily available to a new audience, and allows them to argue, with greater vigor, for their place not only within the vast Simms canon, but also within the collection of American drama.

Works Cited

Collins, Caroline. "Toward a Feminist Reading of Simms." *The Simms Review*. (1995) 3.1: 5-13.

Davidson, James Wood. "William Gilmore Simms, LL.D." *The Living Writers of the South*. James Wood Davidson. Carleton, Publisher, 1869. Rpt. in *Nineteenth-Century Literature Criticism*. Ed. Laurie Lanzen Harris. Vol. 3. Detroit: Gale Research, 1983. *Literature Resource Center*. Web. 13 Jan. 2014.

Hayne, Paul Hamilton. "The Dramatic Poems of Wm. Gilmore Simms." *Russell's Magazine* 2.3 (Dec. 1857): 240-59. Rpt. in *Nineteenth-Century Literature Criticism*. Ed. Laurie Lanzen Harris. Vol. 3. Detroit: Gale Research, 1983. *Literature Resource Center*. Web. 13 Jan. 2014.

Holman, C. Hugh. *The Roots of Southern Writing: Essays on the Literature of the American South*. Athens: U of Georgia P, 1972.

Hoole, William. "Simms's *Michael Bonham*: A 'Forgotten' Drama of the Texas Revolution." *Southwestern Historical Quarterly* 46 (1942): 255-61.

Johanyak, Debra. "William Gilmore Simms: Deviant Paradigms of Southern Womanhood?" *Mississippi Quarterly*. (1993) 46.4: 573-588.

"Mr. Simms's *Norman Maurice*." *The Literary World* 9.242 (20 Sept. 1851): 223-24. Rpt. in *Nineteenth-Century Literature Criticism*. Ed. Laurie Lanzen Harris. Vol. 3. Detroit: Gale Research, 1983. *Literature Resource Center*. Web. 13 Jan. 2014.

Okker, Patricia. "Gender and Secession in Simms's *Katherine Walton*." *Southern Literary Journal*. (1997) 29.2: 17-31.

Parks, Edd Winfield. *William Gilmore Simms As Literary Critic*. Athens: U of Georgia P, 1961.

Quinn, Arthur Hobson. *The Literature of the American People: An Historical and Critical Survey*. New York, NY: Appleton-Century-Crofts, Inc., 1951.

Richter, Erma. *Southern Quarterly*. "A Rumpus, to Be Sure: Simms's *Michael Bonham*." (2003) 41.2: 100-09.

Shillingsburg, Miriam. "The Battered Woman Syndrome in Simms's Fiction." *Studies in the Novel*. (2003) 35.2: 219-230.

——. "Simms' Benedict Arnold: The Hero as Traitor." *Southern Studies: An Interdisciplinary Journal of the South*. (1978) 17: 273-89.

——. "West Point Treason in American Drama, 1798-1891." *Educational Theatre Journal*. (1978) 30.1: 73-89.

Simms, William Gilmore. *Benedict Arnold: The Traitor. A Drama, in an Essay. Magnolia Weekly* 1 (16 May 1863): 165-67; (23 May 1863): 173-75; (30 May 1863): 186-87; (6 June 1863): 194-95; (13 June 1863): 202-03; (20 June 1863): 210-11; (27 June 1863): 218-19; (4 July 1863): 226-27; (11 July 1863): 234-35; (18 July 1863): 242-43; (25 July 1863): 250-51; (1 Aug. 1863): 258-59.

——. *The Letters of William Gilmore Simms*. Ed. Mary C. Simms Oliphant et al. 6 vols. Columbia: U of South Carolina P, 1952-2012.

——. *Michael Bonham; or, The Fall of Bexar*. Richmond, VA: John R. Thompson, 1952

———. *Norman Maurice; or, The Man of the People. An American Dream.* Charleston, SC: Walker and Richards, 1852.

Taylor, William R. *Cavalier and Yankee: The Old South and American National Character.* New York: Oxford UP, 1993.

Watson, Charles S. "Simms's Use of Shakespearean Charaters." *Shakespeare and Southern Writers: A Study in Influence.* Ed. Philip C. Kolin. Jackson: UP of Mississippi, 1985. 13-28.

NORMAN MAURICE;

OR,

THE MAN OF THE PEOPLE.

An American Drama.

BY

W. GILMORE SIMMS, ESQ.

AUTHOR OF "THE YEMASSEE," "KATHARINE WALTON," ETC.

FOURTH EDITION, REVISED AND CORRECTED.

CHARLESTON:
WALKER AND RICHARDS.
1852.

Entered, according to Act of Congress, in the year 1851, by
W. GILMORE SIMMS,
In the Clerk's Office of the District Court of the United States, for the District of South-Carolinn.

STEAM POWER-PRESS OF WALKER AND JAMES.

TO

HENRY GOURDIN, ESQ.

OF SOUTH-CAROLINA,

I INSCRIBE THIS DRAMA.

THE AUTHOR.

DRAMATIS PERSONÆ.

Norman Maurice.
Robert Warren, *his kinsman and enemy.*
Richard Osborne, *an attorney and creature of Warren.*
Harry Matthews, *a friend of Warren.*
Col. Blasinghame, *a fire-eater.*
Ben Ferguson, *a leading politician.*
Col. Mercer, } *Politicians of opposite party.*
Col. Brooks, }
Major Savage, *friend of Blasinghame.*
Capt. Catesby, U. S. A., *friend of Maurice.*
   Citizens, Lawyers, &c.
Mrs. Jervas, *a widow.*
Clarice Delancy, *her niece, afterwards wife to Maurice.*
Widow Pressley, *a client of Maurice.*
Kate Pressley, *her grand-daughter.*
Biddy, *a servant girl.*

Scene—First, in Philadelphia; afterwards, in Missouri.

NORMAN MAURICE.

ACT 1.—SCENE 1.

A parlour in the house of Mrs. Jervas, in Walnut street, Philadelphia. Mrs. Jervas and Robert Warren discovered—the latter entering hastily and with discomposure.

 Mrs. Jervas, [*eagerly.*] Well?
 Warren. It is *not* well! 'Tis ill! She has refused me!
 Mrs. J.   Has she then dared?
 Warren. Ay, has she! Something farther—
She does not scruple to avow her passion
For my most worthy cousin, Norman Maurice.
 Mrs. J. She shall repent it—she shall *disavow* it,
Or she shall know!—I'll teach her!—
 Warren.   She's a pupil
With will enough of her own to vex a master!
 Mrs. J. I have a will too which shall master her!
Is she not mine?—my sister's child?—a beggar,
That breathes but by my charity! I'll teach her,
And she shall learn the lesson set for her,

Or I will turn her naked into the streets,
As pennyless as she came. But, wait and see,—
You shall behold—
 Warren.   Nay, wait 'till I am gone,
Then use your best severity. She needs it—
Has no sufficient notion of her duty,
And—
 Mrs. J. No, indeed!
 Warren.   But you must make her wiser.
 Mrs. J. I will!
I've treated her too tenderly!
 Warren.   But show her
Some little glimpse of the danger in her path,—
Shame and starvation—
 Mrs. J.   She deserves them both.
 Warren. And keep my worthy cousin from her presence.
 Mrs. J. He darks these doors no more! The girl, already
Has orders to deny him.
 Warren.   You've done wisely.
A little time,—but keep them separate,—
And we shall conquer her;—ay, conquer *him* too,
For I've a little snare within whose meshes
His feet are sure to fall.
 Mrs. J.   What snare?
 Warren.   No matter!
Be ignorant of the mischief 'till it's over,
And we enjoy its fruits! Meanwhile, be busy,—
Pursue the plan you purpose, and to-morrow,
We shall know farther. I shall use the moments,
'Twixt this and then, in labours which must profit,
Or fortune grows perverse. See you to *her*,
While I take care of *him*.
 Mrs. J.   Oh, never fear me—

I'll summon her the moment you are gone,
And she shall know—
   Warren.   That you may summon her—
For we must lose no time,—I take my leave.
                            Ex. Warren.
   Mrs. J. The pert and insolent baggage! But I'll teach her!
I'll let her know from whose benevolent hand
She eats the bread of charity—whose mercy
It is, that clothes her nakedness with warmth.
                    [*Rings. Enter Biddy.*
Go, Biddy!—send my niece to me. [*Ex. Biddy.*] A beggar,
That fain would be a chooser!—So, Miss!

              Enter Clarice.

   Clarice. Dear Aunt!
   Mrs. J. Ay, you would *dare* me in another fashion,
But you have met your match; and now I tell you,
Clarice Delancy, 'tis in vain you struggle—
   Clarice. What *have* I done?
   Mrs. J.   Oh! you are ignorant,
And innocent seeming as the babe unborn,
If tongue and face could speak for secret conscience,
That harbors what it should not. So, you dare
Avow a passion for that beggarly Maurice,
Whom I've forbid the house!
   Clarice.   Forbidden Maurice!
   Mrs. J. Ay, indeed! forbid!
   Clarice.   In what has he offended?
   Mrs. J. His poverty offends me—his presumption.
   Clarice. Presumption!
   Mrs. J.   He has the audacity to think of you
In marriage—he would heir my property;—
The miserable beggar! who, but lately—

Clarice. And, if the humble Clarice might presume,
There were no fitter husband! From the Fates
I do entreat no happier destiny
Than but to share, o'er all that wealth may proffer,
The beggary that he brings!
 Mrs. J.   But you shall never!
I am your guardian, in the place of mother,
And I will turn you naked from these doors
If you but dare—
 Clarice. Ah! that *were* guardianship,
Becoming the dear sister of a mother,
Who, when she left her hapless child to earth,
Ne'er dream'd of such remembrance, in the future,
Of what beseem'd the past. I've anger'd you,
But cannot chide myself because my nature
Does not revolt at homage of a being
In whom no virtue starves. Suppose him poor!
Wealth makes no certain happiness to hope,
Nor poverty its loss. In Norman Maurice
I see a nobleness that still atones for
The lowly fortunes that offend your pride.
None richer lives in rarest qualities,—
More precious to the soul that feeds on worth,
Than all your city glitter. Do you think
To win me from a feast of such delights,
To the poor fare on common things that make
The wealth of Robert Warren? Madam—my aunt,—
I thank you for the bounty you have shown me!
It had been precious o'er most earthly things,
But that it hath its price, at perilous cost
To things more precious still. Your charity,
That found a shelter for this humble person,
Were all too costly, if it claims in turn

This poor heart's sacrifice. I *cannot* make it!
I will *not* wed this Warren,—for I *know* him—
And, if it be that I shall ever wed,
 Will wed with Norman Maurice—as a man,
Whom most it glads me that I also know.
 Mrs. J. Never shall you wed with *him* while I have pow'r
To keep you from such folly. You're an infant,
That knows not what is needful for your safety,
Or precious for your heart. Be ruled by me,
Or forth you pack. I cut you off forever,
From fortune as from favour.
 Clarice. Welcome death,
Sooner than bonds like these!
 Mrs. J. Ungrateful girl!
And this is the return for all my bounty?
But you shall not achieve your own destruction,
If I can help it. This Maurice never darkens
My dwelling with his shadow. He hath made you
Perverse and disobedient—but he shall not
Thrive by your ruin. See that you prepare
To marry Robert Warren.
 Clarice. With the grave first!—
Its cold and silence, and its crawling things,
Loathsome, that make us shudder but to think on,
Sooner than he!—a base, unworthy creature,
Who steals between his kinsman and the friend,
That gave him highest trust and held him faithful,
To rob him of the treasure he most values.
The reptile that keeps empire in the grave
Sooner than he, shall glide into this bosom,
And make it all his own.
 Mrs. J. Silence, I say!—
Before I madden with your insolence,

And lose the memory of that sainted sister
That left you in my trust.
  Clarice.   My poor, dear mother!
She never dream'd of this, in that dark hour
That lost me to her own!
  Mrs. J.   I'm in her place,
To sway your foolish fancies with a prudence
You will not know yourself. Once more I tell you,
You wed with Warren—Robert Warren, only!
This Maurice— [*noise without*] Ha! That noise?—
  Maurice, [*in the hall without.*] I *must*, my girl!
  Clarice. 'Tis Maurice now.
  Mrs. J. The Insolent! will he dare!
  Biddy, [*in the hall without.*] Mrs. Jervas says, sir—
  Maurice, [*without.*] Ay! ay! she *says!*—
But when a lady means civilities,
'Tis still my custom to do justice to her,
By seeking them in person. There, my good girl,
You've done your duty as you should. Now, please you,
I will do mine. [*Entering the room.*] Madam—
  Mrs. J.   Was ever insolence—
  Biddy, [*entering.*] Mr. Maurice *would*, ma'am.
  Mrs. J.   This conduct, sir—
  Maurice. Would be without its plea at common seasons,—
And he whose purpose was a morning visit,
The simply social object of the idler,
Who finds in his own time and company
The very worst offence, could offer nothing,
To plead for his intrusion on that presence,
Which, so politely, shuts the door against him.
  Mrs. J. Well, sir?
  Maurice. But I am none of these.
  Mrs. J.   What plea, sir?—

Maurice. Some natures have their privilege—some passions
Demand a hearing. There are rights of feeling,
That art can never stifle—griefs, affections,
That never hear the civil "Not at home!"
When home itself is perill'd by submission.
He's but a haggard that obeys the check,
When all that's precious to his stake of life
Is fastened on the string. Necessity
Makes bold to ope the door which fashion's portress
Would bolt and bar against him. 'Tis *my* fate,
That prompts me to a rudeness, which my nurture
Would else have shrunk from. But that I have rights
Which move me to defiance of all custom,
I had not vex'd your presence.
  Mrs. J.   Rights, sir—rights?
  Maurice. Ay, madam, the most precious to the mortal!
Rights of the heart, which make the heart immortal
In those affections which still show to earth,
The only glimpses we have left of Eden.
Behold in her, [*pointing to Clarice,*] my best apology—
One, whom to gaze on silences complaint,
And justifies the audacity that proves
Its manhood in its error. Clarice, my love,
Is there in any corner of your heart
An echo to the will that says to Maurice,
Your presence here is hateful?   [*Takes her hand.*]
  Clarice.   Can you ask?
  Maurice.   Enough!—
  Mrs. J. Too much, I say. Let go her hand,
And leave this dwelling, sir! I'm mistress here;
And shall take measures for security
Against this lawless insolence.
  Maurice.   Awhile! Awhile!
2

You *are* the mistress here;—I *will* obey you;—
Will leave your presence, madam, never more
To trouble you with mine. You now deny me
The privilege, that never act of mine
Hath properly made forfeit. You behold me
The suitor to your niece. You hear her language,—
How different from your own—that, with its bounty
Makes rich my heart with all the gifts in hers!
Sternly, you wrest authority from judgment,
To exercise a will that puts to scorn
Her hopes no less than mine! I would have pleaded
Your calm return to judgment;—would entreat you
To thoughts of better favour that might sanction,
With the sweet blessing of maternal love,
The mutual passion living in our hearts;
But that I know how profitless the pleading,
Which, in the ear of prejudice, would soften
The incorrigible wax that deafens pride.
I plead not for indulgence—will *not* argue
The cruelty that finds in charity
Commission for that matchless tyranny
That claims the right to break the orphan's heart
Because it finds her bread.
  Clarice, [*aside to Norman.*] Spare her, Norman.
  Maurice, [*aside to Clarice.*] Oh! Will I not! Yet wherefore
   need I spare,
When, if the Holy Law be not a mock,
The justice which must break this heart of stone,
Will send her howling through eternity.
'Twere mercy, which in season speaks the truth,
That, in the foretaste of sure penalties,
May terrify the offender from his path,
And send him to his knees.

Clarice, [*aside to Maurice.*] For my sake, Norman.
Maurice, [*to Mrs. J.*] Yet, madam, in this freeest use of pow'r,
Which drives me hence, be merciful awhile,
And, if this heart, so dearly link'd with mine,
Through love and faith unperishing, must turn
Its fountains from that precious overflow
That kept my flow'rs in bloom—yet, ere the word,
That leaves me sterile ever thence, be said,
Suffer us, apart awhile, to speak of parting!
Words of such import still ask fewest ears,
And words of grief and hopelessness like ours,
Must needs have utterance in such lowly tones,
As best declare the condition of the heart,
That's muffled for despair. But a few moments
We'll walk apart together.
    Mrs. J.   It is useless!
What needs—
    Maurice. What need of sorrow ever? Could earth speak,
Prescribing laws to that Divinity,
That still smites rock to water, we should hear,
The universal voice of that one plea,
That claims for man immunity from troubles
Which make proud eyes o'erflow. Who should persuade
His fellow to opinion of the uses
That follow from his tears? What school, or teacher,
Would seek to show that chemistry had art,
To fix and harden the dilating drops
To brilliants as they fall,—such as no crown
In Europe might affect? One finds no succour,
Sovereign to break the chain about his wrist,
From all the fountains that o'ersluice the heart;
Yet will he weep, though useless. He who stands,
Waiting upon the scaffold for the signal,

That flings him down the abyss, still hoards each minute
That niggard fate allows. That single minute
Still shrines a hope;—if not a hope, a feeling,
That finds a something precious even in pain,
And will not lose the anxiety that racks him,
Lest he make forfeit of a something better
Which yet he cannot name. And, at the last,
I, whom you doom to loss of more than life,
May well implore the respite of a moment,
If but to suffer me to count once more,
The treasure that I lose. A moment, madam?

 Mrs. J. [*walks up the stage.*] A single moment, then.
 Maurice.   Oh! you are gracious!
A single moment is a boundless blessing
To him you rob of time! Clarice, my love.
 Clarice.   My Norman!
 Maurice. Oh! is it thus, my Clarice—is it thus?
 Clarice. We have been children, Norman, in our dreams;
We are the sport of fate!
 Maurice.   And shall be ever,
If that there be no courage in our hearts
To shape the fates to favour by our will.
 Clarice.   What mean you, Norman?
 Maurice.   What should Norman mean,
But, if he can, to grapple with his fortune,
And, like a sturdy wrestler in the ring,
Throw heart and hope into the perilous struggle?
What should I mean but happiness for thee,—
Thou willing, as myself? Who strives with fate,
Must still, like him, the mighty Macedonian,
Seize the coy priestess by the wrist, and lead her
Where yet she would not go! Suppose me faithful
To the sweet passion I have tender'd you,

And what remains in this necessity,
But that, made resolute by grim denial,
I challenge from your love sufficient courage,
To take the risks of mine!
    Clarice.   Within your eye
A meaning more significant than your words,
Would teach me still to tremble. That I love you,
You doubt not, Norman! That my heart hath courage
To match the love it feels for you—
    Maurice.   It hath—it hath!
If that the love be there, as I believe it,
That love will bring, to nourish needful strength,
A virtue that makes love a thing of soul,
And arms its will with wings. Oh! read you not,
My meaning—
    Mrs. J. [*approaching.*] Your moment is a long one, sir.
    Maurice.   Ah, madam!
Who chides the executioner when he suffers
The victim his last words—though still he lingers
Ere he would reach the last? But a few moments,
And I have spoken all that my full heart
Might not contain with safety.
    Mrs. J. [*retiring up the stage.*]   Be it so, sir.
    Maurice.   You hear, my Clarice. We've another moment:
But one, it seems, unless your resolution
Takes its complexion from the fate that threatens
And shows an equal will. If then, in truth,
You love me—
    Clarice.   Oh! look not thus!
    Maurice.   I doubt not;—
And yet, dear Clarice, if indeed you love me,
The single moment that this woman gives us,
Becomes a life;—to me, of happiness,—

To thee, as full of happiness as thou
Might hope to gain from me. She would deny us,—
Would wed thee to that subtle Robert Warren—

    Clarice.   I'll perish first!
    Maurice.   No need of perishing
When I can bring thee to security.
I knew thy straits—the tyranny which thou suffer'st
Because of thy dependence; and my struggle,
Since this conviction reached me—day and night—
Was, that I might from this condition snatch thee,
And, in thy happier fortunes, find mine own!
I have prepared for this.

    Clarice.   What would'st thou, Norman?
    Mrs. J., [*approaching.*]   Your moments fly.
    Maurice.   I soon shall follow them.
    Mrs. J., [*retiring again.*] The sooner, sir, the better.
    Maurice.   She would spare me,
The argument which shows thee what is needful.

    Clarice. Speak! I have courage equal to my love!
    Maurice. I try thee though I doubt not! If thou lov'st me,
Thou'lt yield, without a question, to my purpose,
And give me all thy trust.

    Clarice.   Will I not, Norman?
    Maurice. Then, with the night, I make thee mine, Clarice!—
Steal forth at evening. There shall be a carriage,
And my good hostess, whom thou know'st, in waiting.
Our future home is ready.

    Clarice. Let me think, Norman?
    Maurice. That's as your excellent aunt, who now approaches,
May please:—but, surely, when to my fond pleading
You sweetly vow'd yourself as mine alone,
The proper thought that sanctions my entreaty
Was all complete and perfect.

Clarice. But Norman how—
How should I, in your poverty, encumber
Your cares with a new burden?
   Maurice. There is no poverty,
Which the true courage, and the bold endeavour,
The honest purpose, the enduring heart,
Crowned with a love that blesses while it burdens,
May not defy in such a land as ours!
We'll have but few wants having one another!—
And for these wants, some dawning smiles of fortune
Already have prepared me. Trust me, Clarice,
I will not take thee to a worse condition,
In one whose charities shall never peril
The affections they should foster.
   Mrs. J. [*approaching*] Sir,—again!
   Maurice. Yes, yes—most excellent madam—yes—again!
There's but a single syllable between us,
Your niece hath left unspoken.—My Clarice!
   Clarice. I'm thine!
   Maurice.   *'Tis spoken!*
And now I live again!
   Mrs. J. Well sir—art done at last?
   Maurice. Done! Ay, madam—done!
You've held me narrowly to a strict account—
And yet, I thank you. You've been merciful
After a fashion which invokes no justice,
And yet may find it, madam. Yet—I thank you!
The word *is* said that's needful to our parting;
And that I do not in despair depart,
Is due to these last moments. Fare you well!
Be you as safe, henceforth, from all intrusion,
As you shall be from mine. Clarice—farewell!
   Clarice. Norman.

Maurice, [*embracing her.*]　　But one embrace!
Mrs. J.　　Away, sir.
Maurice.　In earnest of those pleasant bonds hereafter,
That none shall dare gainsay.　Clarice—Remember!

　　　　　　　　　　　　　　　　　[*Exit Maurice.*

Clarice.　Go, Norman, and believe me.
Mrs. J.　　Get you in!　　　　　　　　*Exeunt.*

SCENE II.

A Lawyer's office in Philadelphia.　Richard Osborne at a desk writing.

Enter Robert Warren.

Warren, [*eagerly.*]　Hast drawn the paper, Osborne?
Osborne.　　　　It is here.
Warren.　The copy this?—
Osborne.　And this the original.
Warren, [*examining papers.*]　'Tis very like!　You've done
　　　it famously:
One knows not which is which; and Norman Maurice,
Himself, would struggle vainly to discover
The difference 'twixt the words himself hath written,
And these your skill hath copied to a hair.
We shall deceive him.
　　Osborne.　　Why would you deceive him?
　　Warren.　Eh!　Why?　It is my instinct!　Are you answer'd?
I hate him!　Would you have a better answer?
　　Osborne.　Why hate him when his kindness still have served you?

This very obligation which hath bound him,
And given us cruel power o'er his fortunes,—
His purse—perhaps his honour—
    Warren.   Why, perhaps?
Is it doubtful, think you, that this fatal writing,
Made public,—will disgrace him?
    Osborne.   An error only,—
The thoughtless sport of boyhood—wholly guiltless
Of all dishonest purpose, We have used it,—
You rather—and the profit has been ours!—
Why, if he pays the money as he proffers,
Why treasure still this paper? More—why hate him?
    Warren. Let it suffice you that I have my reasons!—
And let me tell you, Osborne, that I love not
This sympathy which you show for Norman Maurice.
Beware! who goes not with me is against me!
    Osborne. I'm in your power, I know—
    Warren. Then let your wisdom
Abate its fond pretension as my teacher!
I'm better pleased with service than tuition;
Will hold you as my ally, not my master!
I have remarked, of late, that you discover
Rare virtues in my cousin! He hath fee'd you;
Employed you as attorney in his cases—
    Osborne. Not more than other counsellors.
    Warren.   No matter!
It is enough that you are mine!
    Osborne.   This jealousy—
    Warren. Is only vigilance! Each look of favour,
Bestow'd on him I loathe, is disaffection
In him that's bound to me.
    Osborne.   This document?—
    Warren. The *real* one,—the *original*—is mine;

The *copy* you will yield him when he pays you;—
That he will do so, now, I make no question,
Though where his money comes from is my wonder.
    Osborne.   The case of Jones & Peters, just determined,
Brings him large fees.   Another action,
The insurance case of Ferguson & Brooks,
Secures him handsome profits.   Other cases,
Have lately brought him, with new reputation,
Liberal returns of money.
    Warren.   We'll have all!
See that you pile the costs—crowd interest—
Expense of service; tax to the uttermost
The value of your silence and forbearance—
Leave nothing you have done without full charges,
While, what has been forborne, more highly rated,
Shall sweep the remaining eagles from his purse.
    Osborne.   What bitterness is yours!
    Warren.   Oh! quite ungracious,
Contrasted with the sweetness of your moods!
Once more, beware!   Do as I bid you, Osborne,
Or you shall feel me.   Yield him up this *copy*,
Which we shall see him, with delirious rapture,
Thrust in the blazing furnace,—little dreaming,
That still the damning scrawl that blasts his honour,
Lies here, in the possession of his foe!
    Osborne.   Will nothing move you, Warren?
    Warren.   His funeral only,—
To follow—while above his burial place,
I show this fatal paper,—still lamenting
That one with so much talent should have falter'd,
When virtue cried "Be firm!"—O! I will sorrow,
So deeply o'er his sad infirmity,
That they who come to weep above his grave,

Will turn from it in scorn. But, get you ready ;—
You'll sup with me ; and afterwards we'll seek him.
We must look smiling then as summer flowers,
Nor show the serpent crouching in the leaves.   [*Exeunt.*

SCENE III.

Evening : Chestnut Street.   Enter Maurice with Clarice.

Maurice.   Thou'rt mine, my Clarice.
Clarice.   Wholly thine, my husband.
Maurice.   Now let the furies clamour as they may,
That the capricious fortune which had mock'd
Our blessings with denial, has been baffled
By the true nobleness of that human will,
Which, when the grim necessity looks worst,
Can fearlessly resolve to brave its fate.
Thou'rt mine, and all grows suppliant in my path,
That lately looked defiance.   We are one !—
This is our dwelling, Clarice :—let us in.
              [*They enter the house of Maurice.*

SCENE IV.

The parlour of a dwelling in the residence of Maurice, handsomely and newly furnished.   Enter Warren and Osborne.

Warren.   I am amazed.
Osborne.   'Tis certainly a change

From his old lodging house in Cedar street.

    Warren. His run of luck hath crazed him, and he fancies
The world is in his string.

    Osborne. He's not far wrong!
His arguments have made a great impression;
Their subtlety and closeness, and the power
Of clear and forcible development,
Which seems most native to his faculty!
He was born an orator! With such a person—
A voice to glide from thunder into music,
A form and face so full of majesty,
Yet, with such frankness and simplicity,—
So much to please, and so commanding—

    Warren. Pshaw!—
You prate as do the newspapers, with a jargon
Of wretched common-place, bestuffed with phrases,
That, weighed against the ballad of an idiot,
Would show less burden and significance.
We'll spoil his fortunes—

    Osborne. Hark! He comes.

    Warren. Be firm now!
See that you do it manfully—no halting.—

    Osborne. You still persist, then?

    Warren. Ay! when I have him here. [*touching his breast.*]
             Enter Norman Maurice.

    Maurice. Be seated, sirs.
You bring with you the paper? [*To Osborne.*

    Osborne. It is here, sir. [*Giving copy of document.*
And here the separate claim—the costs and charges.

    Maurice. 'Tis well! This first!—I pay this money, sir,
In liquidation of this wretched paper,
To which my hand appears, and, for which writing,
The world, unconscious of the facts, might hold me

A most unhappy criminal. Your knowledge
Includes this person's agency—my cousin—
As still, in moments of insidious fondness,
It is his wont to call me.
 Warren. Norman, nay!
 Maurice. [*impatiently to Warren.*] Awhile, awhile, sir! we
   shall deal directly!—
I said [*to Osborne,*] your knowledge of this boyish error,
Betrayed the agency of Robert Warren,
Which does not here appear. He made *that* guilty
Which in itself was innocent. These moneys,
Procured by him upon this document,
Were all by him consumed. You were his agent,
Perhaps as ignorant of his vicious deed,
As I, who am its victim. Was it so, sir?
 Osborne. I sold for him the bill, sir, knowing nothing,
And still believed it genuine.
 Maurice.   He will tell you,
That, what I utter of his agency,
In this insane and inconsiderate act,
Is true as Holy Writ! Speak, Robert Warren!
 Warren. I have admitted it already, Norman.
 Maurice. [*To Osborne.*] Be you the witness of his words
   hereafter.
Here is your money,—and I take this paper,
The proof of boyish error and misfortune,
But not of crime, in me. Thus, let it perish,
With that confiding and believing nature,
Which gave me to the power of one so base! [*putting it in the
 fire, and putting his foot on it while it burns.*
 Warren. Norman! Cousin!
 Maurice. You cozen me no more!
And if your agent has the wit to gather,

A lesson from your faithlessness to me,
You will not cozen him. Take counsel sir,
And never trust this man! [*To Osborne.*

    Warren. Norman Maurice!

    Maurice. [*To Osborne*] Our business ends! Will it please
        you, leave us now!

[*Exit Osborne: Warren is about to follow when Maurice lays
  his hand on his shoulder.*

    Maurice. Stay *you!* There must be other words before we part,
Not many, but most needful.

    Warren.   Let me pray you,
To fashion them in less offensive spirit.

    Maurice. Why, so I should, could I suppose one virtue,
A life to leaven a dense mass of vices,
Remain'd within your bosom. You *shall* listen
Though every syllable should be a sting!
'Twould not offend me greatly, Robert Warren,
If, as I brand thy baseness on thy forehead,
Thy heart, with courage born of just resentment,
Should move thee to defiance! It would glad me,
In sudden strife, to put a proper finish,
To thy deep, secret, foul hostility.

    Warren. You have no reason for this cruel language.

    Maurice. Look on me as thou say'st the monstrous falsehood;
But lift thine eye to mine—and, if thy glance
Can brazen out the loathing in mine own,
I will forgive thee all! Thou dar'st not do it!
No reason, say'st thou?—Thou, whose arrant cunning,
Hath taken the profits of three toilsome years
To pay thy wage of sin,—and smutch'd my garments,
That else had known no stain!

    Warren.   Have I not
Confess'd that wrong and folly?—

Maurice.   Wert repentant,
When making thy confession—
     Warren.   So I am!
     Maurice. Traitor! I know thee better! Thy confession
But followed on detection! While thou mad'st it,
The busy devil, dwelling in thy heart,
Was framing other schemes of crime and hatred,
Outbraving all the past. Ev'n while my pity
Was taking thee to mercy, thou wast planning
New evil to my fortunes!
     Warren.   Never, Norman!
By Heaven! you do me wrong.
     Maurice.   Pure Innocent,
The very angels look on thee with sorrow,
To see such virtue suffer such injustice!—
But hearken, while I paint another picture:—
The fiends exulting in thy ready service,
A voluntary minister of evil,
As, with a spirit born of hell and hatred,
Thou pluck'st the flower of hope from happiness,
To plant the thorn instead.
     Warren. What crime is this?
     Maurice I heard thy plea for mercy! I believed thee,
And, as thou wert the child of that dear woman
Who called my mother, sister, I forgave thee,
Most glad to listen to thy deep assurance
Of shame for each sad error. So, I took thee,
Once more, to confidence—my bosom open'd,
And show'd thee, shrined within its holiest chamber,
The image of the being that I lov'd!—
I led thee to her—taught her to behold thee,
My friend and kinsman; and, misdoubting never,
Still saw thee bend thy footsteps to her dwelling,

Nor dream'd that to the flowers that made my Eden,
Myself had brought the serpent!

    Warren. What means this?

    Maurice. What! Thou know'st nothing? Thou hast no
        conjecture
Of what the serpent sought within the garden!
Why, man, he whispered in Eve's innocent ears,
The oiliest nothings,—mingled with such slander
Of him who sought to make himself her Adam,
That—

    Warren. 'Tis false!—I swear! I never did this mischief!

    Maurice. Liar! The oath thou tak'st is thy perdition!
Behold the evidence that proves thy blackness,
In contrast with its purity and truth!
Clarice! Come forth! My wife, sir!
                      [*Enter Clarice from within.*

    Warren. Damnation!   [*Warren rushes out.*

    Maurice. Thus fled the fiend, touch'd by Ithuriel's spear,
Even from the reptile rising to the fiend,
And speeding from the Eden that his presence
Shall never trouble more. Henceforth, dear wife,
Our paradise shall still be free from taint;
A realm of sweetness unobscured by shadow,
And freshening still with flow'rs that take their beauty,
As favour'd still by thine. From this blest moment,
Our peace shall be secure!

    Clarice.   And yet I fear,
This bold, bad man.

    Maurice. Bad, but not bold! Fear nothing!
I've plucked his sting! Thou know'st the cruel story;
I told thee all,—suppressed no syllable—
Of his perversion of a simple paper,
Wherein, in vain display of penmanship,

I gave him power for practice which he seized on,
Exposing me to ruin. In those embers,
The fatal proof lies buried. I am free;—
And in the freedom I have won from him,
And in the bondage I have sworn to thee,
I write the record of my happiness!
This day I feel triumphant as the hunter,
Who, on the wild steed that his skill hath captured,
Rifle in grasp, and bridle rein flung loose,
Darts forth upon the prairie's waste of empire,
And feels it all his own!

 Clarice.   I share thy triumph—
Would share that waste with thee and feel no sorrow,
For all that love foregoes.

 Maurice.   I take thy promise—
Will try thy strength, thy courage and thy heart,
As little thou hast fancied! Clarice, dear wife,
With dawn we leave this city.

 Clarice.   How! to-morrow?
And leave this city, Norman?

 Maurice. Dost thou fail me?

 Clarice. No! I am thine! My world is in thy love;
I wish no dearer dwelling place—would ask
No sweeter realm of home! Go, where thou wilt,
I cling to thee as did the Hebrew woman
To him who had his empire in her heart.

 Maurice. I bless thee for this proof of thy affection!
This is the city of thy birth and mine,
But that's our native land alone which suffers
That we take root and flourish;—those alone,
Our kindred, who will gladden in our growth,
And succour till we triumph. Here, it may be,
That, after weary toil, and matchless struggle,

When strength subsides in age, they will acknowledge,
That I am worthy of my bread,—may bid me,
Look up and be an alderman or mayor!—
And this were of their favour. The near neighbours,
Who grew with us, and saw our gradual progress,
Who knew the boy, and all his sports and follies,
Have seldom faith that he will grow the man
To cast them into shadow, We'll go hence!—
    Clarice. Whither, dear Norman?
    Maurice. Whither! Dost thou ask?
Both in God's keeping, Clarice—thou in mine!
I'll tender thee as the most precious treasure,
That city ever yielded wilderness.
    Clarice. I know thou wilt;—but what thy means, my husband?
Thou told'st me thou wast poor.
    Maurice. Means! I have manhood!
Youth, strength, and men say, intellect—
    Clarice. You have! You have!
    Maurice. A heart at ease, secure in its affections,
And still the soul to seek each manly struggle!
Wide is the world before me—a great people,
Spread o'er a realm, along whose verdant meadows
The sun can never set. I know this people—
Love them—would make them mine! I have ambition
To serve them in high places, and do battle
With the arch-tyrannies, in various guises,
That still from freedom pluck its panoply,
Degrade its precious rites, and, with vain shadows,
Mock the fond hopes that fasten on their words.
    Clarice. Could you not serve them *here?*
    Maurice. No! No!
    Clarice.   Wherefore not?—
And O! they need some saviour here, methinks!

Maurice. Ay! They do need! But I am one of them,—
Sprung from themselves—have neither friends nor fortune,
And will not stoop, entreating as for favour,
When I would serve to save! They lack all faith
In him who scorns to flatter their delusions,
And lie them to self-worship. In the West,
There is a simpler and a hardier nature,
That proves men's values, not by wealth and title,
But mind and manhood. There, no ancient stocks,
Claim power from precedence. Patrician people,
That boast of virtues in their grandmothers,
Are challenged for their own. With them it answers,
If each man founds his family, and stands
The father of a race of future men!
Mere parchment, and the vain parade of title,
Lifts no man into stature. Such a region
Yields all that I demand—an open field,
And freedom to all comers. So, the virtues
Flourish according to their proper nature;
And each man, as he works with will and courage,
Reaps the good fruitage proper to his claim;—
Thither, dear wife!

   Clarice. I'm thine!

   Maurice.   Thy ready answer,
Completes my triumph! Wings are at my shoulders,
And more than eagle empires woo my flight!
Yet, do I something fear,—Clarice—

   Clarice. What fear?

   Maurice. *Thou* art not ambitious.

   Clarice.   But for thee, Norman;
If that, in service at thy shrine of glory,
Thou dost not lose the love—

   Maurice.   Be satisfied

That, when my state is proudest, thou shalt be
The one, whom, most of all, these eyes shall look for,
This heart still follow with devoted service.
But, to thy preparations : I will follow ;—
Before the dawn we shall have left this city. [*Clarice going.*
That reptile, [*musingly.*]
   Clarice. [*returning.*] Norman!
   Maurice. My Clarice! [*embracing her.* [*Exit Clarice.*
His fangs are drawn!—
Yet, somehow, he is present to my thoughts,
As if he still had power. But, let him dare,
Once more to cross my path, and he shall feel
His serpent head grow flat beneath my heel. [*Exit within.*

END OF ACT FIRST.

ACT II.—SCENE I.

*Scene: Missouri. A room in the cottage of Norman Maurice.
Enter Maurice and Clarice.*

   Clarice. Oh! Norman, this is happiness.
   Maurice.   'Tis more,—
Security in happiness. Our blossoms
Fear not the spoiler. On your cheek the roses
Declare a joyous presence in the heart,
That makes our cottage bloom.
   Clarice.   You triumph too,
In favour as in fortune. On all sides
I hear your name reëchoed with a plaudit,
That fills my bosom with exulting raptures
I never knew before.
   Maurice.   Ah! this is nothing,
Dear heart, to the sweet peace that crowns our dwelling,
And tells us, though the tempest growls afar,
Its thunders strike not here. The fame I covet
Is still in tribute subject to your joys;
And, these secure—you, happy in my bosom—
My pride forgets its aim! Ambition slumbers
Nor makes me once forgetful of the rapture,
That follows your embrace.   [*Knock without.*
   Clarice. The widow Pressley.
   Maurice. Quick, welcome her.—Poor woman, we will save her.

Clarice. I joy to hear you say so.—Come in, madam.
[*Enter Widow Pressly and Kate.*
Maurice. Welcome, dear madam; you must needs be anxious;
But still be hopeful. I have brought the action,
And doubt not, from my study of your case,
That we shall gain it—put the ursurper out,
And win you back some portion of your wealth.
The truth is on our side,—the evidence
Sustains your claim most amply. We shall gain it!
Widow. Alas! sir, but the power of this bad man
Maurice. Need not be powerful here.
Widow. You know it not;—
His wealth, his violence—
Maurice. Will scarce prevail.
Widow. He buys or bullies justice at his pleasure;
No lawyer here would undertake my case
Lest he should lose a friend or make a foe;
And thus, for fifteen years—
Maurice. He buys not me,
And scarce will profit by an insolence,
That hopes to bully here.
Widow. Oh! sir, I tremble,
And cannot help but doubt. I know your talents;
All people speak of them,—and yet I fear!
With hopes so often lifted and defeated,
How should I dream of better fortune now?
The widow and the orphan find small favour,
In struggle with the strong and selfish man;
And this success you promise—
Maurice. None may take
The sovereign accent from the lip of Fate
And say—this thing is written certainly—
But, if I err not, madam, better promise,

Of the clear dawn and the unclouded sunshine,
Ne'er waited on the night. I trust the Jury.
They have no fears to nurse, and seek no favours,
As do that class of men, the mean ambitious,
Who, for the lowly greed of appetite,
Or hungering for a state they never merit,
Cringe with a servile zeal to wealth and numbers,
And nothing show but baseness when they rise.
My faith is in the people.

 Widow. Mine in you, sir.

 Maurice. I will deserve your confidence. This person,
Who robb'd you of your fortune, would but vainly
Attempt to bully me. I am no bully,
But something have I in my soul which strengthens
Its courage, when the insolent would dare
Usurp the rights that I am set to guard.
Be hopeful, madam. Take no care for the morrow,
Though, with the morrow, our great trial comes!
God and his angels keep the innocent,
And, in his own good season, will redress
Their many wrongs with triumph.

 Widow.   Sir, I thank you;—
And this poor child, the child of bitterness,
If not of wrath, shall bless you in her prayers,
That nightly seek her mother in the heavens!

 Maurice. [*kissing the child.*] Your name is Kate, they tell
  me—a sweet name!
You'll, pray for us to-night, Kate. With the morrow.
If my heart's hope do not deceive my heart,
Your prayers shall all be answer'd.—I'll think of her,
And of her sweet and innocent face to-morrow,
When striving with her enemy.

Kate. I'll pray, sir,
As if you were my father.
Widow. She has none, sir.
Maurice. Losing or winning, daughter, still in me,
Look for a father who will cherish you.
Widow. Farewell, good sir, I have not words to thank you.
Maurice. You have a heart that overflows with speech,
And swells into your eyes! No more, dear madam,
Be hopeful and be happy. [*Exeunt widow and child.*
We must gain it.
The proofs are clear—I cannot doubt the issue,—
And still a prescient something at my heart,
Awakes its triumph with assuring accents
That never spoke in vain. But, who are these?
[*Enter Col. Mercer and Brooks.*
Welcome, gentlemen.
Mercer. We trust, sir, that you see in us your friends.
Maurice. Such, since our brief acquaintance you have seemed
sir,
And mine's a heart preferring to confide;
That still would rather suffer wrong of faith,
Than not believe in man.
Mercer. You'll find us true;—
And thus it is, that, sure of our good purpose,
We come to counsel with you as a friend.
Maurice. As friends, I welcome you. Be seated, sirs.
Brooks. We do regard you, sir, as one to help us,—
In public matters. From our knowledge of you,
We've said among our friends, this is our man;
And, looking still to you to serve our people,
We hear with grief that you are in a peril
Whose straits, perchance, you know not.
Maurice. Peril, sir?

Brooks. You have brought action for the widow Pressley,
For the recovery of a large possession,
Withheld by Colonel Blasinghame—
   Maurice.   'Tis true, sir,
   Mercer. You do not know this man.
   Maurice. I've heard of him.
   Mercer. But not that he is one whom men find prudent
To pass with civil aspect, nor confront
With wrath or opposition. He has power,
Such as few men possess, or dare contend with—
Has wealth in great abundance—is perhaps,
Most fearless and most desperate in battle,
Who better loves the conflict with his fellow
Than any gifts that peaceful life can bring;
Endow'd with giant strength and resolution,
And such a shot, from five to fifteen paces,
As still to shatter, wavering in the wind,
The slenderest wand of willow.
   Maurice. Famous shooting!
   Brooks. It were not wise to wake his enmity!
We look to you to serve our cause in Congress—
Make him your foe, and he opposes you;
His wealth—his popularity—the terrors,
His very name provokes,—all leagued against you—
You still a stranger.
   Maurice.   Patiently, I hear;
And though I feel not like solicitude
With that you show for me, am grateful for it!
And now, sirs, let us understand each other.
I am a man who, in pursuit of duty,
Will hold no parley with that week day prudence
Which teaches still how much a virtue costs.
Of this man, Blasinghame, I've heard already,—

Even as you both describe him. It would seem,
Lest I should fail in utter ignorance,
He took a patient trouble on himself,
To school me in his virtues. Read this letter. [*gives letter.*

   Mercer.
   Brooks. } His hand!—his signature! [*they read.*

   Maurice. Well, gentlemen, you see it written there,
What are my dangers, if I dare to venture
This widow's cause against him. Favour me,
And read the answer which has just been written.

   Mercer. [*reads aloud.*] Sir:—The suit of Pressley *vs.* Blasinghame will be prosecuted to conclusion, without regard to consequences, with the best strength and abilities of
                                     NORMAN MAURICE.

   Maurice. It is brief, sir."
   Brooks. 'Tis a defiance!
   Maurice. 'Twas meant so, gentlemen. I am a man,
Or I am nothing! This poor widow's cause,
The very insolence of this Blasinghame,
Hath made my own! I'll die for it if need be.

   Mercer. Art principled 'gainst the duel?
   Maurice.   Rather ask,
If, when my enemy takes me by the throat,
I do oppose him with an homily.
No man shall drive me from society!—
I take the laws I find of force, and use them,
For my protection and defence, as others
Employ them for assault.

   Mercer. You've practised then?
   Maurice. Never shot pistol.
   Brooks. Nor rifle?
   Maurice. Scarcely!
   Mercer. You are very rash, sir!

Maurice.   Ay! but rashness, sir,
Becomes a virtue in a case like this;
And the brave heart, untaught in human practice,
Finds good assurance from another source
That prompts its action right. This letter's written,
And goes within the hour. Let Blasinghame
Chafe as he may, and thunder to the terror,
Of those who have no manhood in themselves;—
He thunders at these portals still in vain!
To-morrow comes the trial—after that!—
But let the future wear what look it may,
I'll find the heart to meet it—as a man!
  Mercer. Then you are firm?
  Maurice.   As are the rocks,
In conflict with the sea.
  Mercer.   We joy to find you thus!
We'll stand by you through danger to the last.
  Brooks. Ay, Maurice, we are with you.
  Maurice.   Friends, your hands!—
I am not used to friendship, but I love it,
As still a precious gift, vouchsafed by heaven,
Next best to love of woman! For this danger,—
Fear nothing! we shall 'scape it! Nay, 'twill give us,
Or truth is not of God, new plumes for triumph!

SCENE II.

The law office of Richard Osborne. Osborne discovered writing.
Enter Warren.

  Warren. We're on the track at last, Look at that letter;
It comes from our old comrade, Harry Matthews,

And tells us miracles of Norman Maurice!—
Our worthy cousin has the run of fortune;—
She seems to crown him with her richest favours,
As some old bawd, grown hacknied in the market,
Adopts a virgin passion in her dotage,
And yields to her late folly, all the profits
That followed the old vice. He's growing finely;
But I shall dock his feathers.

    Osborne. [*reading.*]   In Missouri.

    Warren. Ay, in St. Louis, that great western city,
Our worthy cousin, Norman, has grown famous!
You read what Matthews writes. In one short twelvemonth
He springs above all shoulders.

    Osborne.   I look'd for it!
He's not the man whom fortune can keep under.

    Warren. What! you forget our precious document?

    Osborne. You will not use it *now?*

    Warren.   Ah! will I not then?
If ever useful, *now's* the right time for it!
See you not that he rises like an eagle,
Already is in practice with the ablest,
Wins popular favour without working for it,
And stands i' the way of better politicians?
They fit his name to music for bad singers,
To whom none listen save at suffrage time.—
We'll spoil the song for him.

    Osborne. What would you do?—

    Warren. You are dull, Dick Osborne! Have I yet to tell
        you,
That, over all, conspicuous in my hate,
This minion of Fortune stands. His better luck
Hath robbed me of a prize which most I treasured—
His better genius trampled mine to dust,—
Humbled my pride when at its height, and crushed me,

Until I learned to loathe myself, as being
So feeble in his grasp.
 Osborne. He crushes you no longer!
 Warren. Can I forget the past? This memory
Becomes a part of the nature o' the man,
And of his future makes a fearful aspect,
Unless he cures its hurts. My path is where
My enemy treads in triumph! I shall seek it,
And 'twill be hard if hate, well leagued with cunning,
Is baffled of his toil. I seek St. Louis!
 Osborne, Beware! You'll make him desperate!
 Warren. I hope so!
 Osborne. It brings its perils with it! Norman Maurice
Will rend his hunter!—
 Warren. If he be not wary!
But, fear you nothing. You shall go with me,
And see how deftly, with what happy art,
I shall prepare the meshes for my captive.
 Osborne. Me! go with you?—and wherefore?
 Warren.   A small matter!—
While I shall drive the nail, you'll clinch the rivet.
I'd have you there to prove this document!
 Osborne. Spare me this, Warren!
 Warren. I can spare you nothing.
 Osborne. I do not hate this man! He hath not wrong'd me,
Cross'd not my path, nor, with a better fortune,
Won from me aught I cherish'd.
 Warren.   Enough! Enough!—
Me hath he robb'd and wrong'd—*me* hath he cross'd—
His better fortune still a fate to mine!—
My injury is yours! You love me, Osborne,—
Will do the thing that I regard as needful,
The more especially as you have secrets,

No less than Norman Maurice. We shall go,
Together, as I fancy, to St. Louis!
    Osborne. This is mere tyranny, Warren.
    Warren.   Very like it!
Guilt ever finds its tyrant in its secret,
And, twinn'd with every crime, the accuser stands,
Its own grim shadow, with the scourge and torture.
    Osborne. A dark and damnable truth! Would I had perish'd
Ere I had fallen, and follow'd, as you bade me!
    Warren. Spare the vain toil to cheat a troubled conscience,
And to your preparations. By the morrow,
We'll be upon the road.
    Osborne. But, for these papers?
    Warren. Confound the papers! They will wait for us,
But opportunity never! Get you ready,
And hush all vain excuses. If my sway
Be somewhat tyrannous, still it hath its profits :—
Be you but true, and from the Egyptian spoil,
There shall be still sufficient for your toil.   [*Exit Warren.*
    Osborne. I'm chain'd to the stake! He hath me in his pow'r!—
How truly hath he pictured my estate!—
Thus he who doth a deed of ill in youth,
Raises a ghost no seventy years can lay!
I must submit; yet, following still his lead,
Pray Providence for rescue, ere too late :—
'Tis Providence, alone, may baffle Fate!   [*Exit Osborne.*

SCENE III.

The house of Mrs. Jervas in Walnut Street. Enter Mrs. J. and Robert Warren.

   Mrs. J. Art sure of what you tell me?
   Warren. Never doubt it!—
Matthews, who writes me, is an ancient friend
Who knows this Maurice well. He sees him often,
Though it would seem that Maurice knows not him.
His rising fortunes favour you! 'Twere well
You sought your niece. You are her kinswoman,—
The nearest,—and the loss of all your fortune,
By failure of the Bank—
   Mrs. J. But Maurice likes me not!
   Warren. Natural enough! You still opposed his passion;
But things are altered now. You've but to show him
'Twas for your niece's good, in your best judgment,
That you denied his suit. But, go to her;—
He's doing well—is popular—grows wealthy;
And now that Fortune lookes with smiles on him,
He well may smile on you! You'll live with them,
And we shall meet there.
   Mrs. J. We? Meet?
   Warren. Did I not love her?
   Mrs. J. Ah!—
   Warren. And should *he* die?—Should accident, or—
   Mrs. J. I see! I see!
   Warren. You are my friend, and you will show her—
   Mrs. J. Ah! trust me, Robert Warren—
   Warren. That's enough!

We understand each other. You will go,—
Her only kinswoman—to seek her out.
You have but her in the world! Say you have err'd;
It was because you loved her that you strove,
'Gainst one, who, whatsoe'er his worth and talent,
Was not o'erbless'd by Fortune! He may frown,
But cannot well deny you; and, for Clarice—
She will not, sure, repel her mother's sister.

 Mrs. J. I'll go! I need the succour of my kindred.

 Warren. We'll meet then; but you must not know me there!
'Tis not my policy to vex my rival,
Provoke suspicion, move his jealousy,
Or startle her by any bold renewal,
Of pleadings late denied. Should you discover
That he who, in their presence, stands before you,
Is other than he seems, you will know nothing;
Since that may spoil your game as well as mine.

 Mrs. J. You are a deep one!

 Warren. When I have your counsel!
This Maurice thought but humbly of your judgment.
He knew you not as I do. He was blinded
By his own proud conceit and arrogance,
And held himself an oracle. 'Twere wise
If still you suffer'd him to fancy thus—
Check'd him in nothing—never counsell'd him—
For still I know he holds your wisdom cheaply,
And scorns the experience which might rise against
His own assured opinion. Such a person
Needs but sufficient cord—

 Mrs. J. And he shall have it!

 Warren. I'll seek your counsel soon, and you shall teach me
What is our proper action. You will find me
More ready to confide in your experience,

Than him whose cunning seem'd to baffle it.
Farewell then, madam, 'till we meet again.   [*Exit Warren.*

  Mrs. J.   Farewell, sir! A most excellent young man!
This Maurice shall not carry it at will,—
He scorns me,—does he? He shall feel me still!   [*Exit.*

SCENE IV.

*The Hall in the Cottage of Norman Maurice.   Time—midnight.
Enter Maurice in night-gown, as just started from his couch.
His hair dishevelled—his manner wild and agitated—his whole
appearance that of a man painfully excited and distressed.*

  Maurice.   That I should be unmann'd! That a mere dream,
The blear and frightful aspects of a vision,
Should rouse me to such terror,—shake my soul
From the strong moorings of a steadfast will,
And drive it, a mere wreck, upon the seas,
No hand upon the helm! Ah! my Clarice.   [*Enter Clarice.*
  Clarice.   My husband—
  Maurice.   I would thou had'st not seen me thus, Clarice.
  Clarice.   What means this terror—wherefore did you cry?
  Maurice.   Surely I did not.
  Clarice.   Yes, a terrible shriek,
As one who rushes desperate on his foe!
  Maurice.   No mortal foe has ever from my lips,
Sleeping or waking, forced acknowledgment,
That humbles me like this—
  Clarice.   What dost thou mean?
What fear?

Maurice.   What answer shall I make to thee?—
How tell thee, my Clarice, 'twas a mere dream,
That filled me with that agonizing fear,
Whose shriek thou heard'st.   Yet, such a dream, my wife,
As still pursues me with its fearful forms,
And shakes me yet with terror.   That a man,
Conscious of strength and will, with conscience free,
Should, in a mere disorder of his blood,
In midnight sleep, feel all his soul unsinew'd,
And sink into the coward!

Clarice.   Thou art none!

Maurice.   Yet such a vision—and methinks I see!—
Hist,—is there nothing crawling by the hearth,
Crouching and winding, and with serpent folds,
Preparing its dread venom?

Clarice.   There is nothing, husband—
The hearth holds only the small jar of flowers.

Maurice.   The reptile ever seeks such crouching place,
And garbs his spotty hide with heedless blossoms,
That know not what they harbour.   Fling it hence!
'Twas on the hearth it crouch'd.   But, hear me, wife;
That dream!   'Twas of a serpent on our hearth,
Thou heedless, with thy hand upon the flowers,
Disposing them for show.   Unseen and soft—
It wound about thee its insidious coil,
And, at the moment when I first beheld,
Its brazen head was lifted, its sharp fang
Was darting at thy heart!   'Twas then I shriek'd
And rush'd upon the monster thus, and smote!—

              [*Dashing the vase to pieces.*

Heedless of every sting, I trampled it;
But, even as it writhed beneath my heel,
Methought, it lifted up a human face
That looked like Robert Warren!

Clarice. What a dream!

Maurice. I cannot shake it off. Did'st hear a sound,
Most like a hiss?

Clarice. Nay, nay! 'twas but a dream!
Come—come to bed.

Maurice. Why should I dream of him?

Clarice. You think of him, perchance.

Maurice. And, as a reptile!
The terrible image still before me crawls—
Oh! that I might, with but a bound and struggle,
Though still at life's worst peril, trample him!

Clarice. Yet wherefore?

Maurice. There are instincts of the soul.
That have a deep and true significance,
And, though no more in danger from his malice,
I feel within me that he works unsleeping,
In venomous toils against me.

Clarice. But, in vain.
Come, Norman, come to bed. You frighten me.

Maurice. Forgive me! There! I have thee at my lips,
I strain thee to my bosom with a joy
That leaves no rapture wanting—yet, methinks,
I hear a sound of hissing, and still see
Glimpses of folding serpents that, behind,
Crawl after us—

Clarice. My Norman!

Maurice. I grieve thee!
I will forget this vision in the blessing
This grasp makes real to rapture. Let us in.

[*He folds his arm about her, and they leave the apartment, he still looking behind him suspiciously—she looking up to him.*

SCENE V.

The edge of a wood. A cottage in the distance. Enter Robert Warren, Osborne, and Harry Matthews. The former disguised with false hair, whiskers, &c.

 Matthews. [*pointing to cottage.*] Look!—you may see it now
 Warren. There, then, he harbours?
A goodly cottage—he's a man of taste,
Not yet too old for sentiment, it seems;
Loves flowers and shade trees, and around his porches
I fancy that we see some gadding tendrils,
That wanton, with full censers, in his homage!
He should be happy there!
 Matthews. Why, so he is.
 Warren. You think so?
 Matthews. There's everything to make him so. He's young—
Is on the road to fortune and to fame,
And has a handsome wife.
 Warren.   The landscape's fair,—
Looks bright beneath the sunshine and exhales
A thousand delicate odours rich in life;
But, sometimes, there's a tempest in the night,
And where's your landscape then?
 Matthews.   Be this his case,
It shall not cost me one poor hour of sleep,
For all the coil it makes. This man's our foe,—
Goes with our enemies in politics,
And will, though now he knows it not himself,
Be run, against our crack man, for the Senate.
 Warren. Who's he?

Matthews. Ben Ferguson.
Warren. Plain Ben?
Matthews. Colonel Ben!
'Tis only when the man's a favourite,
We take the formal handle from his name
And sing it short for sweetness.
Warren. Is he able?
Matthews. We thought him so 'till this your Maurice came;—
Since then our favourite loses in the race.
Ben is a lawyer in first practice here
And had the field to himself since I have known him,
'Till now—
Osborne. Maurice and he have grappled then?
Matthews. To Ferguson's defeat.
Osborne. Before the Jury?
Matthews. Ay, every way—before the judge and jury,—
In court and out of court. At public meetings
They were in opposite ranks, and, with each issue,
Maurice hath risen still in popular favour,
While Ferguson declines. It will rejoice us,
If, as you say, you have some history
To floor this powerful foe!
Warren. You need not doubt it.
But who are friends to Maurice, here,—the people?
Matthews. Were it the people only, it were nothing.
They have not yet arisen to Self Esteem,
And, kept full fed on vanity, are heedless,
Hugging their shadows, how they lose the substance.
Here, all their sympathies are held by others;
Men of much wealth and some ability,
Who, gladly, in this Maurice find an ally,
And join with him to use him. There's a party
Who long have lacked a leader. Norman Maurice

Brings them the head they seek. He guides their councils,
And, with such prudent skill and policy,
That still they fancy he is but their mouth-piece,
Even while he gives the breath of life to them.
I know that they will run him for the Senate.

    Warren. Can they elect him?

    Matthews. It is somewhat doubtful.
They never yet succeeded with their man,
Not having had the man to make success.
What they can do *for him* is not the question,
So much as what he may achieve *for them.*
I tell you, though not fearful for the issue,
It makes us something anxious. Now,—this secret—
If it be true, indeed, that,—

    Warren.   Be you ready;—
I'll see your friends to-morrow. We'll sleep on it.
To-night, I'll fathom Maurice if I can,
And see how he enjoys his western life.
Enough! I have him in my power! To-morrow!—

    Matthews. But what's the secret?

    Warren.   It will keep till then.
Be sure, that when your game is to be play'd—
When Norman Maurice, at the height of favour,
Waits but the will to rise up Senator—
A single word shall damn him down to ruin,
And stifle every voice that shouts his name.

    Osborne. Yet, once more, Warren, ere it be too late,
Let me entreat and counsel—

    Warren.   You are doting!
Go you with Matthews, and, should I be missing,
You both can tell whither my steps were bent,
And what my power upon him.

    Osborne. [*aside to W.*]   Why incur

This danger,—for you too must see the danger,—
To feed this foolish malice.
    Warren. [*aside to O.*] Is it foolish?—
Not when the profit's yours, the pleasure mine;—
And I, if fortune mocks me not with fancies,
Shall find a pleasure in the game I play at,
That you may never dream of! Be you easy—
There's little danger! I've securities
'Gainst *him* in *you*, and in his secret fears,
Not less than in the policy I use;
Besides, my habit, does it not disguise me?
    Osborne. He has the eye of an eagle!
    Warren. Pshaw!
    Osborne.   Beware!—
His genius—you yourself confess it, Warren—
Hath always, when the final issue came,
Soar'd over you triumphant!
    Warren.   Oh! Good night.
We'll meet again to-morrow!   [*Exit Warren.*
    Osborne.   He'll pay for it!
He runs on ruin!
    Matthews. Not his own, methinks!
    Osborne. His own, though now it seems not. I've an instinct
That tells me Maurice cannot be o'erthrown.
Baffled he may be;—you may torture him—
Deny him his just place and high position,
One or more seasons; but he'll rise at last,
So firmly, that the very hands that struggle
To tear him from his throne, will help to build it.
There are some men to whom the fates decree
Performance,—and this man is one of them!
What was his prospect when I knew him first?
He had no friends,—he had no fellowships,

No heedful care of parents—no tuition;—
He stood alone i' the world—unknown, unhonour'd—
Nay, something hated, as I hap to know,
For that he had some innate qualities,
Of pride, of strength, of soul and character,
That would not let him stoop! In spite of all,
He hath struggled through the strife and the obstruction;
Won friends; won homage; high position won;
And still hath grown, the more erect and noble,
At each assault upon his pride and fortune!
I *feel* that he *must* triumph!

  Matthews.   You speak well,
The promise of our enemy! You differ,
Somewhat, from Robert Warren; yet, you know
This secret.

  Osborne. Ay—as Warren's; and I know,
The rise of Maurice is his overthrow!   [*Exeunt.*

SCENE VI.

The interior of the cottage of Norman Maurice. A table spread as if supper were just concluded. Maurice and Clarice discovered seated. Maurice balances a spoon upon the cup. Clarice watches him.

  Clarice.   You muse my husband.
  Maurice. [*pushing away the cup.*] 'Tis with happiness!
Know you, Clarice, that fifteen months have pass'd
Since we were married.

Clarice. Is it possible!
I had not thought it!
Maurice. Time is wing'd with pleasure,
When that the heart, reposing where it loves,
Finds strength for fresher love in faith secure!
The world would seem to smile on me at last!
'Till we were wedded, such had been my fortune,
I questioned still the sunshine when it came;
And, in its sudden and capricious beauty,
Still dreaded something sinister and hostile.
But now I feel secure! With you beside me,
A fair, free world before me, and employment,
Grateful at once to intellect and feeling,
Affording Thought due exercise for triumph,
Methinks, I have from Fate a guaranty,
That she foregoes at last her ancient grudges;
And, it may be, despising our ambition,
Thus easily satisfied with love and quiet,
Turns her sharp arrows on some nobler victim,
Whose young audacity offends her pride!
Sure, Clarice, this is happ'n ss.
 Clarice. It is more!
Such happiness as well might task the fancy,
To wing with words of sweetest poesy.
 Maurice. Then sing for me. I'm in the mood for music;
My heart is glad; my thoughts would wander freely;
Commercing with the indistinct, but sweet.
 Clarice. Nay, Norman, nay: I'm selfish in my gladness;
You sing not; but a something more than music
Swells in the verse that gathers on your lips;—
And this reminds me of the little ballad
You promised me,—once half recited me,

And fain would have me think your heart conceived it
When first it grew to mine!
    Maurice.   And I said truly!
Thoughts passing fair had floated through my fancy—
Thoughts born of warmest tastes and pure affections,
Which yet had found no name! I had strange visions
Of grace and feminine beauty, such as never
The world had shown me living. Then I met thee,
And, on the instant, did they take thy image;—
And thus I first knew how, and whom, to love!
These fancies did I body forth in verses,
As one records a vision of the midnight,
That fills his soul with marvels; and the hour,
That brought me first acquainted with thy beauties,
Taught me what name to write above my record,
Which, until then, had none.
    Clarice. Norman—*was* it mine?
    Maurice. Thine, only, my beloved one!
    Clarice.   Now, the verses,
In thy best manner, Norman.
    Maurice. What! repeat them?—
Would'st ruin me, Clarice, in public favour;
Sap my distinction, lose me my profession,
Draw down the vulgar laughter on my head,
And make grave senators and learned statesmen
Shake reverend brows in sorrow at my folly?
    Clarice. Nay, you mock me now?
    Maurice.   Woulds't have a lawyer,—
Subtle, and stern, and disputatious, still,—
Full of retorts and strange philosophies;
Whose dreams by night are of the close encounter
With rival wits and wary adversaries,—
Whose thoughts by day are still upon indictments,

Flaws, fees, exceptions, old authorities,
And worldly arguments, and stubborn juries,—
And all the thousand small details that gather,
Like strings about the giant Gulliver,
Dragging and fettering down to lowly earth
The upsoaring mind that else might scale the heavens !—
Wouldst have him, in the vagrancy of fancy,
Possess his soul with spells of poesy ;
Having no fear that, lurking at his threshold,
His neighbour Jones or Jenkins, Smith or Thompson,
Some round and fat, but most suspicious client,
Bringing great fees,—his heart upon his action,—
Seeking the sourest aspect in his lawyer,—
Stands, rooted, with strange horror, as he listens
To most ridiculous rhymes, and talk of flow'rs,
Moonbeams, and zephyrs—all that staple sweetness,
That makes the fancies of young thoughtless bosoms ;—
When most he hoped to hear of *Chose in action,*
Trespass, assumpsit, action on the case,
And other phrases, silly as the rhymester's,—
But that they sound in money, not in music !
No ! No !—no poesy ! 'Twere loss of client !

  Clarice. Nay, Norman, but you jest now ! Speak the verses,
If need be, in low accents.

  Maurice.   Lest Jones or Jenkins,
Should turn about, possess'd with holy horror,
And seek some other lawyer ! You shall have them !
They are yours, Clarice, for, truly, they embody
What still meseem'd the virtues of your nature ;—
Tastes, sweet and delicate as evening glories
That tend upon the passage of the day,
And, twinn'd with gleam and shadows, through the twilight,
Betoken, as it were, the unknown beauties,
That make a happier future in the far.

Clarice.   You describe the verses?
Maurice.   It needs I should!
They take a mystic tone and character,
And ask the key-note. You will hardly like them:
Thoughtful, not lyrical, nor passionate,
They need that you should pause upon each accent,
Or they will lose their due significance!
But, next to the grave folly of such doing,
Is the grave preface that still pleads for it.
You lead me erring, Clarice, to these trifles—
You, and the exulting feeling at my heart,
That deems this happiness sure!—Ha! That knock!
                    [*Knock at the door—he starts.*
Methinks it hath a meaning!   A sharp instinct
Tells me that evil at our threshold lurks.   [*Whispers.*
    Clarice.   Evil, my husband!   Let me open it!
                            [*Goes toward the door.*
    Maurice. [*interposing.*]   You, Clarice!   You mistake me.
        There's an instinct,
That, though it speaks of evil, hath no fear!—
Who's there? [*Aloud.*]
    Voice without.   A friend!
    Maurice. [*throwing open the door.*]   Enter, friend!
    [*Enter Robert Warren as before, with valise in his hand.*]
    Warren.   Pardon me this intrusion, but I'm wearied,—
I've travell'd far,—the last seven miles afoot,
Having lost my horse by the way.
    Maurice.   You're welcome, sir,
To our poor fare, the shelter of our dwelling
'Till you recover.   Clarice, see to it.
[*Maurice points her to the supper table. She turns and leaves
    the room,—Warren follows her with his eye, while that of
    Maurice observes him.*
    Warren.   I thank you, sir.

Maurice. Meanwhile, sit down and rest.
Give me your burden. 'Twill require some minutes
To get your supper, make your chamber ready;
'Till then, forget your travel.
Warren. You are kind!
How far, sir, are we from St. Louis, here?
Maurice. Four miles only.
Warren. You, perhaps, can tell me
Something of persons living in St. Louis:
I'm a collector from an Eastern city.
And have a claim upon one Harry Matthews.
Maurice. [*His brow slightly contracts.*] *Harry* Matthews!
Warren. Or *Henry* Matthews: is he good, sir?
Mauirce, [*coldly.*] It may be, sir; I know not!
Warren. You know the man?
Maurice. I have seen him often, sir, but know him not.
Warren. The house I represent has had suspicions;—
A Philadelphia house.
Maurice. Of Philadelphia!
Warren. A famous city, sir; but you have seen it?
Maurice. I know it well, sir. [*Catches the eye of Warren,
   which suddenly drops at the encounter.*
Warren. Ah! you've travelled thither?
Maurice. Have *lived* there, sir; and, now I think of it,
It may be that you can answer *me* of persons,
Whom once I knew there;—there was Mrs. Jervas—
Warren. A widow, sir, who lived in Walnut street?
Maurice. The same!—
Warren. I've heard of her. She lost her fortune lately
By failure of the Bank.
Maurice. Indeed!
Warren. And has left the city,
'Twas said, to seek her kindred in the West.

Maurice. [*To Clarice, who reënters.*]   Hear you that, Clarice!
　　Clarice.　　　　　Is it possible?
It cannot be she means—
　　Maurice.   Perhaps.   'Tis like.
　　Warren.   She has a niece and nephew in the West—
'Twas so reported—who have sent for her,
They being very wealthy, she in want.
　　Maurice. [*with a smile.*]   Indeed!
　　Clarice.   She has no nephew living, sir.
　　Warren. [*smiles.*]   Ah! you know her, then?
　　Maurice.   She is this lady's aunt, sir;
And, it may be, this excellent Mrs. Jervas
Comes hither to her niece, who is my wife, sir.
I suppose, that, as the husband of the one,
I may be held a nephew to the other;
And loving, too, makes kindred.   Well, Clarice,
You'll make the good lady welcome if she comes,
Which, *now*, I scarcely question.
　　　　　Tell me, sir,
Of other persons in that goodly city;—
There was a mute, I knew, one Nicholas Foster,
Whom much I fancied—
　　Warren.　　　　A rare machinist,
Though few conceived his talent.
　　Maurice. [*aside.*]   Yet, *you* knew it!
　　Warren.   He's well as ever.
　　Maurice.　　　　Sully, the master-painter,
A pure, good man, whose exquisite art endows
The beauty with a charm beyond her own,
Caught from his delicate fancy.
　　Warren.   He's still famous.
　　Maurice.   I would you could say fortunate as famous,
As still his art deserves.—I know not why,

But these enquiries sadden me, and yet—
There was one Richard Osborne—

    Warren.   An attorney—

    Maurice. A most obscure one, though of certain merits,
Who might have been distinguish'd, having pow'rs
To raise him into something high and worthy,
But for his evil genius—

    Warren. [*quickly.*] Ha! sir! He?—

    Maurice. Were you a student—an anatomist
Of character—instead of a collector;—
But—

    Warren. Yet would I hear, sir.

    Maurice.   *He*, sir, I mean,
Were one whom it were well to analyze,
Did one design a new philosophy,
And sought in strange anomalies to embrace
The opposite things in nature. Fancy a creature,
Having the external attributes of man,—
The capacious brow—the clear, transparent eye—
The form erect—the voice most musical—
Quick talent, ready art and specious language,
And something winning in his natural manner,
Beguiling still the unwary to belief—
Yet, as if made in mock of heaven's own purpose,
Having, in place of heart, a nest of vipers;
Whose secret venom, mastering all his powers,
Taints ever his performance—makes his doings,
When most they favour virtue, tend to vice—
Corrupts the word he utters, makes him false,
When most the truth should be his policy,—
And keeps him ever lothely in pursuit
Of purposes most loathesome. Know you, sir,
One Robert Warren? [*Laying his hand on Warren's shoulder,
                      and eyeing him closely.*

Warren. [*shrinking and stammering.*] Me, sir—Warren!
No!

Maurice. [*flinging him away and rising.*] Liar and reptile, as
thou still hast been,
'Twere thousand times more hopeful to endow
The serpent with the nature of the dove,
To graft the fruit of Eden on the tree,
That, with its bitter, blights the Dead Sea shore—
Appease the tiger's thirst—the leopard's spots
Pluck from his side, and bind him with a straw—
Than change the designing devil at thy heart!

Warren. What mean you, sir?

Clarice. [*seizing his arm.*] Oh! Norman, wherefore this?

Maurice. What! See you not? Hath sense of happiness
So totally obscured the sense of wrong,
That memory lacks each faculty, and nature,
Losing the subtle instinct which still counsels
The innocent of its peril, stoops to wanton
With the fang'd viper in his villainous coil.
The dream! the dream! my Clarice. Get thee hence!
Leave me to deal with him. Away!

Clarice. What's he?

Maurice. What! do his looks not answer as the reptile's,
That speak his subtle snare and silent venom!
Doth not his coward crouching show his nature,
As now I stretch the arm of vengeance o'er him?
Must I confer a name upon the victim,
Even in the moment when I strike the blow,
Lest, in their ignorant blindness, men should fancy
This were a kinsman whom in wrath I slew!

Warren. Beware!—this violence! [*Snatches a knife from
the table.*

Maurice. Is justice only—

Clarice. [*interposing.*] Norman! Husband!

Maurice. What! See'st not still!

Clarice. I see! I know!—and yet—

Maurice. And yet, and yet, and yet! is the child's wisdom!
Shall we not be secure—never find refuge!
Shall hate pursue, and vengeance turn not on him!
Must we be driven from each world of peace,
To burrow with the hill fox and the wolf,
When but a stroke is needful—

Clarice. Oh! thou must not:
He shares our hospitality—our shelter!

Maurice. [*hurling the table over.*] He hath not touch'd the
    bread and sacred salt,
He shall not claim the Arab privilege,—
He dies!—

Clarice. For my sake, Norman, spare him!
Let him go hence; the past is over now.

Warren. She counsels wisely, Norman. Lift no hand
Against me, for I come to you in peace.

Maurice. In peace! In peace! And wherefore this disguise?
Thy fraudulent tale of travel—this false semblance,
False hair, false speech—unless with heart and purpose
False as of old! Did'st think, that I, who knew thee,
By such damn'd treachery as thou still hast shown me,
Could be deceived by wretched arts like these?—
My blindness and my confidence so perfect,
That I should sleep and dream, while at my pillow
Thou crep'st at midnight, from the hearth that warm'd thee,
To fasten on my heart! Thou com'st, an outlaw!—
What hinders that I slay thee?—that I take thee,
Thus, by the throat, and, stifling fear and feeling,
Slaughter thee, as a bullock at the altar,
Thy blood would still profane!

Clarice. [*interposing.*] Norman! Norman!

Oh! must thy Clarice plead to thee in vain?
Spare him, if but in gratitude to heaven,
For that we prosper in his hate's despite.

 Maurice. 'Tis for that very reason I should slay him!
He comes to blight our brief prosperity,
To compass all our sunshine with his cloud,
And taint our flow'rs with poison.

 Warren.   Yet, beware!
She counsels thee with wisdom, Norman Maurice;
I am not friendless here. Did aught befal me,
Here, in thy dwelling, to my mortal hurt,
'Tis known that I came hither—'tis known farther,
That I have that to speak against thy fame,
Shall blacken it forever.

 Maurice.   Ha, say'st thou that!
Well thou would'st something more!

 Warren.   Only a word—
And lest thy prudence should not check thy passion,
My providence—[*showing pistol.*]

 Maurice. What! thou hast weapons then!
Now, by my hopes—if it were possible,
To find thee but one moment flush with manhood!—
Look on me, villain, as I now confront thee,
But, lift thine eye to mine, and let thy aim
Be deadly as thy malice! Wretched coward—
Thus do I mock thy impotence. [*Rushes upon him and
   the weapon from his hand.*

 Warren. Spare me, Norman!
 Clarice. Husband, let him live!
 Maurice. Outlaw! that masks him with deliberate purpose—
     [*Takes Warren by the throat.*
 Warren. Mercy, Norman!
 Maurice. That seeks by night my dwelling with a lie!—

Clarice. Husband—dear husband!
Maurice. That lifts his deadly weapon 'gainst my bosom—
Warren. Thou stranglest me!
Clarice. Have pity, Norman!
Maurice. For thy sake, I spare him?—
Warren. Thanks—oh, thanks!
Maurice. Yet feel how better 'twere to crush him now,
Than suffer him—
Warren. I swear!
Maurice. Oh!—if thou durst
Take name of God in vain to do hell service,—
I'll slay thee with a certainty of vengeance
That leaves no limb unhurt. For well I know
Thy heart is never then less free from malice,
Than when thy lips declare thy innocence.
Hence, ere I change my purpose. I will spare thee,
And fling thee from my threshold, but to show thee
How much I still forbear. [*Hurls him out headlong.*
Clarice. Oh, how I thank thee.
Maurice. If evil follows on this mercy, Clarice,
Thine is the fault.
Clarice. Oh, Norman, this man's hate—
Maurice. While we can tear the falsehood from his brow,
Is nothing, but—
Clarice. Why should he follow us?
Maurice. Oh! for some hellish purpose. But go in;
Leave me awhile.
Clarice. Wilt thou not close the door?
Maurice. Let it stay wide all night.
Clarice. You go not forth?
Maurice. One sleeps not when the wolf is in his close,
Lest that his howl should stir his infant's sleep—
And when I doubt if ill is at my threshold,

'Twere base to sleep upon the pillow of doubt.
But, go you in, dear wife!—you must not hear,
The voice in anger you have heard in love.
Leave me awhile. This thing still troubles me,
But should not trouble you. Go to your prayers,
And leave the watches of the night to me.
God still presides o'er all. I see not yet,
The evil that this evil spirit brings,
But trust that we shall lack no help of angel,
Whene'er the struggle comes.
 Clarice. Norman.
 Maurice. Dear wife!
 Clarice. Forget not that my life is in thy hands.
Oh, do not rashly purpose.
 Maurice. Never fear! [*Embrace. Ex. Clarice within.*
 Maurice. What can he mean! That paper is destroyed·
Why should I fear his malice? Yet, so truly,
I know his equal baseness and design,
I feel that he hath purposes of mischief,
Which, if he lack'd the agencies of evil,
He ne'er had underta'en. No sleep for me,
When that the dark suspicions in my soul,
Engender still the foe. I must go forth!— [*looks out.*
Oh! God, how beautiful the calm o'er earth,—
How soft the night, that, with a veil of brightness
Wraps all the subject creatures—peace and sleep,
Sharing the dreamy blessing, as if Evil,
Sped not malignant spirits through the air,
And never flower of earth had felt a reptile!
           [*Goes forth.*

END OF ACT SECOND.

ACT III.—SCENE I.

A chamber in the dwelling of Harry Matthews, in St. Louis. Robert Warren and Richard Osborne discovered.

 Osborne.   I warn'd you of the peril.
 Warren.   Yet your wisdom
Had scarcely fancied that his glance could fathom
Disguise so good as mine!
 Osborne.   I said his eye
Was like an eagle's. It were hard to say,
What, with his mind once roused into suspicion,
It could not penetrate.
 Warren.   'Twould better please me,
If one, who should be in my service only,
Could find my foe less perfect.
 Osborne.   And, to do so,
Should prove himself less true.
 Warren.   Oh! your truth,
Were better shown in service than opinion!
My habit was good; and I had been secure,
But that, to sound him, I unseal'd myself;
And, like a witling, answered all his questions,
Of persons whom we once had known together.
 Osborne. Be sure, he first suspected ere he question'd.
 Warren. 'Tis like enough! At all events he floor'd me;—
Disgraced me as he still hath done before

In frequent strife. The mask is thrown aside;
He knows me, here, his enemy; and now—
The open conflict!

Osborne. What is now the game?
The open conflict he would never shrink from!
Why, when his hand was fix'd upon your throat,
Did you forbear the weapon?

Warren. Ask me rather,
Why one is still superior to his fellow;
Why one is brave, another impotent;
Why I am feeble just where he is strong;—
And why, with will to compass his destruction,
My heart still fails me in the final effort!
Such still hath been the sequel of our issues!
He still hath mastered me with such a will,
My spirit droops before him, and I shudder,
To feel, that, with a hate so fixed and fearful,
I lack the heart to drive the weapon home!—
But I shall do it yet!

Osborne. And why the conflict,
Thus ever urged with fate so full of peril?
Now, while you may forbear, and pause in safety,
Forego the struggle, which hath still been hopeless;
Give him repose, and leave yourself at peace.

Warren. Peace! with these passions!

Osborne. They will wreck your own!
A something tells me such must be the issue,
In any strife with Maurice.

Warren. Vain the counsel—
I cannot leave the conflict!

Osborne. Why?

Warren. *Will* not do so!
While still my hate must go unsatisfied—
My pride,—to say no more of other passions.

Osborne. This woman—
Warren. Not a word of her!
Osborne. Smiles she,
That still you prosecute this doubtful struggle?
Warren. She may, perchance, when she is duly tutor'd,
That, on my whisper, hangs her husband's honour.
Osborne. This is your purpose, then?
Warren. You do not like it?
Osborne. I am your slave,—the creature of your mood,
More at your mercy far than Norman Maurice,
Since he is innocent and I am guilty;—
What matter what I like?
Warren. Why, that's well said!—
Enough for you I must pursue my victims,
While hate conceives a hell for him, or passion
Dreams still of heaven from her! This day, when Maurice
Leaves for the city, I shall seek his dwelling.
Osborne. Again! untaught by late experience!
You seek his wife then?
Warren. Why, not exactly.—
Perhaps you do not know that Mrs. Jervas
Arrived last night at midnight.
Osborne. How can she
Assist you in this mad pursuit? You tell me
That Maurice still suspects her.
Warren. Never matter—
She is my ally;—but, here's Harry Matthews:
He comes to take me to the secret council,
Where other plans mature against our foeman.
Osborne. You will not breathe this secret to these people?
Warren. I will *but* breathe it.
Osborne. And withhold the proof?
Warren. As suits my purpose. It is very likely,

I shall not call on you till the last hour,
When all is ready for his overthrow!
Of this be sure, Dick Osborne: I will pamper
My several passions as I can, and stint them,
In nothing, that may gratify their rage.

[*Enter Harry Matthews.*

  Matthews. Art ready, Warren?
  Warren. Will be in a moment!
  Matthews. [*to Osborne.*] You'll go with us.
  Osborne. Excuse me.
  Warren. [*aside to Osborne.*] Why not go?
  Osborne. [*aside to W.*] Sufficient, as they tell us, for the day
Its evil; when I can no longer 'scape it,
I'll mix in this conspiracy;—till then,
Let me go idle.
  Warren. [*aside to Osborne.*] Hark you, Richard Osborne,
No faltering when the moment comes to speak;
The rod that does not yield to me, I break!

[*Ex. Matthews and Warren.*

  Osborne. And no escape! I dare not run on ruin,
And face the shame with which he threatens me;
Yet, with a tyranny so terrible,
That plies me with its torture night and day,
'Twere better throw increase of weight on conscience,
And, by embrace with deeds of deadlier aspect,
At least secure escape from sway like this!
Had I the heart for it! Could I find the courage!
'Twere but a blow!—a blow! I'll ponder it. [*Ex. Osborne.*

SCENE II.

An apartment in the house of Col. Ferguson. Ferguson, Blasinghame, Matthews, Warren, and other persons discovered.

Blasinghame. The matter then resolves itself to this—
We know for certain, now, that this man, Maurice,
Will be the opposition candidate :—
Ben Ferguson is ours.
　Ferguson. And why not you?
　Blasinghame. For the best reasons. No! my private business
Needs careful nursing now. This woman, Pressley,
Is like to give me trouble.
　Matthews.　　　　　　Her new lawyer
Is stubborn, then?
　Blasinghame. He seems to be a man;
And we shall suffer him to prove his manhood!
I wrote him of the merits of my case,
Concluding, with a civil exhortation,
As he was young, and but a stranger here,
That he should spare his teeth, nor peril them,
On nuts too hard to crack.
　Matthews. What said he then?
　Blasinghame. Oh! with an answer bold enough, I warrant.
　Matthews. He did not know his customer, I fancy.
　Blasinghame. I think not; and to lesson him a little,
One of my lambs was sent to him this morning—
Joe Savage!
　Ferguson. Joe's a rough teacher, Colonel.
　Blasinghame. As God has made him, Joe. He'll do our business
As tenderly as if it were his own.

Ferguson.   But was there not some whisper of a secret
Touching this Norman Maurice, which, if true,
Would render any messages of honour,
Impossible, to him!

Blasinghame.   I did not hear;—
Unfold your budget.

Ferguson.   Harry Matthews, there,
Speaks of a secret in his friend's possession,
That's fatal to this man!

Blasinghame.   Ha! out with it!
'Twill save a monstrous trouble in our wigwam;
For, to say truth, this man is popular,
Grows every day in strength in the assembly,
And, I confess to you, I have my fears,
Touching the play before us.   Our new members
Are not what I would have them; and old Mercer,
Catesby and Brooks, gain daily influence,
Under the cunning counsel of this Maurice.
If we can crush this fellow, who has talent,
And shows more stubbornness than I can relish,
'Twere better done before we lose our headway.
This man disposed of, they can find no other
To take the field with Ferguson.

Matthews.   Speak, Warren!

Warren.   There *is* a secret, gentlemen; a dark one
Which, told, *were* fatal to this Norman Maurice!
I will *not* tell it *now;* but wait the moment,
When, over all, conspicuous most, he stands,
With triumph in his prospect, and his spirit,
Exulting in the state he deems secure!
Then will I come between his hope and triumph;
Then show the guilty secret that degrades him,
Confound him with the proofs which now are ready,

And hurl him down to ruin, the more fatal,
For that I suffer'd him to rise so high.
   Blasinghame. But why not now? The man is high enough!
   Warren. The secret's mine, sir. When I'm done with it,
I'll bury it as did the Phrygian barber,
Where every reed that whistles in the wind
Shall make it into music for his ear.
Be sure of this, I'll yield it you in season,
Ere Maurice sits a Senator in Congress!
   Matthews. Well—that's sufficient!
   Blasinghame.   Yes! Let him do that!
Meanwhile, there is a way to save himself.
This Maurice has my message—
   Matthews. He'll not fight!
   Blasinghame.   If he would—
   Matthews. His honour would be rescued by his death?
   Warren. Scarcely; since 'tis for me to keep the secret,
Or free it, if I please! But, let me tell you,
That Maurice will not shrink from any combat!
I know him well. He is mine enemy,
But let me do him justice. He will fight,
Though all the devils of hell stood up against him.
Look to it, sir; [*to Blasing.*,] your reputation's great,
But Maurice is no common opponent;
And you will need your utmost excellence,
To conquer him when once he takes the field!
   Blasinghame. Well, that's good news! My lamb is with
           him now;
We'll hear from him by noon.
   Ferguson.   Before we part,
'Tis understood we put our troops in motion;
The strife will be a close one! Blasinghame
Hath truly spoken of this new assembly;

It puzzles me to fathom it. This Maurice,
Is, questionless, a man of wondrous power;
And, though I much prefer that we should beat him,
In a fair wrestle, with the usual agents,
Yet this is not so certainly our prospect,
As that we should forego this fatal secret,
That makes our game secure.
    Warren. You shall have it.
    Blasinghame. We meet to-night at Baylor's.
    Matthews. [*to Warren.*] You'll be with us?
It may be that your fruit will then be ripe.
    Blasinghame. Ay, come, sir, with your friend.
    Warren. [*to Matthews.*]   Perhaps! We'll see;—
There may be other fruits upon that tree.
                    [*Exeunt several ways.*

SCENE III.

An apartment in the house of Norman Maurice. He appears seated at a table with books and papers before him. After a pause, he closes his books, folds and ties the papers in a bundle, pushes them from before him and rises.

    Maurice. [*solus.*] It is the curse of insecurity!
That cruel doubt that hangs upon possession;
Glides with the midnight to the sleepless pillow,
And, with the laurel wreath that crowns the triumph,
Sows thick the thorns that make the brow to ache!
Did the endowment not imply the service,

Were we not each enjoin'd with a commission,
The task decreed, the struggle thrust upon us,
Making it manhood to comply with duty;
How better far—the treasure in our keeping,
Love at our bosom, peace upon our threshold,
When bliss can never hope increase of rapture,
And fear begins to dream of unknown danger,—
To fly the world—the conflict,—nay, the triumph,
And, bearing off the trophy we have won,
Hush the ambitious spirit in our hearts
That whispers, "Life hath more!"   Have I won nothing,
That I should toil, as unrequited Labour
Still hoping yet to win?   Am I a beggar,
Who, perilling nothing in each fearful venture,
Stakes all his hopes on change?   With goods so precious,
Should I still venture in the common market,
Where Malice stands, with gibe of cruel slander,
And Envy lurks in readiness to steal?—
When the still shelter of the wilderness,
The depth of shadow, the great solitudes,
Beckon the heart with promise of their own,
Still singing, "here is refuge!"
                Wretched folly!—
As if the serpent could not find the garden;
As if the malicious Hate, by hell engendered,
Had not an equal instinct, how to fathom
The secret haunt where rapture hopes to hide!
Hate bears a will as resolute as love,
A wing as swift, an eye as vigilant,
And instincts, that, as still they keep it sleepless,
Prompt the keen search when Rapture stops for rest!
A sad presentiment of coming evil
Stifles each generous impulse at my heart,

That ever spoke in confidence. This Warren,
Is here for mischief; with what hope to prosper—
That single proof destroy'd—I now divine not.
This woman, coming close upon his footsteps,
Confirms my apprehensions. They are allies—
She false as he, but feeble—his mere creature,
To beat the bush, while he secures the game!
Well! I must watch them with a vigilance,
Due to the precious treasure in my trust;
And, swift as justice in avenging mission,
With the first show of evil in their purpose,
Crush them to earth, and———Well?   [*Enter servant.*

   Servant. Major Savage, sir.
   Maurice. Show him in.   [*Enter Savage.*
   Savage. Your name is Maurice?
   Maurice. 'Tis sir. Yours?
   Savage. Mine is Joe Savage,—Major of militia.
You got a letter, sir, a week ago,
From Colonel Blasinghame.
   Maurice. And answer'd it!
   Savage. That answer did not please him, Blasinghame.
   Maurice. I'm sorry for it, sir; but you'll believe me,
When I assure you, that, in penning it,
I never once conceived it necessary
To ask what were his tastes.
   Savage.   Eh, sir: you did not!
Well, let me tell you, those who know him better,
Are something curious never to offend him.
But you, sir, are a stranger—do not know him
So well as others, born here in Missouri—
And so, he sends me to enlighten you.
   Maurice. I thank him, sir.
   Savage.   Well, you have need to do so;

He does not use such courtesy in common,
But usually the blow before the word!
   Maurice. I'm lucky in his new-born courtesy.
   Savage. You are, sir! He's a rough colt, Blasinghame.
   Maurice. Kicks, does he?
   Savage. Kicks, sir! Why do you say kicks?
   Maurice. Surely, no act more proper to a colt.
   Savage. You are something literal, sir. I'm glad of it,
Since 'twill be easier to be understood!
Well, sir, I come to you from Blasinghame.
You know not, sir, in taking up this case
Of mother Pressley's, sir, that you are doing
That which, until your coming, not a lawyer
Had done here in Missouri.
   Maurice. Shame upon them!
   Savage. Shame, say you? Wherefore, when the right of it
Is all with Blasinghame!
   Maurice. Or with his cudgel!
   Savage. [*laughs.*] Something in that, too. Well, sir—I say!—
   Maurice. Well, sir!
   Savage. Now, as you something seem to know already
Of my friend's mode of managing his case,
I need not dwell upon the policy
Of stopping all proceedings ere the trial;—
In which event I'm authorized to tell you
That Blasinghame forgives your insolent letter,
And spares you as a stranger.
   Maurice.   Merciful,
As he is powerful! But what if—having
No such afflicting terror of this person,
So terrible to his neighbours, in mine eyes—
I do reject this liberal grant of mercy.
   Savage. Then, sir, I bear his peremptory challenge,

Which leaves you, sir, without alternative,
Takes no apology, no explanation,
And only seeks atonement in your blood. [*giving challenge.*

   Maurice. Or his!
   Savage. Or his! But that's no easy matter, sir;
He's fought some thirty duels in his time,
Wing'd nineteen combatants, and slew the rest,
Nor had a scratch himself.
   Maurice.   Why, he may say,
As Thumb, in the great tragedy—" Enter Thumb,
And slays them all!"
   Savage. You mock, sir!—
   Maurice. Not a bit, sir!
I marvel only, after hearing you,
That still I have the courage to resist.
   Savage. You will not, sir?
   Maurice. I fear me that I shall!
   Savage. What! you accept the challenge, then?
   Maurice. I'll keep it, sir, until this trial's over.
   Savage. Beware, sir, of evasion.
   Maurice.   You, in turn, sir,
Beware of insolence. You have my answer;
When I have gain'd this suit of Widow Pressley,
I'll see to that of Colonel Blasinghame.
   Savage. I must have your answer now, or—
   Maurice.   The door, sir,—
Unless, indeed, you should prefer the window.
   Savage. Well! You're a man, that's certain! Give us your
            hand.
I'm a rough beast, and like you not the less,
Because you keep a muzzle for the bear;
I *feel* that you will meet with Blasinghame,
And I shall see it. [*Shakes hands.*

Maurice. Very like you will! [*Exit Savage.*
The game becomes of interest! [*tap within.*
Clarice! [*Opens to her, she enters.*

Clarice. Art busy, Norman?
Maurice. Have been. But,—this lady?—
Clarice. Will you not see her?
Maurice. Not if I can help it.
Clarice. She is my only kinswoman, my husband—
You will not drive her from me?
Maurice. Your only!—
You were *my* only, Clarice—I *your* only,
Until her coming! *Only* to each other,
Was the o'erprecious bond that most endear'd you
To my affections, wife. I cannot suffer
That she should pass between your heart and mine—
She who loves neither.
Clarice. Nay, Norman!
Maurice. Nay, Clarice!
This cold, coarse, selfish, this dishonest woman,
Who strove to keep us separate—
Clarice. Her error,
She pleads, was but in a mistaken fondness;
To find a suitor, for her favourite niece,
With better hope of fortune than yourself.
Maurice. Who broke the sacred seal upon our letters,
Mine read,—yours hurried to the flames, unsent—
And would have sold you to this Robert Warren,
My enemy—
Clarice. She confesses all, and weeps!
Maurice. Tears of the crocodile! Believe them not.
Plead for her nothing more! I tell you, Clarice,
I cannot hold my table sure and sacred,
With one so false beside me at the board!—

7*

I cannot yield my home, now pure and peaceful,
To such a treacherous heart as that she carries.
My home is not my home, when doubts of safety
Haunt still my thoughts by day, my dreams by night.
She must go hence!
  Clarice.   Oh! husband, pardon her!
She urges abject poverty!
  Maurice.   More falsehood still!
But we'll provide her;—she shall never suffer,
From cold, or thirst, or hunger, my Clarice.
I will to-day seek lodgings in St. Louis;
To-morrow—
  Clarice. But, should her pride?—
  Maurice.   She has no right
To nurse her pride at peril of our peace!
No more! I will not mock her poverty,
Offend her pride, reproach her evil doing—
Will speak her kindly, and will care for her,
So long as I have strength for any care;—
But will not suffer, for a single moment,
Her shadow on the sunshine of my house. [*Knock without.*
Come in!
    Enter Cols. Mercer and Brooks.
Friends, welcome!
   [*Clarice curtsies as they bow, aud is about to retire.*
  Mercer.   If we be welcome,
Your lady need not leave us.
  Brooks.   That which brings us,
Is business of your own, no less than ours,—
A grateful business still, we trust, to you—
Which, doing honour to your worth and virtue,
It may be grateful to your wife to hear.
  Clarice. If such its burden, I were glad to linger.

Maurice.   Do so, Clarice!—we, gentlemen, are one!
Marriage, with us, fulfils its ample mission,
Making a mutual need for both our hearts;
Whose sweet dependence knows no other refuge,
Than that which each bestows.   It is our fortune,
To have no kindred which may pass between us,
To take from either heart the sweet possession
We hold in one another.   But, be seated.
   Mercer.   Court now in session, sir, your time is precious,
And this great case of yours, 'gainst Blasinghame,
Comes on to-day?
   Maurice.   It does.
   Mercer.   A moment then!
Our friends, sir, conscious of your great endowment,
Assured of your just principles and conduct,
Your sense of public trust and public duty,
Have, with unanimous voice, in a full caucus,
Deputed us to bear you their request,
That you will be our candidate for Senator,
In the next Congress.
   Brooks.   And we now entreat you,
Suffer this nomination.
   Maurice.   Friends, believe me,
I feel with proper sense, this compliment;
And, if my own desire, my young ambition,
Were the sole arbiter to shape my conduct,
Then would I say to you, with hearty frankness,
My wing and eye are set upon the station,
To which your accents now implore my flight.
But, though 'twould give me pride to serve our people,
In any station where their rights are vested,
I have some scruples—
   Mercer.   Pray deliver them.

Maurice. To be a candidate in common usage,
To take the field and canvas with the voter,
To use or sanction fraud—to buy with money,
Or other bribe, the suffrage of the people—
Is to dishonour them—degrade myself!
   Brooks. We ask not this.
   Mercer. It needs not.
   Maurice.   Hear me, sirs.
Our liberties are in the popular vote,
Their best security, the popular heart,
Their noblest triumph in the popular will,—
And this can never be expressed with safety,
Until the unbiass'd voice of public judgement,
Flinging aside each intermediate agent,
Rises, with proper knowledge of its person,
And cries—"Behold our man!"
   Mercer.   You are our man!
Such is already what is spoken loudly
By thousands in Missouri.
   Maurice.   I'll not deny it—
If I had one ambition o'er another,
One passion, prompting still a search for pow'r,
'Twas for a station, such as this you show me,
Where, standing on the platform of the nation,
I might stand up for man! And so, my studies,
The books I read, the maxims I examined,—
The laws I conn'd—the models set before me,—
All had some eminence like this in view,
That, with my training, should the occasion offer,
I might be ready still! But, in my progress,—
The better knowledge I have learn'd from men—
My doubts increase—my scruples grow—and now,
A sense of duty prompts me to declare,

Though each fond idol of the ambitious nature,
Be, from its pedestal, forever thrown,
I will not seek for office on conditions
Adverse to right and manhood. I will never
Become the creature of a selfish party—
Never use wealth or fraud to rise to pow'r,—
Never use power itself to keep in power,
Nor see in him who favour'd my ascent,
A virtue not his own! Nor can I offer
One tribute to the vulgar vanity!
I will not bow, nor smile, nor deference yield,
Where justice still withholds acknowledgment.
 Mercer. We feel the justice of your sentiments.
 Brooks. They're needful to us now, when all's corruption.
Oh! could we but inform the popular mind.
 Maurice. This can be done where virtue is the teacher.
No students learn so quickly as the people.
They have no cliques to foster—no professions,
Whose narrow boundaries, and scholastic rules,
Frown on each novel truth and principle,
And, where they can, still hunt them down to ruin.
They take a truth in secret to their hearts,
And nurse it, till it rises to a law,
Thenceforth to live forever!
 Brooks.   We are agreed—
The people must be taught—what should we teach them?
 Maurice. In politics, to know the proper value
Of the high trusts, the sacred privileges,
They do confide their statesmen. Show to them,
On these depend their liberties and lives,
The safety of their children, and the future!
To yield such trusts to smiling sycophants,
Who flatter still the voter's vanity,

At the expense of his most precious fortunes,
Is to betray the land's security;
To sell the wealth most precious in our keeping,
And, for the thing most worthless, yield to fortune,
What fortune cannot purchase! We must teach,
That he who cringes meanly for the station,
Will meanly hold him in the nation's eye;
That he who buys the vote will sell his own;—
That he, alone, is worthy of the trust,
Who, with the faculty to use it nobly,
Will never sacrifice his manhood for it.
If, with these principles and these resolves,
Thus freely shown you, and invincible,
Our people, through their representatives,
Demand my poor abilities,—'twill glad me,
To yield me at their summons. This implies not
One effort of my own. You, sirs, may make me
A Senator, but not a Candidate.

Mercer. This suits us well. On your own terms we take you;
We feel with you, a stern necessity
To check the abuse of the Elective Franchise!

Brooks. But should we call a meeting to enlighten
The people, in respect to public measures,
You'll not refuse to meet them?

Maurice. No, sir, surely!
I still have done so, upon all occasions,
Whene'er a novel principle demanded
Discussion.

Mercer. Thanks, sir! There will be to-morrow,
A general meeting at the Capitol,
Without respect to party.

Maurice. I will be there!

Brooks. Our quest is satisfied to our desire.

 Mercer. We will no longer trespass. Farewell, madam,
Farewell, sir, We shall meet again at Court.
        [Exeunt Mercer and Brooks.
 Clarice. [*embracing him.*] Husband, you triumph! There
   should be no care
Upon your forehead now! Last night, you slept not.
 Maurice. And now, *you* dream! But clouds *will* come, Cla-
   rice,
Still, with the morrow! Care that flies the forehead,
Still finds a secret shelter in the heart!—
That timid knock!   *[Knock without.*
 Clarice. It is the widow Pressley.
 Maurice. [*opening.*] Come in, madam!
      [Enter Widow Pressley and Kate.
 Widow. Oh! sir, the day has come!
 Maurice. That brings you back your property, I trust.
 Widow. Alas! sir! You encourage me to hope,—
And yet I fear!
 Maurice. It is that we are liable of fear,
That we must hope. If judgment be not erring
No less than justice, madam, mine's a hope
That grows the bolder with each hour of thought.
Be of good heart, dear madam. Check these sorrows,
That wear such needless furrows in your cheeks.
 Widow. They're old ones, sir, plough'd twenty years ago.
 Maurice. Renew them not!
 Widow.   And yet, if what I hear!—
Oh, sir! they tell me that this cruel man
Hath sworn a horrible oath against your life,
If he should lose his case.
 Maurice.   Ah! swears he then!
That looks as if he felt some cause of fear!
 Widow. Do not make light of it, I do entreat you!

He's a most desperate ruffian when he's thwarted,
And has the blood of many on his hands!
'Twas said he left the army for his murders,
And in his duels—
    Maurice.   Let me see,—" of thirty,
Wing'd nineteen combatants, and slew the rest!"
    Clarice. Oh! horrible! How can you jest upon it?
    Maurice. I jest!
    Clarice. In truth, you smile not!
    Maurice.   Do not fear!
I do not think that he will murder me.
    Clarice. Yet be not rash, my husband; take precautions,
This weapon—   [*hands him a small dagger.*
    Maurice. What! your dagger, my Clarice,
This pretty Turkish trifle from your bodice,
The blade mosaic—handle wrought in pearl—
The sheath of exquisite morocco, dropp'd
In gold and green! This ornament for masking,
Were a frail weapon for a man's defence!
Nay, keep your dagger, child, I shall not need it.
    Clarice. Be not so confident.
    Maurice.   Be not so timid!
Who looks for danger surely happens on it!
My papers there! You go with me, dear madam. [*To widow.*
    Widow.   Thanks, sir!
There was a time I kept *my* carriage!
    Maurice. Be hopeful: you shall keep it once again!
[*Aside to Clarice.*] I feed this hapless woman with a promise,
Such as it glads me to indulge myself,—
Yet, should I err in judgment!
    Clarice. [*aside.*] Oh! should you fail!
'Twould break her heart.

Maurice. 'Twere something worse than death!
                              [*Aside to Clarice.*
But we'll not fail! [*aloud*] The courage born of virtue
Hath still a holy sanction for its hope;
And he who strives with justice on his side,
May boldly challenge fortune for success,
If he be true himself!—*We will not fail!*
The carriage there! Come, madam—for the Court House!
                                        [*Exeunt.*

END OF ACT THIRD.

ACT IV.—SCENE I.

A Garden in the rear of the house of Norman Maurice. Walk through a thick shrubbery. Enter Robert Warren and Mrs. Jervas.

    Warren. So! So! You heard it all, then?
    Mrs. J. Every syllable.
    Warren. Glorious! But how did you conceal yourself?
    Mrs. J. An ante-room couducts us to the hall
Where they were secretly at conference;
Thither, when she descended from my chamber,
I softly follow'd. The convenient key-hole
Gave me the means, at once to hear and see them.
    Warren. Your foresight shames my thought! And so, this
        Maurice,
Denies that you shall harbour in his dwelling?
But this you must do! Your security
Lies in his household only! He might promise you
Your lodging in St. Louis,—board and clothing—
Ample provision for your state in future—
But once you free his household of your presence,
He whistles you down the wind. No obligation
Would bind him to the care of you hereafter!
    Mrs. J. What then?
    Warren. Why, to be sure! The very thing, dear madam—
Your sickness will not suffer your removal :

Fatigue of travel, grief, anxiety,
Will have their penalties; and your prostration
Is such, that all the world would say 'twas monstrous
To drive you,—you, a stranger in the country,—
The home of the one kinswoman that's left you!
Your notion is a good one! Norman Maurice
Is not the man to urge the matter on you—
An invalid,—with feeble frame,—hot fever—
Confined to bed,—mind somewhat wandering!—
You're right! Methinks you need no counsel, madam.

Mrs. J. I see! 'Twill do!

Warren. 'Tis excellent! So, Maurice
Accepts the Senatorial nomination,
Though still his pride revolts at working for it.
Well! He's not Senator yet. The widow's case
Will bring its perils too; and, at the finish,
I'll interpose to blight his growing glories,
And show him———Hark! a footstep—

Mrs. J. Here she comes!

Warren. Auspicious! Here, away; and, while you leave us,
I'll open a brief conference with her.
Meanwhile, 'tis well you put your scheme in progress;
Take to your bed, and get your nostrums ready;
Spare not your groans and sighs—a little faintness
Might well arrest you suddenly in your speech!
And—but enough. The thicket! Here, away!

[*They retire behind the copse.*
Enter Clarice.

Clarice. Now all my sorrows sink into the sea,
Since Norman rises to such noble height,
The first in his desert and his desire!
Methinks, till now, I doubted of his fortune,
Nor ever felt secure from sad mischance;

The gibe of envious tongues, the jeer of malice,
The snares of bitter foes, and those dark meshes,
That still the treacherous hands of Warren spread!
These do not fright me now, and, though his presence,
So apt with coming hither of my aunt,
Would seem to shadow forth some evil purpose,
Yet can I not esteem it cause of fear,
Since it were vain for such as he to struggle
Against the noble fortunes of my husband.

 Warren. [*coming out behind her.*] Indeed! and yet the shaft
   that slew the lion,
Was but a reed beside the sedgy stream!

 Clarice. [*seeing him and starting.*] Ah!

 Warren. The little scorpion issuing from the rock,
First slew the steed whose skull he 'habited.

 Clarice. Thou here again!

 Warren. If but to teach thee in philosophy!—
A pebble in the hand of shepherd slinger,
Smote, so we learn from Sacred History,
The proudest giant in Philistia's ranks.

 Clarice. And he whose presence still offends a woman,
But little dreams what champion she may call.

 Warren. I knew *your* champion absent ere I ventured.
Your highest pitch of voice, and greatest need,
Would never bring him timely to your succour.

 Clarice. What means this threat?

 Warren.   It is no threat, Clarice;—
You will not need a champion when I'm near you.

 Clarice. And if I did, methinks, in Robert Warren
I should be loth to seek one! Why come hither,
My husband's foe, pursuing still his fortunes,
And mine, with bitter malice!

 Warren. *Thee* with love!

Clarice. Who wrongs the husband, cannot love the wife!
Warren. Clarice, 'twas in my passionate love for thee,
First grew the passionate hate I bear thy husband!
'Till thou, with fatal beauty, came between us,
He was the twin companion of my pleasures.—
My first associate in each boyish frolic,
We still together went, by hill and valley,
Beside the stream, and through th' untrodden forest,
Having no faith but in our youthful friendship,
No joy, but in the practice shared together.
'Twas thou that changed my kinsman to a rival—
'Twas thou that changed our friendship into hate;
We fell apart, suspecting both, and loathing,
When first our mutual hearts inclined to thee!
Clarice. He did not hate thee—had no jealousy,
But still confided to thee, even his passion;
And thou—alas! audacious that thou art,
How can'st thou still forget that I too know thee,
A traitor to his trust.
Warren. Have I denied it?
I would have won thee from my dearest kinsman.
My treachery to him was truth to thee!
Clarice. And yet 'twas fruitless! Was it not enough
That thou should'st fail? Why now—
Warren. Enough!
Was every passion to be wreck'd forever,
In that which had denial in thy scorn?
With love denied, was vengeance—
Clarice. Vengeance! Ha!
Is it his life thou aim'st at now, or mine?
Warren. Neither!
Clarice. What then? We're separate forever,—
Our lots are cast apart,—our lives divided,—

Why, when no profit comes to thee—no pleasure,
To us, at this dark crossing of our footsteps—
Why art thou here?—Why vex us with thy presence,
To thy own deep defeat?
    Warren.   In your own thoughts,
Look for the answer to this teeming question.
You know me well—enough of me to know,
Whate'er my vices or deficiencies,
I am no simpleton, but have a cunning
That scarce would keep me profitlessly working,
Still drawing fruitless waters in a sieve!
That I should press upon your husband's footsteps,
Would prove I still had hope of my revenge!
That I should seek thee in thy secret bower,
Would show me still not hopeless of thy love!
    Clarice. Oh! vain and insolent man!
    Warren.   Hold, a little!
If hopeful still of you, 'tis through the prospect
Of vengeance on your husband.
    Clarice. Face *him* then!
    Warren. You but increase my eager thirst for vengeance,
When you remind me of the frequent struggle,
Which ended in my overthrow and shame.
    Clarice. Is't not enough, thus baffled and defeated?—
Why thus encounter still the shame and danger?
    Warren. And if my hope lay only in my fortune—
If still my vengeance waited on my strength,
And, to the skill and vigour of mine arm,
I looked to win the vengeance that I covet—
I should forego the conflict, as you counsel,
And leave your world in peace, concealing mine!
    Clarice. Well, sir—you pause!
    Warren. I would have had your thought

Supply the words of mine; but, as it does not—
Know that I look to other means of vengeance;
Not through my strength, but in his feebleness—
Not in my virtue, but your husband's vices!

Clarice. Oh! hence!

Warren. Yet, hear me! at this very moment
Your husband seeks the pinnacle of power;
He stands conspicuous in the public eye;
The highest place awaits him in the State—
The highest in the nation! At a word,
I can o'erthrow him from his eminence,
Can make his name a by-word and a mock,
Degrade him from his rank, and, with a secret—

Clarice. Shallow and impotent, as base and worthless!—
Hence with your secret! Me can you delude not,
Though you delude yourself. I know this secret!

Warren. What! Your husband's forgery?

Clarice.   Your forgery?
Think not to cheat me with your foul contrivance.
You prated of his skill in penmanship—
Defied it,—placed examples in his eye—
And he, confiding—dreaming not that one,
The kinsman who had shared his home and bosom,
Could meditate a falsehood or a crime—
Wrote, at your bidding, sundry names of persons;
And, with these names, without his privity,
Your hand devised the drafts which got the money—
Your hand expended what your guilt procured,
On your own pleasures, in his grievous wrong—
And he hath paid the debt. The fatal papers,
Which might have been a means of his undoing,
Were burned before mine eyes!

Warren.   Your eyes deceiv'd you

I'll not deny your story of the fraud;
But, for the papers—let me whisper you—
They were *not* burn'd—they live for evidence—
Are now in my possession—damning proofs,
For the conviction still of Norman Maurice.

    Clarice. Oh, false as hell! These eyes beheld them burning.

    Warren. Hark, in your ear! What you beheld destroyed,
Were but the copies of originals,
The neatly written forgeries of forgeries:
The originals are mine!

    Clarice. Have mercy, Heaven!
What will you do with them?

    Warren. What you determine.

    Clarice. What mean you?

    Warren. What! can you not conjecture?

    Clarice. No, as I live!

    Warren. What should I do with them?
Appease my hatred, pacify my vengeance,—
Wait till this still triumphant enemy
Puts foot upon the topmost ring of the ladder,
Then cut away the lofty props that raise him,
And let him down to scorn and infamy.
Another day would make him Senator,
But that I step between, and show these papers,
And then the thousand voices in his honour,
Pursue him with their hiss!

    Clarice. Hellish malice!
Oh, if there be a human nature in thee,
Forbear this vengeance.

    Warren. If it pleases thee!

    Clarice. How, if it pleases me?

    Warren. See you not yet?
The alternative is yours to let him perish,

Or win the eminence that still he seeks.
    Clarice. Tell me!
    Warren. Be mine!
    Clarice. [*recoiling.*]   Thine!
    Warren.   Ay! for nothing less
Than the sweet honey dew that lines thy lips,
The heaven that heaves in thy embracing bosom,
Will I forego this vengeance.
    Clarice.   God have mercy!
Yet no! I'll not believe this cruel story;
Thou hast no papers! I must see—
    Warren.   Thou shalt!
Meet me, Clarice, at sunset, in yon thicket.
    Clarice. I dare not. In yon thicket—
    Warren.   Dare you, then,
Behold your husband perish?
    Clarice.   You but mock.
    Warren.   Wilt have me swear!
    Clarice. What oath would bind a wretch
So profligate in sin? I will not come!
My husband's honor still defies your arts,
And mine defies your passion.
    Warren. You have doomed him!
    Clarice. Oh, say not so! You would not have me madden.
    Warren. I swear it! what I tell you is the truth.—
I have these papers, own this fearful pow'r
Upon his fame and fortune, and *will* use it—
    Clarice. And—if I come?   [*Looking vacantly.*
    Warren. And yie'd you to my passion,
The papers, with the fatal evidence,
Shall all be yours.
    Clarice. [*aside.*]   Be resolute, my soul!
Heaven help me in this strait and give me courage.
[*Aloud.*] Bring you the papers, Robert Warren; and—

Warren. [*eagerly.*] You'll come?
Clarice. If I have strength and courage, I will come.
　　　　　　　　　　　[*Exit Clarice, slowly.*
Warren. Then mine's a double triumph! Fool!—these papers
Shall serve a twofold purpose: win the treasure,
And yet confound the keeper when he wakes!
　　　　　　　　　　　　[*Exit Warren.*

SCENE II.

The porch of the Court House of St. Louis. Norman Maurice about to enter, accompanied by the Widow Pressley and Kate, is detained by Mercer upon the threshold.

　Mercer. A word with you, if you please.
　Maurice.　　　Go in, madam,
And find yourself a seat until I come:
I'll follow soon.　　　[*Widow and child enter.*
　Mercer. This case will keep you late,
And we this evening hold a conference,
Touching the course of the debate to-morrow;—
Were it not better you took bed with us,
And, in the meanwhile, lest your wife grows anxious
Advise her, by a billet, of your purpose?
　Maurice. Well thought of. I will do so.　　[*going.*
　Mercer.　　　　Something farther:
Catesby here tells me—but he comes: here, Catesby.
What's this of Savage?　　　　[*Enter Catesby.*

Catesby. [*to Maurice.*] You've won the Savage heart.
It seems that Blasinghame misdoubts your courage,
And, as you gave no reference on his challenge,
Inclines to violence; and has bid his lambs
Gather about him to behold the sport.

Maurice. Ah, sport!

Catesby. And this in utter scorn of Savage,
Who counselled patience till the time is over,
Fixed by you for your answer. Blasinghame
Growls sullen, and shows Savage a cold shoulder:
'Twas he himself advised that you be watchful.

Maurice. I thank him, and feel grateful to the Savage.
As for this Blasinghame, he'll have need to growl,
When we have done with him. But farther—Catesby—
Be you convenient, and, when court is over,
Meet us at Mercer's.

Catesby. I shall stay the trial.

Maurice. Good. Let us in then.
[*Exeunt within.*

Enter *Blasinghame, Savage and others.*

Blasinghame. That's enough, Joe Savage.

Savage. Ay, if it answers.

Blasinghame. Answers or not, I tell you, still enough.
Your counsel's something quite unlike yourself.

Savage. And, for that very reason, may be wisdom.

Blasinghame. Perhaps!—but I'm not used to sudden changes.
I will take further counsel with myself.

Savage. Doubtless, to find the way to wise conclusions.
I wash my hands of the business.

Blasinghame. Pray do so!
But, see you Ferguson?

Savage. He follows us,
Yonder, with Matthews and the stranger, Warren.

Blasinghame. Well, if all fails to bring this Maurice down,
That fellow hath a secret.
 Savage. What is it?
 Blasinghame. Why, something that should please you,—quite
      pacific—
For final overthrow of this man, Maurice:
But let us in. I should be rather anxious,
Having at stake a fortune on this trial.
            [*Exeunt within.*

Enter Ferguson with books and papers, accompanied by War-
      ren.

 Warren. You have it all, sir. At the public meeting
You boldly challenge him with forgery,
Call on me to produce the fatal papers,
And summon Richard Osborne to confirm them.
 Ferguson. We'll crush him at a blow.
 Warren. 'Till then, nothing!
The shame must be complete, beyond recovery.
Let him stretch forth his hand to gain the station,
In sight of all, then, in remediless ruin,
Hurl him down headlong.
 Ferguson.   You are sure of him—
Your facts—your proofs, your persons?
 Warren, Sure as fate!
 Ferguson. You will not fail us.
 Warren.   Would you have me swear?
Have I been wrong'd, and do I hate this Maurice?
Will hate forego the prospect of revenge?
Revenge reject the draught that quenches thirst,
And he who long has dream'd of hidden treasure,
Turn from the golden prize, at last his own?
Not, if the hell that feeds this passion fiercely,
Bestow the needful resolution for it!

Ferguson. And this man, Osborne?

Warren. He has had his lesson—
He'll answer when you call him.

Ferguson. All then is true?

Warren. As true as need be for a lawyer's purpose,
As for a foe's.

Ferguson. 'Tis very pitiful—
For, though I like him not, this Norman Maurice
Is still a man of wondrous qualities;—
But for this lapse from virtue he had been
Most perfect.

Warren. It is well he is not perfect,
Or he had put Humanity to the blush,
By showing, in rough contrast, to her shame,
The meaner value of the coin she carries.

Ferguson. I do not like this business, but our need
Will not permit that we discuss its merits;—
We'll see you with the morrow.

Warren. With the hour,
That hears your accusation!

Ferguson. Good! [*Exit Ferguson within.*

Warren. Ay, good!
It could not well be better for our purpose.
The mine is sprung, the victim still approaches,
Unconscious, and my hand must fire the train!
But here comes Osborne. I must speak him sternly;
He cannot silence me with womanish scruples,—
He shall not!—Well, our scheme works famously.

Enter Osborne.

Osborne. *Your* scheme; not mine!

Warren. When will your wisdom, Osborne,
Conceive that scheme of mine is scheme of yours,—

Or should be?   Now, then, hear our present purpose.
Ferguson brings the charge!

 Osborne.   What! you have told it?

 Warren.   Only to him; and he will keep it safely,
'Till comes the proper moment for explosion.
When our young Senator, in public meeting,
Rises to answer to the public summons,
And take the coveted laurel to his brow,
Then will we loose our thunderbolt, whose bursting
Tears him to atoms.

 Osborne.   What am I to do, then?
What wretched part must I play in this business?

 Warren.   A minor one, 'tis true, but quite important.
You'll be my echo.   When I give the signal,
Confirm my statement and complete our proofs.

 Osborne.   Are you not under pledges to his wife,
To yield her up these proofs?

 Warren.   Ay, on conditions.

 Osborne.   Well!

 Warren.   What of that?   Another means of vengeance!
See you not that I strike him, through her virtue,
But not the less denounce him to the public.
I'll wheedle *her* with a promise to my arms,
Then mock the easy confidence that listen'd
To one she dared despise.

 Osborne.   Oh, Warren! Warren!
Whither would you carry me—where go yourself?

 Warren.   To hell, if need be, so I gain my object!—
Achieve the conquest that to me is heaven,
Comprising, as it must, in equal measure,
At once the joys of passion and of hate!
For you—remember, Osborne—no more scruples!

You are mine—soul, body, thought and feeling, mine—
And these shall ply as still my passions counsel,
Or wo betide the rebel.
    Osborne. Better slay me!
    Warren. Nay, you're not fit to die yet; nor could serve me
Hereafter, half so usefully as now.
At dusk, I keep the meeting with our beauty,
And thence with Matthews to a secret meeting.
Look for me home at midnight; and to-morrow—
Remember! no evasion. Fix'd as fatal,
My will nor brooks dissuasion nor defeat.   [*Exit Warren.*
    Osborne. Had I the heart to perish, 'twere less pain,
Than bend beneath this scourge and bear this chain.
                                        [*Scene closes.*

SCENE III.

An apartment in the dwelling of Norman Maurice. Enter Clarice, reading a note.

    Clarice. Not with me 'till to-morrow! 'Tis an age!
The first night separate since we were married.
Yet better thus. How could I meet my Norman,
Having this deep concealment in my heart,
Nor shudder with a weight of shame, whose crimson
Would set my cheeks on flame! How stifle feeling,
To cling in fondness to his manly bosom,
Nor speak the terrible purpose in my heart,
That said, would stifle his. 'Tis better thus!

Enough, that when I meet him—meet him—yes!—
When his dear voice is sounding in mine ears,
Full of the conscious triumphs that await him,
I then may fling myself upon his breast,
And show the dire necessity that made me
The thing I dare not name,—and plead with him,
For each prompt sacrifice of feminine feeling;
The nerve that rose above the woman weakness,
As still the tribute to his fame and safety.
He will forgive—will bless;—and if he does not!—
Should he recoil from my embrace, and show me
The crimson proof of shame upon my garments,
And cry, " thy hands, that once were white and spotless,
Are red with guilt :"—but no—I dare not think it.
Let me not look that way. Impossible!
Shall I not, while they threaten, steel my heart,
Against this dread necessity, nor tremble,
Though on the altars of his fame and glory,
I bathe this white and innocent hand in crime!
I shudder, yet I shrink not. Give the power,
God, to this heart, against the coming hour!

SCENE IV.

Open space before the Court House of St. Louis. Groups of Lawyers and Citizens.

1st *Lawyer.* Didst hear the speech of Maurice in this case?
2nd *Lawyer.* 'Twas terrible!

1st Lawyer. I never heard the like!
And when he did discourse of Blasinghame,—
His first wrong to the widow—his denial
Of the poor orphan's right—his violence
To those who strove to serve her interests—
The picture that he painted was so monstrous,
That every heart grew cold.
 3rd Lawyer. And Blasinghame,
Himself—didst note him?
 2nd Lawyer. 'Twas another picture!
 1st Lawyer. He sat a spectacle of ghastly fury,
That had moved pity, could we have forgotten
His looks at the beginning of the case.
At first, how bold he seem'd—with what defiance;
Next, with what doubt; then follow'd his dismay—
And last, his fury; while, with impotent rage,
And something, as it seem'd, of shame and horror,
In his own spite at what the other drew,
He crouch'd at last beneath the terrible scourging,
And half escaped from sight.
 2nd Lawyer. I saw him clutching
The panel that he lean'd on, as for help,
While, beaded on his forehead, the big sweat
Still gather'd as it fell; and, on his lips
The stain of red that mingled with the foam,
Show'd how he had even bitten through his lips,
In his great agony, and knew it not.
 1st Lawyer. The Judge has charged the jury?
 2nd Lawyer. He was charging
Just when I left. I could not stand it longer—
As much exhausted at the stern excitement,
As Blasinghame himself.
 1st Lawyer. For Ferguson,

The up-hill work was pitiful. To follow,
With such a case, a speaker such as Maurice,
Was quite as killing to himself as client.
No body heard, or cared to hear, his pleading—
Not even the jury.
 2nd Lawyer. What will be the verdict?
 1st Lawyer. Why, who can doubt? The insuppressible groan,
That broke from every breast—the gaze of fury
That blazed in every eye, when, pointing slowly,
And shaking with such dire significance,
The hand of Maurice fix'd on Blasinghame,
As still, with holy horror in his accents,
He spoke his wonder, that, with guilt so hideous,
He still could brave the gaze of man and justice!—
That groan and glance declared the popular judgment,
And such will be the verdict.
 2nd Lawyer. Hark! that cry—
 1st Lawyer.   Declares it.
[*Shouts in the porch as the people rush out of the Court House.*]
 1st Citizen. Hurrah for Norman Maurice!
 2nd Citizen. The widow's friend!
 3rd Citizen. The people's man forever!
 2nd Lawyer. There speaks the popular heart.
 1st Lawyer.   A glorious voice,
That makes him Senator.
 2nd Lawyer. Hark! he comes forth,
Enter Maurice, with widow Pressley and Kate, followed by Mer-
  cer, Brooks, Catesby and others. Shouts.
 Widow. Ah! sir. God's blessing on you,—make us happy,
And take the half of all you've got for us!
 Maurice. Not for the world, dear madam! I'll not forfeit
The pure delight I feel in serving virtue
For its own sake! In lifting the down-trodden,
For sake of wrong'd humanity! No more. [*People shout.*

1st *Voice.* Hurrah for Norman Maurice!
2nd *Voice.* The widow's friend!
3rd *Voice.* The people's man forever!
Maurice. [*to Mercer.*] Let us get hence.
Dear madam, take my carriage,
And bear the grateful tidings to my wife;
Remain with her to-day while I am absent;—
To-night, as still it's like, I shall be absent.
Rejoice her with our triumph. She expects you!
Widow. I have no thanks—no words,—my tongue is frozen.
Maurice. 'Tis that the thaw is wholly at your heart!
Go hence. Escort her, Mercer, to the carriage.
[*Exeunt Widow, Kate and Mercer.*
Catesby. [*whispering to Maurice.*] Look to it Maurice—here comes Blasinghame!
Enter Blasinghame with others.
Blasinghame. Where is he! Let me see! Ha, give me way!
[*Forces through the crowd, rushes upon Maurice, striking him with a stick.*
Villain, my blows make answer to thy speech!
Maurice. A blow—and I no weapon! But it needs none—
When, with such powerful passions in my heart,
I feel my sinews fortified with strength,
To drag a thousand tigers to my feet.
Thus, monster, that hast trampled on a people,
Defied their virtues—at their sufferings mock'd—
Thus, with my foot upon thy stubborn neck,
I trample—I degrade thee to the dust! [*Seizes Blasinghame by the throat, hurls him to the ground, and stands upon his neck. Shouts of the people.*
1st *Citizen.* Hurrah for Norman Maurice!
2nd *Citizen.* The people's friend!
3rd *Citizen.* The champion of the widow!

Catesby. [*interposing*.] Enough, sir. Let him rise. I'll whisper him
Where he can find us.

Maurice. Now, within the hour!
[*Catesby and Savage lift Blasinghame.*

Catesby. Colonel Blasinghame!

Blasinghame. Where is he? Give me way!

Maurice. [*confronting him.*] Here!

Savage. [*interposing*.] Enough of this!
I see! You'll be at Mercer's. [*To M.*]

Maurice. Ay, now!

Savage. No more! Come, Blasinghame.

Blasinghame. You, Joe!
Well, you are true, boy, and I did you wrong.
Forgive me! You will see to this. This man
Hath had his cursed foot upon my neck!
You saw it!—ha! You saw it!

Savage. He will meet you!

Blasinghame. Ha, Joe! Your hand. But when?

Savage. Within the hour!

Blasinghame. Good! See to it. Ha, ha. Methinks—

Savage. No more!—
Away with me at once; you must not linger.

Blasinghame. Methinks I could drink blood. I'm very thirsty.
[*Exeunt Blasinghame and Savage.*

Catesby. Come, let us get in trim. Are you a shot?

Maurice. No!

Catesby. Ah! that's unfortunate!

Maurice. You think so?—
Never you matter, Catesby: I will kill him!

END OF ACT FOURTH.

ACT V.—SCENE I.

A chamber in the house of Col. Mercer. Norman Maurice and Catesby discovered.

 Catesby. The challenge comes from Blasinghame. This gives us
Advantages, which we should rightly use,
'Gainst one so old in practice.
 Maurice.   We shall use them :—
The weapon for example. Mine's the small sword.
 Catesby. The small sword! Blasinghame expects the pistol.
 Maurice. We have the right in this and other matters ;—
I waive the rest; but this we must insist on.
'Twas still my fancy, upward from my boyhood,
That, next to lance and spear, the proper weapon
For honourable combat is the sword ;—
Admitting grace of movement and decision,
Allowing still discretion to the champion,—
Obeying all the changes of his temper,
And, as the enemy betrayed his purpose,
Giving him power to spare or slay at pleasure,
Or simply to draw blood and to disarm.
 Catesby. You've learn'd to use the weapon?
 Maurice.   But a little!
Some confidence, at least, in eye and motion,
Grew from my youthful practice ; and a passage,
With the bright rapiers flashing in the sunlight,
Was ever such a pleasure to my spirit,
That I am half content to risk the duel,

For the excitement of the keen dispute!
'Tis long since I have exercised, but nature
Hath so endow'd me, that a play acquired,
I never yet have lost. 'Tis fortunate,
That I have made provision for this practice,
And have with me two reeds of Milan steel,
In all respects so equal, that a swordsman
Would linger long to choose.—But here comes Savage!
Enter Savage.

Savage.   Save you, gentlemen.
Maurice.   Your hand, sir. We are ready:
We know your business. Here is Captain Catesby,
Who will discuss with you the needful matters.
Catesby.   Our policy demands the immediate issue,
Lest friends or officers should interpose.
Within the hour,—or, at the least, by sunset,
This meeting should be had.
Savage.   You cannot have it
Too soon for Blasinghame. You know the man!
Well! what the weapon?
Catesby.   We shall choose the small sword.
Savage.   The small sword! Why—'tis not the usual weapon.
Maurice.   As much as any other. France and Poland—
Indeed, most countries of the continent,
Where'er society allows the duel,—
Employ it—
Catesby.   And, you know, in Louisiana?—
Savage.   The pistol's the more equal.
Catesby.   Were Blasinghame,
Or Maurice, feeble, and the other strong,
That were, perhaps, an argument, but—
Maurice.   And, if the question's courage, Major Savage,
As I am told your friend is pleased to make it,
Somewhat at my expense, then, let me tell you,

Cold steel will better try the manly bosom,
Than any decent distance with the pop-gun.
If I remember, Colonel Blasinghame
Hath served in the army, worn the soldier's weapon,
And will not scruple at its use in season.
 Savage.   Your words decide it:
You have the right—the small sword be it then.
 Maurice. [*giving swords.*] Here are two noble weapons—better never
Play'd in the spiral and conflicting circle,
Above the head whose life was made the forfeit
In the delirious conflict. Take them with you;
Your friend can choose from them, or note the measure
Of that which I employ.
 Savage. At sunset, then.
 Catesby. The place ?—
 Maurice.   If you will suffer me—there is,
By Baynton's meadow, a sweet bit of copse,
East of it, through which runs an Indian trail :—
It leads us to a patch of open lawn,
Level, and smooth, and grassy—a fit place
For one to fight, or sleep on !
 Savage.   Be it there, then.
And now I leave you, gentlemen : an hour
Remains for preparation ere we meet ! [*Exit Savage.*
 Catesby. You are the coolest person—for a person
That never was in combat. You will kill him !
 Maurice. Not if I'm cool enough ! I fain would spare him,
Now, that I see him not. But when before me,
And I behold in him the insulting tyrant,
That robs the feeble and defies the strong,
I feel a passionate anger in my heart,
That makes me long to trample him to dust !

Catesby. What more, but seek the surgeon and the carriage?
Maurice. I'm ready when you please.
Catesby. Within the hour! [*Exit Catesby.*
Maurice. My poor Clarice! she sits beside the window,
And with a vacant spirit still looks forth,
Unthinking, yet still dreaming that I come.
What a long night to both—and that to-morrow!
Well! it will chide her tears, and soothe my sorrow.
[*Scene closes.*

SCENE II.

The entrance of a thick wood near the dwelling of Norman Maurice. Sunset. Robert Warren discovered.

Warren. The sun is at its set, and yet she comes not.
Can she have faltered—what doth she suspect,—
What fear! It sinks, and hark—her footstep.
Now comes our triumph—now! [*Retires into the wood.*
Enter Clarice.
Clarice. Oh, if I err,
I that am feeble, and though feeble, loving,—
Devoted, where the sacrifice is needful,—
Willing to die for him whose dear devotion,
Hath made it my religion still to love him—
Oh, God have mercy on the hapless error,
That grows from love's necessities alone!
If in my death his triumph may be certain,
My breast is ready for the knife. I need

No prayer, no prompting to the sacrifice,
That saves him from the wreck of all his hopes,
And honour with them. Let me now not falter!
Forgive me, Heaven, in pity to the weakness
That knows not how to 'scape. If it be crime,—
The deed, which I have brooded o'er, until
My shuddering fancy almost deems it done—
By which I do avoid the loathlier crime ;
Let not the guilt lie heavy on my soul,
As solemnly I do profess myself,
Most free from evil purpose, and most hating
That which meseems the dread necessity
That shadows all my fortune! God have pity,
And show the way, that still unseen before me,
Lies open for my rescue! Ha, 'tis he !

   Warren. [*reënters.*] Methinks, Clarice, you come reluctantly.
Your husband's fate—the dangers that await him,
That do appear so terrible to me,
Would seem to touch you not.

   Clarice.   I'll not believe it!
I tell you I must see these fatal papers—
Must feel them—spell and weigh each syllable,
Ere I believe you!

   Warren. Said I not you should?

   Clarice. Show me them. I'm here.

   Warren. Come hither, then.

   Clarice. What! in the deeper darkness of the wood?
No! Here!

   Warren. What! dost forget my recompense?
Wouldst thou the naked heaven behold our pleasures?

   Clarice. Oh, Heaven! sustain me! Let me not go mad ;
That I may hear unmoved this foul assailant,

Nor show, to baffling of my hope and purpose,
The loathing that I feel! [*Aside.*

    Warren.   The proof is ready—
Wherefore dost thou linger?

    Clarice. [*eagerly.*]   Ha! then thou hast it—
Here, in thy bosom—here, in yonder wood.

    Warren.   Even as thou sayest—here, within my bosom;
But 'tis in yonder wood that thou shalt see it.
Behold!   [*Takes the papers from his bosom and
    waves her to the wood.*

    Clarice. Give me to see them.

    Warren. Yes!

    Clarice. But here!

    Warren. No—there!   [*Waving papers and retiring.*

    Clarice. Show me! I come! [*Following.*

    Warren.   Yet farther. Follow me!
By yon red oak, where the dark thicket spreads,
Where silence, and her twin, security,
Brood ever, and declare for loving hearts
Their meet protection in this lonely shade,—
Thither, Clarice! [*Retires from sight, beckoning with the papers.*

    Clarice.   Thither, then; I follow thee!
Thou dost implore thy fate! I follow thee
Where shadow and silence both invoke with speech,
Too potent for my feeble pray'r and plaint,
A shadow and a silence yet more deep!
They awfully declare a hideous worship
Where Horror sits supreme, and summons me
To make befitting sacrifice. My soul,
Be firm of purpose now. Nerves do not falter,
When that I do demand your resolute office.
I dare not call on Heaven to help my weakness,

But from the indulgent mercy, born of Heaven,
Implore the saving grace I may not merit.
    Warren. [*within.*] Clarice!
    Clarice. Ha, then, I come to thee.
Fool! thou entreat'st a Fury to thy arms,
And not a woman. Thou would'st have my love—
Partake of my embrace—my kiss—thou shalt!
My husband—'tis for thee!
    Warren. [*within.*] Clarice!
    Clarice.   He calls me!
I do but answer to his summons! Ha!
Another voice is sounding in mine ears,—
And many voices! One of them is Norman's,—
He calls!—he, too, implores me to the wood!
There will he meet with Warren. If he meets him,
I know what then must happen. I must thither.
His voice again. It sinks into a murmur—
Mixed murmurs follow of a crowd! What is it,
That rolls so dully in my brain, and makes me
Uncertain of my footstep? Oh! the horror
Of this strange weakness! Ha!
    Waren. [*Within the wood.*] Clarice!
    Clarice.   He calls!
Thrice! Thrice! It is decreed. I come—I come! [*Exit within: a moment after a cry of agony, and then a sound as of a falling body. Reënter Clarice with papers in her hand, and garments all bloody.*
    Clarice. Ha, ha, I have them! I could laugh! Ha! ha!—
But for this horrible silence. Yet, I have them!
He would have kept them from me—he. Ha, ha!
But would I suffer him when he threatened Norman,
My husband, with dishonour—my brave husband,
That even now is rising in the nation,

Among the great, in the high places of power,
Ranked with the men most eminent.   Dear Norman!
Ha!—ha! I'm very happy now.   I have the papers,
The proof, and Norman is made Senator,
Spite of this wretched liar!   He'll lie no more.
He wish'd for my embrace, and sure he had it!
Such close embrace, so sharp, so sudden, sweet,
It made him shriek and shrink with such a pleasure,
As men endure not twice.   [*Groan within.*
God! what is that!
A footstep!   He pursues me for the papers.   [*Thrusts them into
                                          her bosom.*
He shall not have them.   No—I have no papers.
He comes!   Home—Norman—Home!   Home!   Home! my
     Norman!
          [*Exit wildly, looking behind her as she departs.*

SCENE III.

The wood behind Baynton's meadow.   Enter from opposite sides, Norman Maurice, Catesby, Surgeon; and Colonel Blasinghame, Savage, Surgeon.

Savage.   Can nothing reconcile our parties, Catesby?
Catesby.   The invitation to the field is yours:
Yours still must be each overture for peace.
Savage.   What will content you, Blasinghame?
Blasinghame.   His blood!
Savage. [*to Catesby.*]   I'm sorry, but you hear?

Catesby.   To business, then.
Maurice is at his post, so, place your man.
            [*Maurice and Blasinghame confront each other.*
Maurice. Art ready, sir?
Blasinghame. For vengeance! You have foil'd me—
Disgraced me in the eyes of all our people,
So, look to it, for by the God that made me,
I'll write my living tortures on your heart!
Maurice. Your blood upon your head!
                [*They fight. Maurice disarms him.*
Blasinghame. Curse on the weapon!
Maurice. Curse not the weapon!—curse the hand, the heart—
The cause,—which have betrayed you;—not the weapon!
Your life is at my mercy!
Blasinghame. [*folding his arms.*]   Take it, then!
I would not live dishonoured. You may slay me,
But cannot conquer me.—My breast is open!
Maurice. I will not slay you. I *will* conquer you.
Your life is mine. I give it you. Live on,
A wiser and a better man hereafter.
Blasinghame. [*tottering and turning away.*] My strength is
            gone from me; my heart is crush'd.
Look, Savage,—these are tears, and not of blood.
Come with me, for I falter.   [*Going.*
Savage. [*to Maurice.*]   You're a man
Among ten thousand, Maurice. Now, forgive him.
He weeps. The strong man weeps.—I must go with him,
But know me for your friend.
            [*Exit Savage following Blasinghame.*
Catesby.   'Twas nobly done.
When I consider Blasinghame's career,
His brutal murders, his long tyrannies,
The provocation you have had to slay him—

I marvel that you spared him. Sir, your triumph
Is now without alloy.
  Maurice.   I'm glad you think so,
Yet deem the merit of forbearance small.
Had he been bolder, I had never spared him;
But could not strike him when, with folded arms,
He stood to meet the stroke. But—let's to Mercer.
                              [*Exeunt.*

SCENE IV.

The Chamber of Richard Osborne. Enter to him Harry Matthews.

  Matthews. Where's Warren?
  Osborne. I've not seen him.
  Matthews. Not since when?
  Osborne. Noon yesterday.
  Matthews.   Indeed. 'Twas then we parted.
He promised to meet with me last night at Baylor's.
  Osborne. And came not?
  Matthews. No. 'Twas probable his business—
For you must know his hands are full at present—
Was quite too grateful and too full of profit,
To make him leave it soon. I marvel'd not
That he should fail us *then ;* but now, this morning,
When, by agreement, he should breakfast with us—
And here's the hour—that he should still be absent,
Seems something strange. He must be at the meeting,
Or we are done forever.

Osborne. What's the meeting?
Matthews. One of both parties, meant for caucussing,
Popular wholly in its character.
Whose temper will determine our Assembly
As to its choice of Senator in Congress.
 Osborne. Ay,—Indeed.
 Matthews. You'll be there?
 Osborne. Yes; I promised him.
 Matthews. Who? Warren?
 Osborne. Yes.
 Matthews.   I must go look for him.
We must not risk our fortunes by delay.
His voice may help to make our Senator. [*Ex. Matt.*
 Osborne. Would he were dumb or I! Alas! these murmurs,
How feeble—since the fetters are about me,
And but one way remains—to curse and perish.   [*Exit.*

SCENE V.

The open street. Ferguson and Matthews.

 Ferguson. What quest was that, I pray?
 Matthews. [*smiling.*]   I must not tell it—
A lady's in the secret.
 Ferguson.   Keep it then.
But give yourself no farther care for Warren.
His last words, when we parted yesterday,
Implied his absence 'till the latest moment.
He'll be with us to-day, when we are ready.

Matthews. 'Twill do no harm at least to hurry him.
Ferguson. Have you seen Blasinghame?
Matthews. This morning? No.
Ferguson. You know not he and Maurice fought at sunset?
Matthews. Indeed! How did they fight?
Ferguson. With swords.
Matthews. What then?
Ferguson. Why, Maurice had him at his mercy!
Matthews. And spared his life?
Ferguson. He did, but had been much more merciful
To have taken it,—for he has crushed the other!
Matthews. How! Blasinghame!
Ferguson. Has withered in a night.
Matthews. Good Heaven! Impossible! What! Imbecile!
Ferguson. He stares in vacancy—his hair's grown white,—
He trembles as with palsy, and he weeps,
Even as an infant!
Matthews. What a change is this!
Ferguson. He's useless to us now; and Savage grows
More friendly now to Maurice than to me.
Matthews. This Maurice wrecks us all.
Ferguson. But, in an hour,—
Let Warren be but faithful to his pledges,
And we shall see his vessel in a tempest,
Such as no bark can weather.
Matthews. Be it so—
My breath shall not be wanting to the blow! [*Exeunt.*

SCENE VI.

The interior of the City Hall of St. Louis. A raised platform in the centre. Citizens crowding about it. Chairman presiding and seated with other distinguished men. On one hand, Ferguson and others—opposite, Norman Maurice, Mercer, Brooks, &c. Norman Maurice discovered speaking.

Maurice. Thus have we, sir, discussed the several questions
Involved in this upon the Constitution—
I trust that, on this instrument, I speak
The doctrines of Missouri. I would have it
A ligament of fix'd, unchanging value,
Maintained by strict construction,—neither warp'd,
Nor stretch'd, nor lopt of it's now fair proportions,
By the ambitious demagogue or statesman,
Who, with the baits of station in their eyes,
Still sacrifice the State! Our policy,
Should hold ours as a linkèd realm of nations
Where each one sits secure, however feeble,
And, pointing to the sacred written record,
Finds in it her Palladium. Government,
We hold to be the creature of our need,
Having no power but where necessity,
Still under guidance of the Charter, gives it.
Our taxes raised to meet our exigence,
And not for waste or favourites—our people
Left free to share the commerce of the world,
Without one needless barrier on their prows!
Our industry at liberty for venture,
Neither abridged, nor pamper'd; and no calling

Preferr'd before another, to the ruin,
Or wrong of either. These, sir, are my doctrines!
They are the only doctrines which shall keep us
From anarchy, and that worst peril yet,
That threatens to dissever, in the tempest,
That married harmony of hope with power,
Which keeps our starry union o'er the storm,
And, in the sacred bond that links our fortunes,
Makes us defy its thunders!—Thus, in one,—
The foreign despot threatens us in vain.
Guizot and Palmerston may fret to see us
Grasping the empires which they vainly covet
And stretching forth our trident o'er the seas,
In rivalry with Britain. They may chafe,
But cannot chain us. Balances of power,
Framed by corrupt and cunning monarchists,
Weigh none of our possessions; and the seasons
That mark our mighty progress, East and West,
Show Europe's struggling millions, fondly seeking,
The better shores and shelters that are ours.
Enough, sir—I have yielded my opinions,
Freely delivered, frankly argued, fairly,
With deference to the learning and the wisdom,
Shown by my opponent! The rest is yours.
  Chairman. You have heard, citizens; what farther order
Is it your pleasure, that we—
  Mercer.   Sir, it needs not!—
The ample range that this debate hath taken,
The spacious grasp of argument upon it—
How well discussed the questions—how complete
And clear, the several reasons which concluded,—
Leave none in doubt of what should be our judgment.
Methinks there's but one matter now before us,

And th's decided, stays the whole discussion,—
By showing, in our preference for the man,
What still hath been our thoughts upon his measures.
Well have the advocates on both sides spoken,
Not equally, but well! For Ferguson,
His eloquence honours his experience past,
And ancient reputation ;—but, methinks,
That none who listened to the speech of Maurice,
But must have yielded to his clear opinions ;—
Enforced by illustrations near and foreign,
Such full analysis, such profound research—
Statements so fairly made,—objections battled
So fearlessly—and arguments sustained
With so much equal truth and eloquence!
His views are mine—are those of this assembly!
Nay more—I boldly challenge in their favour,
The voices of Missouri! What remains—
But that we speak to her assembled wisdom?
This day they choose a Senator in Congress—
Whom shall we name to them of all our people?

   1st Voice. Why, Norman Maurice!
   2nd Voice. Who but Norman Maurice?
   3rd Voice. The widow's friend—the champion of the people!
   Brooks. Such is the popular will!
   Ferguson.   A moment, sir!
If eloquence and talent, just opinion,
Were the sole requisite, for this high station,
I should be silent here, or probably,
Join with you in the shout for Norman Maurice.
But truth and virtue claim a place with talent,
And he who serves, our Senator in Congress,
Must know no smutch of shame upon his garments.
   Maurice. Ha! shame, sir?

Ferguson. That was the word, sir.
Maurice. Shame of mine?
Ferguson. Of thine!
Maurice. Speak, sir; I listen.
Ferguson. It is charged, sir,
That Norman Maurice, ere he sought St. Louis,
Was once a resident of Philadelphia;
That there he forged a paper on a merchant,
Well known, by which he gain'd two thousand dollars!
Maurice. A falsehood! false as hell! As God's in Heaven,
I never did this thing!
Ferguson. The proof is here!
Maurice. The proof! What proof?
Ferguson. Know you one Robert Warren?
Ha! you are silent, sir—you start, you redden!—
Maurice. With scorn and indignation, not with terror!
I do know Robert Warren; that base reptile
Whom thrice I spared the scourge. Set him before me
And you shall see whose tremors speak the guilty,
And whose the innocent, aroused to vengeance!
Ferguson. Have then your wish! Accuser! Robert Warren!
Stand forth and answer! [*Pause.*
Maurice. He dare not!
Ferguson. He will!
Maurice. Shout for your man again. Set him before me.
Ferguson. Call at the door, there—call for Robert Warren.
Voice without. Ho! Robert Warren, Robert Warren! Ho!
[*Enter Harry Matthews hastily, and in great agitation,*]
Matthews. Who calls for Robert Warren? He is murder'd,—
Stabb'd with a dagger, and was found a corse,
Within the wood behind the house of Maurice.
Here is the dagger, found upon the body,
And crusted with his blood. [*Showing dagger.*

Maurice. Murdered! Give it me! [*Seizes the dagger, looks at and drops it.*

Great God! 'tis hers! [*Aside.*]

Matthews. Behold the murderer!
He staggers! It is he hath done the deed!

Ferguson. Ay, truly,—who so like to do the deed,
As one who needs to silence such a witness.

Maurice. Thy bitter jealousy and hate delude thee,
And make thee but a liar. I convict thee,
Out of the mouths of thine own witnesses.—
When saw you Warren last? [*To Matthews.*]

Matthews. Noon yesterday:
He left me then to seek *your* house.

Maurice. My house!
What would he at my house?

Matthews. I do not know.
But know that from that hour until the present,
When now we find him by your house a corse,
He has no more been seen.

Maurice. 'Tis fortunate,
That we may get the truth from fraud and cunning,
Even when it makes against them. Noon yesterday
Found me in public court-house, on a trial,
Before a thousand eyes, 'till four o'clock!

Ferguson. But after that?

Maurice. My witness here is Mercer.

Mercer. From that hour
'Till sunset, he continued at my house,
Then left with Captain Catesby, to return
With dark, and to remain with us all night,
Most part in consultation with our friends
Who did not separate until near the dawn.

Ferguson. Then, 'till this hour?

Catesby. With me! We slept together!

Maurice. Man of a bitter malice, art thou answer'd?

Ferguson. Thou 'scapest the murder, not the forgery.
Warren was not the only evidence;
Where's Richard Osborne?

Osborne. [*Coming forward.*] Here!

Ferguson. All do not fail us!
Your name is Richard Osborne? You know Maurice,
And know the crime which Warren charged upon him?
He named you as his witness.

Osborne. He did wrong, then!
I know of no offence of Norman Maurice—
Yet know him well, and all I know of him,
Hath still approved him, to my sense and judgment,
The noblest, as he is the first of men!

1. *People shout.* Hurrah for that!

2. *People shout.* Hurrah for Norman Maurice!

Ferguson. Confusion!

Matthews. I'm off. [*Exeunt Matthews and Ferguson.*

People. [*with cries and hisses.*] Away with Ferguson!

Mercer. [*to Maurice.*] Your triumph is complete!

Brooks. All's well!

Maurice. Tell me that!—
All's well!—You spoke! Did you not say, my wife?
What of her—Speak!

Mercer. You're ill! Your lips are very pale!
But courage, all your trial's over now.

Maurice. Art sure of that? Let me but understand it!—

Mercer. 'Twould seem so!—What a foul conspiracy,
So fatally arrested. For this murder—

Maurice. What of it?

Mercer. 'Tis very strange!

Maurice. Very strange indeed!

Mercer. But stranger still the audacious charge against you.
Who was this Warren?

Maurice. [*with an effort.*] Who? but here is one,
To put you in possession of the story.
He knows how dexterously a lie was founded,
Most monstrous, on the basis of a truth,
By this same Warren, to my injury. [*Osborne comes forward.*
Osborne, I thank you for your ready answer,
And good opinion.

Osborne. It was but your right.

Maurice. What is that cry? my fears. [*Noise without.*
      Enter Kate, followed by Mrs. Jervas.

Kate. Oh! Sir! Your wife!

Maurice My wife! Be still my heart. What of my wife?

Kate. She's sick. O! very sick!

Mrs. Jervas. She's broke a blood vessel!

Maurice. [*with a cry.*] God! thou hast sent
This Terror, like a fate into my house,
And wreck'd the hope that nestled there in peace!—
Hence, woman, from my sight!
My wife! my wife! [*Rushes out.*

Mercer. [*to Catesby.*] Follow him with a surgeon.

Brooks. What a day's history of storm and sorrow!
There is some cruel mystery in these doings,
Which we must fathom! This conspiracy,
For such it clearly shows, makes for our party;
Let's hasten to the use of it. They'll never
Hold up their heads again. The people's with us,
The assembly waits us and will crown our triumph!

SCENE VII.

A chamber in the house of Norman Maurice. Clarice reclines upon a couch. The widow Pressley stands at a little distance watching her.

   Widow. Dear lady, you will die.
   Clarice. Do not come near me!
   Widow. You bleed! You suffocate!
   Clarice. And still he comes not.
You promised me to send for him. Oh, God—
Should they behold these papers. Ha! I hear him.
Do you hear nothing?
   Widow. Nothing!
   Clarice. I hear! 'Tis he!
   Maurice. [*without.*] Clarice! my wife!
             Enter Norman Maurice.
   Maurice. Speak! Tell me! Where!—Clarice. [*seeing her.*
   Clarice. Oh! now you come! Heaven bless! I'm dying,
        Norman!
             [*Raises herself feebly to his arms.*
   Maurice. Dying!
   Clarice. I feel it; but——
   Maurice. The surgeon! God of Heaven,—
   Clarice. He cannot help me now. Too late! no succour,—
I've but the words for blessing and farewell!—
I'm sinking;—but you're safe! Safe! Oh! the rapture,
To know it, and to whisper in your ears,
With the last loving words. He would have crush'd you—
Made infamous your name, my noble husband;
But stoop,—your ear—he'll trouble us no more.

He's silent—and I have the fatal papers ;—
No copies—all the originals.—Ha! Ha!—
They're here—now take me,—closer—to your heart;
I leave you—lose you—Norman. Ah! your lips,—
How cold, but sweet, my Norman—cold—sweet Heaven. [*Dies.*

Maurice. Now sink my soul!—since the bright star is gone,
That made thy life and glory from the heavens—
That stored thee with all blessings. I am crushed!
Ha! what are these! (*lays her down gently—the papers fall*
Oh, God! I see it all.   *from her bosom.*
Oh, bloody wretch, whose nature was a lie,
This was thy work,—not hers. 'Tis plain before me.
My poor Clarice! how faithful unto death,
Shielding me at the peril of thyself,
And, in the seeming dread necessity,
Doing the deed that from its delicate props,
Shook the fair fabric of thy innocent life!
My wife! My wife.   [*Sinks down.*
    [*Noise and voices without.*]

People. Hurrah for Norman Maurice!
    Enter Mercer, Brooks and others.

Mercer. Maurice, my friend, we triumph. You are Senator
For the next term, in Congress, from Missouri.

Maurice. Could'st wake her with thy tidings!

Mercer. God! This is death!

Maurice. It lies upon her silent lips like snow.
Oh! do not speak—she hears not! why should I?
Nor sorrow, nor joy shall fill these frozen eyes,
That see not me. She would have listened once,
How gladly,—and found music in the triumph,
That now can bring me none. My wife! My wife!

THE END.

CAIUS MARIUS;

AN HISTORICAL LEGEND.

CAIUS MARIUS;

AN HISTORICAL LEGEND.

I.

The Dungeon of Minturnæ.

MARIUS.   THE CIMBRIAN.

Marius.   What art thou, wretch, that, in the darkness com'st,
The midnight of this prison, with sly step,
Most fit for the assassin, and bared dagger
Gleaming in thy lifted grasp!
   Cimbrian.   I am sent by those
Whose needs demand thy death.   A single stroke
Sets us both free forever—thou from Fate,
Me from Captivity.
   Marius.   Slave, hast thou heart
To strike at that of Marius!
   Cimbrian   That voice—that name—
Disarm me; and those fearful eyes that roll,
Like red stars in the darkness, fill my soul
With awe that stays my hand.   Master of the world,
The conqueror of my people hast thou been,—
I know thee as a Fate! I cannot harm thee.

Marius.   Go to thy senders, and from Marius say,
That, if they bare the weapon for my breast,
Let them send hither one who has not yet
Looked in a master's eye.   'Tis not decreed
That I shall perish yet, or by such hands
As gather in Minturnæ.   Get thee hence!

II.

Public Hall of Minturnæ.

MAGISTRATES.   THE CIMBRIAN.   AUGUR.

Cimbrian.   I cannot slay this man.   Give me to strike
Some baser victim, or restore to me
My chains.   I cannot purchase, at such price,
The freedom that I covet.

Magistrate.   Yet this man
Conquered thy people.

Cimbrian.   He hath conquered me!

Augur.   And he must conquer still!
His hour is not yet come.   The Fates reserve
His weapon for their service.   They have need
Of his avenging ministry, to purge
The world of its corruptions.   I behold
A fearful vision of the terrible deeds
That wait upon his arm.   Let him go free.
Give him due homage; clothe him with fresh robes;
Speed him in secret, with a chosen bark,
To other shores.   So shall your city 'scape
Rome's wrath, and his hereafter.

Magistrate. It is well:
This counsel looks like wisdom.
 Augur. It is more!
So the Gods speak through their interpreter.
 Magistrate. Release him straightway—send him forth in
   honour;
We give him freedom—let the Gods give safety.

III.

Island of Ænaria.

MARIUS. CETHEGUS.

Cethegus. Thou hast slept, Marius.
 Marius. And thou hast watched my sleep;
Ah! truest friend and follower, not in vain!
Dismiss that cloudy trouble from thy brows,
Those doubts that vex thy heart; for know that Fate
Still hath me in its keeping, and decrees
Yet other deeds and conquests at my hand,
And still one glorious triumph. I shall be
Once more, in Rome, a Consul! When a child,
Sporting on summer slopes, beneath old hills,
Seven infant eagles, from a passing cloud,
Dropt clustering in my lap. The Augurs thence
Gave me seven times the Roman Consulate.
 Cethegus. Thou'st had it six.
 Marius. One other yet remains.
 Cethegus. Alas! the Fates but mock thee with a dream;

For know that, while thou slept'st, our treacherous bark
Loosed sail, and left the shores.

   Marius. Gone!

   Cethegus. Clean from sight.

   Marius. Ha! ha! Now thank the Gods that watch my sleep,
And save me when the might of man would fail!
Courage, my friend, that vessel speeds to wreck,
Racked on some lurking rock beneath the wave,
Or foundering in the tempest. We are safe!

   Cethegus. Thou'rt confident.

   Marius. As Fate and Hope can make me.
Yet look! there is an omen. We must fly
This place, for other refuge. See the strife
Betwixt these deadly scorpions on the sands.

   Cethegus. What read'st thou in this omen?

   Marius.   Sylla's soldiers
Are fast upon our heels. Get to the shore;
Some fisher's boat will help us from the land,
And bear us whither the directing Fates
Decree for refuge—safely o'er the seas
That gulph our treacherous vessel.

   Cethegus.   Be it so!
I follow thee whatever be thy fate!

   Marius. Hark! dost thou hear?

   Cethegus. What sound?

   Marius.   The tramp of horse;
And lo! the boat awaits us by the shore!

IV.

Marius, alone, seated, among the Ruins of Carthage.

1

Alone, but not a captive—not o'ercome
By any fate, and reckless of its doom—
Even midst the ruins by his own hand made,
There sits the Exile, lone, but unafraid!
What mighty thoughts, that will not be repressed,
Warm his wild mood, and swell his labouring breast?—
What glorious memories of the immortal strife,
Which gave him fame, and took from Carthage life;
That giant-like, sea rival of his own
Proud realm, still challenging the sway and throne;
Doomed in long conflict, through experience dread,
To bend the neck at last, to bow the head;
To feel his foot upon her lordly brow,
And yield to him who shares her ruins now!

2

How, o'er his soul, with passions still that gushed,
The wondrous past with all its memories rushed;
These ruins make his monument. They told
Of wisest strategy, adventure bold,
Dread fields of strife—an issue doubtful long,
That tried his genius, and approved it strong;
That left him robed in conquest, and supreme,
His country's boast, his deeds her brightest theme;
Written in brass and marble—sung in strains
That warm the blood to dances in the veins;
That make young hearts with wild ambition thrill,

And crown the spirit with achieving will;
That seem eternal in the deeds they show,
And waken echoes that survive below;
Brood o'er the mortal, slumbering in the tomb,
And keep his name in song, his works in bloom,
Till envious rivals, hopeless of pursuit,
Join in the homage, who till then were mute;
Catch up the glorious anthem, and unite
To sing the bird they could not match in flight;
Content to honour where they can not shame,
And praise the worth they can not rob of fame.

3

How, with these memories gathering in his breast,
Of all the labours that denied him rest—
Of all the triumphs that his country bore
To heights of fame she had not won before—
Broods he, the exile, from his state and home,
On what awaits thee and himself, O Rome!
Of what thy hate deserves, and his decrees,
Whom thou hast brought unwilling to his knees.
No sad submission yields he to his fate,
So long as solace comes to him from hate,
Or hope from vengeance. In his eyes, ye trace
No single look to recompense disgrace;
With no ambition checked, no passion hushed,
No pride o'erthrown, no fond delusion crushed;
With every fire alive that ever swayed,
His soul as lordly as when most obeyed,
He broods o'er wrongs, forgetful of his own,
And from his heart hears vengeance cry alone.
Fixed on the ruins round him, his dread eye
Glares, as if fastened on his enemy;

His hand is on the fragment of a shrine
That Hate may henceforth deem a thing divine;
Grasped firmly—could the fingers but declare
How dread the oath the soul is heard to swear!
The awful purpose, nursed within, denies
Speech to the lips, but lightens up the eyes,
Informs each feeling with the deadliest will,
But, till the murderous moment, bids "be still!"

Come read, ye ministers of Fate, the lore
That fills the dark soul of the fiend ye bore;
Reveal the secret purpose that inspires
That deadly mood, and kindles all its fires;
Scan the dread meaning in that viperous glance
Fixed on those ruins in intensest trance,
Which nothing speaks to that it still surveys,
And looks within, alone, with meaning gaze;
Unclose that lip, that, rigidly compressed,
Stops the free rush of feeling from the breast;
And, on that brow, with seven deep furrows bound,
Write the full record of his thought profound.
What future scene beneath that piercing eye
Depicts the carnage and the victory;
The flashing steel—the shaft in fury sped—
The shrieking victim, and the trampled dead?
Say, what wild sounds have spelled the eager ear,
That stretches wide, the grateful strain to hear;
How many thousands perish in that cry
That fills his bloody sense with melody?
What pleading voices, stifling as they swell,
Declare the vengeance gratified too well?
What lordly neck, beneath that iron tread,

Strangled in utterance, leaves the prayer unsaid?
What horrid scene of triumph and of hate,
Do ye discover to this man of Fate,
Which, while his Fortune mocks the hope he bears,
Consoles his Past, and still his Future cheers?

5

He hath no speech, save in the ruins round;
But there's a language born without a sound,
A voice whose thunders, though unuttered, fly
From the red lightnings of the deep-set eye;
There passion speaks of hate that cannot spare,
Still tearing those that taught him how to tear;
One dream alone delighting his desire,
The dream that finds the fuel for his fire;
Let fancy shape the language for his mood,
And speak the purpose burning in his blood.

V.

Marius. "If thou hadst ears, O Carthage! for the voice
That speaks among thy ruins, it would cheer
The spirit that was crushed beneath my heel,
To hear the tongue of thy destroyer swear
To live as thy avenger. I have striven
For Rome against thee, till, in frequent strife,
Thy might was overthrown—thy might as great
As Rome's in days most palmy, save in this:
Thou hadst no soul as potent in thy service,

As I have been in hers. And thou, and all—
The Gaul, the Goth, the Cimbrian—all the tribes
That swelled the northern torrents, and brought down,
Yearly, the volumed avalanche on Rome—
Have sunk beneath my arm, until, secure,
She sat aloft in majesty, seven-throned,
And knew or feared no foe. This was my work—
Nor this alone ; from the patrician sway,
That used her as the creature of his will,
I plucked her eagles, casting down his power
Beneath plebeian footstep. For long years
Of cruellest oppression and misrule,
I took a merited vengeance on her pride,
Debasing her great sons, that, in their fall,
Her people might be men. I loved her tribes,
Since they were mine. I made their homes secure ;
I raised their free condition into state—
And I am here ! These ruins speak for me—
An exile—scarred with honourable wounds,
At seventy years, alone and desolate !

"But the o'er-ruling Deities decree
My triumph. From thy ruins comes a voice
Full of most sweet assurance. Hark ! it cries,
To me, as thy avenger. Thou forgiv'st
My hand the evil it hath wrought on thee,
That the same hand, upon thy conqueror's head
May work like ruin. The atoning Fates
Speak through thy desolation. They declare
That I shall tread the ungrateful city's streets,
Armed with keen weapon and consuming fire,
And still unglutted rage. My wrath shall sow
The seeds of future ruins in her heart,

So that her fall, if far less swift than thine,
Shall be yet more complete. She shall consume
With more protracted suffering. She shall pass
Through thousand ordeals of the strife and storm,
Each bitterer than the last—each worse than thine—
A dying that shall linger with its pain,
Its dread anxieties, its torturing scourge,
A period long as life, with life prolonged,
Only for dire, deservéd miseries.
Her state shall fluctuate through successive years,
With now great shows of pride—with arrogance
That goes before destruction—that her fall
May more increase her shame. The future grows—
Dread characters, as written on a wall—
In fiery lines before me; and I read
The rise of thousands who shall follow me,
Each emulous of vengeance fell as mine,
By mine at first begotten. Yet, why gaze
In profitless survey of the work of years,
Inevitable to the prescient soul,
And leave our own undone? I hear a voice
Reproaching me that I am slow to vengeance;
Me, whom the Fates but spare a few short hours,
That I may open paths to other masters,
For whom they find the scourge. They tutor me
That mine's a present mission; not for me
To traverse the wide future, in pursuit
Of those who shall succeed me in their service,
But to speed onward in the work of terror,
So that no hungering Fate, the victim ready,
Shall be defrauded of its prey. I rise,
Obeying the deep voice that, from these ruins,
Rings on mine ear its purpose. I obey,

And bound to my performance as the lion,
Long crouching in his jungle, who, at last,
Sees the devoted nigh. The impatient blood
Rounds with red circle all that fills mine eye;
A crimson sea receives me, and I tread
In billows, thus incarnadined, from nations
That bleed through ages thus at every vein.
Be satisfied, ye Fates! Ye gods, who still
Lurk, homeless, in these ruins that ye once
Made sacred as abodes, and deemed secure,—
I take the sword of vengeance that ye proffer,
And swear myself your soldier. I will go,
And with each footstep on some mighty neck,
Shall work your full revenge, nor forfeit mine!
Dost thou not feel my presence, like a cloud,
Before my coming, Rome?* Is not my spirit,
That goes abroad in earnest of my purpose,
Upon thy slumbers, City of the Tyrant,
Like the fell hag on breast of midnight sleeper,
That loads him with despair? Alone, I come;
But thousands of fell ministers shall crowd
About me, with their service—willing creatures
That shall assist me first to work on thee,
And last upon themselves! The daylight fades,
And night belongs to vengeance. I depart,
Carthage, to riot on thy conqueror's heart."

---

* The reader will be reminded by this passage, of that noble and solemn speech made by the Ghost of Sylla, at the opening of Ben Johnson's tragedy of Cataline: "Dost thou not feel me, Rome," etc.

VI.

Silent once more the ruins—dark the night,
Yet vengeance speeds with unembarrassed flight;
No fears delay, no toils retard the speed
Of that fierce exile, sworn to deadliest deed;
And thou, O Queen of Empires, now secure
Of state that might be peaceful, were it pure,
Too soon thy halls shall echo with the yell
That summons human fiends to works of hell!
Ambition, long unsated, urged by Hate,
Queen of the Nations, speaks thy mournful fate;
Thy valour wasted, and thy might in vain,
Thy virtues sapped to break thy despot's chain!
Long didst thou rule, in simple courage strong,
The guardian friend of right, the foe to wrong;
Great in thyself, and conscious of the sway
That kept meet progress with the march of day;
That, from all nations plucked the achieving arts,
Which make sway sov'reign in a people's hearts;
Proud on thy heights rose forms to worship dear,
There swelled the temple's crest, the column there,
Each with its chronicle to spell the soul,
And each most precious to the crowning whole;
A world thyself—a wondrous world—that made
The admiring nations silent in thy shade;
Genius and Art commingling in thy cause,
And Gods presiding o'er thy matchless laws.

VII.

But dark the hour impends—the storm is nigh,
And thy proud eagles flaunt no more the sky;
Thou hast not kept thy virtues to the last,
And all thy glories centre in thy past—
Thy safety in thy glories. From beneath
Thine altars swells the midnight cry of death;
The tocsin summons—not to brave the foe,
But to make bare thy bosom to the blow;
From thy own quiver flies the shaft of doom,
And thy own children hollow out thy tomb.
The exulting shouts that mock thee in thy shame,
Were those that led thee once to heights of fame:
The bird that swoops to riot on thy breast,
Is the same eagle that made great thy nest.
Hark! at his shrilly scream, the sleuth-hounds wake,
The bloody thirst which in thy heart they slake;
Thy proud patricians, hunted down, survey
The herds they kept, most busy with the prey.
These are the flocks they fostered from their foes,
And these are first to drink the blood that flows.
Wondrous the arts of vengeance, to inspire
The maddened son to prey upon the sire!
Wondrous the skill *that* fierce plebeian wields
To make this last the bloodiest of his fields.
Vain all thy prayer and struggle—thou art down—
His iron footstep planted on thy crown;
But in thy fate, 'tis something for thy pride,
Thus self-destroyed, thou mighty suicide!

BERTRAM;

AN ITALIAN SKETCH.

BERTRAM.

AN ITALIAN SKETCH.

I.

Scene: *The Dungeon of Bertram in the Castle of Leoni.*

Leoni. Bertram.

Leoni. Thou sleep'st as one who hath no fear—no grief!
Bertram. As one who hath no fear; and, for my griefs,
That they permit me sleep at such an hour,
Would show them much more merciful than thee.
   Leoni. I, too, am merciful—will bring thee sleep,
So deep, as will shut out all sense of grief
From thy unlabouring senses.
   Bertram. Be it soon!
   Leoni. Is this thy prayer?
   Bertram. Dost ask?
   Leoni.   Enough! Then hear!
To-morrow thou shalt have no charge in life—
The fair sky shall reject thee; the bright sun
Lend thee no succour—and the wooing breeze
That sweeps so sweetly through yon window grate,
Shall only stir the long grass on thy grave!
Dost hear what I have spoken? Thou shalt die!

Bertram. 'Tis well!

Leoni. No more?

Bertram. What more wouldst have? Thy power
To which I may oppose nor prayer nor pleading,
Needs not my vain acknowledgment of grief;—
And fears I have none.

Leoni.   Is all sense of hope
Utterly dead within thee? Does no dream
Rise up before thy fancies, fraught with pleasure,
That life prolonged may bring thee—happiest hours,
In sunshine or in shade—such as thy bosom
Was once most blest to dream of? Thou hast been
A very bird of the summer, in thy flight,
No less than music. Thou couldst clip the air
With ever glad embraces; couldst delight
The groves with the spring sweetness of thy song,
And fed'st on all the flowery fields of life,
With never satiate appetite and hope!—
Is thy privation nothing?—the great loss
Of the things visible and glorious, thou
Hast ever sought with such a fresh delight?
The woods and waters—this fair earth and sky,
Glowing in birds and blossoms; and the night
Proud in its starred luxuriance; and that moon,
Whose pallid disc looks mournful through yon bars,
As if to yield thee sympathy. Awhile,
Her beams will gleam upon thy silent grave,
And seek thee through the grasses on its slopes,
And thou know nothing.

Bertram. Be it as thou say'st.

Leoni. I tell thee, by the morrow thou shalt sleep
I' the iron grasp of death.

Bertram.   One word for all!

Time ceased with me to-day—and in *her* grave
Sleep all my earthly morrows.
 Leoni.   Obdurate!
Yet would a prayer become thee.
 Bertram.   Not to thee!
My prayers are not for life—nor yet for death—
And, if for mercy, but to Him, whose power
Leads through the awful future, in whose shadows
I see no sway of thine! Thou could'st not answer
To any prayer I make thee.
 Leoni. Not for life?
 Bertram.   No!
Life were no mercy now. The light which made
My life on earth, now beckons through the gates
Which thou may'st ope, not shut! Thou hast o'erstept
The limits of thy policy. Thy power,
That smote too soon the victim in thy grasp,
Forever lost its sway, in the foul blow,
That rather spoke the madness of thy hate,
Than made its purpose sure. For prayer of mine,
Invoking life for *me*, denied to *her*,
Thou wait'st but vainly. Not to mock thy power
Do I contemn thy mercy; but that blessing
Were now no boon to me. I hear the doom
Thy lips have spoken, and I welcome it!—
Will meet it with no struggle and no prayer,
But, in such meek humility of heart—
Not reft of every hope—which best becomes
These bonds, this weakness—conscious that I breathe
In thy forbearance only. Let the axe
Be sharpened and in readiness—the neck
Is bared, and bent already, for the blow!
 Leoni. Die in thy pride! I would have wrung the prayer

From thy unnatural bosom, to deny thee;
Would first have moved thee to an abject homage,
That shame, as well as death, might fasten on thee,
Defiling thy past honours; and have shown thee,
Clipping with eager arms about my knees,
While my feet tramp thee to the kindred dust
Which stains thy insolent forehead.
 Bertram. Oh! I know thee!
 Leoni. Thou know'st me! Well! it needs not that I tell
    thee,
Thy doom is written! With the sun, thou diest!
                                          [*Exit Leoni.*

II.

Bertram—*solus.*

 Bertram. I will not shame his brightness! He will blaze
For other seasons. He will bring their fruits,
And cheer to song the throats of merry birds,
And ripen yellow harvests for the race,
In multitudinous lands; and I shall lose
These joys, which never failed till now to gladden
This weary heart of mine! But now their sweets
Bring me no hope; nor, with their sweets denied,
Do I feel loss. 'Twas in her love that grew
The season's bounty—and the glorious smile
That blessed me in the rising of the sun,
And cheered me in the music of the bird,

And charmed me in the beauty of the flower,
And taught me, in the fragrance-blessing earth,
The way to countless blessings, which no more
I find in earth or sky, in song of birds,
Beauty in flowers, or glory in the day!
My day is night: my prayer is for that sleep
That sees no more the day from which is gone
The soul's one beauty, giving charm to all!
Nor is the night which now approacheth fast—
Through which my feet must go—the final night,
Whose coming makes men falter, with a fear
That, in th' unknown still dreads the worst of knowledge—
Without its welcoming light! I have o'ercome
The natural fears of Death, who, in our youth,
Must ever be a Terror! Doubt and dread
Grow passive, in that weariness of soul
When life maintains no hope; and death puts on
The aspect of a friend to him who feels
How toilsome and how endless is the day
Consumed without a quest, through barren realms
That Love hath ceased to brighten with his beams,
Or freshen with his flowers. My woes, that brought
Despair for one dread season, and dismay
That still o'erwhelms my heart, hath also taught
Elsewhere to seek the Comforter! And Fear,
That found on earth but Tyranny, beyond,
Looks upward for protection. He whom Power
Drives from the shelter of the Throne, finds strength
In the more steadfast Altar; and the man,
Who knew no safety with his kindred fellow,
Soon finds the need of Him, who, throned apart,
Repairs the wretched sorrows of the race,—
Rebukes the injustice—from the oppressor plucks

The scourge—and to the victim, soon or late,
Atones for the worst sufferings borne on earth.
Oh! Death shall be no pang, though sharp his blow;—
And loss of life, however glad before
In bloom and blossom, bring no sorrow now!

And yet, to tread that passage of thick gloom
Into the world of doubt! To take that plunge,
From consciousness, to the bewildering change
Which may be wo, or apathy still worse,
In loss of that large consciousness, whose hope
Clings to the soul as to its only life,
Secure in joyous certainty of wings,—
High powers, that yield not to the outward pressure,
And, with the will, ne'er-pausing progress keep
To the mind's best achievements! Oh! that doubt!—
Whether, in passage from the state we know,
We rise elsewhere erect, or grow to nothing;
Never know waking—with one pang lose feeling;
Lose, with the sky and earth, all sense and seeing—
The *all* that we have lived for—while the loved one,
Most precious to the heart of all affections,
Lies silentiy beside us, and we know not!—
Hushed each divinest instinct that, while living,
Taught us, unseen, of the approaching footstep,
And, with a breath, infusing still the zephyr,
Quickened each pulse within the trembling bosom
With intimations of that precious spirit
So natural to our own. Oh! my Francesca!
Where glid'st thou?—through what region, breathing glory—
Through what sweet gardens of delight and treasure,—
That I behold thee not?—and drink no promise
Of what awaits me in the world hereafter,

From the sweet whispers of thy passing spirit,
Stealing beside me ? Thou art freed the struggle,
And, in the unlimited province of thy wing,
Why fly'st thou far?—why bring'st me no sweet tidings
To strengthen the dear hope that gave us courage
When we were torn asunder—made us fearless
Of all the tyrant might decree against us—
Assured of that blest future which his power
Might never enter ? Wert thou nigh—about me—
Infusing with thy sweetness the damp vapour
That chills this gloomy dungeon—I had known it !
My soul had felt thy presence, as one gathers
The scent of flowers that grow in foreign gardens,
Whose blooms he doth not see! Didst thou look on me,
I should not droop this hour. Oh ! wouldst thou speak,
I should not feel this dungeon—dread this death—
That, in thy absence from my spirit now—
Thine freed—takes on a shape of during darkness,
That never hopes a dawn ! Who comes ?   [*Enter Friar*

III.

Friar. Bertram.

Friar. My son !
Bertram. Art thou mine executioner ?
Friar.   Thy saviour rather—
If I might execute upon thy pride,
Thy sinful thoughts and passions, and thy fears,

By bringing thee, in penitence and sorrow,
To the white feet of Him who came to save,
And perished, for thy safety, on the cross!
Oh, son! the moments leave thee. A few hours,
Is all the remnant of the time allowed thee.
I would prepare thee for the terrible change
The morrow brings thee—would entreat thy prayers—
The meek repentance of thy evil passions,
And not less evil thoughts—and such confession
Of each foul secret festering in thy soul,
With the due sorrows which should follow it,
As may command thee to the Saviour's grace,
And make thee fit for the Eternal Presence!

 Bertram. Behold me then most guilty. Pride was mine,
And sinful thoughts, and dark imaginings,
And reckless passions, and ungracious fancies,
And all the thousand tendencies to evil
Which ever urge the impatient soul of man
To heedless forfeiture of Heaven's sweet mercy.
What need the dark detail—the nice relation—
The name and character of each offence,
Too numerous quite for name, for recollection—
Too foul for the now blushing consciousness
To summon into sight, or give to speech!
Enough, that I have sinned—that, in my sorrow,
I could weep tears of blood; and that I perish
Forgiving all mine enemies—imploring,
Of all, forgiveness—and of God, o'er all!—
Most doubtful of his mercy, as well knowing
How great mine undesert.

 Friar.   Alas! my son,
This will not answer thee. Thou must disburden
Thy heart of each dark secret. 'Tis thy pride,

And not the shame and grief of thy contrition
That locks thy secret up!
 Bertram.   I have no secrets
From God, to whom for judgment I must go;
No hope from man, of whom I have no fear,
And no confession for his ears, whose judgment
Can do me hurt or service now no more.
 Friar. Beware, my son! This stubbornness! This woman—
Francesca—who hath perished in her guilt—
She was to thee no wife? Her full confession—
 Bertram. Ah! now I know thee! Get thee to Leoni:
I have no secrets for thy keeping, father,
Or thy revealing. Yet a prayer I make thee;
Leave me to God—in quiet.
 Friar.   If I leave thee—
Thy conscience unrelieved—the truth unspoken—
I leave thee to the enemy of man,
Who lurks in waiting for thy soul—
 Bertram. Away!
 Friar.   The curse—
 Bertram. Oh! fit for curses only—hence!
Thou hast usurped the white wings of the dove,
To do the serpent's office! Who is there?
          [*Enter Francesca.*

IV.

Francesca. Bertram. Friar.

 Bertram. Ah! now is Heaven most merciful! She comes!
She glides, a form of light, athwart the darkness;

I see her radiant beauties, starred by Heaven
With supernatural brightness; and I feel
The lightness of a breath, that's balm for angels,
Uplift me as with wings! Oh! blessed being,
That hallowest where thou com'st—how doth thy presence
Prepare me for the sacrifice. One moment;
I shut mine eyes in doubt! I open them,
Once more to rapture! Dost thou see, old man?
Thy lips had spoken curses as from Heaven—
Lo! now, its angel!

Francesca. [*to the Friar.*] Hence, father, to Leoni.

Bertram. Leoni! Can she speak of him—Leoni!

Francesca. [*to the Friar.*] He summons thee! He needs
    thee! Hence with speed!

Friar. Then hast thou answered wisely. All goes well!
I leave thee.

Francesca. [*to the Friar.*] Hence!   [*Exit Friar.*

V.

Francesca. Bertram.

Bertram. Is it Francesca speaks—
And speaks she of Leoni? Thou wert mine,
Francesca—and in robes elect of heaven,
Speak'st thou of him who was thy enemy,
As he is mine? I tremble, with a dread,
That tears my very heart-strings! Oh! Francesca
Pure spirit of the purest of earth's mortals,

Speak, and uplift me, with a voice of mercy,
From this dark sphere to thine.
  Francesca. Bertram!
  Bertram. That name!
Which still was the dear burthen of thy lips
When thou wast mine, and mortal—still to me sounds
As thou hast ever said it. There's no change,
To eye or ear, in thee. Oh, heart! be hopeful;
Since death makes free the living to their mission,
Nor robs the loved one of those precious beauties,
That fashioned thought and sense, and fiery passion,
To one sweet frame of love!
  Francesca. Dost think me dead,
Dear Bertram?
  Bertram. Dead, my Francesca—dead to earth—
But O! not dead to me! They showed thee to me,
Even through these grates, arrayed in innocent white,
And robed as for a bridal with the stars,
In pure white blossoming flowers.
  Francesca. They mocked thine eyes,
As they have mocked my ears. I am not dead . . .
I live as thou hast known me. I am thine,
As still I was before; but, rouse thee briefly,
For we have little space. Reserve thy wonder
Till we go hence in safety. We must fly—
While the dread baron sleeps. Leoni sleeps—
Sleeps soundly! I have left his bed but now!
  Bertram. Thou! Left *his* bed but now!
  Francesca. Marvel not, Bertram,
However marvellous all seemings be
That check us in this dungeon. Thou shalt know
The dark, dread truth hereafter.
  Bertram. Left his bed!

His bed! The lustful murderer—the foul satyr,
Whose very eye but taints the thing it looks on,
Whose every breath is incense of pollution,
Whose every touch is sin! Oh God! I hearken
And live! He lives! . . . She lives! Francesca—mine!—
All live! Yet hath she left his bed but now!—
Death! death! O friend! where art thou? I had lost
The sense of fear! I lived but for one hope—
That the short, rapid interval of time
'Twixt this impatient consciousness, and that
Which made my faith assurance absolute,
Of life with thee hereafter—would be o'er,
With but one shock—one moment of thick darkness—
And then all light and rapture!—and I wake,
To feel the scorpion sting of agony,
That tells me of the death that follows death,
In which all hope lies buried—smothered sure
In loss of that most precious of life's fancies,
Its dream of the pure angel, whit'st of all
Above the cloudy confines of the grave,
Waiting with welcome! Death! O, death! O, terror!
That I should life for this!—that thou should'st tell me
Francesca, with no crimson on thy cheek,
No gushing eyes, no husky, tremulous voice,
That thou com'st freshly from Leoni's bed,
No longer fresh—yet living!   [*Falls on his face.*

 Francesca.   Were thy fears—
Thy dark suspicions true, O! cruel Bertram,
How vain were tears or tremours, conscious blushes,
Or all the broken agonies of speech,
To show my shame or thine!

 Bertram.   Yet didst thou leave
Leoni's bed but now! Thy own lips said it,
Nor faltered in the speech.

Francesca. Oh! had I left
My virtues on his bed, there had been need
For faltering and for tears. I left his bed,
But left no living bed, my Bertram! No!
Look on this dagger—let it speak for me!

Bertram. It bleeds—it drops with blood, The crimson edges
Gleam brightly dark before me. O! Francesca,
I see what thou hast done—yet, do not say it!
I feel the terrible need that stood before thee,
And comprehend the fate that forced upon thee,
The dreadful stroke of death. And yet, Francesca,
I would it had been any hand but thine
To do this deed! [*Covering his eyes.*

Francesca. Thy life was on it, Bertram—
And mine—and something more to me than life;
And, in my soul, a voice that cried—" Be cruel,
Or thou art lost to Bertram and to Heaven!"
Thou hat'st—thou fear'st me! Ah! I see it, Bertram!

Bertram. Hate thee, Francesca? No! How much I love thee,
No words may speak. Yet there's a deadly horror
That shakes my frame—that seizes on my heart!
Look how thy hand is crimsoned!—up thine arm,
Even to thine elbow, drips the clotting current!
God! what a terrible stroke! *Thou* didst *not* do't—
Thou, once so gentle, whom a wounded sparrow
Had brought to feminine sorrows. Thou hast wept
The fate of the cucuyo when I brushed it,
To loss of wing and glitter from thy garments;
And not a beggar's babe, with plaint of hunger,
But, with thy bounty, won a boon of tears,
Sweet as the angels weep o'er woes of mortals;

And thou to strike this blow! I'll not believe it;
Some other hand than thine, Francesca!

  Francesca.   Mine!
Mine only, Bertram. Do not curse or chide me;
Turn not thy face away. 'Twas for thy safety.

  Bertram. As if Death had one terror in his keeping,
To wound a fear of mine!

  Francesca.   Yet, have a thought
Of poor Francesca's danger. See her struggles,
At midnight, in the darkness, with her tyrant;
That bold, bad man, with all his power around him!
Hear her wild shrieks, which all refused to hear:
How vain were all her pleadings! How the danger
Threatened the whiteness of her innocent bosom,
That knew no claim but thine; and think how madly
The spasms of fear and horror in my soul
Impelled the deadly weapon to the heart,
Grown viperous with its lusts—its snakes about me
Ready to sting with deathsome leprosies!
Oh! think of this, my Bertram!

  Bertram.   My Francesca,
Dost think I blame thee! 'Twas a fate that made thee
Thus stern and fearful; yet, to me, thy beauties
Were those of meekness only. In mine eyes,
Thy mould was still of those celestial beings
That find their virtues in their tenderness,
Chastened by love to purity. All passions
Grew modest in thy presence. Every feeling
That ministered to make thy loveliness,
Seemed to have had its birth in angel meekness,
That spread a hallowing moonlight at its coming,
Making the rugged soft. How could I know thee,
Thus terribly incarnadined with vengeance

For any purpose!   Could I dream of thee,
Thus robed in crimson horrors, and believe thee
The pure white thing thou wast, when first I found thee
In groves of green Val d' Arno, singing sweetly,
With eyes of dewy glist'ning, to pale sisters
That watched above in fondness?   Oh! thy nature
Hath been o'erwrought to madness!   May I fold thee
Once more to this lone bosom, and remember
The thing thou wast, but art not?
   Francesca.   Let me save thee,
Even though I lose thee, Bertram.
   Bertram.   Lose me, never!
The flight that saves thy Bertram—
   Francesca.   Saves not me,
Since thus he holds me altered—if he alters
In the dear faith he gave me.   The worst death
Grows up before me, though we fly together,
In these so foreign glances—in this speech,
That tells how much he loses in the change
That outraged what I was, and, in my terrors,
Made me achieve the deed, however needful,
That makes me thus a terror to his love.
Yet must we fly.   These keys undo thy fetters—
See how they fall about thee!   Rouse thee, Bertram!
Thy hands, thy feet are free.   Thy tyrant sleeps,
No more to cross thy fortunes; and Francesca,
If stained with blood, is pure for thee, as ever
In happy vale of Arno.   Yet I ask not
That thou shouldst deem me so—that thou shouldst love me,
As then, in those sweet hours.
   Bertram.   I've done thee wrong
By this ungrateful chiding.   I will take thee,
As all confiding to this hopeful bosom

As when thy hands were innocently white.
We'll fly together. I am thine, Francesca,
Never to wrong thy hearing with a thought
That love may deem rebuke. Let us away!
    Francesca. (*aside.*) Yet is the thought the shadow to the soul,
Though never shown by speech. My doom is written
In the deep horror which his spirit feels,
At what this hand hath done. O! in the future,
I see the icy dread—I hear the accent
That speaks the chilled affection—forced and idle,
As born no more of fondness. I must perish,
In the denial of the love which made me,
At first, a breathing woman. I must perish;
Yet, to the last, in loving him I cherish
The hope, that when the icebolt falls between
Our lives, our hearts shall reunite once more,
And death retrieve the whiteness life hath lost.
    Bertram. Why lingerest thou, Francesca?
    Francesca.   But for prayer!—
Heaven's mercy may be yielded to our flight
If not our hearts. Dear Bertram, let me lead thee;
But take the dagger—I will bear the keys!
    Bertram. Oh! give it me; far better graced in mine,
Than in thy hands, Francesca. Give it me!
Oh, heart! 'tis my infirmity that speaks—
But I could easier strike a host of hearts,
Than see it in thy grasp! And yet, Francesca,
I would not wrong thee by reproach. Thy danger
Made the dread weapon a necessity
Thou couldst not 'scape, and shouldst not. Let my arm
Enfold thee; and should danger threaten now,
Thine eye shall see this arm more red than thine,
In shielding thy white bosom.

Francesca. (timidly.) May I hold
Thy hand, my Bertram?
    Bertram. Heart and hand, Francesca.   [*Embracing.*
    Francesca. Now could I go to death!
    Bertram.   We go to life,
To love and safety, dear one!
    Francesca. (aside.) Through a night,
Where all is cloud before me, never-lifting
Till the last cloud descends. O! love no longer,
As once we knew it—wings and sunniness,
With music in the pauses of the breeze,
While leaves drop down in odors; but a love
That chills while it embraces—and sweet accents
That never warm to meaning.
    Bertram.   What say'st thou?
    Francesca. Of cold and darkness, Bertram.
    Bertram.   Soon, the light
Will gather round us with its cheerful aspects,
That smile among the stars; and Heaven's fresh breathings—
'Scaped from the pestilent atmosphere of death—
Will lift our spirits with a glad surprise.
The bolts unclose! O! see you not, Francesca,
How swiftly darts the messenger of light,
As glad to do us service, o'er the threshold,
And waves his glow-worm torch to guide us on;
While the fond zephyr, through the yawning portal,
Wraps us in sweet embrace, and bears us forward,
On wings made free like his. Come forth, Francesca.
    Francesca. (faltering.) Whither?
    Bertram. To life—from death!—Dost see?
    Francesca.   The blessed stars!
    Bertram. Now fly we with the urgent feet of fear;
This valley must not hold us. To our hills:

There we may breathe in safety. But thou shrink'st!
 Francesca. The light! They see—the stars! These bloody
   proofs—
 Bertram. (*averting his eyes.*) And I—alas!
 Francesca. Lead where thou wilt, my Bertram.
 Bertram. Among the hills! I know where runs a brooklet,
Shall cleanse thee of these stains—Jesu! how black!
 Francesca. How black! how black! (*aside.*) Alas! the stream
   may cleanse—
The arm be white once more as when he took it,
To wrap about his breast!—but O! my heart,
The dread impression fastened on his soul,
Leaves only night to mine! I follow, Bertram!
 Bertram. (*aside.*) How terrible! How had she heart for it!
So fearful, even in her innocent ways,
So tender still, and merciful!
 Francesca.   Thou speak'st?
 Bertram. Of the great debt I owe thee—of the struggle
That nerved thee to this blow! And yet, Francesca,
Would we had died before—together died—
Even at the moment when our lips first met,
In love's first sweet delirium!
 Francesca.   Thou art right!
Would we had died, O, Bertram! in that hour,
And had not lived for this!—Would *I* had died!

THE DEATH OF CLEOPATRA.

THE DEATH OF CLEOPATRA.

Guard. What work is here? Charmian, is this well done?
Charmian. It is well done, and fitting for a princess,
  Descended of so many royal kings.—SHAKSPEARE.

AUGUSTUS CÆSAR. DOLABELLA.

Augustus. Dead! say'st thou? Cleopatra?
Dolabella.   She sleeps fast—
Will answer nothing more—hath no more lusts
For passion to persuade—nor art to breed
Any more combats. I have seen her laid—
As for a bridal—in a pomp of charms,
That mocked the flashing jewels in her crown
With beauty never theirs. Her bridegroom one
Who conquers more than Cæsar—a grim lord
Now in the full'st possession of his prize,
Who riots on her sweets; seals with cold kiss
The precious caskets of her eyes, that late
Held—baiting fond desire with hope of spoil—
Most glorious gems of life; and, on her cheek,
Soft still with downy ripeness—not so pale,
As sudden gush of fancy in the heart
Might bring to virgin consciousness—he lays
His icy lip, that fails to cause her shrink

From the unknown soliciting. Her sleep
Dreams nothing of the embrace, the very last
Her eager and luxurious form may know,
Of that dread ravisher.

Augustus. If it be true,
She still hath baffled me. My conquest sure—
My triumph incomplete! I had borne her else,
The proudest trophy of a myriad spoil,
In royal state to Rome. Give me to know
The manner of her death.

Dolabella. By her own hands!—
That, conscious still, commended to her breast
The fatal kiss of Nile's envenomed asp;
That subtle adder, which, from slime and heat,
Receives a gift of poison, whose least touch
Is a sure stoppage of the living tides.

Augustus. Her death commends her more than all her life!
'Twas like a queen—fit finish to a state,
That, in its worst excess, passionate and wild,
Had still a pomp of majesty, too proud
For mortal subjugation! She had lusts
Most profligate of harm—but with a soul,
That, under laws of more restraint, had raised
Her passions into powers, which might have borne
Best fruits for the possessor. They have wrought
Much evil to her nature; but her heart
Cherished within a yearning sense of love
That did not always fail; and, where she set
The eye of her affections, her fast faith
Kept the close bond of obligation sure.
This still should serve, when censure grows most free,
To sanctify her fault. In common things
Majestic, as in matters of more state,

She had, besides, the feminine arts to make
Her very lusts seem noble; and, with charms
That mocked all mortal rivalry, she knew
To dress the profligate graces in her gift—
Generous to very wantonness, and free
Of bounty, where Desert might nothing claim—
That Virtue's self might doubt of her own shape,
So lovely grew her counterfeit. O'er all,
Her splendour, and her soul's magnificence.
The pomp that crowned her state—luxurious shows—
Where Beauty, grown subservient to a sway
That made Art her first vassal—these, so twinned
With her voluptuous weakness—did become
Her well, and took from her the hideous hues
That else had made men loathe!
     I would have seen
This princess ere she died! How looks she now?
 Dolabella. As one who lives but sleeps; no change to move
The doubts of him who sees, yet nothing knows,
Of that sly, subtle enemy, which still
Keeps harbour round her heart. Charmian, her maid,
Had, ere I entered, lidded up the eyes,
That had no longer office; and she lay,
With each sweet feature harmonizing still,
As truly with the nature as at first,
When Beauty's wide-world wonder she went forth
Spelling both art and worship! Never did sleep
More slumberous, more infant-like, give forth
Its delicate breathings. You might see the hair
Wave, in stray ringlets, as the downy breath
Lapsed through the parted lips; and deem the leaf,
Torn from the rose and laid upon her mouth,
Was wafted by that zephyr of the soul

That still kept watch within—waiting on life
In ever anxious ministry. Lips and brow—
The one most sweetly parted as for song—
The other smooth and bright, even as the pearls
That, woven in fruit-like clusters, hung above,
Starring the raven curtains of her hair—
Declared such calm of happiness as never
Her passionate life had known. No show of pain—
No writhéd muscle—no distorted cheek—
Deformed the beautiful picture of repose,
Or spoke th' unequal struggle, when fond life
Strives with its dread antipathy. Her limbs
Lay pliant, with composure, on the couch,
Whose draperies loosely fell about her form,
With gentle flow, and natural fold on fold,
Proof of no difficult conflict. There had been,
Perchance, one pang of terror, when she gave
Free access to her terrible enemy ;
Or, in the moment when the venomous chill
Went sudden to her heart; for, from her neck,
The silken robes had parted. The white breast
Lay half revealed, save where the affluent hair
Streamed over it in thick disheveled folds,
That asked no further care. Oh! to behold!—
With eye still piercing to the sweet recess,
Where rose each gentle slope, that seemed to swell
Beneath mine eye, as conscious of my gaze,
And throbbing with emotion soft as strange,
Of love akin to fear! Thus swelling still,
Like little billows on some happy sea,
They sudden seemed to freeze, as if the life
Grew cold when all was loveliest. One blue vein
Skirted the white curl of each heaving wave,

A tint from some sweet sunbow, such as life
Flings ever on the cold domain of death;
And, at their equal heights, two ruby crests—
Two yet unopened buds from the same flower—
Borne upward by the billows rising yet,
Grew into petrified gems!—with each an eye
Eloquent pleading to the passionate heart,
For all of love it knows! Alas! the mock!
That Death should mask himself with loveliness,
And Beauty have no voice, in such an hour,
To warn its eager worshipper. I saw—
And straight forgot, in joy of what I saw,
What still I knew—that Death was in my sight,—
And what was seeming beautiful, was but
The twilight—the brief interval betwixt
The glorious day and darkness. I had kissed
The wooing bliss before me; but, even then,
Crawled forth the venomous reptile from the folds
Where still it harboured—crawled across that shrine
Of Beauty's best perfections, which, meseemed,
To shrink and shudder 'neath its loathly march,
Instinct, with all the horrors at my heart.
    Augustus. Thus Guilt and Shame deform the Beautiful!

MICHAEL BONHAM:

OR,

THE FALL OF BEXAR.

A TALE OF TEXAS.

IN FIVE PARTS.

BY A SOUTHRON.

RICHMOND:
JNO. R. THOMPSON, PUBLISHER.
MACFARLANE & FERGUSSON, PRINTERS.
1852.

The tale which follows, was originally prepared with a view to performance. Subsequently, however, I have persuaded myself that it would read better as a story. The reader will find that I have taken some liberties with the historical facts in the leaguer and taking of the town and castle of San Antonio de Bexar; but the history will suffer little from my freedoms, while, I believe, the story gains by them.

DRAMATIS PERSONÆ.

Texians.

COL. MILAM, *Chief of the Texians.*
MICHAEL BONHAM, *Second in Command.*
DAVID CROCKETT, *Ex-Member of American Congress.*
ALABAMA DAVIS, *Orderly.*
RICHARD HARRIS, *A Moody Hunter.*
SPARROW, *A Huge Feeder and Wit.*
KENNEDY: *Sings a good Song.*
TEXIAN SOLDIERS, &c.
ELLEN HARRIS, *Wife to Richard Harris, but in disguise as Billy Harris.*

Mexicans.

DON ESTEBAN DE MONTENEROS, *Governor of Bexar.*
DON PEDRO DE ZAVALO, *Suitor to his Daughter.*
GOVERNOR'S SECRETARY.
BRAVO.
MEXICAN SOLDIERS.
MASQUERS, &c.
DONNA OLIVIA DE MONTENEROS, *Governor's Daughter.*
DONNA MARIA DE PACHECO, *her Cousin.*
DUENNA OF OLIVIA.
JACINTHA, *Attendant on Maria.*
CHARACTERS IN BAL MASQUE.

MICHAEL BONHAM.

PART I.—SCENE I.

Time, Afternoon. Texian Bivouack among the hills—a wild, mountainous country in the back ground. Fires scattered about as in an Encampment of Hunters. Groups of Texians seen disposed in picturesque situations, and in wild and various costume—chiefly the hunting shirt—but some of them clothed in buffalo and deer skins, all armed with bowie-knife and rifle. Songs and laughter, at intervals and from a distance. Sentries disposed in the distance. Enter a group upon the foreground.

Sparrow. No sign of supper yet! My nose brings me no intelligence. Mere smoke, common smoke all, (*snuffs the breeze,*) as if there were any need of the fire before the butcher has dressed the meat.

Davis. What, old fellow, still growling? That stomach of yours keeps you very unhappy.

Sparrow. 'Tis I that keep my stomach unhappy! That I should deliberately put myself in a situation where so excellent a member may never be pacified! Here, too, where I offer so prominent a mark for a Mexican bullet, But did'nt somebody say something about supper?

Davis. No one but yourself; we spoke of fighting, or skulking—any thing but supper.

Sparrow. Not a word of fighting until I am fed. I won't fight on an empty stomach. The Yankee may do that, not I. I'm of the genuine John Bull breed, though I never saw the island—which I suppose furnishes the best grazing country in the world. I may never see it,— but I shall live and die with the pious conviction that it's the only part of the world in which they have any proper idea of what's due to a human stomach.

Davis. Well, certainly, Sparrow, you show the blood if any man; but what was that you said of Yankee fighting? Now, when I'm out of the States, I acknowledge the Yankee myself. When I'm at home, its quite another thing.

Sparrow. Something I heard a hundred years ago in a sort of comparison 'twixt Bull and Jonathan.

Davis. Let's have it.

Sparrow. It's short, my lad, as your mother's blessing. Bull, then, you must know, won't fight till he's had his belly full, while Jonathan will never fight after. Give Bull his breakfast, and he will use his bayonet with as much certainty of victory, as the Mussulmans have of Paradise when going into battle. But beware how you give Jonathan a bite. You must only show him his dinner—let him only smell the smokes from the cook-pot and see the enemy at the same moment, keen of appetite as forty Indians, making after it. Your Yankee will then prove himself an ugly customer. He will fight worse than any Turk.

Davis. Very good, and that was a say—

Sparrow. A hundred years ago, more or less. You remember it was to save *their stores* that they fought at Concord.

Davis. But Lexington?

Sparrow. Well, then it was to save their *bacon!* But, look you, Davis, as you regard my happiness in this life, tell me, hasn't Crockett gone out after game?

Davis. Will he find it? He don't know the country.

Sparrow. Pshaw! I've fed well in the States. Have I lost my nose for roast or boiled, now that I'm in Texas? The good hunter no more loses his sense for hunting on strange ground, than I do for eating. The same instinct is at the bottom of both faculties. You must show that the animal and the appetite change as well as the country: and that we know from sacred writ is out of the question. *Cœlum non animum mutant qui trans mare currunt.*

Davis. What's that?

Sparrow. Camanche, if not Latin. It means that even when a man's half seas over, his nature undergoes no change. He still feeds, and fights, and frolics, as he did before. Hark! what's that? [*Horn sounds.*

Davis. A horn! It sounds like Crockett's.

Sparrow. Now bless the babe! I have an instinct that he brings in something of better flavor than himself. My nose is monstrous keen. My appetite is a marvellous faculty

Richard Harris, [*coming forward and putting his hand on Sparrow's shoulder*] Old man, enough of this! Wait like a man.

Be patient. Don't be howling like a beast,
When meat is scarce in the forest.
    Sparrow.   Like a beast!
Why, true, I have a wolfish appetite.
But, beast! Old fellow: hark you, don't you eat?
    R. Harris. I must suppose I do: I live.
    Sparrow.   Art never hungry?
    R. Harris.   Never!
    Sparrow.   What! Never hungry?
    R. Harris.   Never, that I know.
    Sparrow. Heaven save me from this man! Keep us
        asunder!
Send us apart. See to it, Orderly,
Put me at right or left, the wing or centre,
But never where he goes. He has no bowels,
Is never hungry, or he never knows it.
Can such a man be human? He is surely
A *lusus*—what's the name—a something Latin,
Meaning a monster.
    R. Harris. You're right. I am a monster;
I feel like one—a very savage monster,
The hair growing inward.
    Sparrow. I believe it all. I can believe any thing of a person who is never conscious of the delights of hunger—the keen provocation, the sharp instigation of the bowels, to kill and eat—an inspiration, I verily believe, that comes only from the soul. The soul is, indeed, the true source of human appetite. It is the immortal giving counsel to the mortal nature how to take care of itself. A man who never receives any such divine intimations—do you hear me, Harris?
    R. Harris, [*fiercely.*]   Did you speak?
    Sparrow. Did I speak! Decidedly wolfish. Yes, I

spoke. I said—to think that all my good things have been thrown away upon him. Yes. I say that the man who never receives any divine intimations of appetite, cannot possibly have a soul at all. Chew upon that, old Lupus.

R. Harris. Would it were so. Methinks it *must* be so.

Sparrow. It is so. Never doubt it. Never hungry! To talk after such a fashion when there's not a man in the mess not ready to eat up his grandmother, as the wolf ate up Little Red Ridinghood, bones and all. Why—

Davis, [*whispers.*] No more. The fit is on him.

Sparrow. What fit? Eh, well. But I have my fit too, and just now the symptoms are very earnest about the diaphragm. I must have something to excite one—something. Ah, lad, come forward, [*to W. Harris.*] A pretty little fellow truly, and modest. Hark ye, child, was it not you who regaled my supperless senses last night with a song—a sort of ballad; a most woful, sweet affair, very lovelorn and comforting.

W. Harris, [*coming forward timidly.*] I didn't mean to disturb your sleep, sir. I—

Sparrow. And who tells you that you did? No, no You didn't disturb me. You did me a service. Positively, your song made me half forget my hunger, though I had been dreaming, only a minute before, of canvas back ducks at the Balize. You shall sing for me again. Your name's—eh!

W. Harris. Harris. William Harris, sir.

R. Harris, [*curiously.*] How! Harris! *That* your name?

W. Harris, [*timidly.*] It is, sir.

R. Harris. Where from? What family?

W. Harris. From Tennessee. I have no family.

R. Harris. My name, before I left the States, was Harris, too. Now, it is nothing.

Sparrow. Nothing, indeed! You're a whole State yourself. You represent yours of Mississippi most admirably. An empty stomach in a man is not much unlike an empty treasury in a State, and he who never feels hunger may certainly pass for a most incorrigible repudiator. But sing for us, my boy, sing, though you can find nothing more appropriate to the occasion than

'The cat ran away with the pudding-bag string.'

W. Harris. I'm out of voice. I'm hungry like the rest.

Davis. Truth, lad, you look it. You are both hungry and suffering. Now, that I look at you particularly, I wonder what could have brought you here to Texas.

Sparrow. Why wonder! What brought me, I wonder. The lad heard no doubt of the famous buffalo tongues. Wasn't it the buffalo tongues that brought you boy! If you have the gift of tongue at all, you must answer as I wish.

R. Harris, [*curiously.*] You're but a child yet, boy—
a very weak one.
You'll scarcely do for fighting. With that face,
(It has the favor of some one I have known,)
It would not seem you loved it.

W. Harris, [*drooping.*] I've never fought.

R. Harris. 'Tis easy, once begun. But wait your
time.
It is not hard to die. That truth, once known,
And you will chide the death-shot that goes by,
Seeking all hearts but yours. The danger then
Comes like your sleep or supper.

Sparrow. Not a word
Of either, I beg of you, till Davy comes.
The song, the song. Sing for me little Willy,
You have a singing face, most like a woman's.
And that reminds me of my cousin Sally,
The cleverest creature at an oyster party—
How the soul treasures its first principles—
That ever sung to sauce it. You shall sing me.

    W. Harris. I cannot, sir. I do not feel like singing.

    R. Harris. Yet, last night I heard you,
When no one asked, and no one seem'd to listen,
Piping as wofully as a woman might
Over her buried lover.

    W. Harris. Did *you* hear me?

    R. Harris. I did;
And curse me, but the silly thing you sang,
A something in the language or the music,
Brought back to me a long sad history,
With many a gush of water to the springs
I had thought drained forever. [*He buries his face in*

    W. Harris. Did you then weep! *his hands.*

    Davis. [*aside to S.*] He may well ask him that. It's a bad sign when such a man weeps, or is melancholy before going into battle. He's a marked man, I tell you. He'll get his despatches, among the first, from some Mexican bullet. Such a change! From a rough, quarrelsome fellow, to a sort of good-natured melancholy.

    Sparrow. Pshaw! It's hunger; only he don't know it. A good supper will bring all things right. Hunger shows itself differently in different persons. Some it makes particularly civil; others particularly savage: some it makes mad, while it makes a different class only sentimental and poetical.

    Davis. How does it affect you?

Sparrow. Can't you see? It makes me contemplative and philosophical.

Davis, [*aside.*] Observe them.

R. Harris. 'Tis very strange, perhaps, that I should weep,
But, were all known—

W. Harris. What all? If what were known?

R. Harris. Ha! wherefore do you gaze into one thus?
What art thou, boy; what can it be to thee,
This knowledge? Do you question me?

W. Harris. No, no;
No question. I but heard you say—

R. Harris. Is't strange, do you think, that a grown man should feel
That he has been a monster in his day,
And would be sorry for it.

W. Harris, [*eagerly.*] Oh, are you sorry?

R. Harris. What's that to you, or any man on earth?
What's it to any here? [*Looking round fiercely.*

Sparrow. He'd pipe awhile,
Would any one but dance.

R. Harris. What if I dance,
Or laugh, or sing, or weep, or play the fool,
In any form, with any fool among ye—
Who says me nay upon it!

Sparrow. His dander's up.

R. Harris. There's one it might concern, but she, thank Heaven!
Sees nothing of my madness. She has seen
Enough to cause her own.

W. Harris, [*aside.*] 'Tis well; you do not see.

Davis. So, ho, friend Dick, and runs the story thus;
You left a sweetheart then in Mississippi!

R. Harris. In the whole world, as I'm a living man,

MICHAEL BONHAM.

I never left but one, and, of the world,
She had none left but me.
    W. Harris, [*affected.*]   Ah!
    Sparrow.   What ails the boy?
    W. Harris. Oh, nothing. I but thought—
    Sparrow. How long 'twould be to supper—eh?
    W. Harris.   No. Of a song,
Might suit a case like *his.* I had a ditty,
If I could gather up the words, of one,
Who left the woman he had loved the most,
Suspecting her of little love for him,
Even when she swore the fondest. He grew false,
From falsely doubting her; and in his wrath,
Meeting his friend—
    R. Harris. Don't sing it for your life!
Such were the broken fragments of the song
You smote me with last night. I've had enough
Of tears for one short season. Can't you sing
Some fierce war ballad?
    Sparrow.   Something funny, lad.
    R. Harris. No. Nought of that! Give us a burst
        of war,
Of battle and confusion. Give us a storm,
I' the way of ballad music. Please *me,* boy,
And when the real storm comes,—I mean the battle,—
I'll see you through all dangers. 'Tis my notion,
You'll need some guardian then.
    W. Harris.   I'll sing for you.
    R. Harris. None of your dolefuls. A tempestuous
        strain,
To hush up other tempests.
    W. Harris.   An old song
Was taught me by my mother.

Davis. Give me old songs;
I like them better than newfangled ditties:
They seem to have been made when women had hearts,
And honest men could find them.

W. Harris. So they might now,
If they would only value what they win,
And knew the way to keep as well as conquer.

R. Harris. What can you know about it? Where's your beard!
Sing what your mother taught you.

W. Harris. [*Sings.*]

Hark! the trumpet's voice through all our valleys,
   Red the plains are weeping with the strife;
The song and dance have fled our peaceful alleys,
   And the young warrior leaves the drooping wife;
But will she—

R. Harris. I will not hear to songs about a wife!
Vex me no more. Do I not tell thee, boy,
I will not weep again? Sing me another,
And have no woman in it.

W. Harris. I have no other.

R. Harris. Then sing no more for me.

Sparrow. Now, that's what I call monstrous unreasonable. The song was a good song, and had a certain turn in it, a sort of quivering trepidation, that touched my fancy. I could listen to such a song with pleasure at the table—supper being about half over, and the first—the sharper pains of appetite being somewhat mollified. What say you, Davis? Don't you consider that a song to satisfy any man, not absolutely on an empty stomach?

Davis. Yes, indeed, but just now, I fancy, we are to have much better music. [*Horn sounds.*] Crockett is

here at hand. His horn, blown three times, means that
he has got something for supper.

Sparrow. Supper! Don't quiz me Davis. If you do
I'll make it personal. I can bear being quizz'd
About my wife and children—not having any;
My lands, my goods, my gold, my merchandizes,
But not on matters purely spiritual,
Dinner and drink, the meats that Providence sends us,
The cook that dresses them, the hand that carves—
These are all sacred subjects: upon such
It will not do to trifle.   [*Horn again sounds.*

Davis. 'Tis Crockett's horn.
Sparrow.   Art sure of it?
Davis.   My life on't.
Sparrow.   Hurrah! then—let's hurrah!
My gratitude cries out to Providence
With hundred tongues, from bottom of my heart!
Davis.   Heart! Say you, Sparrow?
Sparrow.   What! You would say too high
By some five inches. Know, good Orderly,
That in the case of the Bull family,
There is but one grand passage to the heart,
And that is through the stomach. Do you hear,
Of meetings for a public charity?
'Tis with your hecatomb of roasted oxen,
Spread forth on dinner table. Is the purpose
Science or art, or strange philosophies,—
A public work—a personal compliment—
The tribute of a people to the warrior,
Who wins their battles,—or the patriot statesman,
Who makes successful treaties with the stranger,
In which, by license of the Levitical law,
He drives usurious bargain for their welfare?

All these acknowledgments still find expression
Only o'er groaning tables. Here speak the virtues,
The public gratitude, and men's affections,—
The sentiments, the sensibilities—
They find their voices all in the abdomen;
Derive their eloquence thence, and in its solace,
Find all their rights secure, their wrongs appeased,
Their duties well performed, their morals active;
In short, their slumbers for the night made certain,
With a clear conscience—thus they realize,
The good—*mens sana in corpore sano*,
Which is the all that human hope can look for
Of human happiness,—so draw the curtain.

 Davis. Good! good! and now the song. Another
  song.

 Sparrow. Deuce take the song. 'Twill do when
  supper's over.
I'll have a quarrel with the first that whistles,
Or makes pretence of music.

 Davis, [*to R. Harris.*]   Whither go you?

 R. Harris. Into some starving corner. You will have
A flock of Sparrows soon.   [*Exit R. Harris.*

 W. Harris, [*aside and following.*] There's hope of
  him! There's hope of him. He weeps!

 Sparrow. Ay, let him go. The man that knows no
  hunger,
That never dreams of dinners of rare dishes,
That has no hope of delicate supper joys,
And lives and festers in the sun, unmoved
By pulses of particular appetite,
Be far from me and heaven! Hearken me, Davis,
Beware of such a man. He's like the serpent,
That poisons his own food.   [*Horn again.*

Davis. The third blast blown.

Sparrow. Heaven bless that fellow, Crockett. He has bowels
That stir the love in mine.

Texians, [*without.*]   Hurrah for Crockett.

Davis.   He's comes. He's here.

Enter Crockett with a Bear on his shoulders.

Crockett. Well, lads, how goes it!

Sparrow. How goes it? As the wheel goes when there's no oil for the machinery : as the watch goes when the main spring's broken : as the team goes when the manger's empty. It's no go at all, Davy, or at best a slow-go. Welcome my old cock of Tennessee. Your coming is the only *go* that's worth the mention. You set all wheels in motion. You bring the true grease for the machinery. The wheels of time had stopped without your assistance. Thrice welcome to you and your companion. All your friends of the forest are welcome at the close of dinnerless days like this. He is your friend, Sir Oleaginous Bruin, therefore I welcome him. I take him by his fist,—rough but hearty ; unclean, perhaps, but honest. He will find a thousand friends among us. We will honor him duly with proper dressing. We will take him and you both to our bosoms. [*Embraces Crockett and the bear alternately.*]

Crockett.   You're a most loving Sparrow, by the Powers.

Sparrow. It is the virtue of our tribe. The warmth of the Sparrow is proverbial. It is an emblem of love in some countries, and might be in all. The dove is a poor emblem. Its fidelity lacks catholicism. It is clearly selfish. But the sparrow's love is universal. It is one of the few birds that keeps a harem. Do not question my love, Crockett, because I share it between you and Sir Bruin.

Crockett. I reckon you don't mean to sarve me with the same sauce as the B'ar.

Sparrow. No fear. My love discriminates according to the deserts of the object. Indeed, I may say that while I love him, I honor you. You both appeal to my affections, though in a different fashion.

Crockett. You always put your butcher in your prayers.

Davis. 'Twould be as easy to put him in his belly.

Sparrow. Avaunt thee, for a cannibal!

Crockett. Ha, Davis—that you? Well, here we are at last; me and my friend, as Sparrow calls him. He gave me as close a hug as Sparrow did, and thought just as much of his bowels all the time.

Sparrow, [*inspecting the Bear.*] What a delicate morsel. What a brisket he carries, and five good fingers of mortal fat upon his ribs.

Crockett. Ay, indeed. Brown jacket has all of that. A fatter varmint never sucked his own paws, or cramped up mine. Tough enough in the fight, you'll find him quite tender, now its over. He gin me more work than I ever had on a Congress Committee. I *treed* him some three hours ago, *creased* him without killing him, and brough him down a little more lively than when he went up. I put in, thinking he was about to kick his last, and found myself in his arms. He hugged mighty close, I tell you, much agin the will of one of the parties, and that warn't him. He's made my ribs ache for it, but thanks to Jim Bowie, I riddled my way into his. And now, Sparrow, the sooner we try his fat, the sooner your trials will be over.

Sparrow. **Verbum sap!** Spoken like an oracle. You have but one fault, Davy; you waste words. You learned that foolish practice in Congress at eight dollars *per diem,* to say nothing of mileage. Waste! waste! waste!

Crockett. And you!—why you're waist itself,—all waist, nothing but waist.

Sparrow. Well put, Dave. Your studies in Joe Miller were your making in Washington. You do not forget his lessons. A shot like that takes a fellow about the middle. That I have some extra extents of territory is very true; but of this be certain, that unlike the majority of great manor holders, none of my grounds are lying out, none at naked fallow. All's under fence, and in a high state of improvement. Ho, there! Halloo within! Halloo! Hear you that, boys? My intestines, you see, do no hurt to my lungs. [*Enter Texians, who take charge of the bear.*

Texian. He's heavy, by the Powers!

Sparrow. Carry him gingerly, and with proper meekness,
He's worth a host of such as ye; will keep
A host of you, when salt would fail to save ye.
Be off! I'll follow and attend his dressing,
And see that in the shape of cook, no devil
Spoils the good gifts of Providence. Begone!
But three men—hear to this philosophy,—
Are needful to an army: He who takes
The prey—and he who dresses it—and he
Who does the dressing justice.

[*Exit Sparrow, tucking up his sleeves.*

Crockett. Where is Bonham?
Davis. Not yet back.
Crockett. He'll get his death, that fellow.

Davis. Why more than you or me?
We're all i' the way of such accident,
Travelling the road to Bexar.
　Crockett. But for him,
The danger's something greater, for he travels
More roads than ours. Where, think you, that I left him?
　Davis. Lassoing some mustang.
　Crockett. A trick worth two of it.
If you'll believe me, he's this very minute
Within the walls of Bexar.
　Davis. A prisoner!
　Crockett. Prisoner, indeed. Would I be standing here
Sucking my fingers like a Congress ninny,
If he, I call my friend, were in such trouble?
　No, no. Bonham's no prisoner, nor like to be one, if he's the man I think him. He's only playing Major André among the Mexicans; looking behind their *curtains* in disguise.
　Davis. They'll Major André him. They'll hang him.
　Crockett. Yes, perhaps, if they catch him napping, but that they're not likely to do. He's playing priest for them, and looks for all the world like the genuine critter. I was most o'-mind to drop down on my marrow bones and ax his blessing myself.
　Davis. You saw him enter San Antonio?
　Crockett. With my own eyes. How would you like, says he to me, to visit Bexar? Thank you for nothing, says I: my neck's not yet ready for a Spanish cravat, which, they tell me, is made of iron. No danger, says, he; I'm going. So up he walked to the sentries. I lay snug in a hollow, with a great bunch of chaparal before me. I watched him all the time, and, sure enough, in he went along with the sodgers.

Davis. Their prisoner!

Crockett. Not he. He carries his toothpick under the priest's garment, and a couple of Colt's time-pieces. Hush! do you hear nothing?

Davis. Nothing!

Crockett. You're no hunter. Jest you part your legs a little, and an old buck would walk between 'em, and nobody the wiser. To your tree. [*They shelter themselves.*] Do you hear?

Davis. I hear.

Crockett. A Mexican, by the Powers! Stand where you are, stranger, and give 's the word, or I'll blow it into you with a bullet.

Voice, without. Washington.

Crockett. Talk of the devil and you see his picture. 'Tis Bonham's self!

Enter Bonham.

Bonham. Oh! you have precious eyes:
Not know your friends!

Crockett. And precious little like a friend do you look now, Major, with these fiery fine Mexican breeches on. Why, Major, you're as fond of change as a young female woman of fifteen. Where's the padre's skin?

Bonham. Without. I kept it over the Don till this moment, then cast it to show you how famously I look when walking the streets of San Antonio.

Crockett. Famous! Are there many more, Major, where they came from?

Bonham. Yes. When you have driven out a regiment or two of these Mexican blackguards.

Davis. What chance of that?

Bonham. Enough to make us busy! It is ours,

That brave old Spanish keep, with all its treasure,
If we but battle as becomes a people,
Sprung from the Old Thirteen!

 Davis. You've been in Bexar?

 Bonham. Ay, have I—in the castle and the city;
Trod the great Plaza, rambled through the highways,
Survey'd the walls, the gates, the guns, the soldiers,
And said, they shall be ours.

 Crockett. Hurrah for that! I believe it all. Major, as good as if I had read it in the Globe newspaper. Look you; when next you put on the skin of the priesthood, I'll go with you as a Bishop or Cardinal. I've a great fancy for fine dresses and other matters, and as Bexar's to be ours, I've a notion to go beforehand, and put the ear-mark on every thing I desire for myself.

 Bonham. Were you but master of the lingo, Davy?
 Crockett. What! Do you talk it?
 Bonham. Almost like a native. I have travell'd much
Beyond the Anahuac; know the tongue,
The people, and a thousand other matters,
That makes it easy to perform the part
That I would play in. Here, I am a Don
Fit for a bridal. At the dawn you saw me,
The priest to mutter o'er the ceremony,
And take the first fee from the maiden's lips.

 Crockett. Smack!
 Bonham. To-morrow I may sell in Bexar's streets,
Th' *Aguardiente* which enflames their passions;
By night you'll see me as a muleteer,
Dancing fandangos with the duskiest damsels
That ever roll'd tortillas, or drew water.

 Crockett. You're too much for me, Major. You're a huckleberry above my persimmon. I can hunt and fight,

MICHAEL BONHAM.

I reckon, as well as any man. I can shake as clever a
leg at a Virginny reel, when I'm a litttle up in sap, as any
native this side of the etarnal ridge : and, though I say it
myself, I have put up as decent a prayer as I ever heard
from any parson in all this nation of Texas, but that was
when I was most mightily scared, as I never expect to
be scared again. But I can't do the many fine things
you're up to. Yet if there's any thing that I *kin* do, say
the word, and let me go with you. I can promise you to
keep the secret, speak the truth, and stand by you with
knife and rifle to the last beat of a big heart.

Bonham. You shall have your wish, comrade.
Crockett. Shall I now, Major ?
Bonham. I shall return this night to Bexar's walls,
Shall need a man to be at my command,
To watch, or pray, or fight, as I think proper,
Still ready when I call and always faithful.
Crockett. That's me—that's Davy Crockett.
Bonham. Be ready when I call.
Crockett. 'Ready' and 'Go-ahead' are just the names
They made for me in Congress.
Bonham. Enough. And now for Milam.
Milam, [*entering.*] He is here, Bonham.
You are safe, I see, and I am satisfied.
What tidings bring you?
Bonham, [*to Crockett and Davis.*] Leave us, comrades.
Remember, Dave, at midnight. [*Ex. Davis and Crock.*
Milam. Goes he with you, then?
Bonham. He begged the favor. He has sense and
 shrewdness
Not less than strength and courage. 'Twill but need
That I should put a curb upon his tongue,
Or he'll convict himself of Tennessee
At the first syllable.

Milam. Your eye upon him:
I dread his blunders.

Bonham. He will play a part,
Whose duties keep him silent. He's the Mute
While he remains in Bexar.

Milam. Yet I fear him:
His tongue will wag. The humors of the woodman
Will still have way. He'll choke else.

Bonham. I'll school him:
And, for the rest—methinks the gates already
Fly wide to give us welcome.

Milam. How stands the count
Touching their numbers?

Bonham. One full regiment.

Milam. Eight hundred men, perhaps; and we but three.
They in their keep, behind their fortress wall,
With best artillery and engineers.

Bonham. But a mean, spiritless race, ill officer'd;
While ours are men, with appetites for conquest,
Shall make each man a hero. Be you ready,
And Bexar is our own.

Milam. I fear for you.

Bonham. For me!

Milam. The dangers you incur.

Bonham. In seeming only;
They wake no other pulses in my breast,
Than such as joy in danger. I am sure—
Know well the game—the people that I visit,
And grasp with ready arm, and iron will,
The weapons that protect me.

Milam. Bonham, the truth!—

MICHAEL BONHAM.

There is some secret treasure in yon walls,
More dear than wealth or glory, that you covet.
 Bonham.   There is!
 Milam.   A woman?
 Bonham.   Ay, by my troth, a woman—
A Spanish maiden, lovely as the dawn,
And precious as the sunlight to the flower,
To Michael Bonham.
 Milam.   Who is the maid?
 Bonham. The daughter of Don Esteban.
 Milam.   The Governor?
 Bonham.   The same!
 Milam. You rob him doubly then of child and lord-
   ship.
 Bonham. But give him what should recompense his
   loss,
A son and nation.
 Milam. How did you know her?
 Bonham. By happiest chance, last season, on the route
To Santa Fé, I rescued her and cousin,
From the Camanches.
 Milam. Is she grateful for it?
 Bonham.   I trust to find her so.
 Milam. She knows you then?
 Bonham.   But as a gentleman of Mexico;
'Twas in the guise of one I did the service.
 Milam. Did'st meet with her to-day?
 Bonham.   Ay, and I promised
To be with her to-morrow.
 Milam.   And you will?
 Bonham. Ay, though I die for it.

Milam. God speed you, comrade!
You're a bold lover, and bring back awhile
The good old days of chivalry, when valor
Mix'd love and battle in such close communion,
One knew not which was sweetest. Yet, remember,
I urge not this upon you. You are free,
This moment, from your pledge. Better far,
We scale the walls of Bexar, all defying,
Than risk your neck upon them.
   Bonham. Mine the peril!
I claim it of my fortune. To my soul,—
When I regard the prize that hangs upon it,—
The danger wears the aspect of a pleasure,
And woos me to embrace it. Be you ready,
When at the gates you hear my bugle's signal,
And all the hunt is ours,
   Milam. We'll not fail you.
   Bonham. Enough! Fear nothing, and farewell the while.
                   [*Exeunt different ways.*

SCENE II.

Midnight. The moon about to rise among the mountains, and looking down from another point on the Texian bivouack. The fires nearly burnt out. Sentinels seen at intervals among the sleeping groups. Enter Bonham in priest's garments.

Bonham. 'Tis midnight, and the moon but palely shines,
To light me to my comrade, as if loth
That we should seek this venture. But the eyes,
That beckon me are warmer to my heart,
Than ever shone her smile; and I will seek them,
Though she should cloud her jealous glance for aye,
And smile for me no more! 'Tis here, methinks,
He laid him down to sleep. These goodly legs,
With yellow, well-stained moccasins, are such
As I have seen him carry, though the bulk
Above, is something portlier than his wont—
Ho! comrade!   [*Pushes one of the sleepers.*]
    Sparrow, [*in his dream.*] But eight dozen among seven
        of us!
    Bonham. Dreaming of oysters! [*Pushes Crockett.*]
    Crockett, [*in his dream.*] Question! I say Question—!
        question!
    Bonham. He dreams of Congress and the Lower
        House—
The politician, not the hunter now!
Ho! Crockett! to your feet and drum up voters.
The question's on the Tariff—item, salt—
Kentucky's licks are threatened!
    Crockett, [*awaking.*] Out you varmint!
To listen to my dream!
    Bonham.   Comrade, up!
    Crockett.   Major—you!
    Bonham. Bestir you—get your weapons—
Put your camanche garment on your back,
And follow with dispatch. I'll wait for you,
Where the path opens on the Lesser Prairie.
                                  [*Exit Bonham.*

Crockett, [*rising.*] Confound the old Congress! that I shouldn't lose myself a moment, but to get back to them diggins, as if I loved them. Well, the people of Tennessee might have done worse when they sent me, and havn't done better now they've left me at home.

[*Exit Crockett.*

Richard Harris, [*rising from the bushes.*] There's danger in this chance, it seems—this Michael Bonham has as keen a scent after mischief as yon feeder, [*pointing to Sparrow,*] has after meat. My appetite for danger is keener than my scent, and I must use the help of other hunters. I shall reach him before Crockett can.

[*Exit R. Harris.*

Ellen Harris, [*emerging.*] Thus still he flies in search
   of death! O! heart,—
When wilt thou sleep—how rest—and where find peace,
For I must follow him, as fondly now,
As he will follow danger. He is gone!

[*Exit after R. Harris.*

Enter Crockett in Camanche habit.

Crockett. All's ready, but to take a buckle in,—
Tighten the girth, and feel the bullet down,
And then upon the trail. What a huge mountain
Old Sparrow makes in the moonlight! How he snores!
What says he in his sleep?

Sparrow, [*dreaming.*] Raw meat for the Camanches—
  raw buffalo beef
Dipped in the gall of the animal! [*Snores.*]

Crockett. Ten pound of it, with just that sort of sauce,
Will he consume per diem. A true bill!

Sparrow, [*dreaming.*] The brains and liver spread
    upon with fat,
And coated with—   [*Snores.*]
  Crockett. The gall! He knows the dish!
But I must leave him without hearing further,
Lest I grow sick of my Camanche habit!
That such a bird of prey should be a *Sparrow*.
                       [*Exit Crockett.*

  Scene closes.

SCENE III.

The edge of the prairie. A dense wood on one side, while all the rest of the scene, far as the eye can reach, is a long dead level of tall grass, waving in the moonlight. The moon at her full and high in heaven.

       Enter Bonham.

  Bonham. How holy is this silence! What a sea
Is here, of green and waving meadow. in the moonlight,
Glittering with thousand flowers of thousand hues
That mock the rainbow's beauties. As the breeze
Sweeps over the wide track, the gentle tops
Heave into tiny billows that beseem,
The billows of the gulf, when, roused from sleep
By the soft zephyrs of the southern wastes,

They yield themselves unmurmuring to the embrace
Of wooers that they love. Oh! gentle night.
Thus honored by the moon, that o'er this sea
Burns with a sweet benignity, and soothes
Its wildest forms to beauty, in my soul,
Shines a like hallowing aspect. Love is there
Above the forms of danger, like some angel
That, through the cloud and tempest, still looks down
Speaking good will to earth. A footstep,—Hark!
Who comes?

Enter Richard Harris.

R. Harris. A friend.
Bonham. He has a name.
R. Harris. 'Tis Harris, Sir.
Bonham. What would you with me, Harris?
R. Harris. Service, sir,
Provided that means peril, which they tell me
You are in quest of.
Bonham. I may meet with it.
R. Harris. Now danger flies from me! I cannot find it,
Whether on sea or land. Most men fear death,
But death fears me—hides from me—will not face me
Though I implore him in the fatalest passage,
Where other hearts have yielded. By day and night,
Hourly, I seek his shaft to stretch me out,
Sightless in sight of heaven. In quest of this,
I come to you, since it is thought your purpose
Takes you in danger's jaws, the worst of danger
Within the walls of Bexar.
Bonham. This is madness!
Life is a precious privilege, too precious,

MICHAEL BONHAM.

In momentary weariness or trial,
To be flung off with scorn.

R. Harris. Look I like one
For such child weakness, to beseech my doom;
It is not weariness that moves, or trials
Such as compel the tear in other men,
But the fixed purpose of a mood whose reason
Lies deeper, is more hideous than the grave.
Help me to human peril which may lose me
The eternal one that haunts me.

Bonham. I would not know your secret; but if true
The blessed faith that's taught us, Death himself
But opes the door for other and worse fiends,
Than those which haunt the sinner to repentance.
Repent, my friend, and live. To share my danger,
One must love life.—on such good terms with it,
That he shall use all prudence to preserve it.
You cannot go with me. Your very temper
Might wholly mar our purpose.

R. Harris. Cannot, sir!
Bonham. Impossible!
R. Harris Then no more's to be said.
Bonham. Abide your time, my friend. Your quest for
 death,
Is sin not less than madness. Soon enough,
Death seeks the very best of us—too soon,
For many of the best. A word more, Harris
Have better thoughts, my friend.

R. Harris. I would I could!
In praying for death, I sometimes pray for them.

Bonham. Pray for *them* always! In another day
Battle awaits us! Pray you to survive it.

It may, perchance, o'ercome the bravest spirit
To meet its probable terrors. You may have
Your criminal prayers vouchsafed you at a season,
When all, the very humblest, could not save you
From dreadfuller dooms than death. Comrade, hither!
    Enter Crockett.
 Crockett. I'm at your service, Major. Harris here?
 Bonham. He goes not with us. To the camp, my
   friend!
You will not shrink from battle when it comes;
Will wait its coming with a patient courage
That makes all strifes successful. 'Tis my task
To strip it of its perils as I may!
Commend yourself to patience! Comrade, on!
    [*Exeunt Bonham and Crockett.*
 R. Harris. Still baffled in my purpose! Should I wait
On time, and chance, and opportunity,
When I can make them all? Here is the chance,
When human eye is none for scrutiny—
The time—what season half so meet for death,
As when the heart has will'd it for itself—
And opportunity is in the weapon here,
Which my own right hand clutches. Wherefore bear
This torture, day and night, that hourly wakes
Its hell within my heart, when with a stroke
I still the strife for aye! I see no ghost!
I strain these balls to see them! Here's the plain,
Ghastly beneath the moon. The midnight hour
Has thrown apart the great gates of the grave,
And they may walk if they will. They covet darkness
I do not seek the light. Whither I go,
They come not, though I bid them to my sight,

With backward prayer and horrible invocation,
I summon them now,—I call them 'neath the moon:
Come ye fell spectres—wherefore do ye mock,
Mine ears with your reproaches? I would see
And dare ye face to face. I hear them still,
Voices that through the void go hurrying on,
Or lurk at hand to scare. Ha! how they mock,
They tell me that I dare not—though they see
My hand that does not tremble, with the weapon
Uplifted o'er the breast that does not shrink,
And know that as I summon them to see,
I strike with mortal sureness, thus—

E. Harris, [*who enters from behind and arrests his blow.*]
   Mercy! mercy!
 R. Harris, [*turning fiercely.*]   To thy knees.
 E. Harris.   Spare me! be merciful.
 R. Harris.   How durst thou on my steps?
 E. Harris.   I came—
 R. Harris. Thou hauntest me like a shadow.
 E. Harris.   Have mercy!
 R. Harris, [*sheathing the knife.*] No! I'll not harm
  thee!—
I will not pluck, with innocent blood like thine,
More curses on my head.
 E. Harris.   Oh! spare me'
 R. Harris. Have I not said I will not harm thee, boy?
 E. Harris.   Oh! but thyself! thyself.
 R. Harris. And what am I to thee? What if I perish?
 E. Harris.   You promised to protect me.
 R. Harris.   Was't for this
You follow'd on my footsteps? Foolish boy.
With fears like thine, a heart so much a coward,
What dost thou here in Texas? To the Camp—

Thou should'st be with thy mother! While I can,
I'll care for thee and save thee,—but no word
Of what thou hast seen to-night.
 E. Harris.   Thou wilt not—
 R. Harris.   What!
 E. Harris.   Do murder on thyself
 R. Harris. 'Twould seem to be in vain that I should
    try—
The ocean yields me up! The gallows scorns me.
The shot strikes down my comrade in his track,
The hopeful slain, the hopeless left to life,
And my own weapon, sure for other breasts,
Fails when I threat my own. A fate is in it.
'Tis meant that life has yet some use for me
'Till then I may not perish. Be it so!
Come! Follow me in silence. Not a word,—
Dost hear,—on peril of thy life.
          [*Exit R. Harris.*

 E. Harris, [*following.*]   I hear!
I follow thee! I thank thee heaven for this!
Oh! still be merciful! On both have mercy!
           [*Exeunt.*

[END OF PART I.]

PART II.—SCENE I.

Interior of Chamber in the palace of Don Esteban de Monteneros, Governor of San Antonia de Bexar. The Governor, solus, in military costume, writing at table. His chapeau bras, and sword lie before him among papers. He looks up from his reading.

Don Esteban. There! *Madre de Dios!* It is done. It is well done! It is written! The record is made. I may now take my rest. I may sleep. I have fought successfully. The battle is over. The field is won. The laurels are gathered. They enwreath my brow for ever! I defy, thee, Time! Immortality, thou art mine! I clutch thee! Oblivion, I mock thy spiteful arts! . . . Yet, let me see! Let me read once more what I have written! Despatches are not like ordinary letters. They belong to history. They make history! They answer all the purposes of fame. They are fame! Through such as these she speaks, and confers glory upon great heads! *Sic itur ad astra!* And I am not alone. Napoleon lives in his bulletins, rather than his battles! Great example that! Let me see how I have followed it.

[Reads aloud.

" *To his Excellency Don Lopez de Santa Anna, President, &c.*

"Excellency! I have the honor to inform you of the complete defeat,—I may almost say, the total annihilation of the Texian invading army, by the small but gallant forces under my command. So complete, so sudden was the rout, that I may, without exaggeration, appropriate as my own, the language of the mighty Roman. We had but to come, and to see, to conquer! It did not even need that he should see us! The enemy disappeared at our approach. He shrunk from every encounter, and is now flying, with all speed, to the barbarian homes from which he emerged. The hateful Yankeyos are gone forever!— Our soil no longer blushes beneath the tread of their infamous and rebellious hordes. This defeat, so utter and complete, is due entirely to the terror inspired by our arms! So conclusive was this terror, that I cannot now be sure that any of them perished. Their slain and wounded have not been reported to me. Their flight was quite too rapid for pursuit. Ours was a victory without a blow; one of those victories in which the Generalship of the leader, sustained by the bearing of his troops, discourages in the enemy every idea or feeling of resistance. Your Excellency will rejoice with me, that the war is so happily ended. San Antonio de Bexar is safe. We ineed no succours. May your Excellency live a thousand years. God and Liberty! Done, at this our Castle of Montaneros, this, &c.

There!   [*Seals the Letter.*
That I say is well done! Simple and expressive. To the point, without childish epithet or womanly circumlocution. In the very spirit of Napoleon's Dispatches! He could scarce have done it better! And, for the facts? Are not the Texian Rebels dispersed? Who can say where they are? Who has seen them for a month? Not I? Can I answer for what I have not seen? No! If I see

not the Texians, and hear nothing more of them, am I not to suppose that they are dispersed? What more natural? And who should disperse them but myself? To my glory be it written! Cæsar was a Captain—Cortez was a Captain—Napoleon was a Captain—there was a Captain among the States of the North, named Jackson or Johnson—I'm not sure which, and rather think that both are the same;—but—What ho! there Luis.

Enter Luis his Secretary.

There! for Mexico,—see that the Courier has dispatch. Life, nay, more than life depends upon his speed!

Luis. Excellency, Señor Don Pedro de Zavalo, has just come in from Tuscasito and begs to kiss your hands.

Don Esteban. What! My son that is to be? I wait him here!—Fine fellow, that [*Ex. Luis*] Son of mine. A little too fiery, perhaps, too warlike, at a season when bulletins can be made so expressive. Ah! here he is. Don Pedro, welcome. [*Enter Don Pedro.*] I rejoice to see you. My household is at your service. All that I have is yours.

Pedro. Your Excellency is too generous. Do I disturb you?

Esteban. Not a whit. I was just closing my despatch for the President, announcing the late glorious victory.

Pedro. Victory!

Esteban. What! do you ask! Have you not heard?

Pedro. Of a victory?

Esteban. Ay, indeed! Can it be that you have heard nothing?

Pedro. Not a syllable!

Esteban. What! nothing of our victory over these Texian Yankeyos!

Pedro. Not a word till now!

Esteban. Oh! Fame! O glory! What is there now worth living for! But, really, my dear Don Pedro, *have* you heard nothing of this glorious triumph?

Pedro. There was some rumor of a small force of Texian rebels, but it was said they were dispersed by famine.

Esteban. Famine, indeed! When will the world do justice! And our valor and skill, by which they were dispersed, must go for nothing.

Pedro. My dear Governor, suffer my congratulations. These are truly pleasant tidings. It was feared that these outlawed wretches would give you trouble. Fortunately, there were few of them.

Esteban. Few! Four thousand men at least.

Pedro. Can it be possible? And your force?

Esteban. But a poor three hundred. But they *are* soldiers as you may suppose. Brave fellows, I admit. You will suffer me to add that they were admirably managed! War is a science, Don Pedro.

Pedro. This alone suffices to prove it! But three hundred to four thousand! Your success was truly miraculous.

Esteban. Miraculous! Is a man, now-a-days, to get credit for nothing? Is Fate to be the enemy of Fame? I shall begin to dread lest the honor of this victory will be ascribed to Saint Iago, as in the days of Hernan Cortez. People will begin to fancy that they saw his white horse leading the pursuit of these cursed Pagan Yankeyos. But, you are surely too wise for such notions, Don Pedro. There was, let me assure you, no other miracle in the affair than such as belongs to good Generalship—such as a true military genius may effect at any moment. The miracle lay in my successful strategy; and that you may call miracle, if you will.

Pedro. Glorious strategy indeed! But tell me, my dear Don Esteban, where was this battle fought? It is so very strange that I should have heard nothing of it before.

Esteban. [*Hesitatingly.*] Fought! Where was it fought? Why, I may say, everywhere! It was a sort of running fight in which, from the panic of the fugitives, the parties did not absolutely come to blows. For that matter, the rebels are supposed to be running still. They have had a prodigious fright, I assure you. It was quite in vain that I endeavored to pursue them. I could not hope to overtake them. Never did panic stricken scoundrels better use their legs. It is through their fears that you have the sufficient proof of their danger.

Pedro. Most conclusive testimony! And now, my dear Governor, of other matters. How is our fair cousin?

Esteban. We shall surprise her as I would have surprised the Texians. With this view, I have said nothing as yet of our little arrangement.

Pedro. Indeed! But my dear Don Esteban—

Esteban. A part of my plan, Don Pedro! I am none of your rude, direct, undiverting, matter-of-fact persons, to speak out abruptly to the simple point before me. This requires no sort of genius. I am for a stratagem in most things, as a matter of art and refinement.

Pedro. But, my dear Don Esteban, where's the necessity of stratagem in a case like this?

Esteban. Necessity! Where's the necessity of my daughter marrying at all? It is matter of taste purely. Now, my tastes lie in stratagem. I never broke my egg, or ate my supper, or kissed my wife, or did any other natural and necessary thing, without a stratagem. Stratagem is to action what the wine is to the feast,—the oil to the dressing; the salt to the salad; the sugar to the cake; beauty to the woman; wisdom to the man; glory to the saints, and tail, hoof and horns to Don Sathanas! If you deny me my strategy, Don Pedro, I deny you my daughter,—and there is an end of it!

Pedro. But, my dear Don Esteban, will you not make some allowance for the impatience of a lover?

Esteban. To be sure! so I do! so I will; but you must suffer me to say too, that I require, in turn, some allowance to be made for my genius as a strategist. This is my life, my passion. You shall have my daughter: but only after a process of my own; and I tell you that, as yet, she does not know you in the character of a lover. I shall surprise her with the fact—an agreeable surprise, as I shall design it—though surprises of this sort usually operate pleasantly on the fancies of young damsels.

Pedro. I hope they may in this instance.

Esteban. Never doubt it, Don Pedro. Only, don't be impatient. Hear my plan! First, for the masked battery.

Pedro. The masked battery?

Esteban. Exactly. I speak in military parlance;— and a masqued *ball* may fairly be considered a masked battery.

Pedro. I begin to see.

Esteban. Don't attempt to anticipate. It's quite impossible that you should divine my expedients. A few explanations shall enlighten you. Now then, and firstly, as she is, by the favor of Holy Mother, a christian damsel, you shall assail her as a Turk!

Pedro. As a Turk! I' faith, Don Esteban, your stratagem promises to be somewhat intricate.

Esteban. Intricate! To be sure. This is the very nature of all stratagem, to be intricate. But patiently. Look you then. I propose a Bal Masquè, at the Palace, this very night, solely to bring about this stratagem.

Pedro. But shall I not see Olivia before to-night?

Esteban. Oh! ay! See her, to be sure, as often as you please; but not a word of your passion, or of our purpose, till I give the word. I am Governor and Commander here, in Chief, and we must proceed in all things, in military fashion. I must give the signal,—my hand must fire the train.

Pedro. Well, Governor, I hope you will not by your stratagems succeed in compelling my cousin to a flight as rapid as that to which you forced the Texians.

Esteban. Well hit that! Very good! No! no! To prevent that danger, let us go to her at once. Ho, within there!

[*Enter Luis.*]

Esteban. Say to the Señorita, Donna Olivia, that Senor Don Pedro de Zavalo of Tuscasito, and myself, present ourselves to kiss her hands.

Luis. The Señorita has gone to the Plaza, your Excellency.

Esteban. To the Plaza! Good! The day is a fine one. We will follow her, Don Pedro. [*Luis assists him with hat and sword.*

Pedro. With all my heart.

Esteban, [*bowing him to advance.*] Your servant, Señor.

Pedro, [*bowing and retreating.*] Pardon me, your Excellency, but your politeness must not make me forgetful of your rank.

Esteban, [*aside.*] Excellent young man! He was born to be a courtier. [*Takes the arm of Don Pedro, and together they march statelily out.*

SCENE II.

The Plaza, or Public Walks in Bexar. A gay scene of trees and shrubery. Prolonged vistas filled with groups of well and variously dressed people of both sexes. The ladies with parasolettes and head-dresses and veils, but without bonnets. A frequent sprinkling of the military, and occasionally a peasant. Bonham enters as a gay Mexican cavalier, while Crockett is garbed as an arriero, or mule driver.

Bonham. All goes as we would have it. You appear
The very person that your habit speaks you;
A yeoman of the States, a wagoner,
May well beseem the Mexic muleteer,
And play the part with all the natural grace
Of our brave western hunters. A good bronze,
Is that upon your cheeks. Renew it often
When the chance favours. We must separate now.
You hurry to our lodging. 'Tis not well
We should be seen together. I will join you
Within the hour and bring your last instructions;
Meanwhile forget not you were born a *Mute!*

Crockett. Mum is the word!—the uncongressional
　　　word:—
It's mighty hard not to forget it, Major,
But I am in for it now.

Bonham. 　　　And must go through!
'Tis but a day. Away! We separate.

Crockett. Ah, ha! You're for staying awhile longer among these beauties. Well! I'm tough and gristly now but I was tender enough once, and there was a time when the very sight of a pretty gal used to make my heart thump agin my ribs, for all the world like a cracked drum at a Nashville muster. I like to look at the critter still,

MICHAEL BONHAM.

but she don't make the old drum beat any longer. But, mum's the word; the Major's looking wolfish! I'm off.
[*Exit Crockett.*

Bonham, [*solus.*] She comes not! And I look for her
    in vain.
Bright eyes, sly glancing through their falling veils,
Like stars through pliant folds of floating cloud,
Shine on me as I pass; and swan-like forms,
Swim in spiritual movement 'mongst the trees.
But hers—among the thousand still supreme,
Leaves them to fruitless triumph. Can it be
That she has play'd upon my foolish passion
And mocks me with her promise? Idle fear!
She cannot thus do wrong unto herself,
And to that angel purity of glance,
Needing no sweet assurance from her tongue—
Though that were angel's too. She *must* be here!
Why do I seek the crowd? In some lone spot,
Hallow'd by solitude from the vulgar mood,—
'Tis there that true maid would receive her lover;—
There, by yon silent groves that skirt the river,
Methinks she wanders now: and—Ha! she comes,
Even now, from thence. I will conceal myself. [*Goes aside, while Olivia enters, looking anxiously around her.*

Olivia. I see him not! No form in all the Plaza,
Tells me of him. He has forgotten me!
How should I move so proud a heart as his?
What charms are mine that I should make this conquest,
Oh! wherefore should I hope—yet wherefore tremble
Lest he forget me? Can it be, my heart,
I love this stranger?
    Bonham, [*behind her.*] If you do, dear lady,
It were the blessing, which, beyond all others,
His inmost spirit prays for.

Olivia. What have I said!
Ah, Señor, you surprise me.
    Bonham. Sweet surprise!
At least, to the offender! Ah, forgive me
If, stealing on thy steps, mine ears grew happy
With what they drank from thy unconscious lips.
Oh! let me make complete the dear assurance,
By the frank homage of a heart that brightens
In the sweet glimpse vouchsafed me of your own.
I love you, lady!
    Olivia. Ah! Señor, do you love me?
    Bonham. With all my heart, with all my strength and soul,
My thought, my hope, mine eyes, I love thee, lady.
    Olivia. Ah, Señor! Oh! my foolish heart be still,
Nor in the sudden trouble of this joy,
Declare your foolish fondness. [*Aside.*
    Bonham. Not a word,
Nor look of blessing, lady? Did'st thou hear,
The faith my worshipping heart has offered there?
    Olivia. Did I not hear! Can I believe thee, Señor?
    Bonham. Say, shall I swear it, lady? By what star,
Brightest and sacredest in Beauty's eyes,
Purest in Heaven's! Prescribe to me the oath,
And by the stars—and by those eyes, I swear,
And on this hand;—nay do not keep it from me.
    Olivia. Oh, do not swear! It needs not—will not prove
What you declare so fondly. Do but speak—
Or look—the words once more, and—
    Bonham. Speak, O! speak!
    Olivia. And—I'll believe you!

MICHAEL BONHAM.

Bonham. Will you believe me!
Ah! sweetest, never did a maiden's faith
Less peril on a lover's! From that hour
When my most fortunate eyes, by Lova's rancho
Beheld your beauty—

Olivia. Señor, by that rancho—
That scene of strife and dread, I still remember,
Never to lose it—when the wild Camanché,
Smote me to earth, and 'neath his savage fury,
Hopeless, I shriek'd for succor, and—I found it!
Nor succor only! You came, you conquer'd, Señor,
More than the desperate savage.

Bonham. Dear Olivia,
The same eventful victory made me yours,—
Captive to those dear eyes, and witching beauties,
That seem to sadden o'er their own swift triumphs,
As if the world had nothing left to win.

Olivia, [*softly and in low tones.*] To me it hath not,
now.

Bonham. My prize, my precious angel!
Olivia. And did you love me then?
Bonham. That very moment!
Ah! sure you must remember how I held you,
Close lock'd in my embrace,—the danger over,—
Feigning belief that, in your feminine terror,
Your strength had left you.

Olivia. And it had, believe me,
Else I had never suffered such embrace,
Even from the one so—

Bonham. Wherefore on the word,
So full of precious promise do you pause?

Olivia. Oh, no, I should not speak; but you were
right,—

The strength of will, at least, if not of person,
Had left me when I trembled in your arms.
Nor would I chide you with a show of rigor
That needed no display. I heard your voice;
Its gentle accents soothed me;—saw your form—
And in your loving tenderness of look,
Felt any thing but weakness. I was strong,
And—but 'twere most unmaidenly to show,
How great my weakness now.

Bonham.   Speak on! Speak on!
Give to each dear emotion fitting speech,
That I may feel, how bless'd o'er other men,
This fortunate moment makes me.

Olivia.   Oh! no more!
Here comes my father.

Bonham, [*aside.*] Then my trial comes!

Enter Don Esteban and Don Pedro.

Olivia.   My dear father!

Esteban. How now, Señorita! It's as hard to find you as the gold mines of Gallipango. We have met with every body in all Bexar, but yourself—among others, with your good aunt, the ever-to-be-loved-and-honored-at-a-distance, Donna Elvira Teresa de los Flores y Banamos, who would have held on to an antediluvian himself had he only come in the guise of a bachelor. These old maids keep their hold upon a single man, as if every nerve had a tooth of its own. It's only when I meet with her that I am painfully reminded that I am a widower. But I shook her off finally, by a stratagem, calling to her side Don Vincente Trueba, who is more certainly a marrying man than I am. She took to him as a hungry serpent to a drowsy frog. A most happy stratagem, that of mine, eh! Don Pedro.

Pedro. Truly, a most happy stratagem!

Esteban. Who have you here, Señorita? Señor, your health.

[*Bonham bows in silence*

Olivia. This, my dear father, is the brave gentleman who saved my cousin Donna Maria and myself from the Camanches, at the fountains of Loro.

Esteban. Indeed, Señor, I rejoice to see you. My daughter has already made me acquainted with your valor, and the great service you rendered herself and cousin. I love men of valor. I am one myself. I hate ingratitude, and will show that I am grateful. Señor, I kiss your hands, and beg to assure you that all that I am, and have, is at your command.

Bonham. You do me too much honor, your Excellency; the small service—

Esteban. Small service, do you call it? What! to save my daughter, Señorita Olivia de Monteneros, from a horde of rascally Camanches, a small service! By the wisdom tooth of my great grandmother, I would not suffer your enemy to speak of it so lightly. It was a great service, Señor, and you managed the rascals famously. It was a nice stratagem! You took them by surprise—I can see that. Pray tell me how you planned it: a very nice stratagem, no doubt—worthy to be studied.

Bonham. Nay, your Excellency, but there was no stratagem at all. I simply heard the screams of women, hurried to the spot, and had the good fortune to extricate your daughter and her cousin from the savages.

Esteban. Bravely done, and told with rare modesty! Still, I should have preferred that you had operated a little more by the rules of art—a little more strategetically. At all events, the affair tells for your valor. No small odds, Don Pedro, one man to some fifteen or twenty Camanches.

Bonham. But *two*, your Excellency.

Pedro. The Camanches are very cowardly scoundrels. One good man, with half a heart, is equal to a score.

Bonham, [*to Pedro.*] Did you ever manage a score of them, Señor?

Pedro, [*fiercely.*] Hey! Señor.

Esteban. Indeed, Don Pedro, but we differ very much in that opinion. But the subject of Camanche valor will serve for future discussion. Meanwhile, this noble gentleman—Señor—[*to Bonham*]—I would bring you to the knowledge of my excellent kinsman, here, Don Pedro de Zavalo, but that I have not the honor of your name.

Bonham. I am known, sir, in Mexico, as Don Armador de Aguilar.

Esteban. Don Armador de Aguilar! A good name—an historical name, as I may say. Your family came in with the conquest.

Bonham. They did, your Excellency.

Esteban. You will inherit their fortunes. You are a conqueror also. You look like a man who has been used to conquest.

Pedro, [*half aside, at Bonham.*] "Great as he is in
    dust he lies,
He meets a greater, and he dies!"

Bonham, [*aside.*] Truly I think, this gallant jeers at
    me :
We'll fathom him anon.

Esteban. What is't you said, Don Pedro?

Pedro. Truth, Señor, nothing of much. A poor jest, On a much poorer subject.

Esteban. A wise business that. But let me bring you to know this gentleman, Señor Don Amador de Aguilar.

You should be friends. Both young, and brave, and of ancient family. Ah, if it had not been for the success of my stratagem—if we had not utterly annihilated these Texian rebels, scattered them to the four winds of heaven, how I should have rejoiced to see you two, rivals for fame and smiting hip and thigh among the runagates.

Pedro. These Texians are no Camanches—not easily driven by fine caparison and the mere show of weapons. It will require blows, absolute blows, with strong arm and good metal, I can tell Don Amador, whenever he shall meet with them! [*Touches his sword.*

Bonham. Don Pedro thinks as I do, your Excellency. He has probably met these Texians in battle. They have felt his sword. He knows them, or rather he has made them to know him by the strength of his arm. Ha! Señor, is't not so?

Pedro, [*haughtily.*] No, Señor.

Bonham. Texians are not Camanches. They will require good weapons, and it is part of my business here to seek them with mine. I am indifferently ready for any enemy, and keep up the practice sometimes with a friend behind the walls of La Guayra. It is my favorite place of practice, when in Bexar, at sunrise every morning.

[*Touches his sword and looks significantly to Pedro.*

Olivia, [*aside.*]   These men mean mischief.

Esteban. Well! well! whether Camanche or Texian, I feel sure of both of you. My strategies, and your valor and vigor, would soon bury the whole banditti of Texas in the Gulf. You must go with me, Señors. My home shall be your home. Don Pedro, it has long been yours. Don Amador, it must be yours from this moment. Come!

Pedro. You must pardon me, your Excellency; but an engagement—*an engagement of honor.* [*Looking to Bonham.*

Esteban. Indeed! but this will never do. We must find another engagement for you. You must home with me. I must know Don Amador better: and you, Don Pedro, must unite with me in securing his friendship. Two such gallants are not met with every day in Bexar. Ah, Señors, we are quite too far from the great centre. The rays of Mexico seldom reach, and never warm us; and when we can lay hands, as now, upon one of its choice spirits, we must not suffer him to escape. Hear you, Don Amador. Come along! Come with me—I have a most delightful stratagem in progress.

Pedro. I too have a stratagem, your Excellency. It is very like, your friend, Don Amador, has his also. If he be the gallant that you speak him, as I do not question, he can scarcely well be without one.

Bonham. True, I have my stratagem, Señor, and am always ready for a good one, such as your Excellency and Don Pedro may propose. It is possible that I may match you both with something in return. At present, however, I have an engagement, your Excellency, and must beg you to excuse me.

Esteban. By'r Lady! but I take this ill, Señors.

Olivia. I see that I must interpose, at last,
To end this struggle. Señor Don Amador,
Give me an arm, I pray you: nay the other—
Don Pedro will support me on the right—
You must attend me Señors; I too have
My little stratagem,—to wake the envy
Of all the Plaza. Not a maid that passes,
And sees me thus so gallantly attended,
But sickens with vexation. 'Tis so seldom
That I have chance to move them to this measure,
I must not lose it now. You are kind, Señor
Don Amador. [*Takes the reluctant arm of Pedro.*

Bonham, [*offering*.]   Cheerfully, I yield me,
Dear lady, to the sweetest despotism,
And know not how to murmur.
   Esteban. Well managed, Olivia. Ha! ha! You have
your stratagems also. It is a gift in the family.
   Pedro, [*to Bonham, looking behind Olivia.*] I trust,
Senor, that you will not forget the claims of your friend.
If my engagements are thus interrupted, I can assure you
they are by no means forgotten.
   Bonham. Never doubt me, Senor. My friend will not,
and I have usually been found true to friend and foe.
   Estaban. Pshaw, gentlemen, your better friends are
           here;
Would you seek truer? Come with me; I'll find
Friendships enough, and, may be, warmer feelings
For any dozen cavaliers. Lead, Señorita,
The day is leaving us.
   Olivia.   My triumph, Señor,
Must be complete. The woman's stratagem
Must make me without rival on the Plaza,
Though the day leaves us. See, they pass us by,
Nor spare the show of inward grief they feel,
At such unwonted conquest. Oh! gentlemen,
You make me proud to-day.
   Bonham.   It is man's pleasure
That Beauty should be proud.
   Olivia, [*bowing first to Pedro, then to Bonham, while
they are respectively menacing each other, and thus they
go forward.*]   Don Pedro!
   Pedro.   Señorita!
   Olivia.   I am too happy, Señors.
   Bonham. That you should be so, with my ministry,
Leaves me still happier, lady. At your will

Let *friend and enemy wait.* As I am true
To Beauty, I will be as true to friendship,
And not less true to hate. Let them both know
That truth and valor need no better plea
Than beauty's laws prescribe. Then take me, lady,
And still the time that keeps me in your service,
My heart shall hold too short.

 Esteban.   Well said! Well said!
How dextrous are these Mexican gallants.
What says't Don Pedro?

 Pedro. Why, that I am no Mexican gallant. Fine speeches are not my vocation; but I can strike hard blows when the time comes for it.

 Esteban. Let the time come before you speak of blows.

 Bonham. At least *my* speeches tell not of *my* blows. They speak for themselves.

 Pedro.   And mine!

 Olivia. Sirs, must I wait you?

[*Exeunt omnes. The Governor leading the way, and the two rivals still supporting Olivia, and preserving an exterior of courtesy in her eyes, pass out, exchanging sinister glances at every opportunity. She turning alternately upon them, and with a smile, watching and striving to discourage their hostility.*

END OF PART II.

PART III.—SCENE I.

An apartment in the palace of the Governor. He appears busy among numerous masks and dominos.

Esteban, [*solus*.] This is a matter to employ all a man's genius were it ever so fertile. But I can never doubt for a moment what I should wear myself. There! Oh! Bald headed Cæsar—laurel-tufted and trophied Roman—there! let it gratify thy awful shade, that I prefer your semblance to that of any other hero. [*Lays aside the war costume of a Roman Captain.*] Ha! who's there! What, my fair niece, my dove. [*Enter Donna Maria de Molina as from a journey.*] My antelope! Welcome! Better late than never. How came you so late? I had quite given you up for the *Bal Masqué*.

Maria. Bal Masqué, dear uncle, and when?

Esteban. To-night. This very night.

Maria. Then I am still in time. I would not have lost it for the world. And how's my dearest Olivia: and you, how do you sleep now—better?

Esteban. Famously. Like a Bell bird of Brazil, with a tremendous ringing in all my ears.

Maria. How terrible! A ringing in your ears?

Esteban. Delightful rather. It is the ringing of the bells of Mexico that I hear, and have heard for the last three nights in honor of my victory.

Maria. Victory! What victory? Over whom?

Esteban. The rebels,—the Texians; these runagate Anglo-Americans—the degenerate sons of Washington.

Maria. What, have you beaten them?

Esteban. Into powder. They are dispersed forever. 'Twas a prodigious affair. I operated upon them in two ways, but chiefly by stratagem.

Maria. How I rejoice.

Esteban. You may well. You may now travel to Santa Fé without an escort.

Maria. You forget the Camanches, uncle, and the scene at the rancho of Loro.

Esteban. No, indeed; and let me tell you that there is at this very moment, and in these very walls, the very cavalier to whom you owed your rescue on that occasion.

Maria, [*with curiosity and doubt.*] Ah!

Esteban. So!

Maria. Possible!

Esteban. That very cavalier.

Maria. This very moment!

Esteban. In this very house.

Maria. And—

Esteban. With Olivia.

Maria. Dear Olivia, let me fly and embrace her.

Esteban. Stop. Hark a moment before you go. I have a little stratagem. The idea takes me suddenly. Quite an inspiration. I have it now.

Maria. Have what?

Esteban. Look you, Maria—do you remember this cavalier? Had you strength and courage in the moment of danger, to open your eyes and see who it was to whom you owed life and honor?

Maria, [*hesitating.*] I am not sure; and yet I think I did see him. I have some notion that he was a person— a sort of a man.

Esteban. A person! a sort of a man! Very good, very definite and particular. Well, you shall see him. He will make you open your eyes. A person—a sort of a man. And this of one of the bravest looking of all the cavaliers of the country.

Maria, [*aside*.] As if I know not *that!*

Esteban. You shall see him. You shall say then. It may be that I may then let you into my new stratagem—may possibly ask you to assist a little in the scheme.

Maria. Again—another stratagem? Always a stratagem, uncle.

Esteban. And why not? What is life itself but a stratagem—a great bundle of stratagems running on from seven years to seventy. We rise with the dawn to plan, to set snares, dig pitfalls, scheme, trap and take the prey, all of us—man and woman alike: man for the conquest of the world, and woman for the conquest of the conqueror! Have you no stratagems, wench?

Maria. Me! Stratagems. Blessed mother, what a question. What sort of stratagems do you think such a head as mine could carry?

Esteban. Simple ones enough, doubtless, unless the heart takes a share in the business, and then a woman is nothing but a stratagem. It may be that mine at present will become yours. We shall see.

Maria. Tell me only—does it concern this cavalier?

Esteban. Yes.

Maria. Must it concern me, too, uncle?

Esteban. Come! come! That is asking quite too much at one time. I must surprise you with it. I like surprises above all things; a passion that proves my military propensities. One of them, by the way—one of the greatest is about to ripen. This very night, girl—hark you, the mine is to be sprung under Olivia, and she will be in the skies when she least expects it.

Maria. Oh, horrible! What a dreadful design. In the skies when she least expects it. Why, uncle, what can you mean? What has Olivia done to incur such a fate. This is a sort of gunpowder business. Blow up! What a horrible idea.

Esteban. Delightful rather. What should I mean by sending her to the skies, but sending her to heaven?

Maria. But what if she don't want to go to heaven at this early warning.

Esteban. But my process will make her quite happy.

Maria. She does not say so. What if she prefers her own time for it, and by a different process. One does'nt like to be hurried, uncle, even on the high road to happiness.

Esteban. A good phrase that. I like it. The High-road to Happiness. Silly creature, what should be a young girl's idea of the skies and heaven and happiness?

Maria. I'm sure I don't know. I never thought much of either.

Esteban. Oh, what a simpleton you are. Why, what should be a young girl's idea of happiness but marriage; of heaven but a husband; of the skies but a region where all day long she might be catching the sweetest rose-colored loves, and boxing them up for winter. Heaven is only the marriage state under good regulations.

Maria. What! and you are going to marry Olivia to this strange cavalier? Ah—

Esteban. No, indeed. She must find her happiness from another quarter. You know our kinsman Don Pedro de—

Maria, [*eagerly.*] Zavalo. Is he the man?

Esteban. The same.

Maria, [*curiously.*] Will she marry him?

Esteban. Doubtless. But I have yet to surprise her with the arrangement. In that consists my stratagem.

The explosion takes place to-night: Scene, the *bal masquè;* time, midnight. 'Twill be a most famous *coup de theatre.*

Maria. I rejoice that I am in season for it. I feel relieved. I had begun to tremble for my stranger cavalier. [*Aside.*]

Esteban. What think you of my plan.

Maria. Excellent. Don Pedro is just the person for Olivia.

Esteban. Is he not? So brave.

Maria. So handsome.

Esteban. With so much spirit.

Maria. And so much money.

Esteban. He will cover his family with honour.

Maria. He will cover his bride with jewels.

Esteban. He fences splendidly.

Maria. And waltzes like Myrtillo.

Esteban. Has so much talent.

Maria. And such a lovely hacienda.

Esteban. Is such an adroit diplomatist.

Maria. And wears such a beautiful moustache.

Esteban. Is it not a charming prospect? Was there ever such a plot? What a joyful surprise for Olivia.

Maria. It should make her very happy.

Esteban. Should it not? Ah, you puss. But, hark you, this is all secret. Mum's the word; and, when all's over—then, hey! for my other stratagem.

Maria, [*indifferently.*] That concerns the stranger.

Esteban. Yes, indeed. And another of my acquaintance of the other sex. How ignorant and innocent the creature looks. She little dreams my purpose to blow her up also—send her to the skies after the fashion of Olivia. [*Aside.*

Maria, [*aside.*] He is transparent enough, Heaven knows. Well, Heaven prosper it. I am prepared for a blow up, in such company, at a moment's warning.

Esteban. And now, Maria, for Olivia, with whom you will see this strange cavalier—this person, this sort of a man. Ha! ha! ha! Such a description of Don Amador—

Maria. Don Amador: is that his name?

Esteban. Don Amador de Aguilar; as brave a looking gentleman as comes from Mexico. Come. But mum! Remember—not a word to Olivia. My hand, that prepared the mine, must fire the train. [*Exit Esteban.*

Maria, [*following.*] To all my hopes auspicious, grant
    it, Blessed
Maria; for since I've seen this man, I see
No other. [*Exit Maria.*

SCENE II.

A Saloon in the Governor's Palace. Bonham and Olivia discovered.

Olivia. You will come fashioned like a monk.

Bonham. And you?

Olivia. A nun in solemn sables; on my arm
This antique cross, a relique of my mother,
Will teach you to distinguish me from others
In a like habit.

  Bonham. 'Twill not need, Olivia;
That shape, that air; I shall not fail to know you
Among a thousand nuns all dress'd in sable.

Olivia.   Ah!
Bonham.   Hark! those voices?

Enter Esteban and Maria.

Maria, [*running to Olivia.*]   My dear Olivia.
Olivia.   Dearest cousin, welcome.
Esteban. Don Amador, you see here another damsel who owes her safety to your valour. My niece, Donna Maria de Molina, of the Molinas who came in with the conqueror. The family is as old as your own. An old tree, but with precious fine fruit upon it yet.

Maria, [*to Bonham.*] My brave deliverer! Oh, how many thanks
My heart holds for you.

Esteban. Let it empty them. Don Amador is such a modest man, that you cannot say too much to encourage him. He is the person, the sort of man, you know.
                        [*Half aside to Maria.*

Maria. Oh, fie, sir. Hush, this is no stratagem.
Esteban. I have half a mind to tell, but I spare you. I leave you with him that your acquaintance may ripen. I have all the world to attend to. The *Bal Masquè* to-night is enough to give me a week's employment. And then; but mum! [*Looking significantly to Maria and whispering,*] not a word. Don Amador, I kiss your hands. Ladies a thousand.   [*Exit Governor.*

Maria, [*to Bonham.*] So soon your flight after your gallant service,
We had no time for thanks.

Bonham.   Good service in the cause of youth and beauty,
Brings its own tribute, lady.

Maria. But the duty
Is not the less of those, who win the service,
To yield the grateful homage of their hearts:
Senor, pray honor me by wearing this
Poor token of my bosom's gratitude,
Upon the bosom whose impulsive valor,
Deserves a nobler tribute. [*Giving a jewel.*
   Bonham. Dearest lady,
Reward or token of acknowledgment
My service needs not. I will wear this jewel,
Not as the proof of virtue in my bosom,
But generous worth in thine.
   Maria. Senor, nay,
Disparage not the gallantry which makes
The woman's heart do homage; all her pride
Forgotten, and no feeling in her soul,
Save as it tends to worship. Do not shame
With much too humble estimate the gift,
Which heaven makes doubly precious in success.
   Olivia, [*aside*] How charmingly she looks; how earnestly
Eye, lip and brow according. Should he see
Her loveliness as I do.
   Bonham, [*to Maria.*] To hear more
Were to grow vain of common properties:
The common strength of man, skill in his weapon,
And the spontaneous impulses which drive him
To use them for the succour of the feeble
By brutal might oppress'd.
   Maria, [*earnestly and with subdued tones.*] How much I envy
The better fortunes of my lovely cousin,
To have known you so much longer. To have seen you,
And so much better to have shown the feeling

Both hearts must own forever.
 Bonham.   You but pain me,
By such too lavish bounty of your praise,
That mocks my service. 'Twas a happy fortune
That led me to the humblest deed of manhood.
The meanest boor of Mexico had striven,
With heart and hand like mine, were the occasion
So dear to him as mine.
 Maria.   'Tis all in vain,
Don Amador, you undervalue service,
We value not enough. We know too well
The boors of Mexico, to look for succour,
So measureless as thine. The age of valor,
That generous passion, which, in search of glory,
Seeks evermore the paths of strife and danger,
Heedless of any recompense, but only
Smiles of the lovely, praises of the good,
Is of rare finding now. We must not lose it
When in the sight it walks. Pray let me know you,
When other cares will suffer, and the smiles
Of our dear cousin here, will grant you absence;
My father. Don Fernando de Molina,
Will joy to show, in welcome that he gives you,
How much he loves his daughter.
 Olivia, [*aside.*] How well she speaks.
 Bonham, [*to Maria.*] A not unnatural love. Believe
  me, lady,
'Twill make me proud to know him. [*Prepares to go.*
 Olivia, [*timidly.*] You leave us, Senor?
 Bonham, [*aside to Olivia.*] Oh, how unwillingly!
 Olivia. [*aside to Bonham.*] One word more—
Beware of Don Zavalo. For my sake
Seek him not, Amador.

Bonham, [*aside to Olivia*] Fear nothing, my beloved.
Maria, [*aside.*] They whisper! O, my jealous soul,
   I tremble
Lest they should love! I hate her! How I hate her!
 Bonham, [*approaching Maria.*] Thanks, lady, for
   your kindness. It will gladden
To make me useful in your future service:
Command my sword and honor.
 Maria, [*in low tones musingly.*] Alas! for woman,
   Senor,
That cannot well believe, yet dare not doubt.
 Bonham. Ladies, farewell: we meet again to-night.
       [*Exit Bonham.*
 Maria.   To-night!
 Olivia.   To-night!
 Maria. You echo me, dear cousin.
 Olivia. Methought it was Don Amador that said,
To-night.
 Maria, [*aside.*] Even as I feared, she loves him!—
Why so he did; and so did both of us.
You seem bewildered cousin. As you live,
You scarce have bid me welcome.
 Olivia.   Sure I have.
I feel a thousand welcomes, my Maria.
 Maria.   Art sure?
 Olivia. You cannot doubt, but tell me, my Maria,
What think you of Don Amador?
 Maria.   What think you?
 Olivia. I fear to tell you.
 Maria, [*quickly.*] Tell me not you love him!
 Olivia.   Wherefore?
 Maria. 'Twere your misfortune, cousin.
 Olivia.   Wherefore, still?

Maria. Come with me to your chamber; I have something
To pour into your ear, of such strong power,
Shall either make you very sad or merry,
Shall lift you into happiness, or sink
Your baffled heart and hope, as low from hope,
As hell can be from heaven.
 Olivia.   You affright me!
Give me this fearful secret; speak your tidings,
Lest in my terror I conceive them worse
Than human wo can make them.
 Maria.   Love not this man!
 Olivia. Amador!
 Maria.   Oh, feeble heart—
Caught at a glance, snared by the passing vision,
Without a hope to cling to. To the chamber—
Oh, cousin—wherefore—
 Olivia. Mock me not thus, Maria. Oh! my heart,
One moment,—now—speak out and do not trifle;
You do not sport with me,—you cannot, cousin.
 Maria. Look on me, dear Olivia—do mine eyes
Lighten with merry thoughts—upon my cheek,
See'st thou the laughing spirit of mischief there—
Eager in malice, or thoughtlessness to revel,
In the sweet misery of a sister's heart.
 Olivia.   Oh, no! I will not doubt thee. 'Tis in earnest;
Those eyes now fill with tears—those words now falter:
Come with me to my chamber. There!
         [*Exit Olivia.*
 Maria, [*following.*]   Ay, cousin—
And there I'll cozen thee with such a tale,
Shall make thy head to ache, thy heart to ail.
         [*Exit Maria.*

SCENE III.

A Wild and Mountainous region. The Texian army in movement. Groups pass over the stage, partisan fashion, and in picturesque costume. Enter Sparrow, Davies and other Texians in the foreground.

Sparrow. Though a man of some bulk, I am yet a man of movement. I have no passion for a quiet life. I'm for action, whether the object for assault be foe or food, soldier or supper. I have a large territory to endanger, as well as to supply; but that makes me no more cautious than if I were a Calvin Edson. Let the battle come when it pleases. The sooner the better. This city of San Antonia de Bexar, they tell me, is a sort of little Mexico, where the gold may be had for the gathering.

Davis. You are too old a bird, Sparrow, to be seasoned by that salt. For my part I never yet found more gold in one place than another, and I think with the preacher, that gold is the root of all evil.

Sparrow. Indeed! I would I had many such roots to set out in my garden. The cotton crop might go hang for me, and the Liverpool market along with it. The preachers, too,—but let them say what they will, I never yet found one of them who found his salary clogged with too many such roots. They were never too numerous for his religion.

Davis. This is rather dull talk, Sparrow, just as we are about to have cracked crowns and broken noses. Can't we change the music in some manner, and hurra for something.

Sparrow. Ay! You may. We will hurra! Here goes! Hurra for nothing! Will that suit? Change the music, to be sure; but do you see the singer in my visage? Do I sing small like a woman. That's not my vocation, Davis. Look about you as the boys come by and get a singer; but the Anglo-Norman breed is better at shouting than singing. Of our three hundred now, not ten of us can turn a ballad, but not one of us that can't scare a Mexican's soul out of his breeches by one hallo!

Davis. Here's the very man, Joe Kennedy, from Alabama. He sings famously, and makes his own songs as he goes.

Sparrow. Such a fellow has his uses, even as a singer. I can understand him. Let him make us something now to warm the fellows for a brush.

Enter Kennedy and Texians.

Davis. In season, Joe. A song to shorten the journey. We have been talking here about that root of all evils, gold; which we are to gather here in this little Mexico, San Antonio, until, somehow, we've got the dolefuls. Give us something fine and fiery.

Kennedy. I heard you! Get your ears ready and your hands. If I am to sing, I must be clapped, mark you, just as they clap your theatre fellows who sing well, as all theatre fellows would sing, were they—

Davis. What?

Kennedy. Joe Kennedy.

Sparrow. Put your spirit into your song, my lad, and blaze away.

Kennedy, [*sings.*]

1.

My banner to the breeze,
  And my bowie at my side—
My barque upon the seas,

And the single star my guide;
I shall lay the oyster bare,
  To pluck forth its precious fruit,
And these evils that ye fear,
  I will gather at the root.
And the evils, &c.   [*bis.*

2.

We are soldiers of the north,
  And we know like men to fight;
We have gone to battle forth,
  With old England in her might;
We have spirits born to dare,
  We can smite and we can shoot,
And the evils that ye fear,
  We will gather from the root,
And the evils, &c.   [*bis.*

3.

Do you speak of coming hours,
  When to battle we must go;
We are ready, by the powers,
  To awaken any foe;
We shall teach them that the bold,
  Still inherit all the fruits,
And their moustaches and gold,
  We shall pluck up by the roots.
And their moustaches, &c.   [*bis.*

Sparrow. Good I say. Three cheers for amateur Kennedy. He has done the thing famously. Such a song as that would give a fellow an appetite for any thing, eating or fighting. It meets our case exactly. Kennedy, your hands. I shall think well of you forever after, and whenever an extra delicacy offers—a sleek tongue of a young buffalo bull,—you shall be in for a slice. A good chorus that. [*Sings.*

"And their moustaches and gold,
  We shall pluck up by the roots."

My fingers feel as if they were at it already. [*Sings.*

"Their moustaches and gold
  We shall pluck up by the roots;
We shall pluck."

Davis. Stop your hurraing—here's the Colonel, boys.
  Enter Milam and others.
Milam. Ye loiter men. Ye should be on the march;
By midnight we must be at Bexar's gates,
If we would find them open. Ye must haste,
Ye have no wealth, no gold, no cumbrous baggage
To weigh your shoulders down—your rifles only,
And you will lighten them at every shot,
That brings an enemy down. Away, our friends
Are busy now in Bexar. 'Tis my hope
That we shall win the spoils of yonder town,
With scarce a struggle—follow fast, my lads.
      [*Exit Milam and aids.*

Sparrow. Talk of a struggle with these Mexicans!
Fellows that never tasted British beef,
Know nothing of a steak, and *à la mode,*
Have never in their wildest fancies dreamed of.
Tortillas are but poor provocatives,
And all the *chile* in Chili could not warm them

To a death struggle with a beef-fed soldier.
Where are their limbs and sinews?
  Davis.   Eyes to shoot,
A rifle, or the dexterity to use
The knife Jim Bowie gave us.
  Sparrow.   I could eat
A dozen for my supper,—with a dressing,
Made up of all their thirteen thousand generals,
From the Napoleon of the west himself,
To Senor Ampudia. I feel wolfish,
With cannibal convictions. On, away,
We'll think of supper as we smite and slay.
                  [*Exit Sparrow, Davis, &c.*

    Chorus of Texians as they march off.

    " We shall teach them that the bold
      Still inherit all the fruits
    And their moustaches and gold,
      We shall pluck up by the roots."

    Enter R. Harris and E. Harris.

  R. Harris.   They're on the march, and battle is at hand
A desperate struggle. Something tells me now,
My hour is near at last. The fate's at hand
Shall lay me in the silence I have sought.
I have had warning of it. Hither, boy, [*To E. Harris.*
I somehow like you. You have hung about me
More than I wished. I could not quarrel with you,
For, as I tell you, something in your face,
It may be, in your voice, has made me like you!
My head ached and you chafed it. I was lonesome;
You sat beside me, and you talked with me,—

MICHAEL BONHAM.

Albeit you talked of subjects foreign to me,
Of God, repentance, hope, lessons too late,
For one so old a learner as myself.
Your voice was pleasant to me. It had something,
That minded me of other times and persons,
I never more shall see. Come closer, boy.
   E. Harris. What would you with me, sir.
   R. Harris. A kindness only—
I have not often done them, but, to you,
I would not have you perish.
   E. Harris. What mean you, sir.
   R. Harris. A battle is at hand.
   E. Harris. Ah.
   R. Harris. A fearful one perchance. You are no
      soldier:
You'll prove, I'm sure, a coward in the action,
And that were dreadful. You must stay behind.
   E. Harris. Stay behind! I cannot.
   R. Harris. Can you fight then?
   E. Harris. I know not. I have never fought before,—
Never took life, never as I remember,
Hurt hair on human head; but—
   R. Harris. Well—and what.
   E. Harris. Sooner than not go on. Sooner than leave
      you,
I'll try to kill.
   R. Harris. You havn't soul for it.
Your lips belie your tongue. Your very tones
Betray your terrors. You are not the creature
For such wild doings. You must stay behind
In silence, while the troop is on the march;
The night will favor you, and with this money—[*Offers
      purse.*

E. Harris. I cannot take your money, sir.

R. Harris, [*fiercely.*] You must.

E. Harris, [*firmly.*] Never.

R. Harris. What! not remain behind, nor take the money.

E. Harris. No, though I perish, though I prove the coward
You hold me, and I sadly think myself,
I must go forward. It may be my arm
Will shrink from doing hurt to human foe,
But I can stand and suffer. I'll not fly,
But perish where you place me.

R. Harris. What good in that?
In battle to stand idle, is worse danger
Than cowardice and flight. You must not go.

E. Harris. I must. If in your heart a warning voice
Tells you of coming death, in mine another,
Compels me to encounter any peril
Sooner than leave my comrades.

R. Harris. You are foolish.
You have no comrades. I'm the only man,
That you have mixed with.

E. Harris. You're my comrade then.

R. Harris. And do I not assure that for me
Death even now stands waiting.

E. Harris. I'll see you die.

R. Harris. You're obstinate, boy.

E. Harris Oh, firm sir, nothing more.

R. Harris. Poor lad. I pity you. You little dream
The dangers that await you—little guess
The shock, the carnage, bleeding men and blood,
Hoarse cries of hate, and vengeance, and of pain—
Here, take the money, linger in some cabin,

MICHAEL BONHAM.

Such as you'll find among these hollow dales,
And there await the action.

E. Harris. Sir, forgive me.
But I must seek and see it; all the peril
Which you incur I share in. In this purpose
My soul, though feebler, fearfuller than any
In all our little army, still is firm.
I go with you.

R. Harris. On then, in heaven's name, on;
We may delay no longer. Follow close.

[*Exit R. Harris.*

E. Harris. In heaven's name be it, for I dare not think,
Heaven will not shelter us on danger's brink.

[*Exit.*

SCENE IV.

The groves near the convent of La Guayra. The walls of the convent shining white from the hills in the distance.

Enter Don Pedro.

Pedro. He comes not. Curses on him. Should he fail me,
Let him not hope to 'scape me. I will slay him
Without remorse, though grasping on the altar,
He called upon the Blessed Host for succor.
My dearest hope he perils. All my heart
Is full of her perfections, and her's only.
And shall he rob me of them? Have I lived
And toiled, nor seemed to seek, and loved at distance,

Still unpresuming lest I should endanger
The precious gift I coveted, for this?
But no. It shall not. I will to the palace
And drag him from her presence, though she pleaded
With all the eloquence of love and beauty,
And—but it needs not. My impatient spirit
Be hush'd. He comes, mine enemy comes, to perish.

Enter Bonham.

Oh! you are here at last. I've waited long
And somewhat dreaded lest my hints, too guarded,
Had failed to touch your valor. 'Twas my fear,
That I should have to press upon your pleasure,
Disturb you in the presence of your mistress,
And goad you by impatient word and buffet
To do your weapon justice.

 Bonham, [*coolly.*] Angry, Señor?
 Pedro.   I am. I hate you.
 Bonham.   Wherefore?
 Pedro. Enough. I hate.
Hate to destroy.
 Bonham. Nay! Nay! I trust not, Señor;
I'm in no mood to perish at this moment.
Now when the sun shines brightly on my future
That never shone before. What angers you?
 Pedro. My answer's in my sword.
 Bonham. To fight you now
Were only to assail you at advantage—
You're feverish now, scarce master of your weapon,
Let us forbear a season while you tell me,
Wherefore your wrath.
 Pedro. Enough! It is my humor.
 Bonham. That's not enough for me. Why should I
   fight

MICHAEL BONHAM.

To gratify your humours? You must show me
Some cause of provocation.
   Pedro.   Will a blow do it.
   Bonham. Nay 'twill not need! If you're so desperate,
You force the fight. I will not be dishonored;
Will fight you when you please.
   Pedro.   Be it now then.
   Bonham. Be it so; and yet I would 'twere otherwise.
My cue is not for fighting. On this weapon
Hangs fifty times the value of your life.
   Pedro.   Dost mock me?
   Bonham. Such madness might deserve my utmost scorn.
Most like I do.
   Pedro. My taunt shall break thy teeth. Come on.
Come on,
And hear me Señor,—such is my conviction,
That you are in my path, the deadliest foe
That ever fate rear'd up against my fortunes,
That I have sworn, by all I prize the most,
To slay you without pity, even as the hunter,
Spears the wild boar that griding on his weapon,
In death betrays the malice of a passion
That death alone defeats.
   Bonham.   Child fury, Señor,
Unworthy of a man. Your oath is idle,
If you rely on such. We are apt to fight,
If right I read your anger, for the favor
Of the fair lady in the palace here.
   Pedro. And if the prize be precious **in your sight**,
As still it is to mine, I challenge you
Fight like a man.

Bonham. I have been thought a man;
Will fight as one, but not one blow to prove
My love for her. I will not wrong her beauty
To make her youth, her charms, her innocence,
The prize of ruffian strife. 'Tis for your humor
That I make bare my weapon. I am ready—
Now stand we point and foot to foot,
And play your game as all your wealth were on it—
Your blood upon your head.
 Pedro.   The blood of both,
If need be, but no words.
 Bonham. Let the steel speak. [*They fight.*]
It makes a merry music—
Might touch with fear the maids in yonder convent
Could they but see our danger, and know farther,
That we are young, both bachelors and fighting,
Because there still are beauties in the land,
And love is not an exile.
 [*This is spoken merrily, in broken sentences as the play of the duel will allow. Bonham being quite playful, while Pedro becomes more and more furious.*]
 Pedro. [*Fight and pause.*] Scha! is this fighting?
 Bonham. It is the mode I use when the mood suits me;
You are too angry, Señor, for a swordsman,
Your play is rash and wild. In cooler moments
Your weapon were a good one.
 Pedro.   You laugh at me.
 Bonham. I can't do else. You are no match for me.
 Pedro. Demonios! We shall see. [*Resumes the fight more desperately and Bonham disarms him.*
 Bonham.   The day is mine.
Your life is at my mercy.

MICHAEL BONHAM.

Pedro. Take it then.
Bonham. Away! You are a madman.
Pedro. I shall be
'Till I have vengeance. [*Draws a dagger and rushes on Bonham.*

Bonham. Fool. [*flings him off and wrests the dagger from him.*]
For this too, as you see, I am prepared.

Pedro. Hell's curses on thee. We shall meet again.
[*Exit Pedro.*

Bonham. [*Solus—putting up his sword.*]
'Tis well the time is short. A few more hours
And we may laugh to scorn the single danger
Of one man's jealous rage. Yet 'twas a risk
I did not idly covet—did not seek.
Upon the safety of this single life
Hangs the best hope of Texas—hangs the fate
Of San Antonio. Bexar, to her fall,
Nods at my signal. The Alamo's walls
That now frown darkly on the distant plain,
Shall, in a few brief hours, obey my voice
Or silence me forever in her keeps.
How heavy grows this silence. As if night
Were burden'd with its weight of doom already.
Would it were over. Be but Milam true
And I grow happy in the loves I win,
Or tremble with the doubts of love no more.
The hour awaits the man, and he is here.
[*Exit Bonham.*

PART IV.—SCENE I.

Night. Within the Ramparts of Bexar. The sentries lie sleeping by the gate. Enter Bonham and Crockett with the keys.

Bonham. The gates are ours, the sentinels asleep—
Your work is ended, comrade, barely ended—
Milan is on his march. In three hours more
Comes the grand struggle. Meanwhile for the mask;
You, garb'd as the Camanche, are secure,
In silence; but beware of speech to any—
Your tongue were fatal to us. You can play,
The masker, as a hunter, happily,
By signs and action;—but the tongue, the tongue;
Keep that in bonds, dear comrade.
    Crockett. A needful warning enough, major, to an ex-member of Congress. But if I was Quincy Adams now, you would lecture me in vain. He, poor fellow, can't help his tongue. But the hunter who has properly larned his rifle to make his speeches, knows pretty well when he ought to keep silent himself.
    Bonham. Do so, to-night, and all goes as it should.
Now to your preparations. Bring your weapons,
Be in full costume, as an armed Camanche,
The masque will sanction it. Beneath my cassock,
I am a Texian. When you hear my bugle,
Make answer with your own. 'Twill waken Milan's
And the full chorus of our shouting comrades
Will waken Bexar, not again to sleep,

'Till she or we are silent, or subdued.
Away 'Tis victory or death to-night.

[Exit Bonham.

Crockett. Well! Who's afraid of victory? Not I,
And as for death—we'll *call* it victory.

[Exit Crockett.

SCENE II.

The chamber of Donna Maria. She is preparing for the Ball, with Jacintha in attendance.

Jacintha. There Señorita, you are ready. Truly you are a princess. The great princess Papantyin, whose dress you wear, never looked half so beautiful in the times of Montezuma. You will win every heart in Bexar.

Maria. Have you done your best? I tell you, Jacintha, my fate hangs upon this night.

Jacintha. Oh that's what you 've said a thousand times before.

Maria. But never 'till now in earnest. On this night I peril all my hope.

Jacintha. What to a man?

Maria. Ay but one among a thousand. But go forth,
See if my cousin's ready. I would see her.
See if she's ready! That I know. She is not.

[Exit Jacintha.

And will not be to-night. The blow I've struck,
Will keep her in her chamber. To make certain,
'Twill need another. I will urge upon her

A frank submission to her father's will,
Show her the hopelessness of any struggle,
Dwell loudly on the sinfulness of passion,
That wars with filial duty; and in painting,
Make doubly odious, to her shuddering spirit,
These nuptials that she loathes! Ah! if I err not,
The arrow from my bow, already shot,
Sticks fast and deep, and, humbled in her terror,
She keeps her chamber close. The *Bal Masqué*
Shall be *my* field of triumph. Do I look
Prepared for conquest? Are my charms displayed,
In happiest fashion? Is there, in my habit,
My glance, the free array of linkéd beauties,
The smile that smarts, the danger that invites,
The flowing tresses that, in youthful fancies,
Beguile and lead them wanton,—'till the heart
Clings to the one perfection it beholds,
And knows one faith forever? Are these mine?
Look I, indeed, the princess, born for sway
O'er hearts and o'er affections,—prouder sway,
Than sovrans over subjects?
—Mock me not—[*addressing the mirror.*]
Thou bright misleader of the weak heart's passion,
That, through the blinding spells of vanity,
Presents a lovelier image to the owner,
Than charms the stranger's eye. Delude me not,
Bright mirror, nor abuse that easy faith
That woman gives thee still. I must believe thee!
This form, these eyes, this port of regal splendor,
Were made for conquest. Shall it be to-night!
I wait not for thy answer.
                Re-enter Jacintha.
Speak Jacintha! My cousin?

MICHAEL BONHAM.

Jacintha. Why, Señorita, your cousin's not dressed: And does not mean to dress for the *Bal Masquè*.

Maria. I'll go to her. Auspicious to my prayer, The field is won—I have no rival there.

[*Exeunt Omnes.*

SCENE III.

The chamber of Olivia. She sits in a desponding attitude—her hands crossed in her lap—her head drooping upon her bosom. Duenna in attendance.

Duenna. My child, shake off this sadness. Take the counsel of one who honors the world—who loves you dearly, as if she were your mother. You're too quick, to hearken evil tidings.

Olivia. Stay! she comes!

Enter Maria followed by Jacintha.

Maria. Can it be possible, my dear Olivia, You do not go to-night?

Olivia, [*with a sad smile.*] You see, my cousin.

Maria. But why this, Olivia?

Olivia, [*reproachfully.*] Can *you* ask?

Maria. Ah! but your father's wishes—well, you know How much his fond designs—his dearest hopes, The all that he has schemed for, hang upon it.

Olivia. 'Tis for that very reason I remain.

Maria. Surely you will not then oppose your father.

Olivia. I know not—cannot think. I must have time. Let us not speak of it now. I sent for you To see your dress. 'Tis very beautiful. You look the princess. You were born for conquest— Will conquer. Go, my cousin; I'll not keep you.

Maria. It makes me sad to see you so—to leave you—
It vexes me, I told you.
    Olivia. Let it not.
'Twere a worse sadness, cousin, unto me,
To have a suitor forced upon my hand,
In presence of the goodly company,
Against the natural feeling of my heart.
    Maria. Surely, my cousin, you do wrong Don Pedro;
He seems to me a proper gentleman—
Well formed and brave—a handsome cavalier.
    Olivia. No more, dear cousin—not to theme like this
Can I give ear. Go you to easy conquest
If such as he find favor in your sight—
I doubt not you will conquer where you choose:
You cannot choose but conquer. You were made
For queenly station—brow and eye commanding,
Stately and beautiful.
    Maria. You do but flatter, cousin.
    Olivia. Alas! I have no heart for flattery—
You may believe me. You are beautiful,
And will be sovereign in all eyes to-night.
    Maria. It deepens my regret for your own sake,
You are not there on mine. I'd have you see
My conquests, dear Olivia. What you say
Fills me with hope. I hasten to secure them,
For you must know that, like Don Esteban,
I too have plots and little stratagems,
And,—but you do not hear me.
              Well! I leave you.
Good night. Good night.
                    [*Exeunt Maria and Jacintha.*
    Olivia. Good night. Be prosperous, cousin.
    Duenna. You wish against yourself, my child!

Olivia. How so?
Duenna. Your last words to your cousin.
Olivia. And they?—
Duenna. Still wish'd she might be prosperous to night.
Olivia. Do I not wish it?
Duenna. At your own expense?
Olivia. What is it that you mean?
Duenna. Your cousin's *not* your friend.
Olivia. Fie, mother; Fie.
Duenna. She knows not friendship. Has not, in her heart,
A single feeling for you; loves herself,
And has her stratagems to help herself;
Why counsel you to give up Amador,
Marry Don Pedro, at your father's bidding,
Without a word of pleading in his ears,
Though well she knows he loves you in his heart,
Above all other objects? 'Tis my notion,
She loves Don Amador herself—
   Olivia. Oh, no!
Duenna. Yes, but 'tis very probable, my child.
The cavalier's a noble gentleman,
None like him in all Bexar—just the man,
That she would like to have. Why should she take
This time to tell you of your father's scheme,
But just to keep you from the ball to-night,
To have him to herself.
   Olivia, [*rousing herself.*] You half persuade me.
   Duenna. I am sure of it.
Olivia. Such was my own suspicion, swift and sharp
As summer lightning from the cloud unseen,
But that my heart repelled it in its fondness,

Lest I should wrong my cousin. We have slept
On the same couch together fifteen years—
Linked in each other's arms; we've prayed together,
Confessed our mutual cares to one another,—
Our loves, our fears, our hopes, and still I fancied
The early link that knit our hearts in childhood,
Time never could have broken. Could I think it—
Could I believe?—but no! I will not wrong her
By any doubt like this.

  Duenna. You do not wrong her.

  Olivia. I will not, but I'll baffle her, if wrong
Lurk in her heart to me. Go, dear Ursula,
Get me the gipsy garb I wore at Rosas;
She has not seen it, will not know me in it,
I'll habit me in that;

                                [*Exit Duenna.*

I'll watch her movement,
And see the joys I have no heart to share.
Ah! bitterness, to find the colors fade,
The brightness from the day, the balm from night,
Sweet from the evening air, and scent from earth;
The parent heedless—the friend false—the heart,
In peril and dependence, needing succor,
Yet with no faith in him that offers it.
Nay, Amador, I wrong thee, thou shalt have it,
My heart, my faith, my hope, my all of being
Unquestioning if thou wilt. Within thy bosom
I'll place the trust, by father and by friend
Equally wronged—that never questions love,
And looks to love and heaven for all its succor.

                                  [*Exit Olivia.*

MICHAEL BONHAM.

SCENE IV.

Splendid saloon in Governor's Palace for the Bal Masqué. Individual masques and groups discovered. They engage in the Spanish dance. Enter Governor as Julius Cæsar, and Don Pedro as the Grand Turk.

Pedro. You make a famous Roman.
Esteban. The famous Roman—I am Julius Cæsar.!
Pedro. You look the hero famously! But she,—
Where's your fair daughter—how does she appear?
Pedro. You'll find her somewhere, as a nun, in sable.
Pedro. I see a dozen such.
Esteban. Then must you try your wits in seeking her.
I've nothing more to tell you.
Pedro. This Don Amador,
Does he come here to night?
Esteban.   Be sure of it.
Pedro.   How habited?
Esteban. Nay, nay, Don Pedro, you must pardon me,
That is a question out of precedent.
Pedro. Save in particular cases; this is one of them;
Knowing your admiration for him, I desire
To show him marked distinction, as a stranger,
During the progress of the festival.
Esteban. Ah! that indeed. He comes, then, as a
      monk,
There—you will find him in yon group,—dost see him,
His head above the others?
                  [*Exit Esteban.*

Pedro, [*gloomily.*] It is he!
The instinct of my hate had taught me truly.

Now will I set a blood-hound on his path,
Who shall not sleep until his fierce pursuit
Avenges my dishonor.

Enter Canales the Bravo, in the garb of a mulcteer.

 Canales.   You see me here.
 Pedro. Hist! 'Tis he! Thou'lt do it? [*pointing to* Bonham.
 Canales.   The monk!
 Pedro. He is no monk. He is mine enemy,
The dearest to my hate.
 Canales.   His grave is dug.
 Pedro.   To-night.
 Canales. Ay! When he leaves the palace.
 Pedro, [*draws him aside.*] It cannot be too soon for
  my hurt honor;
His shadow chills my path. He stands between
My heart and all its sunshine.
 Canales. Take your sleep—
His shadow will be less before to-morrow!
The sun that sets for him, shall rise for you;
He troubles you no longer.
 Pedro, [*giving money.*] Be this the earnest
Of that which follows when the deed is done.
 Canales. Account it done.
[*Exit Bravo who is thence seen to hang upon the footsteps
  of Bonham.*

 Pedro. Then shall I sleep . . . . and thou,
My proud and powerful enemy,—thou too
Shalt take thy sleep in death, accursed foe!
The first to teach me what it is to tremble
With loss of hope in love, and loss of faith,

In mine own weapon. Be the earth upon thee
Before the smiling sunlight blesses earth.
[*Exit Pedro.*

Bonham Advances.

Bonham. She fails me—and the hours are waning fast:
Should Milam fail me too.

Enter Crockett.

Ah! my dear comrade.

Crockett. Major, this is famous fine. My head is a swimming fairly in the blaze of glory, jest as it used to swim when I looked on old Hickory's. It's wonderful handsome. I never seed the thing better done at the White House, even in Van's day, when Ogle got frightened at the gold spoons. Lord, what a shine of dresses. There's gold and silver enough about 'em to build a church, not leaving out the steeple. And look at the diamonds; I reckon, Major, them's the ra'al grit, jest sich as we'll git out of the gold mines if we ever git into them.

Bonham. In truth, good comrade, there is much to dazzle
Such simple eyes as ours. But we've a purpose
That must not suffer mind or thought to wander
From the great duty we have here in hand.
Let not the brightness blind you to the loss
Of proper prudence. See, and smile, and idle,
As the mood prompts you; but beware of speech.
You're a Camanche and a warrior comrade—
No more a politician. Let your speeches
Be only in your actions. For the warrior
Blows are the proper language; swords and rifles
The proper parts of speech. Our eloquence
We will deliver, with due voice, in season,
Through our shrill bugles. Once more be counselled;

Keen eyes, even now, are watching us—we must not
Again be seen together, 'till the moment
When we must work together. Now leave me
And keep aloof with caution. If you will speak,
Choose you some uncouth Indian dialect,
Cherokee, Choctaw, Chickasaw, or Creek,
Either will suit the habit that you wear;
Say little even then. Would you make love,
'Tis but to sign with fingers on the lip,
Sigh hoarsely as a savage might, and mutter
With something of a panther's tenderness,
Whom the fit seizes 'twixt his sleep and supper.
Enough! and now let's separate.
  Crockett.   Right, Major.
You're always right. We'll make different tracks, then,
And hunt our game apart.
         [*Exit Crockett.*

 Bonham. [*Solus.*] I see her not. I know not why it is,
But something seems to speak of treachery,
As if a busy tongue beside mine ears
Kept ever more one croaking chaunt of evil.
But who comes here? so gallant in attire,
Like a proud vessel with her full sails set,
And the gay streamers, from her lofty tops,
Coying with heaven's own breezes.

  Enter Donna Maria as the princess Papantzin.
    [*Bonham recedes at her approach.*

 Maria. You fly me, father.
 Bonham. Not so, fair princess. I but shrink in wonder
At such a vision.
 Maria. You do injustice
To the most holy vestments that you wear,
To shrink from mortal sovereign.

MICHAEL BONHAM.

Bonham. But, if true,
The lesson that were taught me, you are not
A mortal sovereign, Lady. If I err not,
You rank among that royal race, which perish'd
In Mexico three hundred years ago,—
The race of Montezuma.
   Maria. You have read
Our story but imperfectly: the race
Of Montezuma perish'd; but one Princess
Survived, in state of trance, and still survives.
   Bonham. Princess Papantzin!
   Maria. The same, good father;
And, by the virtue of that sacred trance,
Which keeps her spell'd by sleep, alternate seasons,
She reads your secret.
   Bonham. What secret, Princess?
   Maria. The heart that beats beneath that peaceful habit
Is scarce so peaceful!
   Bonham. In your spells alone,
Lies the deep guilt of its inquietude.
   Maria. Could I believe it, Senor. 'Neath that cowl
The soldier's front is hid. That garb conceals
The Cavalier, whose brave but callous heart
Could rescue beauty from the savage arm,
Yet fling it from his own.
   Bonham. You wrong me, Lady.
You do not know this heart.
   Maria. Oh, would I did.
   Bonham. And why the wish?
   Maria. Ah, vain, cold tyrant, man!
Would'st force me to confession? Must I bend,
And, spite of maiden modesty and shame,
Lay my fond bosom bare. The simple wish,
Speaks the heart's secret.

Bonham. This habit, noble Princess!
Your royal state—your ancient family—
The wondrous mystery of your own repose,—
Three hundred years in life, yet blessed with youth,
And beauty—as I doubt not—to this hour,—
Are each enough to guard me from the sin
Of the poor vanity, such as, in your thought,
Has triumph'd over mine.
   Maria. No more! No more!—
I am no Princess, Amador—and you
No monk! No monk! I am a woman,—fill'd
With all her passions and infirmities—
Loving as woman seldom loves, and freeing,
Before the man she loves, her secret bosom,
As tame and common love could never free it!
Your arm has saved my life; and in that triumph
Achieved another. Look upon your conquest,
And trample on it with your eyes of scorn,
Or lift it with your love. [*Lifts her mask.*]
   Bonham. Donna Maria!
   Maria. Ay, Señor—
The proudest heart that beat in Mexico,
Until it met with yours.
   Bonham. Why do we meet?
   Maria. Nay, tell me not you love, and love another!
Say not that to my cousin's feebler beauties,
Her sad and sighing passion, illy suited
To the brave spirit of ambitious valour,
Your heart is yielded. Know, that, if no Princess,
Such as my habit speaks me—in my bosom
There dwells a regal spirit, whose impatience
Brooks not a rival—brooks not that the heart
It seeks, should not, with ardour like its own
Burn to requite its passion.

MICHAEL BONHAM.

Bonham.   Dearest Lady,
I am not worthy of this high distinction.
You know me not! My home is desolate,
My fortunes overthrown! My name!—my sword—
My honor, and my will, alone, are mine.
  Maria. Why speak to me of fortune? Dost thou fancy,
That she who dares, as I have done, thus boldly,
Beyond the solemn state that guards her sex,
And makes each step, without the narrow pale,
A step along the precipice! dost think,
That such as she gives heed to such obstruction—
Shrinks from the form of poverty, and joys
Only in sleek delights and idle passions!
No, Amador! thy name, thy sword, thy honor,
Are wealth enough for me. If that thy *will*
Be also thine,—thou hast thy answer ready!
I ask thee not to spare me! Speak thy purpose:
I speak to thee as woman cannot speak,
Save, when her heart, filled with one image only,
Forgets the world beside,—its slavish prudence,
And all its worldly policies,—but one.
If thou wilt take me from myself, I am thine!
And, O! believe me, never heart like mine,
Will cling about thy fortunes,—will partake them,
Through scorn, and shame, and grinning poverty,
And smile at all denial—all save thine!
—Speak to me, Amador,—my own speech fails me!
  Bonham. Oh! Lady, how you humble me. In vain
Would I essay to answer thee, in language,
Meet in expression, full of thought and feeling,—
Which love like thine deserveth;—but, I cannot!
  Maria. I understand thee, Senor. Thy reluctance,

To speak, is my reproach. Thou hast no answer
For burning words like mine! Thou feel'st the shame
That I should feel! Look on my face once more—
Not for its beauties, Senor! See the tide,
Of crimson, that rolls over it. My heart
Feels just such burning billows o'er it now!
My woman nature—maidenhood's deep shame—
For that the desperation of my heart,
Moved one to bare what others would conceal,
Through pangs of fiery torture!—Hear me, Señor—
Thou knowest my secret.

 Bonham. It is sacred, Lady.

 Maria. It *shall* be sacred, Señor. Dost thou think,
That I were mad to leave in mortal keeping
Such secret of my shame. Impossible!
It must be razed from out thy memory,
Pluck'd from thy heart;—lest, in thy future hours,
It serve, when nights are dull, and sports grow tame,
To cheer, with provocation to new mirth,
Olivia and her Lord.

 Bonham. You wrong me, Lady—
Nor less your cousin—

 Maria. Señor, on a cast,
I set my maiden fortunes—all my wealth
Of feminine hope, and heart and confidence,
Love that was like devotion—truth without fear,
Even of the cold world's bitter mockery!
The fates make war upon my luckless cast,
Through thee, their scornful minister! What more!
Cans't thou not read the dread necessity,
That drives me, where I would not—into hate!

 Bonham. Why hate?—

 Maria. Or hate, or love, or—nothing!

MICHAEL BONHAM.

Bonham. Nay!
This is but madness, Lady.
   Maria. Amador!
Farewell!—Hereafter, when we chance to meet,
Thou'lt mourn, it may be, that so fond a heart,
So full, to its own sorrow and o'erflow,
Was slighted off so coldly.   [*Going.*
   Bonham. Lady, stay!
   Maria. If thou relentest, Amador, but lift
Thy finger; but if not, no words—no words!
Thy hand still keeps thy side. Farewell! Farewell!
                                         [*Exit Maria.*
   Bonham, [*solus.*] Was ever such a woman! Soul so proud,
And yet so passionate, was never seen!
So prompt at each extreme; in love and hate,
Equally raging; ready with her life,
To prove her heart's devotion; not less ready,
That heart's devotion set at nought or wronged,
Avenging it with life! I pity her,
From my whole soul; would fear her, but that time
Is hurrying onward to that precipice,
Which, overleapt, between her world and ours,
A mighty track of chasm and cloud prevails,
Must separate our steps, forever more!
Give me the gentler heart, who, loving, trembles
With fear, not less than hope; that has no pride
Save in the loved one; whose humility,
Lofty at lowest, with a grace most winning,
Entreating still, where most it may command;
Takes, as a bounty, its best right, and blessing
For favour shown, is favour'd with love's blessing,
With every show of love. But who comes here!
       [*Enter Olivia as a Gipsey Girl.*]

Olivia. Shall I read your thoughts, Father!
Bonham. A hard task,
And a sad volume, pretty sooth-sayer.
 Olivia. I like to read sad volumes, at merry seasons.
I'm sometimes sad myself. Your palm, good Father.
 Bonham. There! Read it quickly, damsel.
 Olivia. Do not hurry me!
Oh, Señor, you're no monk!
 Bonham. What am I then?
 Olivia. A Cavalier! a gallant gentleman!
And what is more, beloved of a fair lady,
The greatest beauty in this gay saloon.
 Bonham. Indeed! But one, my damsel.
 Olivia. Oh, me! What vanity!
As if 'twere not enough to win from Bexar
Its highest prize, at once of wealth and beauty,
But you must have a score.
 Bonham. But who's the lady, damsel?
 Olivia. She who wears
The garb of the great Princess of Papantzin,
She who lies tranced at Mexico, they say,
Even to this hour, still young, still beautiful,
Though twice two hundred years have seen her birth:
—She spoke with you but now
 Bonham. You err, my girl!
That lady loves me not.
 Olivia. 'Tis you that err,
Through modesty, perchance. your sex's failing;
I know she loves you! By my art, I know it,
And all that live in Bexar will inform you,
How great her loveliness, how vast her wealth:
But you have seen her; have you not?

Bonham.   I have!
Olivia. Is she not beautiful?
Bonham.   Very beautiful!
Olivia, [*mournfully.*] Ah! I knew you'd think so!
Bonham. Wherefore do you sigh?
Olivia. At your good fortune, Señor. You will be
The envy of all Bexar! 'Tis not often
A stranger makes such conquest. Doubtless now,
You have forgot some other vows: I know it:
Some other maid, in secret sighs—forsaken,
For your new passion.
   Bonham.   'Tis I that am forsaken!
Were you, indeed, the mistress of your art,
You'd know that true to all my bosom's pledges,
The maid I loved. who vow'd to me her heart,
Has failed me, and is false!
   Olivia. She is not false!
   Bonham. Ha! Speak!
   Olivia, [*aside.*] Ah, me! my soul; she comes again!
—Senor, behold your conquest, where she comes,
Princess Papantzin. On this talisman,
I close your hand. 'Twill keep you to your faith,
If even in your heart the flame of love,
Burned for another.
[*She closes his hand upon the antique cross, and disappears just as Donna Maria enters.*

   Bonham, [*seeing it.*] Ah! can it be! Olivia!
She's gone! I'll seek her!   [*Is about to go.*
   Maria. Senor, stay!
   Bonham. Princess!
   Maria. Nay! not another word of mockery!
You know me as the woman that I am,
Most weak when strongest, or I had not come,

Once more, to bare the weakness of a heart,
Already too much scorned!
   Bonham.   Cruel Lady!
Ungenerous as unjust. Too well you know
Such feeling in this bosom never yet,
Mock'd the fond heart in yours.
   Maria.   Hear me, Senor!
I said I had your secret. Until now,
I knew not that, beneath this priestly garb,
Other than gallant Cavalier was hid;
But now, indeed, your secret is my own!
You are a traitor here. I know you now,
A Texan rebel; whose position here,
Dooms him to death, a sudden and a sure,
From hands of hate and vengeance!
   Bonham.   Ha!
   Maria. Dost hear!
Your comrade, the Camanche, has betrayed you!
   Bonham. How know you this! By whom! How!
       Where!
   Maria. To me he has betray'd you. Thoughtlessly,
Beguiled to speak, he answered me in English,
A tongue I little know; but in the ears,
Of keen suspicion, wrought upon by passion,
The understanding quickens: a brief sentence,
Fell from his lips; but that sufficed to show me,
Your secret, and his own.
   Bonham. What secret, Lady?
   Maria. Would you evade,—deny? Are you not then,
A Texan? One, who, found in Bexar's walls,
Stands in the two-fold danger of the spy
As well as rebel!

MICHAEL BONHAM.

Bonham. To other ears than yours,
Dear Lady, it were easy to deny
Connexion with the man you deem my comrade.
  Maria. Himself declared it!
  Bonham. Impossible!
  Maria. How Senor: my own ears—
  Bonham. Deceived you, Lady.
  Maria. Nay, Senor, that were more impossible.
My heart was on his accents, for I knew him
Your comrade. I had seen you both together,
Whispering in seeming confidence. At noon
You were in close communion on the Plaza,
Too close to seem the common chance encounter,
Of unconnected strangers.
  Bonham, [*aside.*] It needs but time!
How must I play the masquer with the heart,
And lull to sleep the vigilance of hers.
  Maria. You muse: You meditate!
  Bonham. Methinks it needs,
I should not answer rashly. Grant it said,
This person is my comrade. If I err not,
You are not here in simple mockery,
To tell me of the doom, the shot, the scaffold!
You have a purpose!
  Maria. I have a purpose, Senor!
Down woman pride; down, swelling heart; be still,
Ye struggling thoughts of shame, that threaten me,
With worst of human scorn—the scorn of him,
Whose love is all I seek. Oh, gaze not, Senor,
While I declare this purpose. I am come
To buy you with your secret.
  Bonham. Do I hear!
You cannot mean it, Lady.

Maria. By my shame,
I do! I do! How low this passion sinks me,
To what abasement of my soul and feeling,
My sex's pride, my maiden modesty,
I need not more describe! Fatal passion,
That flings me, shameless, on unwilling arms!
 Bonham. Let me have time to think—to—
 Maria. Not an hour!
Speak in your peril, in your hate, your passion;
With all your doubts upon you; all your fears:
—With thought, you will despise me.
 Bonham. But one hour!
 Maria. Why a moment? The question is your fate
   or mine:
—Your safety from a doom—a death of shame:
Mine from a life more full of it.
 Bonham. One hour;
Give me one hour for thought.
 Maria. Alas! I give it;
But you speak coldly. You will play me false:
You meditate escape! Oh, bitterness!
That I should sink to this.
 Bonham. One little hour.
 Maria. Be it so. 'Tis now eleven; at twelve!
 Bonham. My life then, Lady—
 Maria. Your love! Your love! O, Senor,
I cannot now be generous! Do not hate me,
If, to the very moment of your promise,
In my despair, I hold you! [*Exit Maria.*
 Bonham. Be it so.
The hour must find the answer! I have none.

   Enter Crockett.

 Bonham. Ah, David, you have ruined me: your tongue!

Crockett. Dang the tongue, say I. I've never been quite the master of it since I went to Congress. But Lord love you, Major, how could you hear of it? It was the merest slip; a fag end of speech; a sort of little eend of an argument. The truth is, I was taken in by that Queen, or Empress, or whatever she is. In the very midst of her Spanish talk, not a word of which did I understand, and so warn't bound to answer, you know, what does she do, but pops out upon me some broken English about you, and before I could say Jack Robinson, I had said a great deal more. I hope there's no harm done!

Bonham. Ay, but there is.

Crockett. What shall be done! Suppose I go and make love to her, out and out—in airnest.

Bonham. Do nothing. Be in readiness. Be prudent. Let not your tongue be trapp'd again. An hour Will end your doubts and mine. Away, and leave me: Be not remote; but keep aloof from me.

Crockett. Dickins! But I wish 'twas well over. I feel for all the world as if I was walking in the dark, in a snake country, every step among stings and rattles. [*Going, but returning.*] Oh, look you, Major, I'm thinking you're watched rather closely by that sailor looking critter, yonder; him there by the urn, or vase, or whatever fine people call that great drenching jug. You see him! He turns his head away, as I look towards him.

Bonham. He may mean evil. Keep your eye upon him, And that may save you from a second lapse. But let us separate, now.   [*Exit Bonham.*

Crockett. Only give me work to do, if you wouldn't have me in mischief. That sailor's after no good. He turns just as the Major turns, and now he follows him! Well, as there's no lady in the business, I'll play a third.

Any hand but Dummy's, which no man can play after he gets popular. That fellow's after no good. He dogs the Major mighty close; but I'll be the dog for him. He shall have teeth, but no tongue! [*Exit Crockett.*

Enter Olivia. Still as the Gipsey.

Olivia, [aside.] My cousin does not conquer! Her impatience
Speaks in her gesture. Whither has he gone?
Ah, there she comes, again! She seems to seek him:
I must not meet with her.
[*Exit Olivia.*

[*Enter Maria and Jacintha—the latter as a Shepherdess.*]

Maria. Can it be true! She here!

Jacintha. True, Senora, every word of it; and there, as I live, she's going now! This very moment.

Maria. Where!

Jacintha. There!

Maria. What, the Gipsey?

Jacintha. The very same!

Maria. And they have met: these eyes have seen him with her;
His hand in hers, conversing with their palms.
Oh! Hate! they love. I see his purpose now:
She flies to meet him. Married in an hour,
He will disarm the anger of the father,
By pleading through the daughter. But I'll balk them;
Come vengeance, to thy work. Away from me,
All weaknesses of love. Though scorn'd, though baffled,
Hopeless in heart, exposed to mock and shame,
Revenge shall yet be mine. Hither Jacintha.
Where did you see my uncle?

Jacintha. With Don José and Don Velasquez, at the Monti tables.

Maria. Auspicious: follow me!

[*Exeunt.*

SCENE V.

A gaming apartment. The Governor, with several persons in military guise, at the table. Don Pedro standing against a column, looking on sullenly. Don Valasquez, of the Cavalry, and Col. Don Sanchez, of the Artillery, at the table, with the Governor.

Governor. I shall surprise you, yet! Upon the red!

Velasquez. The black for me! If I have luck at all,
'Tis in that colour.

Sanchez. Colour of luck for me,
Seems in no colour of the cards to-night.
Methinks, Don Pedro frowns upon our sport:
He does not play.

Governor. Ah, my brave son-in-law,
Don Pedro; where's your spirits?

Pedro. In the red;
If that be deep enough to look like blood.

Governor. You're too bloody-minded! Where's the humour
Of savage thoughts like these? Look to the ladies,
Unless you care to play.

Pedro. Is it not time
That *you* should look to them?

Governor. Ay, very soon: the hour—
Is close upon the signal! There! [*Flinging a card.*]

Velasquez. And there! [*Flinging cards.*]
Sanchez, [*flinging cards and money.*] And there
    am I. The old predicament!
I'll play no more!   [*Rises.*
  Velasquez.   An hundred ounces gone!
  Governor.   Ha, ha! my worthy colonel.
  Sanchez.   Done, sir, done.
*Enter Maria suddenly. They all rise but Esteban, who
    does not see her. She touches his arm.*

  Maria. Sleeps Cæsar, when conspiracy awakes,
And treason, far apart, with mask and dagger,
Watches the fatal moment when to strike.
  Governor. How's this. What's this. Ha! my fair
    princess,—you!
What! with *your* secrets and your stratagems.
  Maria. Even so. Away with me: your ears awhile;
I'll ope them with a vengeance.
  Governor.   What's all this!
    [*Exeunt Gov. and Maria. Scene closes.*

SCENE VI.

*As in Scene I. The Bal Masqué. Enter Olivia hur-
    riedly.*

  Olivia, [*solus.*] His life! The life of Amador! A
    traitor—
A Texian rebel! He, my love—my soul!
Where shall I find—how save him—from this danger?
Oh, cruel cousin, failing to usurp
The love that was mine only, must thou rob
Him of his life and me of all the hope

MICHAEL BONHAM.

That made life precious to me? I must find him—
Save him, or perish with him!

Enter Bonham.

Bonham. My life! My love!
Olivia. My Amador! My heart! You are in danger.
You are betrayed! My cousin, to my father,
Reveals your secret. By a happy chance,
Concealed behind a column in the chamber,
I heard her cruel story—saw the passion
Which, in her face and voice, disclosed the fury
Of woman's passion baffled. She has told him
That, by her arts detected, you confess'd
Yourself a Texian rebel—spy in Bexar,—
You and your comrade. Oh, my Amador,
Even now they threaten. Tell me, is it true:
Are you this traitor?
Bonham. What, if I confess?
Olivia. Ah, me, my heart!
Bonham. The foe to Mexico,
But not to you, Olivia. False, perchance,
To all beside but thee.
Olivia. Alas! my Amador,
What is it that you tell me.
Bonham. That I am true to thee.
Olivia. Are you a Texian?
Bonham. I am.
Olivia. But not a Texian rebel.
Bonham. A Texian citizen! The friend of Freedom,
Rebellious 'gainst injustice—born to fight
'Gainst every tyrant that between the sun,
And man, his victim, rears his giant shadow.
This was the earliest lesson of my youth
Taught by rare ancestors. Among the States,

Honored among the empires of the North,
Stand two fair sisters. On the map behold
The Carolinas! She that nearest lies
To your own land, my love, is land of mine.
Upon the hills of Congaree, I first
Drew breath of freedom. Thence I came to succor
Our friends in Texas. Seeking for the foe,
By Loro's springs, in place of him, I found
A trembling fawn, and Love.
 Olivia.   My Amador!
 Bonham. If still I wage the war with Mexico,
I do it with half a heart—with fettered hands,
For love, that takes the place of hate, disarms
My soul of half its fury. Thou know'st all—
Dost hate me now, Olivia?
 Olivia.   Hate thee? Oh, no!
How should I hate thee.
 Bonham.   Hear me, Olivia—
An hour will make me captive to my foes,
Or see my triumph over them. Even now,
Behold, the crowd is stirring. They prepare—
The women disappear. The masques
Survey us from afar. All things declare
For the approaching struggle. Art thou mine?
Wilt thou be mine?—mine only—let the fates
Declare them as they may!
 Olivia, Thine—only thine.
 Bonham. Then come the foe. Let the wild storm
   begin;
I'm cased against its dangers. In my heart,
Whate'er the evil without, sits smiling hope,
Secure in sweet communion with the thoughts
That wait on happy love. But hasten thou,

MICHAEL BONHAM.

And, in the costume of the nun, prepare
To mate with me in flight. Away! they come.
                              [*Exit Olivia.*
[*Bonham retires to one side of the stage, leans against a column in an indifferent attitude. Enter on the opposite side the Governor, Don Pedro, Don Velasquez, Col. Don Sanchez, the Bravo, and other masques.*
  Pedro, [*to Esteban.*] What! shall we scruple now!
        Hold parley here,
In presence of the spy?
  Esteban.   He hears us not.
  Pedro. But sees us, and that's quite enough for shame,
If we stand gazing at him through our fears,
When that one cry, from fiery hate should be,
Upon him, Braves, at once!
  Esteban.   You are too rash;
Leave it to me. I'll manage it, my friends,
So that no danger—to the ladies, mark me—
  Pedro.   They are all gone.
  Esteban. Patience! A little stratagem—
  Pedro. And where the need of little stratagem
To take or slay one man? We've but to rush—
  Esteban. Indeed! and get his bullet in your brains.
No, no. We'll act more wisely. Go you, Sanchez,
And bring a score of men, with muskets ready;
Meanwhile we'll parley with him.
  Pedro.   Parley with him:
Parley with shame and cowardice!
  Esteban. You're but young, Don Pedro, wait the
        event,
And see the uses of my stratagem:
I'll show you reasons for it.

[*He leads Pedro and the rest up the stage, while Bonham advances, and rests against a column in the foreground. While this takes place, Olivia, in the guise of a nun, has rejoined him; placing herself on the opposite side of the column upon which he leans, and partly behind him.*

Olivia, [*whispers him.*]   I am here, Amador.
Bonham, [*with a glad start.*]   Ah, faithful! You are
   here.
Olivia.   To die with you!
Bonham. Nay, never say to die. We shall *not* die;
Life is too precious now to me, my girl,
With such a treasure. I have friends at hand;
Have weapons in my grasp. We shall not perish.
   Olivia.   Harm not my father, Amador.
   Bonham.   His head
Is sacred in my sight. I will not hurt
A single hair that claims thy love. But hence;
Hide thee within yon niche. They come.
                        [*Exit Olivia.*

   Esteban, Pedro and others re-approach.
Pedro.   To falter thus,
With but one foe against a score of us.
   Esteban. Ah, but the benefits of stratagem.
You are but young, my son; art brave, but lack
The wisdom that still teaches how to venture,
And calculates the blow before it strikes.
Never press closely on a desperate man;
He drives an ugly bargain for his life,
And gains the odds before he loses it:
We'll parley with him.
[*Advances to Bonham, slowly followed by the rest. Bonham retains his position.*

Esteban. Most reverend father, I implore your blessing.

Bonham. You have it, son.

Esteban. Most fitly answered—with becoming grace,
And holy unction. But most reverend father,
There are about me those, my counsellors,
Sage, grave, and potent gentlemen, brave chiefs,
Famous in battle, next in great repute
To him, the warrior more than all renowned,
Whom Fame has styled " Napoleon of the West"—
I say there are, who somewhat doubt your zeal,
Who make some question of your holiness,
And strangely do proclaim you nothing better—

Bonham. Than hungry wolf in wool of meeker beast.

Esteban. How excellently said. But, reverend father,
Though not without some curious doubts myself,
Methinks they wrong you much; and, with your leave,
I'd ask you certain matters.

Bonham. Cæsar may speak!

Esteban. Full of discernment! Upon your arm, my father,
You bear the holy symbol of your faith,
But do you ever lift it to your lips?

Bonham, [*kissing the cross.*] Behold!

Esteban, [*aside to Pedro.*] He could not do it better,
were he the Archbishop
Of Mexico. Tell me that any heretic will kiss
Holy Cross. I know better.

Pedro. Pshaw!

Esteban. Mark the further progress of my stratagem.
Hem!
And now another question, Holy Father,

Bonham. It needs not, Senor. I will spare you trouble,
Spare you some breath, and answer ere you ask me—
I am suspected, first!

Esteban. No, not exactly, but—

Bonham. 'Tis so. I see it in the eyes of all,
And hear it in your accents.

Esteban. Nay, good father! You are too quick, but say that something of this sort is the difficulty, and you will at once see the propriety, and the prudence, and the necessity, of accepting my protection! My officers, you perceive, are furious: it will not be possible to restrain them; they are terrible as lions in rage, and your only hope of safety is in—

Bonham. There needs no parley, Senors. Your fierce warriors,
Are not so dreadful in mine eyes, to make me
Seek your protection. You would have my secret.
'Tis yours! Know me a Texian, and your enemy!

[*Throws off the monkish disguise, and appears as a Texian warrior, with hunting shirt, bowie-knife, sword and belt with pistols.*]

Esteban, [*recoiling.*] My eyes! Was ever such a stratagem!

Pedro. Upon the traitor!

Bonham, [*presenting a revolving Colt.*] Upon him with what appetite you may!
This little weapon counts a score of lives:
Each ready jaw is open for its victims.
Who first? Is't you—or you—or you? What, none!

[*They severally recoil as the pistol is presented.*]

What, Cæsar, are these cohorts from Pharsalia?

Pedro. Oh! shame; shall this one traitor mock us thus.

Upon him all at once—but one can perish!
    Bonham. And you that one! But ere you muster
        courage
For deed so brave, I'll summon to the game
An equal set of players.   [*Winds his bugle, and
    that of Crockett's sounds.*
Hear ye that?
And that?   [*Another bugle: from the rear.*
    Pedro.   Treason is busy!
    Esteban.   What a stratagem!
Ring the alarm bell. Bring up the troops;
Fly you, Don José, for the cavalry;
Look, Don Velasquez, for the infantry;
Don Sanchez, see to the artillery:
At once unmuzzle! I will take command.
See you, Don Pedro, to Don Amador;
Let him not escape you. Set upon him, fellows—
Do not fear danger. Fly to it as I do!
                [*Exit Esteban.*
    Pedro, [*to Canales, the Bravo, aside.*]
Get thee behind him. When we charge in front,
Make in upon him, and with shortened dagger
Make the work short!
    Bonham.   Ye are slow to quarrel!
Ye lack the violent spirit of your chief,
And do not fly to danger.
    Pedro, [*aside.*]   He disappears—
Another moment brings him through the chamber,
And the game's ours!
Ho! my brave fellows, must we stand defied
By one foul traitor! Shame upon this baseness;
Give me your hearts and hands. From all your throats
Send up the cry of death—Death to the traitor!

Mexicans. Death to the traitor!
Pedro, [*whistle heard.*] The signal! He is there.
Upon him *now!*
[*Olivia shrieks from behind.*
Bonham. That voice! That shriek!
Crockett, [*from behind.*] Hurrah! She's safe!
[*Struggle heard, and blows, within.*
There's for you, leather jacket;—
A feather for your cap, or I'm mistaken!

[*Bonham is about to turn, when the shout of Crockett re-assures him. The Bravo is driven in, staggering from a wound in the head, at the very moment when the attack is made on Bonham in front. The Bravo passes between him and Pedro, and receives the shot meant for the latter. At this sight, and the entrance of Crockett, the assailants recoil.*]

Bonham. What, do ye pause! Is all your courage
gone,
With one poor puff of battle? Lo, we stand,
My comrade and myself awaiting you—
But two to twenty!
Pedro. Were our weapons equal,
I'd mate with you alone.
Bonham. Ha! say you so?
Upon these dastards, Davy, like the rush,
Of the flame-torrent o'er the prairie's waste;
Sweep them from sight, while I—This gallant seems
More valiant than his comrades; we must hold
Meet conference together; point to point,
In private. Art thou satisfied? [*To Pedro as he
puts up his pistol and draws.*
Pedro. I am!
Look to it! [*Rushes on—they fight.*

MICHAEL BONHAM.

Crockett. You have the best of it, Major; you've the man,
But there! I'm good for any twenty.
  [*Swings his rifle over his head, and rushing upon them, drives them out.*
 Bonham, [*while fighting with Pedro.*] Bravo, comrade,
You've done your work to shame me. Now for mine!
But fly you to the Alamo. It is ours.
I hear the signal. I will follow you!
      [*Presses Pedro back.*
 Pedro. Hell's curse upon my weakness!
 Bonham, [*disarming him.*] 'Tis already. Behold!
A second time, my mercy
Has suffer'd you to live. Beware the third!
 Pedro. Demonios! I am blasted. [*Exit.*
 Bonham. Now for Olivia,—to a place of safety
She must be borne, and then—my life! my love!
    Enter Olivia.
 Olivia.   Art safe?
 Bonham. As love could wish.
 Olivia. What mean these clamours, Amador?—that shouting.
 Bonham. The sound of combat: said I not, Olivia,
That I had friends and arms? We shall not perish.
 Olivia. Ah! but my father.
 Bonham. We shall care for him.
But let me bear you to a place of safety.
 Olivia.   Where?
 Bonham. The Convent of La Guayra. Come—away!
The moments now are precious: precious lives
Depend upon them. Fear'st thou me, Olivia?
This Texian rebel, traitor, spy!

Olivia.   Ah, no more—
I love thee; fear thee not: will fly with thee!
  Bonham.   We shall be happy!   [*Exeunt.*
          Enter Donna Maria.
  Maria.   The Convent of La Guayra!
All is not lost to vengeance as to love;
The serpent now must overcome the dove.   [*Exit.*

          END OF PART IV.

PART V.—SCENE I.

The streets of San Antonio. The clamor and confusion of a rout, mixed with the occasional uproar, keen and quick, of a melée à outrance. Mexicans, half-armed and in great consternation, flying across the stage, pursued by the Texians. Enter Alabama Davis, Richard Harris, William Harris, and others, with signs of blood and battle.

Davis. This is no fighting, comrade.
R. Harris. Fighting! No—
I'm scarcely breathed for battle.
Davis. Wait awhile;
We soon shall hear from Milam.
R. Harris. He has gone
Against the Alamo.
Davis There'll be fighting there:
It is their citadel.
R. Harris. Let us join him then.
We can do nothing here. We find no foe
Worthy the name. Such panic-bitten wretches
But sicken me to see. What wait we for?
Davis. The signal.
R. Harris. Would it sound then. How I pant
For danger!
[*Bugle sounds livelily at a distance.*
Davis. Hark! We have it now.

R. Harris. Let's away.

W. Harris, [*to R. Harris, putting his hand on his arm.*] Why haste you thus to death?

R. Harris. I seek it, boy.
But you! You follow closely. So much fear,
Yet so much rashness.

W. Harris. My rashness comes from fear;
I dread to stop behind.

R. Harris. You should be with your mother.

W. Harris, [*aside.*] Would I were!

R. Harris Follow me closely. You are, at my side
Much safer than behind.

Davis. [*Sounds of conflict.*] They're at it now.
The shot is sharp and heavy.

R. Harris. Hurra for death!
The old King Death that takes the crown from all,
Whose subjects are the living; throne's the tomb,
Whose columns compass earth. Hurra for Death!

Davis. For victory rather. On, brave comrades, on!

W. Harris. I must go forward. Heaven have mercy
on me!

[*Exeunt Davis, Harris and Texians.*

Enter Governor still as Julius Cæsar, with his sword drawn, making desperate passes in the air. He stops breathlessly.

Governor. Phew! Was ever such a stratagem! That fellow has a head for a prime minister. With what skill, what coolness, what audacity, he lied through the whole scheme; and so brave too—that is another merit. Holy Mother! But he looked fierce enough to swallow a regiment. Jesu send that Pedro make mince meat of him. It were my ruin if he does not. What will his Excellency, Señor Don Lopez de Santa Anna, say? Say! He will read my despatches—the rebel army annihilated!—and lo! here it is anew, with San Antonio in their hands. Who could have thought it? But there is the Alamo yet. They **will eat bullets before they get that.** [*Shouts.*] Ha! more shouts. The enemy in front—between me and the Alamo. Cæsar help me! I am good only at the strategic part of the warfare. The subordinate parts—the mere physical struggle,—blows and shouting,—these are for the common soldier. Santa Maria! They are on all sides. They are here, and there, and everywhere. They come. The sounds thicken. At least they shall find me sword in hand.

[*As he is about to rush out, Enter Sparrow, who confronts him. Sparrow is out of breath and almost speechless.*

Sparrow. Ho! ha! who—who are you? An enemy at all events. Have at you, breath or no breath. [*Governor flies, and encounters Crockett at the wing, and is thrown down in the concussion. Sparrow, who has been pursuing him, falls upon and grapples him.*] Ha' ho! The captive to my bow and spear. Shall I *spear* him, or *spare* him?

Crockett. Don't eat him, Sparrow, at all events.

Sparrow. Let him holler 'nough, then.

Crockett. I reckon he would if he could talk English, or if he could talk at all, with such a mountain upon him. Rise, old fellow, you are not upon a horse that you should keep up such an awful joggling. Do you know who you've got under you?

Sparrow. Ay! a fat fellow like myself—with more bulk than breath. Eh! Who?

Crockett. You are straddling no less a person than his Excellency, the Governor of San Antonio.

Sparrow. The devil you say!

Crockett. No. I say the Governor. Up, terrapin, and give him breath.

Sparrow. Breath! By the powers! but that's impossible. Give what I hav'nt got myself? The thing's beyond my generosity. But I'll tell you what I will give him Davy.

Crockett. What?

Sparrow What he wants quite as much—quarter. He lies quiet enough, all but the blowing.

Crockett. And reason equally good for both quiet and blowing, with such a mountain of meat upon him. But don't be too sure of his quiet. He's a famous fellow for stratagems.

Sparrow. Ah, say you so? Then I'll rise with caution and deliberation. [*Rising with difficulty.*] It's one reason why I never like to get down; i's so very troublesome to get up again. [*Governor groans.*

Crockett. He seems to be relieved. He's coming to. That grunt was good English.

Sparrow. Yes. I understand it. He will probably understand me now. [*Governor rises assisted by Sparrow.* Hark ye, Don Buffalo, your sword, or you shall have mine.

[*Solicits the sword of Esteban with the left hand, while threatening with his bowie knife. The Governor recoils, but yields his weapon.*

Crockett. He takes you at your word. Who says these fellows don't understand English?

Sparrow. Ah, when one speaks *pointedly* to them. We've only to use a steel pen. I'll try him again in English—he gets on so well. Hark ye, Don Buffalo, set forward, or I'll— [*Makes a show with bowie.*

Crockett. He learns famous fast—does jist as you wish him.

Sparrow. I'faith, yes. It's wonderful. Hereafter we'll call an American bowie, an English grammar—an accidence—a sort of first Beginner for young Mexicans;—the very *rudi*ments of the language.

Crockett. Ay! and a handful of rifle-bullets, the seven parts of speech—seven is it, or nine?

Sparrow. It don't matter much. They're to learn the language, not we. But I must give this great fellow his third lesson. On, Don Buffalo! [*Pricks him with bowie. Governor winces and goes forward.*

Crockett. That's what you call a bloody noun, Sparrow.

Sparrow. Clearly. You see how he likes to *decline* it. But look you, Davy, what chance of breakfast in these diggings? After such a night as we have had, one is apt to hunger a little.

Crockett. Well, there was a famous fine supper cooking in the Governor's kitchen last night, but I reckon it's all burnt up afore now.

Sparrow. Burnt up, while we stand here doing nothing, literally nothing—for the country. I'll save it though I perish! Show me to this kitchen—this palace. Let them fight who want to. I have done enough for this bout. A man of my years is not expected to be everywhere. My prisoner will answer for me—what I have done. On, Don Buffalo! I'm mighty sorry to hurry a man of your dimensions; but look at mine—and I am in a hurry. But I will be amicable, even while I push you, and I promise you that we will breakfast together at your own tables.

Governor, [*aside and going.*] What a stratagem! What a stratagem! Bexar lost, and Esteban de Montaneros a captive! It is something to be able to say that I was taken sword in hand.

Sparrow. Slide, my good Don of Buffaloes, your speed
Is needful, if we both again would feed.
  Crockett. Give him more grammar, Sparrow. Blood and 'ouns,
Try him in verbs, and lesson him in nouns,
Until he learns my maxim which, if spread
Through Mexico, would send 'em all ahead!
[*Exeunt omnes. Sparrow pressing Don Esteban with the point of his bowie knife.*

SCENE II.

The flight approaches the walls of the Alamo. A contested battle field. Alarums. The Mexican infantry recovering under Don Sanchez.

  Sanchez. We yet outnumber the rebels. We are two to one.
Fear nothing, men of Bexar. It needs only one
Bold effort. Follow me. We'll meet them at the
Northern gate of the Alamo.
  Mexican soldier. They're *in* the Alamo!
  Sanchez. What then! We'll drive them out. They are but
Few. We shall keep them fighting on both sides—
Within and without. Come on! God and the republic!
                    [*Exeunt Mexicans.*
    Enter Milam and Texians.
  Milam. They fly before us. They can hold no ground

MICHAEL BONHAM.

With the old Saxon stock. My merry men,
But one more tug and the whole field is ours!

Enter Crockett.

Crockett. Hurrah! hurrah! the Governor's in our hands,
Captured by Sparrow!

Milam. Hear you that, brave fellows,
The Governor's in our hands. The biggest beast
In Bexar captive to the smallest bird
That ever flew from Georgia.

Texians, [*cheering.*] Hurra for Sparrow!

Milam. Here's Crockett too—
Brave Dave, himself a host.

Texians. [*cheering.*] Hurra for Davy Crockett—Congress Davy.

Milam. Where's Bonham?

Crockett. Is he not here!

Milam. I have not seen him.

Crockett. We parted soon after your first bugle. We had it, tooth and nail, in the ball-room. Twenty to two; and lathered 'em like all the world. I left the Major with his prize.

Milam. What prize?

Crockett. A woman. The Governor's daughter! He's a fellow that can love and fight in the same breath.

Milam. No doubt he's in the Alamo! Harris there,
With less than thirty men, maintains his ground,
In full possession. The foe without, o'ercome,
And town and citadel alike are ours.
One gallant effort more my merry men,
And you may sleep on glory!

Crockett. Ay, or in it!

[*Exeunt.*

Chorus of Texians as they follow.
We will show them that the bold,
   Still inherit all the fruits,
And their moustaches and gold,
   We will pluck up by the roots!

SCENE III.

A wood under the walls of the Alamo. Mexicans partially seen within it. Enter Milam, Crockett and Texians.

   Milam. Behold the enemy! They seem prepared,
But will not stand our ouset. Follow me,
To victory, and, if I fall, avenge me.
[*Rushes on. A shot strikes him down. The Mexicans shout—the Texians waver.*
   Enter Bonham.
   Bonham. What! shrink ye from these dastards—men of straw.
That fight in vapour—never show red-blood,
Or sicken at sight of it. For shame!
The old Thirteen, the great Southwest, the North,
The Carolinas, Georgia, Tennessee,
Countries of Bunker Hill and Saratoga,
Cowpens and Eutaw, Moultrie's isle, Savannah,
Are looking to your actions, as their sons,—
They must not be dishonored! To that howl
Of these faint-hearted Mexicans—these braggarts,

MICHAEL BONHAM.

Give answer, my brave comrades, with another,
Shall make them shake with agues. Milam's down!
Stone dead! But what of that: his spirit rises
Above us now, and summons us to vengeance.
Out, bowie knives, and let the work be close;
I'll show ye to begin it. Follow me!

[*Charge. Texians rush onward with a shout. Battle fluctuates. At length the Mexicans disappear—the Texians following, leaving in the field of battle a group, Richard Harris dying, and William Harris supporting his head.*

R. Harris. My head swims round. The shadows on my sight
Grow darker. What I've pray'd for is at hand—
I'm dying! Who is it that holds my hand?

W. Harris. 'Tis I—Will Harris.

R. Harris. Faithful to the last;
You've clung to me in danger. But it's over;
The victory is ours—that's sure;—you're safe.

W. Harris. But you!

R. Harris. Will soon be safer still. I'm dying fast!

W. Harris. Oh, God forbid, and spare you!

R. Harris. Wherefore? I
Have rather need of mercy than of life!

W. Harris. May God have mercy on you!

R. Harris. That's right,
Pray for me. I have need of every prayer.
I've been a cold and cruel criminal—
Have spurn'd all natural ties.

W. Harris, [*sobs convulsively.*] Alas! alas!

R. Harris. How is this boy! You sob—you weep for me,
As if I were some dearest relative.

W. Harris. You are! you are! Oh, Richard, look
   upon me;
Do you know me *now?*
   [*Throws off her cap and lets down her hair.*
 R. Harris. My reason's gone, I think—or, is it Ellen?
 W. Harris.   It is! It is!
She that was once your own, your only!
 R. Harris.   Is
My own—my only still! Hear me, Ellen,
I'll buy your last forgiveness. In my bosom
Search for the packet. It contains the papers
That prove your marriage—the certificate;—
You'll find it sealed with blood!—from Parson Baker.
Believing you had played me false, I slew him,
To hush for ever the last living proof
Of our unhappy union.
 W. Harris. Merciful Heaven!
 R. Harris. Nor he alone! Your brother John pur-
   sued me,
Because of your dishonor—so he deemed it;—
He perish'd by these hands!
 W. Harris. Have mercy on him, Heaven!
Let not these murders hang about his soul,
Dragging it downwards.
 R. Harris   Pray. I'm failing fast.
I loved you all the while—believe me, Ellen;
And when, at last, I found that you were true,
I would have come to you again, but dared not,
Your brother's blood upon my hands and soul.
Come closer—let me hear you; in my ears
Still tell me of forgiveness. Christ! have mercy!
Look down upon me! Would that I had time
For pray'r; but no! I cannot. Death is rushing

Fast on my heart. His icy fingers grapple
My throat. I choke! My dearest Ellen! [*Dies.*
  W. Harris. His lips are cold. He stiffens in my
    arms.
I hear his voice no more. Have mercy Heaven!
Mercy on both! Oh, take us both together!
    [*Sinks upon the body as the scene closes.*

SCENE IV.

A court of the palace. Pedro and Donna Maria.

  Pedro.   Art sure of what thou tells't me?
  Maria.   Ay, as sure,
As pride and hate made jealous of the object
Can make eye, ear and spirit. To Laguayra,
I saw them speed together. Seek her there.
Clothed in the habit of some fallen Texian
One of your followers. Let him bear a message
As if from Amador. Bid her forth to him,
And take her to herself. Bear her away,
Fast as your love may carry you, to Rosas,
There wed her as you may.
  Pedro.   The plan's a good one.
  Maria.   'Tis the only plan.
  Pedro.   I'll do it.
  Maria.   And do't at once!
Or, ere another hour he does it for you,
And we are baffled still.
  Pedro.   I half despond—

So oft already baffled!

Maria. Because too slow!
You linger now, when on the wings of love,
As I on those of hate, your arm should snatch
The pride of conquest from the unwilling fortune.
Go to! are you a lover and a man,
And talk of being baffled. Man or woman,
True to the lordly instincts of their souls,
Are never baffled.

Pedro. You should have been a man.

Maria. Oh! would I had been. Even now, a woman,
Had I but sway'd in counsel—had you listened,
This night had never happ'd. Delay no more,
Lest that the grinning fortune mock you still
With baffled love and vengeance, in full cry,
With " Hadst thou been a man!"

Pedro. I am a man!

Maria. Prove it then,
In 'haviour of a bold one.

Pedro. In one hour,
She shall be mine forever.

Maria. Yield no hour,
But take the fortune in its moment mood,
Or all the golden opportunity
Goes to the common loss. Away with you,
Nor linger at her pleadings. Hearken not
Her cries and supplication. Make your ears
Deaf to all plea, all passion but your own;
And with most absolute certainty make her yours,
In spite of hell or heaven!

Pedro. By Heaven, I will! [*Exit Pedro.*

Maria. Ay! had I been a man, this night of shame
Had never left such record. I have sunk

MICHAEL BONHAM.

Deeper than plummet's cast in the deep sea,
In all that makes the glory of our sex;—
Its holy calm, its whiteness, purity—
The all, that far beyond its hope's fruition,
Were needful to its life. I cannot live,
Unless for vengeance. Vengeance must be mine!
And I will have it, if, faithful to his strength,
This man obeys my counsel. She shall fall
From her high pride of place. She knows my secret—
But shall not gloat, in future state secure,
On the possession. And for him!—for him!
Alas! I love him still!—the fatal passion
Works quivering in my heart, where still one hope
Looks to his passion for the generous sunshine
To gladden it with growth. [*Distant cannon is heard.*
                      The battle rages,
And the deep roar of the destroying cannon
Proclaim the assault upon the Alamo now.
Let them roar on! My soul, in a like tempest,
Glads in the echoes that still speak for passions
As terrible as mine own. But hark!—these voices!
And he—he here already! He pursues her.
Her flight discovered! I must thwart him now—
By proper artifice must check his search,
While Pedro takes the prey. We must gain time,
Or all is lost once more.
            [*Veils herself and seems to retires.*
      Enter Bonham with Texians.

Bonham.   Who's here?
  Maria, [*in affected terror.*] Spare me! Protect me,
      Señor, from this danger—
These ruffian soldiery!
  Bonham.   Donna Maria!

Bonham,   Yes, 'tis well,
Dear lady, that we meet. These are not hours,
When, without proper guardianship, your sex
May rove the streets of Bexar. Be't my care
To have you guarded to a place of safety,
Where you will find your uncle.
   Maria.   Ah, Señor! can it be
That I have forfeited the happy claim
I had upon you in less hapless hours?
   Bonham.   What mean you, lady?
   Maria.   Do I hear aright?
You yield me to the fierce and brutal soldier,
For guardianship, at this all-licensed hour,
When plunder keeps the city, and blind fury
Whets every fearful passion known to man!
   Bonham. The men who shall attend you—
   Maria.   Better none.
I thank you, Señor: leave me to my fate!
   Bonham. Oh, lady, how you wrong me: but with *me*
I pray you be secure. Wilt suffer me,
To guard you to Don Esteban?
   Maria.   Señor, perchance
I cross more pleasant duties. You have cares
That need your presence elsewhere.
   Bonham.   None to suffer,
By seeing you in safety.
  Mara, [*aside.*] Ay, cheat thyself with that, until too
         late,
Thou wakest, to know that woman conquers still,
And, weak in vulgar weapon, works by will!
                   [*Exeunt Omnes.*

SCENE V.

A chamber in the castle, the Alamo, Governor Don Esteban de Montaneros seated at a table. Writing materials before him.

Don Esteban. [*Solus.*] Was there ever such a stratagem? And how to report it to his excellency, Señor Don Lopez de Santa Anna? That *I* should live to be surprised—surprised in my own castle. Taken prisoner. Captured by a single man. Nay, he was no *single* man. His name was Legion. Besides there were two, and I was taken *sword in hand.* Not taken until I was overthrown, with a matter of twenty men upon me. That is a point of which something must be made. The dispatch must be eloquent when I reach that part. But to account for the surprise. What shall be said about that. Ha! I have it. Treachery in Mexico. Don Amador de Aquilar—an assumed name perhaps; but, assuredly a Mexican; a native born citizen of Mexico—one of the deadly enemies of Santa Anna; seeking to sell the country to the Texians, as the Yucatanese have already sold theirs. It was no Texian force at all—very far from it. Mexicans all, every man of them—creatures of some chief conspirator in the great city. Let Santa Anna look to it—captured, sword in hand, overthrown. I see his danger. I will warn him of it. No want of vigilance can be charged on me, I'm thinking. Ha! here he comes, Don Amador.

Enter Bonham and Maria.

Bonham. Your excellency I kiss your hands.

Governor. Don Amador, you are very welcome.

Bonham. Señor, I bring your niece as to a place of safety.

Esteban. What, my princess. Ah! you see me not as when we met last night. Such is the fate of war. Julius, himself, was not superior to its vicissitudes. The great Hannibal yielded to stratagems. Scipio was not always successful; and shall I be so presumptuous as to expect from fortune what she did not always grant to Cæsar, Pompey, Hannibal and Scipio. No, no, modesty forbids the notion. It would be sheer vanity. I must look for adverse winds. I must expect an occasional cloudy day. My own genius is not always equal. The warrior sometimes sleeps as well as the poet. There was a luckless moment which found me napping. Unhappily, just then, my enemy was wakeful. What a coincidence. But a single moment, and see the consequences. Behold me now, a prisoner. But where's your cousin—where's my child, Olivia.

Bonham. In safety at the convent of LaGuayra, Whither I go to bring her.

Maria. Nay, you need not.

Bonham. Need not, lady.

Maria. You will not find her there,
Because of certain stratagems of mine,
To make her safety certain. Ere this hour
She is Don Pedro's bride, and speeds away
To the fair town of roses, or perchance
To Tuscasito.

Bonham. Ha! Don Pedro's bride—
In flight to Tuscasito.

Esteban. Well, let them go—
I always meant her for Don Pedro, and don't
See why they should have fled at all.

MICHAEL BONHAM.

Maria. Ay, but our conqueror does, if I mistake not.
He meant her for his own.
    Bonham. I did. 'Tis true. I should have asked your
        blessing
Upon our mutual loves.
    Esteban. Don Pedro has been hasty. A good fellow,
But with no taste for stratagem
    Maria. There you mistake. It was by stratagem
He won his bride at last. Don Amador,
'Twas I that counselled him, that, at LaGuayra,
Olivia lay secure. 'Twas I that taught him
To clothe his follower in the Texian garb,
And with a specious message, as from you,
To win her to his arms. 'Twas I that next
When you were pressing on his flying steps,
Arrested yours and gave the needful time,
To make the stratagem sure. I crossed your path,
Pretended woman fears I never felt,
And we are here together while they fly,
Unchecked to Tuscasito.
    Bonham. Say no more.
Oh! treacherous woman, hateful to the last.
What has your malice wrought?
    Maria. My dear revenge,
The only triumph of defrauded love.
    Bonham. 'Tis not too late.
    Maria. Before you reach La Guayra,
They will have wed.
    Bonham. False prophetess, in vain
Your hateful story. Never will Olivia
Consent to his demand.
    Maria, [*in low tones, approaching him.*] He asks her
        not.

Nurse not this flattering fancy in your thought,
For resolute to make my triumph sure,
And leave your heart as desolate as mine,
I whispered him that woman, in her mood,
Is never more consenting than when most
She makes denial. Bade him never heed
The outward show of anger in her eye,
Or its sharp, bitter accent on her lips;
These, did I say, were natural to the weak,
The frail protectors of the woman's secret.
So stubborn is he made by my tuition,
I tell thee, Amador, he will make her his,
Though the last accent on her palsied tongue
Be gasped in mortal agony.

  Bonham. No more.
Woman, away. I'll hearken thee no more.
         [*Bonham rushes out.*
 Maria. He has it here. Ha! Ha! he has it here.
 [*Presses her hand upon her heart, and suddenly sinks, swooning into the arms of Don Esteban.*]
  Esteban, [*supporting her to sofa.*] Jesu! Was ever such a stratagem!
          [*Scene closes.*

SCENE VI.

A wood near the convent of La Guayra. The convent seen in the distance. Pedro discovered in the wood.

 Pedro, [*watching.*] He's lost within the gate. 'Tis my last hope—

The project is a good one. That old fool,
And dastard, Esteban, would surely name it
A stratagem. 'Tis something more than his;
More like to be successful. How my soul
Burns with impatience. Love and hate unite
To goad me into phrenzies of new passion,
That will not let me rest. Thanks to this woman;
Her subtle wit be honored, that, at last,
When most I felt despondency could rouse me,
To hope and to performance. Whence her malice,
I neither know nor care, but if it prospers,
I'll take her as my counsellor through life.
Holy Maria, be my patroness,
Give me to triumph now above my foe,
That fierce and wily enemy, and claim
My homage ever after.

   Mexican soldier. The gates unfold, my lord.

   Pedro. Thanks, holy virgin. Thanks! We have her
      now.
She's ours. She comes. And victor in the end,
Though Bexar and the Alamo both be lost,
I bless my happy fortune. Hark, aside,
Spread yourselves, soldiers, but concealed be nigh,
So that we lose her not again. She comes.

   Enter Olivia and Mexican in disguise.

   Olivia. Where do you lead me? Where is Amador?

   Pedro, [*emerging from shade.*] Here's one who loves
      you better.

   Olivia. I am lost, Don Pedro.

   Pedro [*takes her hand.*] Nay, saved.

   Olivia. Unhand me, Señor.

   Pedro. You strive in vain. My arms are thrown
      around you,

Never to loose again. Your father's rights,
And mine, beneath his sanction, both demand
That, with a gentle force.
  Olivia. This violence—
  Pedro. Is but the action of a faithful love
That will not lose its labor.
  Olivia, [*screams.*] Ambassador! Ambassador.
  Pedro. How like a child,
You waste your feeble strength in feebler struggles.
You call in vain. Within the Alamo's walls
Your traitor lover lies. Would you oppose
Your woman strength to mine?
  Olivia. Ay! though I perish.
Sooner than yield to thee, I welcome death.
My Amador. Oh! come to me and save.
  Pedro. Your shrieks are vain. Your struggles! I must use
The needful force for safety.
  Olivia, [*faintly.*] Amador! Help.
      He carries her out struggling. Scene closes.

SCENE VII.

Another part of the wood. Enter Bonham with Texian soldiers.

  Bonham. Methought I heard a cry. A woman's voice.
'Twas from this wood it rose, and look, the marks
Of strife upon the ground.

MICHAEL BONHAM.

1st Texian. A woman's track.
Bonham. 'Tis hers! 'Tis hers! That fury's tale was true.
Follow me, comrades, as you love me, follow.
[*Exeunt Omnes.*

SCENE VIII.

The Forest. Pedro and party hurrying Olivia in flight.

Pedro. We are past all danger, and you strive in vain,
Submission now were wisest. You are mine.
Olivia. Oh! hateful, how I loathe thee. Never in vain
The struggle against injustice—never wise
Submission to the criminal. If I call
Vainly on him I love, the God who hears
Will send me a deliverer. Hear me, heaven—
My Amador. Where are you, Amador?
Bonham, [*from the forest.* Here, my Olivia, here.
Pedro. Pursued? Demonios!
Olivia. Safe, O! safe.
Bonham, [*bursting in—Pedro releases Olivia and turns upon him.*] Ah, villian, you are sped.
Pedro. Fiends light upon you.
Olivia, [*passing behind Bonham.*] Oh! Amador,— you save me twice.
Bonham. [*To Texians.*] Drive out this scum while I dispatch this ruffian.
Texians with a shout rush on Mexicans and drive them out.

Bonham. [*To Pedro.*] Twice have I spared you, villain. When but late
You sunk before my arm, I bade you then
Dread our third meeting. We *have* met and now
Look to your weapon. Mercy from my breast
Is banished. This last villainous assault
On one who hates and scorns you, has rooted out
All seeds of pity. On your sword your life.
Be ready.

Pedro. I am ready. 'Tis my weapon
And not my will that fails me. If I perish,
Know that in death I hate thee still, as now,
While living, I defy thee.

Bonham. This sounds well.
Stout manhood somewhat qualifies the shame
That stamps the villain's brow. Yon tree, Olivia
Will shield you from the sight of bloody strife—
The man who dreads not foes his crimes have made
Is not unworthy of them. Sob not thus
 thou would'st not unman me, dear Olivia,
And make my heart as tender as thine own.
(To Pedro) Art ready. Fix thy foot upon the turf,
Thou soon shalt sleep on. Look thy last to heaven,
Thou soon shalt face for judgment. To thy prayers
As well as weapon. Now say.

Pedro.   Point.

Bonham.   Guard—
And now good sword be true,—good arm be strong,
Good eye be vigilant, and heaven be good.

[*They fight. The sword of Bonham snaps suddenly.*]

Pedro. Ha! Ha! 'Tis mine. The day is mine.

Olivia, [*rushes out from tree.*] Spare him. Oh! spare.

Pedro.   Death.

[*Thrusts vengefully—Bonham parries with left arm, closes—draws bowie knife and stabs Pedro to the heart.*]

Bonham. Ay, death, but 'tis to thee
Fool! did'st thou think
My life was placed on worthless steel like that.
   Pedro, [*falls.*] Hell's curse upon thee. Thou hast won the game
At mine own color—the red. Help, ere I fall. [*Dies.*]
   Bonham. From this spot, Olivia.
   Olivia. Thou art hurt.
   Bonham. A scratch.
Thou safe and in these arms, I feel no hurts—
Let us away. Look not upon this sight,
'Twas needful for my safety as for thine
We're victors now. I will recall my soldiers,
Then bear thee to thy father.
   Olivia, [*sounds bugle.*] He is safe.
   Bonham. [*To Texans who reënter.*] As thou could'st wish him.
Take up the body,
See it well bestowed,
With honorable burial. Follow me.
                              [*Scene closes.*

SCENE IX.

A court in the Alamo. Crockett and Sparrow meeting.

Crockett. The very bird I have been looking for, the smallest of birds, and the most pert. Sparrow, I've a message for you. You are wanted.

Sparrow. Where! For what! Is a man never to have rest. Is he always to be marching and fighting, without rhyme or reason, song or supper.

Crockett. Ah! there I have you. I can put you in the best of humors by a single word. You are bidden to the supper.

Sparrow. I'll come! What's for supper?

Crockett. You do not ask who gives it?

Sparrow. I do not care. There are only two parties to a supper. The man that eats and the thing that is eaten. I am willing to be the one, and I've done all that is decent and civil in asking after the other.

Crockett. Well, it will be a rare supper.

Sparrow. That'll please me. I'm rather an Englishman in that respect. I can't bare your *done* meats. No, the blood nicely trickling still from under the brown edges, and I am pacified. A rare supper for me always.

Crockett. Bonham gives it, and the governor has a hand in it; so it ought to be good.

Sparrow. Why the devil should the governor have a hand in it before any body else?

Crockett. Good reason. It's his daughter's wedding supper.

Sparrow. Ho! Ho! I see. Bonham's to marry her. Well, he's a good fellow. I'm sorry for him.

Crockett. Why sorry. She's a good fellow too.

Sparrow. There's a pair of them, and that's reason enough for some people why they should be paired. But except the supper which comes with it, and which, I suppose, reconciles so many persons to the thing, I could never see any fun in a wedding. It's a melancholy solemnity always.

MICHAEL BONHAM.

Crockett. But you hav'nt answered me. Will you come?

Sparrow. Count certainly upon me. I never disappoint good suppers. I am never cold when they are warm.

Crockett. You'll be at the wedding also, won't you?

Sparrow. Ah! that's another matter. I'll think of that.

Crockett. [*Bugle sounds—enter Davis.*] That bugle, Davis.

Davis. 'Tis Travis. He takes command. Bonham is to leave us; to take despatches to Sam. Houston. Have you heard the news?

Crockett. Any from the States? Old Tennessee, or Congress.

Davis. D—n Congress. It's made up of old men's souls and old women's tongues, and a buzzard is the only means of communicating between them.

Sparrow. That's only since David left. He was the leader of that body, and his decency went so far that he refused to spit in the president's silver spittoon, and emptied five finger basins at a draught. Say you, Davy, is it true that when the waiter brought you a soupplate of soup, you ordered him to bring the tureen?

Crockett. God bless you for a sweet singing Sparrow. But many a fool has left on record the report of his own braying, printed under the name of a better man. But let's hear the news that Davis brings.

Davis. The news is nearer home. They say that Santa Anna is marching down upon us with twenty thousand men.

Crockett. We must stand a siege then?

Sparrow. Never think of it without laying in a plentiful stock of provisions. A six months siege, for a force like ours, would need eight hundred beeves, one hundred barrels of buffalo tongues.

Crockett. Enough! you shall be made commissariat to see to these things. You'll be at the wedding, Davis.

Davis. Ay! and the supper too.

Sparrow. You'll ask too many, Crockett. A supper table should be select. I hate to see it crowded.

Crockett. Except with meats! Has any one seen Kennedy? We want him for the singing.

Davis. He'll sing no more! He fell at the first rush. Poor Harris, too: you heard about his wife?

Crockett. A sad story that.

Davis. He was a bad fellow, by all accounts, but died repenting,—and died fighting.

Sparrow. Let me die eating. If any thing can lessen the pangs of death, it is that you have the means of satisfying the pangs of appetite. You'll see a bird, or beast, dangerously wounded, still eat ravenously. Some famous naturalists have gouged out a buzzard's eyes, and plucked off a bird's wings, and, by seeing them eat freely have convinced themselves that the poor devils were not a bit conscious of suffering or loss. I confess, however, I'm not exactly satisfied. If the thing be true, it only proves that God gave the poor things very unnecessary and burdensome appendages.

Crockett. By the powers, Sparrow, before you became a sparrow, you must have been a wolf. What you'll be hereafter, it's hard to guess. You'll be at the supper, I suppose?

Sparrow. In some shape,—yes.   [*Ex. Sparrow.*

Davis, [*to Crockett.*] We'll go together Davy. I have something for your own ear.   [*Exeunt.*

SCENE X.

An apartment in the Alamo, splendidly prepared and lighted brilliantly. The Governor in state, with Bonham, Crockett, Davis, Sparrow, and other Texians, with Mexican officers, &c. Olivia, with Duenna and Ladies, appears in the back ground.

Esteban, [*coming forward.*]   Señor Don Amador
          these are all your friends;
They know the full conditions made between us
Touching the town of Bexar and its people.
You leave us, and, at parting, take from me
My heart's best treasure. You will honor her,
Protect her, love her; be to her what I
Have toiled to be through seventeen happy years,
While I have been her father. You'll find in her,
If that you use her rightly, such a treasure,
As man can find in woman's love alone,—
In her's not always. Here, my child, Olivia:
Give me your hand. 'Tis yours, Don Amador.
Be witness Señores.
    Bonham.   Sir, I take the gift,
Not ignorant of its value. 'Tis a treasure
Such as I still shall cherish in my heart,
Secure from spoil without, secure from hurt
From erring mood of mine.
               In other lands,
Where'er our lot is cast—whether we build
Our cabin here in Texas, or afar,
Among my native hills of Congaree,
Erect our happy roof-tree, in my heart,

As fondly as in yours, her happiness
Shall be the creature of my busy thought,
From sunny dawn of morning until night.
To this, with solemn pledge, in sight of heaven,
I bind my soul forever.

   Esteban.   She is yours!
   Olivia.   My father, O! my father!
   Esteban.   Speak, my child.
   Olivia.   If I have vex'd you, father—If, capricious,
I've given unheeding ears—
   Esteban.   Never! Never!
You still have been a child most dutiful;—
Will be a wife. Go to him. Make him yours
By love, by duty, and by gentleness,
As you were mine. My faith is in his pledges;
He will not wrong the venerable white
Of this old head, by harming hair of thine.
Kiss me, my child. I bless you ere I yield you!

   Crockett, [*to Sparrow.*] Dang it, Sparrow, he's a sensible old gentleman after all. I can't tell what he said exactly, but I understand what he meant to say.

   Sparrow, [*to Crockett.*] He's giving away his daughter—that I see, and he behaves well. I'm a little sorry I squeezed him so hard, when I had him down. But stay! Who's this?

   Crockett, [*to Sparrow.*] Dickins! The Princess.

Enter Donna Maria, supported into the midst and laid
                upon a sofa.

   Bonham, [*aside.*]   She here!
   Olivia.   My cousin!
   Esteban. My poor Maria! You were wrong to come. You only harm yourself.

MICHAEL BONHAM.

Maria. I know it, uncle;
But could not bear, at such a time as this,
My childhood's first companion and my friend
To lose forever, with no word, no prayer,
For pity and forgiveness. You, too, Amador,
Ah! look not thus upon me. Never more
Shall my wild passion, wrought to madness, vex
Your generous nature. See the ravage here
Of twelve short hours. A week—another day—
And you will yield that tear upon my grave,
Your heart denies me now.
  Bonham, [*aside.*] There's mischief in her eye!
  Maria. Olivia! Cousin!
  Olivia. Dearest Maria!
  Bonham, [*aside to Olivia.*] Stay! Do not go!
  Maria. Alas! you love me not. My moment madness
Has turn'd your heart aside from me. A life
Is blasted in a moment. Fifteen years
Of childish play and prattle—girlhood's dreams
Still nightly interchanged—dear confidence
Such as youth only cherishes—all gone—
Forgotten, as if never known, or worthless!
Will you not grant forgiveness? I have wrong'd you,
But that was in my madness! See you not
I cannot wrong you now. This face no more
Shall wear the smiles of conquest—as this heart
Must banish all those feeble hopes and feelings
That led it once astray. Speak to me, cousin;
But say that you forgive me.
  Olivia. Why forgive?
You've never wrong'd me, cousin.
  Maria. Ay! but I have;
Cruelly wrong'd you. But that time is past.

I've wakened from my dream, I loathe myself,
Now that 'tis over. Cousin, think of me
With sorrow and with pity, when beneath
Your foreign roof, secure in happy love,
You think on me no more.
   Olivia.   Ah! speak not so;
Still must you live—still conquer.
   Maria.   Amador,
Tell her it cannot be!
   Bonham.   Wherefore, lady,
So very young—so beautiful as thou?
   Maria.   No more! I must not hear you! Blessings,
          cousin,
Be on you. There! now bear me to my chamber—
My work is done—the latest task is ended—
Now welcome death.
   Olivia.   Oh, cousin, speak not thus!
You rend my heart.
   Maria.   I would not—yet I must!
Farewell! Be happy! Yet we should not part
Without one fond embrace, one farewell kiss.
   Olivia, [*approaching Maria.*]   Sister—cousin!
   Bonham, [*anxiously—aside.*] I like it not—beware!
   Olivia, [*aside to Bonham.*] Oh! sure we cannot now
          deny her this.
I have ever loved you, cousin. In my heart,
Where'er I go, will think of you with fondness,
Having a thousand things in memory,
Of what we were together. This embrace—
   Maria.   Is death!
Ha! There!   [*Attempts to stab her, rises from the
          sofa and draws forth a concealed dagger.*
   Sparrow, [*arresting the blow.*]   The woman's mad!

Esteban. Jesu! Was ever such a stratagem!
Maria. Still baffled!
Bonham. Disarm her!
Maria. That ye shall not. See!
[*Stabs herself.*
Bonham. Horrible! It is a fatal blow!
Maria. Or it were mockery.
Go to your beauty, Amador. She faints!
I die, but faint not! Yet one look! I loved you;
I love you to the last! Oh! Amador,
She cannot love as I have done. This hand,
That smote its kindred heart, had, in your cause,
Borne weapon 'gainst a thousand foes—but now!
Support me, Amador. Your arm; yours only—
God! how I loved this man! [*Dies.*
Bonham. 'Tis over now—
Olivia!

Curtain drops while the characters group themselves around her.

BENEDICT ARNOLD:

THE TRAITOR.

A DRAMA, IN AN ESSAY.

BY W. GILMORE SIMMS, ESQ.

Author of 'The Yemassie,' 'Richard Hurdis,' 'Border Beagles,' 'Eutaw,' &c.

Written for the Magnolia Weekly.

RICHMOND:
1863.

BENEDICT ARNOLD.

O N the course of an essay, written many years ago, discussing the epochs and materials in American History, most suited for the uses of art and fiction, I said--
"Perhaps, were the questions put suddenly, without concert, to a group of literary men, promiscuously assembled throughout the country-- were they required at once to designate the one man of the Revolution, whose history, beyond that of all others, furnishes the most striking materials for the Romance writer-- the probability is that they would fix, with one common voice, upon Benedict Arnold."-- No other series of events, in any one life, seem more naturally to group themselves into the form of a story. None were of a more important nature; none endowed with a more tragic interest.

The fate and fortunes of Benedict Arnold are, indeed, such as, beyond all others, seem meant to "point the moral and adorn the tale." Brave to desperation, heroism was, with him, a natural and a noble instinct. Among the first to take up arms in the cause of his country, he was ever the first to force his way into the thickest ranks of danger. Privations only seemed to heighten his capacity for endurance; while the sense of opposition warmed his valor into a flame which his own streaming blood could never extinguish. Gallantly leading on the charge, vigorously heading the assault, the epic hero of antiquity never presented a more exquisite example of fortitude, conduct, and audacious valor, such as bestows animation upon songs, and imparts inspiration to the creative art of the enthusiastic genius. We behold him at Quebec, and at Saratoga, and still he appears the same generous and fearless hero -as bold as Hector, as unyielding as the greater Ajax. What a character for the first grand opening scenes of the drama--what swelling acts for the great theatres of patriotism and song! Sure to secure the admiration of the spectator, as Arnold himself most certainly did, at this period, secure that of the American people. Doubtful of their great hope--suffering from privation--harrassed by frequent defeat—is it wonderful that the brilliant career of Arnold—particularly the great share which he had in winning the field of Saratoga—should have dazzled their eyes and baffled their judgments. His star continued to rise in the ascendant, like the sun,—

"——— When his beams at noon
Culminate from the equator,—

till, almost alone, it fixed the admiration of the people, who began to regard the calmer and colder Washington as the stalking horse of the pageant—wanting in heroism as conduct—the presentment of the king—the Agamemnon, perhaps, but not the Achilles—the Æneas, but not the Hector, of our Troy! And the cry runs on Arnold! Even those who possess an abiding faith in the true virtues and the real greatness of Washington, begin to address him in the language of expostulation, such as the Prince of Ithaca employs when he would provoke Achilles to exertion:

"Then marvel not, thou great and complete man,
That all the Greeks begin to worship Ajax;
Since things in motion, sooner catch the eye,
Than what not stirs! The cry went once on thee,
And still it might; and yet it may again,
If thou would'st not entomb thyself alive,
And case thy reputation in thy tent."

It was the good fortune of America, as it was the true greatness of Washington, that he was not impatient of himself—that he could resist equally the entreaties and the arguments of his friends, and the goadings of his own ambition—that, heedless of the cry which ran on Arnold, (or rather Gates,) he could content himself, cased in his tent, waiting his hour until the time for proper action should arrive; while his less circumspect rival, encouraged to presumption by success, and the adulation of blind worshippers, maddens with an equal blindness; and first intoxicated by hope, then furious by disappointment, grasps the torch of the incendiary for the destruction of the high temple in which he had been sworn the officiating priest. His hand is lifted, but his deed still cloaked, and the hour is speeding whose entire revolution is to bring about the catastrophe, equally fatal to his honest fame, and to the liberties of his country! The interest grows naturally with the struggle which is in progress; equally in his own mind, and between the advocates of the rival heroes. The people, like the ancient chorus, clamor their wishes, and bemoan their disappointments. Unlike the ancient chorus, however, they soon begin to take an active part in the events of the drama. The result is doubtful. Ambition begins to rear his crest in triumph, while patriotism trembles with the numerous and growing apprehensions. Faction exults in confidence, while affection falters in the trust which it once had in the genius of Washington. For a moment—for a moment only— the fate of this great nation swings doubtfully in the balance!

The catastrophe follows!— none more sudden—none more complete in the whole wide world of scenic exhibition. The fall of a great man!—not by death, for death is no foe to the fame that is already sure in past performances!—not by the jealous rival, or the dark assassin; but by the rapid spreading of the single plague-spot—the inherent baseness in his own soul.

And such a fall!—To what utter perdition, not only of all future fame, but of all past achievement—the annihilation of that hope which lived in coming days and deeds, and the overthrow of those high monuments which men had raised up as trophies to denote the deeds already done! A mighty, an irrevocable fall—total to the hero—terrible to the spectator—like that of Lucifer—"never to rise again"—yet not such a fall as would satisfy the catastrophe, or furnish an appropriate denouement for the dramatic Muse. A fall to be stigmatized by the curses of the chorus—to be moralized by the didactic poet, into a thousand homilies, for the ears of reverent youth; but utterly insusceptible of use upon the stage—having no outward action, no results corresponding with the crime—no punishment which human eye may follow, proportioned to the extent of his deserving; a fall of the *soul*, rather than of the frail body which it informs—a conflict of the wild, benighted heart, ending in moral discomfiture and shame, not of the muscular and mighty frame, overborne by superior skill and power, and yielding, but fighting bravely to the last!

And with what adjuncts of poetry and feeling—of tears and tenderness—of pride and passion—may that dark conflict be allied! His was not the single ruin. It is coupled with the fate of Andre—a mournful story of the blight of early promise.

Young and full of genius—loving and full of hope—brave, and burning with ambition—he, too, falls with the traitor—is dragged down to the same dreadful moral death! He perishes—a sad catastrophe—but one from which the human spectator recoils with horror.

The chorus must close the narrative. The scene which degrades the hero must not offend the sight of the audience!

Andre, upon the dishonoring tree, like Hector roped to the car of Achilles, is a spectacle which may be spared the eyes which have previously been delighted with his youth, his beauty, his generous virtue, and his noble valor and devotion!

There is surely much that is dramatic in this history. The leading events, thus grouped in general terms, to the entire exclusion of details, are particularly imposing in their aspects—many of them are startling and full of consequences. The deeds of the hero are as brilliant, as his treason is utter and unqualified. Arnold was no imbecile in action. He was only so in morals. His courage was unquestionable; and he exposed himself personally in battle, as was the case with the valiant man in ancient warfare. His audacity was immense, and he entertained, along with it, a love of approbation, an appetite for praise, which, had his culture been of a better sort, in a community of higher moral, would have been the most impassioned love of glory. But, with all these circumstances in its favor, his story, as at present known, is essentially undramatic.

It will always remain so. The objections to its present employment, for the drama, arise from our familiarity with the details; many of which, to make the subject available for the stage, must be made to yield place to others more tractable and appropriate.

When these details shall be no longer present to the memories of men—when but little more shall be remembered than the bold, but impressive fact, that one among our bright and shining lights—one of the noblest in seeming and in promise—went down from our sky, in shame and darkness, at the very moment when all eyes were fastened upon it in hope and admiration—then, doubtlessly, the future Shakspeare of our land—if we are ever to be blest with such an advent—will seize upon the event, and shape it into some long and endurduring chronicle. And this he will do, however his details may vary from the history, by no such violations of *general* truth as should outrage propriety. He will be conscious of no such barriers as restrain us now. He will exercise such privileges of art, legitimate for his purpose, as the living generations will not tolerate; such as the now living author, conscious of the true facts, will not venture to assert. He will depict the hero in the day of his completest triumph—no stain upon his shield—watched, almost worshipped, by the admiring multitude; and with none of those misgivings of success which embitter the hope and disturb the moral equilibrium of the ambitious nature, the philosophic observer alone may be permitted to see, lurking close, possibly in the shape of a virtue, the single plague spot in his soul, which is destined to spread, with a rank rapidity, over the growth and freshness of the better nature—latent, however, not spreading—perhaps not to spread—but depending for its growth or its suppression upon the chances of a wild and never-to-be-satiated appetite for sway! Grant him what his ambition seeks, and seeks worthily, and we shall see no more of his inherent canker. It will be wholly conquered by the triumphant virtues, which have no need to succumb in the easy gratification of his heart's prevailing passion.

Such is the moral portrait of Arnold, as he appears, and may be made to appear, in the opening scenes of the drama. It may be that the future poet, who thus undertakes his delineation—uninfluenced by that feeling of reverence which fills *our* hearts, when we approach the great hero of civilization—will venture to delineate, as in honorable conflict for the ascendancy, the rival stars of Washington and Arnold. The one calm, cold, and haughty in his serene pride of place; the other fiery and impetuous, hot with haste, spurring forward, sleepless always, to that glorious eminence which the jealous fate denies he shall ever reach. It will not perhaps be difficult, a hundred years hence, to make it appear that Arnold was the victim of some great injustice—to show that his rightful claims were denied; at all events, to make it appear that such at least was his own conviction—a conviction not uncommon to the nature covetous of fame and jealous of any division, however small, of those rewards of glory, on the attainment of which the whole affections of his being have been set. He shall be baffled in these desires. He shall be defrauded of these hopes. Fate shall war against him—his best merits shall fail of their fruits —he shall aim in vain—he shall toil honorably and without purpose; while the better fortune of his rival shall carry him onward with swelling sails, in his own despite, to the haven of their mutual ambition. The star of Washington rises, and gathers hourly increasing lustre, in due degree as Arnold's declines from the summit—waning away, under a cruel destiny, in mockery of all his merits and all his achievements!

Such are the frequent vicissitudes of fortune, and no probabilities would be violated by the artist who should thus depict, to remote ages, the career of this unhappy hero. What follows from such a history? The bitterness of a proud heart denied! The misanthropy, the jaundiced green of envy and mortification, discoloring to his mind all the objects of his thought, and working, subtly and strongly, upon that little, latent, plague-spot in his soul, till his passions break all bonds —unleashed tigers--a gnawing fury and a howling hate urging them on, scorning the reason that would guide and mocking the power that would restrain.

The temptation follows--and the fall! That temptation may be made to work upon nobler feelings than any we are accustomed to associate with the *auri sacra fames!* In this respect, alone, the true history of Arnold should be ennobled for the sympathy and commiseration of less knowing periods. The tempter, clothed in the British uniform and armed with the signet of his king, shall be made to approach the denied and wronged ambition with the deference of an admiration only so far subdued as to forbear offence---he shall dilate only upon unappreciating injustice of a country which refuses to recognize, and properly to honor, such superior merits; shall adroitly exaggerate, to the proud, vain man, the paramount importance of his services; the wonder of his achievement, and the glory which they have rightly gathered in the world's esteem. Then, by adroit insinuation, the better justice shall be shown which rewards such heroism in the opposing service. It will be part of the tempter's scheme to insist that the war is merely a civil contest between rival parties in the same nation— a dispute involving only the success of contending factions; not a principle; not the liberties or safety of a people bravely contending for their rights! It will not be difficult for the spectator to imagine how such a man as the poet has already described, stung by a sense of injustice and neglect, which, in the case of merit, is the worst injustice; will give greedy ear to the solicitations and suggestions of the tempter. Supposing the serpent to approach his task with even ordinary ingenuity, it will not be difficult to see that such a man, thus endowed, and with a latent defect of the moral nature as already shown, *must* fall!

Thus far the story, even as we read it now, is dramatic in its character. The difficulty lies in what remains. The treason of Arnold was that of the Cabinet—of the politician—and not of the hero. It involved no show of heroism. There is no grand action addressing itself to the eye of the spectator, corresponding with the extreme self-sacrifice of the subject, and the general alleged importance of the events. The mere surrender of an impregnable post, though the key of the country, and the delivery of a brave army into unmerited captivity, are not events which can be made imposing before an audience, however great may be their real interest to the fortunes of a nation. They equally lack the two greatest essentials of dramatic art, individuality of development, and an action continually rising in interest, to the catastrophe.

The flight of Arnold from the scene, and the degrading death of Andre upon it, are other difficulties which can only be overcome by the dramatist who shall address himself to an audience totally ignorant of, or indifferent to these details; which the dramatist may then so vary as to accommodate them to the requisitions of the stage. When the grandson of the last revolutionary soldier shall be no more—when the huge folios which now contain our histories and chronicles, shall have given way to works of closer summary and more modern interest—the artist will find a new form for these events, shape all their features anew, and place the persons of the drama in a grouping more appropriate for scenic action.—There will be a more individual character given to the history, the general events will be thrown out of sight, the personal will be brought into conspicuous relief in the foreground—the rival heroes of the piece will be forced into closer juxtaposition; and the treason, detected in the moment of its contemplated execution, will be crushed by the timely interposition of Washington himself! He will be made to have seen the true nature, and to have suspected the purpose of the traitor, even from the moment of his very first lapse of honor,—to have had his eyes upon the tempter, a stern, cold, silent watch—keen and vigilant, and the more terrible from its very silence and unimposing calm. His watch will have been maintained with an interest no less personal than patriotic. It will not impair the character of Washington, to show that he too had his ambition; and serving glory as well as his country, was filled with a two-fold jealousy of *him* who, in striving with him for the one was doing so, fatally and criminally, at the expense of the other. It may be, that in the hands of the future dramatist, the sword of Washington himself, shall be made to do justice upon the head of the traitor, as, by a similar license, Richmond slays Richard, and Macduff, the usuper of Scotland, in the presence of the audience, and no doubt in conflict with the absolute fact. It will only be doing justice to the real merits of Arnold to show him at least fighting bravely to the last, and proving the possession of a stout spirit, even though he falls the victim of a corrupt and dishonest heart! Or, with a slight variation from this denouement, and with some nearer approximation to the historical fact, while the sword of Washington achieves the death of the foreign emissary (Andre,) his stern voice, rising pre eminent over all the sounds of battle, shall send the baffled traitor (Arnold) — hell in his heart, and curses on his lips—to the inglorious scaffold which the audience does not see!

The fate of Andre may be woven in with such a history, in the form of an under plot, by a process well known to the dramatic artist. You have but to endow Arnold, or his wife, with a sister, who, won by the love of Andre, shall be made the instrument in bringing about the treachery of the hero. The exercises of her affections, and their defeat, may be employed to impart tenderness and animation to the subordinate scenes; while the wife of Arnold, whether described as a patriotic matron, like Portia, or a woman devoted to her lord, like Medora, whether "guilt's in his heart" or not, will, like the Belvidere of Jaffier, or the unsexed companion of Macbeth, furnish all that is needful for the interest in the domestic relations of the hero. Such departures from the absolute history, as are here suggested, will not offend the spectator some hundred years hence. They would not, even now, offend a British or a continental audience, which knows nothing more than the simple fact, if they know even that, that the American Revolution was distinguished by one great traitor, whose name was Benedict Arnold. But such freedoms with details with which we are all familiar, would scarcely do with *us*. So fresh in our memories are all the facts in this connection, that any such violations of the written record would convert into a hostile critic every sturdy militiaman from Maine to Mississippi.

The history and material thus discussed, long ago arrested my attention as affording admirable dramatic material, and perhaps no one subject in American history has been half so frequently employed already by authors of art or fiction. I should hardly exaggerate were I to assume that the story of Arnold and Andre has been woven into fictitious tale and narrative more than twenty times; and, in singular confirmation of what I have said, this has been done in almost every instance in *the dramatic form*, showing that the subject itself naturally suggests its own uses through this medium. I have in my library several dramatic works, where Arnold or Andre is the hero; but can now lay my hands on three only.

The first of these, in the order of publication, is a fragment by Mr. George H. Calvert, of Baltimore, a gentleman of fine talents, the writer of several interesting volumes of travel, and the translator of Schiller's Don Carlos, which he has very happily rendered into English blank verse. His more recent translation of the "correspondence of Goethe and Schiller," is in honorable proof of his own merits as an English, as well as German scholar; while his critical writings are highly creditable to his various tastes and studies. displaying generally an accurate and ample knowledge of his subject, and a nice acumen that has suffered none of its essential interests to escape him. In mentioning these general claims of this writer, I have only to add that his dramatic fragment of Arnold is a failure, and that subsequent experience led him to the abandonment of a subject with which he could take no liberties. It may be well to note, however, what he says in respect to his performance. In his preface he thus remarks—"The attempt to work an historical drama out of Arnold's treason, exhibited to the author the barrenness of the subject for dramatic development; and as therefore he almost despairs of accomplishing his original design, the fragment is now published as it was written several years since."*

I agree with the author in the *difficul'y*, but not in the *barrenness* of the subject. The reasons for the difficulty have been stated already. There is *no* barrenness—there can be none—for the material is full of the tragic; full of the means and matter of passion; full of startling events and striking incidents, and bold salient character; and the author needs only to be permitted that ordinary license of the old dramatist, dealing with subjects of *remote* date, of supplying the details at his own pleasure, and varying them according to the requisition of the stage; supplying gaps in the narrative by invention, and introducing subordinate personages in an under-plot. But this is the very difficulty, and the reader of the fresh history would be perpetually comparing and contrasting the facts in his books, with the course and conduct of the counterfeit presentments of the scene. Our histories in fact tell us too much, and furnish details which are not helps but obstacles.

The sample published by Mr. Calvert does not so much reveal the *barrenness* of his material, as his own deficiency as a dramatist. Nothing can well be less dramatic than the fragment he has published. His mind is *essayical* of cast, not dramatic. He began badly, and one had better, in such cases, always recast his plot, and begin anew rather than encounter the wearisome and uphill progress which follows from a bad beginning. Lord Byron somewhere compares himself to a tiger, who, failing in his first spring, slinks back into his jungle. I do not counsel thus the abandonment of one's prey; but, if a second effort is made, it should be a new eminence from which the leap should be taken.

I have already admitted the embarrassments of the subject, and, in the introduction to this paper, indicated all the reasons for it; but I am equally sure that Mr. Calvert, truly able as

---

*Miscellany of Verse and Prose; By George H. Calvert, author of Count Julian, Cabiro, &c. Baltimore—1840.

I hold him to be in some provinces, has not in this shown himself capable of dealing with such materials. He has given us rather a versified dialogue from the history, than a dramatic writing. His personages generalize beyond the occasion. They deal in such matters as is set down at large in all the histories. Most of this material should be taken for granted—should be assumed to be known to the spectator, or only used sparingly, to connect the threads of the story, or to develope the characteristics of leading personages. True art asks only such portions of the *known* as are absolutely necessary to a right comprehension of that which it wishes to convey, additionally, to the reader or spectator. Mr. Calvert was too literal, and left nothing to the imagination of the audience. The little blank verse essays, which are spoken by 'Col. Robinson' and the 'Old Soldier,' are insufferably tedious, though marked by some vigorous lines, and here and there by an original thought or fancy. The 'Old Soldier,' who is of no use in the scene, and certainly was not needed by any exigencies of the subject, proves himself especially a sad proser, and would soon do the business for any tragedy before any audience. All the fine things in the world, which he might say of Washington, would not reconcile even an American audience, and would never avert the catastrophe certain to attend the play!

Another tragedy, on the same subject, published by Horatio Hubbell, lies before me now.† This is more dramatic of plan, but shows little of the artist besides. As a composition it is bald and feeble, and the rhythm of the blank verse is very faulty. The adjuncts provided by the author are very few.—It requires action, incident and conflicting struggles of passion, which in a tragedy needs incessant play, like the lightning of the South in dog days. But the piece exhibits more dramatic resources on the part of the author, and time and training might have prepared him for converting it into a successful *melo-drama*. Some of his original matter is of this nature.

---

*Arnold, or the Treason at West Point. A Tragedy, in five acts. By Horatio Hubbell. Philadelphia—1847.

A third, and more recent performance than either of these, has been put forth in New York, by Mr. W. W. Lord, a gentleman who has won considerable reputation by several volumes of Poetry. This production* is a far more ambitious effort than either of the two preceding. It is more graceful and correct as a poem; and, though still not likely to attract attention, by its susceptibility for the stage, is decidedly more dramatic than either of the preceding performances. It reads well in the closet, and is highly creditable to the talents of the author; but it lacks warmth, animation, and the characterization seems to me unsystematical in certain parts. The interest is made to turn rather upon Andre than Arnold; and this I regard as a mistake. Even thus, however, the author has failed to make Andre a hero. He is a mere love-stricken youth, who takes up the character of the conspirator without any of the requisite qualities. As a lover, he lacks ardency. The whole piece is deficient in what is called in stage language situations. The author has not sufficiently taxed his invention in the preparation of such incidents as would bring out his characters in scenes of action and passion. All of the writers have been hampered, not by the barrenness of the subject, but the fear of violating the details of history. To be successful in this material, one must assert a certain degree of audacity— must be content with looking to the history for the main facts —the treason—the conspiracy—the detection and disgrace— but must boldly conceive for himself the events, incidents and situations.

Let me now proceed to acknowledge my own sins of performance. I do not dilate on the failures of my contemporaries with any complacency but that which comes from sympathy. I too have shared their experience, and my confession must follow that which has been made by others. In the days of my rash and errant boyhood, in the variety of my schemes, for poem, tale and drama, I too laid hands upon the subject of

---

*Andre: a tragedy in five acts. By W. W. Lord. New York: Charles Scribner. 1856.

Arnold's treason and Andre's fate, resolved upon a drama.—My experiment, though it did not end in the same conviction with that of Mr. Calvert, namely, that the subject was barren, was yet of unsatisfactory result in my hands. I was baffled by the details of history. I had no sufficient freedom. There was too much known to suffer invention its privileges. I was stopt by stern barriers of fact, such as do not oppress us in the ancient histories. The skeleton fact in the old chronicles suffered for Shakspeare. He reclothes it with flesh of his own, fills its veins with his own blood, and clothes it in the habilaments which his fancy chooses. The record of Macbeth in the chronicles, from which Shakspeare drew, hardly occupies three pages, and even the few facts which are given, are perverted by the dramatist. Macbeth has a son for example, while Shakspeare makes one of his most felicitious points in the story from his denial of children to the barren womb of his wife.—So with Lear, Cymbeline, and even Richard the Third. The chronicle is just striking enough to attract the dramatist to the subject, while it is so denuded of its details as to leave the author at full liberty to choose those which he might deem most passionate and picturesque in the development of the story. The terrible facilities of the modern press has shorn the poet of his materials, while crowding those of the historian upon him.

Briefly, my experience in the treatment of the subject of Arnold forced me to the conclusion that it was insusceptible of dramatic uses, unless by such violations of the known history, as the present generation would be unwilling to tolerate. I labored on through the performance, however, and fragments from my experiment were given to the press anonymously, as far back as 1830. These fragments were accompanied by a preface, in which the author admitted the work to be a failure for stage purposes. It said, among other things, that "the incidents were not sufficiently rapid for the quick succession of action required on the stage; and there is no proper catastrophe. . . . . The death of Andre cannot be exhibited on the stage. . . . The events are quite too fresh in the memories of the people, not to maintain the ancient objections to the use of a subject so near home, &c., &c."

But thirty-three years have elapsed since the date of that preface. Old things have passed away; all things are becoming new. New wars have superseded the old. Those of former days are obliterated, or sink into insignificance, compared with the stupendous efforts of our own times. Instead of an army of forty thousand men, the greatest number that Great Britain ever employed, at any one time, for the subjugation of the colonies, the North puts 1,000,000 into the field for the subjugation of the South. There is no parallel for might and panoply, the number of men in the field, and of those who perish, between past and present. The public mind is swallowed up in the vastness of its own state, of life, security, peace and independence, and few care now to trouble themselves with the petty details of the past. These facts suffice, in some degree, to relieve the Romancer from much anxiety as to his freedom with history. Besides, we have learned to lose our faith in Northern historians. We have bared their falsehoods; we have developed their true characters. We have discovered that their Arnolds, and their Putnams were traitors; that Charles Lee was a traitor; and where there was not treason there was imbecility and cowardice.— Their historians are of a piece with their generals; and "falsehood be thou my faith," might well become the motto, as it seems to be the rule of conduct of the whole of them—their Everetts, Sumners, Sabines, Headleys, Hildreths, *et id omne genus*. The privileges of the Dramatist expand, as the reputation of the Historian falls, and in the decline of our confidence in the character, we shall accord a higher degree to the artist. And there is a good moral in doing so, since honest fiction is at all times more moral and more enduring than any history. He who shall take up the subject of 'Arnold and André,' in some future day, will find it more malleable in his hands, especially if he shall heed the lessons afforded him by the experience, in failure, of all preceding writers.

And now to *our* drama; the first scene of which opens at "Governor's Island," New York, and discovers Sir Henry Clinton, General Robertson, and 'Old Thurston,' a Royalist and Quaker, an uncle of Mrs. Arnold, and a man even fanatical in his loyalty. He has long been a secret emissary of the Royalists in Philadelphia; has been the chief agent in bringing about the marriage of Margaret Shippen with Arnold; though her own preferences are supposed to have inclined her to another; and he has, through the pretexts of traffic, beguiled Arnold, writing under the name of 'Gustavus,' into the correspondence with Andre, who wrote the signature of Anderson; for all which correspondence the name of Mrs. Arnold furnished a decent cover. These facts will suffice for the present. Thurston, as we shall see hereafter, notorious as a loyalist, has been forced to fly from Philadelphia. He can only appear in that city in disguise and secretly.

SCENE I.

Sir Henry Clinton
Thurston, we must be secret as the gravel.
There is too much at stake; and England's honor
Must be unsmutch'd by censure! 'Tis enough
That our ill-fortune so impairs our strength,
As makes it needful that we now subdue
Those we should rather conquer. On your oath,
See that this traffic shall be sped so safely,
That never a track shall show where we have trodden!
No writings, mark you! — And the fewest words—
And these delivered only to such parties
As shall be sure, from fear or sympathy,
In the King's interest!
     Thurston.
      His Majesty
Shall find me not a laggard--not a traitor—
True, and, I trust, not witless! I shall tender
His state and honor, and the pride of Britain,
As sacredly as things, o'er all most precious,
To my own soul's security with God!
You have full pledges of *my* loyalty,
Given to such hands as carry credit
To him who bears them; proofs of earnest faith;—
The will to serve; experience in his mission;
Known by long service to the King's advisers—
As to yourself, Sir Henry; my Lord North,
And—
    Sir Henry.
Enough! I doubt not your credentials!—
Your will, your wisdom, wit and loyalty;—
But much I question of your passion, Thurston.

BENEDICT ARNOLD.

Thurston.
Passion! Sir Henry! Do these thin white hairs
Give promise of much passion!

Sir Henry.
                        The hottest head
Is sometimes carried upon palsied shoulders;
And where the passions pass into the brain,
They're fiery as a powder magazine!
You have not school'd *your* brain, though three score years,
May well have cooled your blood. Your loyalty,
Impatient zeal, and hatred of Republics,
All work in you like Passion; and you speak
Even when you counsel, with a tongue that rages,
When such may be your theme! The proof is found
In your expulsion from your native city,
Where, even when Prudence counselled most your silence,
The hot blood, scathing in the reckless brain,
Lost all reserve of caution. This I fear;
And we've too much at hazard!—a great cause;
The issues of an empire—seas of blood;—
And there's that awful sacredness of State,
Lodged in a nation's pride and purity,
That makes me tremble, lest the deeds we work in
Should spread upon the winds! 'Twere to dishonor
Long ages of achievement—to tear down
A thousand laurell'd busts—a thousand panels,
With grand escutcheons blazon'd; -to acknowledge
Our Empire's feebleness of arm and aim;
Decay of national genius; of our strength;
The weakness of our cause, or of our virtue;
And show us basely in the world's wide eyes,
Piercing with the fox's tail the lion's garment!
We must be wary, lest we come to shame;
And you must humble your imperious blood,
And tame your temper down to common methods,
If you would work for us, and work to profit.

Thurston.
I will be schooled, Sir Henry. You shall find me
No wanton prattler to the winds of summer,
Of fruits behind the hedge. I know the danger;
The mighty interests that wait upon us!
I feel the trust as sacred which you give me;
And zeal, itself, shall take, between her teeth,
The curb which guides her to the proper goal,
Where the prize waits upon the enterprize!
Just your rebuke, Sir Henry. I'm of temper
To chafe and rage, perchance; and shout my passion;
When nought is left to feebleness *but* rage;
When I had nought to lose but life; no object
To teach the blood obedience to the will!
But now!———

Sir Henry.
 Enough! This letter that your bring
To Beverly Robinson, perchance, you know,
Is from the pen of Arnold.
    Thurston.
     He wrote it, Sir,
'Neath mine own eyes. It may be, you remember,
In marrying Margaret Shippen, he became
The husband of my niece?
    Sir Henry:
     Another reason
Why we should counsel caution to her uncle.
Know you the cause of Arnold's discontent?
He writes of popular ingratitude;
And hints at other subjects of complaint;
Of Congress; men in power, and selfish factions;
Repents of his rebellion, and aspires,
Henceforth, to do good service to his King!
Can we believe him? Is it not a *ruse*,
The better to ensnare us?
    Thurston.
     Not so, Sir Henry,
He may be trusted. Reasons may be found,

Enough, in his own character, to show
What makes him discontent. He's a vain man—
Ambitious of the highest round of the ladder;
Yet fails—and evermore must fail, to win it!
He at last sees this; and now he despairs,
While Washington shapes Congress to his will,
And takes to favor Greene and Lafayette!
Arnold's voluptuous; profligate; loves pomps;
The gay society; the splendid show;
Wastes money; yet, with constant greed of gain,
Seeks it in doubtful schemes, which profit nothing;
And wounds his reputation by small traffic,
That squares not with the honor of the soldier,
Or the nice sensibility of one,
Born gentleman, and bred in courtly laws!
Wasteful, luxurious, lustful, and more vain
Than any bird that spreads a lacquer'd wing,
He forfeits, in society, the fame
He still had won in battle field and camp!
Hated by the commons, his imperious sway
Hath vex'd the gentry; and even now it is thought
He will be charged, to trial by court martial,
For such offences 'gainst the State and city,
As will degrade to name! That danger waits him;
And, if I am not in the signs, will seize him;
And then he's *ours* forever! He's brave and skilful;
Not wise or virtuous! 'Twas his evil lot
To pass his youth in such communities
As knew no moral where no profit grew.
His training, in the lowest walks of trade,
Have made him a strange mixture—good and bad,
Most strangely blending; yet in conflict ever;
'Till all his actions serve but to perplex
Men's judgments; and to make his bitterness
The foil to all that's noble!

     Robertson.
     You know him well;
How came he then to marry with your niece?

Thurston.
The work was mine, *because* I knew him well,
And felt that time and circumstance would favor
His prompt return to loyalty. An ingrain'd rebel,—
And such the girl herself had in her eyes,—
My niece had never wed!

Sir Henry.
Money will then
Appease his appetite?

Thurston.
Nay, something more,
For he's a man of *many* appetites!
He must have ranks—such rank as now he holds
Among the rebels.

Sir Henry.
What! a Brigadier?
This must be thought of.

Thurston.
He will do good service—
His zeal made eager by the thirst for vengeance!
Has fierce resentments to appease; and gloats
Upon the thought that, heading British Legions,
He'll rage with fire and sword among the people
He still hath led to victory.

Sir Henry.
'Tis well!
We'll think of the details some other season
As the plots ripens. Meanwhile, you remember,
No written pledge. He whom you describe,
Will, in the eagerness of appetite,
Find them all needless. You may promise money—
Be liberal—but, as touching the commission—

Thurston.
Be not too chary of your promises!
He must have *army* rank—will never take
A lower grade than he now fills —

Sir Henry.
Well, be it so!

Thurston.
Those are the least conditions. He may ask
For something more.
Robertson.
What! Would he have the Peerage?
Thurston.
'Tis like he'll ask it
Sir Henry.
He's a blockhead then!
You have your limits! Could he give us all,—
Washington, army, Generals, arsenals, empire;—
We may not give him *title!* He, whom we purchase,
We *use*, not honor! Nothing more of this.
Thurston.
Twill need you send an agent forth to meet him,
One with official sanction—one of rank—
To crown the assurances that I shall make—
And they must meet.
Sir Henry.
This must be thought upon—
'Tis perilous.
Thurston.
Great enterprise must be so!
Who stops at venture rarely reaches gain!
But, hear me; and we'll strip it of the peril!
Should General Arnold be assigned West Point—
Robertson.
West Point?
Thurston.
This powerful fortress in his hands—he there
In sole command—facilities were easy—
Your ships upon the river—
Sir Henry.
Ha! I see!
Thurston.
That citadel, esteemed impregnable--
With all its numerous garrisons; vast depots;
The storehouse of the rebels; where they keep
The national stock of arms and ammunition;

The powder of the army; in itself
The master key of the continent! Methinks,
'Twere a great prize!—at thirty thousand pounds,
A most cheap purchase!

Sir Henry.
He shall have the money!
Shall be a British Brigadier! See to it!
You rouse a hope that you must pacify!
See to it, Thurston. I will make the purchase!

Thurston.
And when I do report to you the hour,
And the man--ready--you will straight dispatch
One of good rank, commissioned to confirm
My cash assurance?

Sir Henry.
Would we might avoid
This last condition.

Thurston.
'Tis impossible!

Robertson.
Send Andre out to him! He's our expert,
Has had much practice, and is deuced dextrous!
Besides, the way is opened him already;
This correspondence, through the charming lady,
Of this most gluttonous Brigadier; why Andre
Will leap to it, with a Platonic ardor,
That finds the moonshine fiery! He'll rejoice
In such a golden opportunity,
To find fresh fuel for his ancient flame.

Thurston.
I pray you, General, keep it in remembrance,
That lady is *my* niece. I'll serve my King,
To *his* great honor may be; but not, mark you,
To loss of any of mine own. Were Andre
To show himself presumptuous in his mission,
He'll find that three score years, and a white head,
Were three score powers; the head not lacking hands,
To punish his presumption!

Sir Henry.
                    There spoke out
The hot blood seething in the grey beard's brain!
Pshaw, Thurston, would you flame up at a jest?
Be wary, man! How can I trust your prudence,
When like the powder at the spark, you blaze!
Enough, it shall be Andre—if he likes it!
'Twill help the work that he *doth* know the lady,
And holds her in esteem. You would not have him
Forego the courtier—nay, the gallant, Thurston,
Because the lady is your niece? Pooh! Pooh!
You must not be too harsh on youthful fancy;
And the flirtation of two silly people
Will serve to cover many a subtle scheme;
The statesman, or the soldier, quaintly working
In Cupid's silken armor for the nonce!
'Tis this the General thinks of.

Robertson.
                    Nothing farther!
But Thurston's quaker fancy will not suffer
His drab to dress in purple.

Thurston.
My quaker notion, gentlemen, is briefly,
That but to jest upon a woman's honor,
Let her be never so virtuous, is to smutch it!

Sir Henry.
Come, let us to the ramparts; where, no doubt,
As the night's soft and beautiful, we'll find
Our Major waiting for the rising moon;
Conning a difficult line in song or sonnet,
To be employed, at more auspicious season,
Im promptu, where the lady smiles in waiting
The sentiment she fancies she inspires.
We'll teach him what we need; and you shall show him
What proper courage he should have; what favor
Put on; how shape his progress; and so, briefly,
Con o'er together, each his several part

BENEDICT ARNOLD.

In this brave drama. I'm impatient, Thurston,
To win this Arnold back to his allegiance.
Putnam we have, and Lee--
     Thurston.
       You may have many,
If you'll but pay the price that vanity
Puts on its own pretensions in the market.
We've many a Patriot, blatant in the Congress,
Who only needs such jingle of your guineas,
As makes his voice impossible.
     Sir Henry.
  [*Putting his hand on Thurston's shoulder.*]
       Can we buy,
At any price, the master-traitor, Washington?
     Thurston.
No! for that monster-miracle of manhood
Hath self-esteem so blended with his virtue,
It riseth to a virtue of itself,
And is, in time, the substitute for passion!
It chafes me to declare him what he is--
The pure and native-born aristocrat;
The natural gentleman; so truly noble
As, without the consciousness of sway, yet sways,
To the perpetual consciousness of others;
And see not that, in measuring all besides,
His own eyes are cast down! He should have been
A monarch; yet, in rising to the King,
He would make forfeit of some qualities
That best become the man!
     Robertson.
      Why, you depict him
As the fond lover paints the loving mistress,
Ere the first kiss hath taken the edge from fancy.
     Thurston.
Ay; but I *hate* him!--hate because I fear him;
And fear him because I know him. He, alone,
Suffices to confer on this rebellion
Some character of virtue. That I hate him

Compels me to be just. You have not wealth
To buy him; nor has any mortal pleasing
The art to win him; since cash—common medium
By which we make approach to common men—
Passion, or Greed, or Lust, or Vanity,
All seem in him to lack. His icy nature
Affolds no single avenue to Guile
In working on his virtue.
      Sir Henry.
       He might have
A seat in the Peerage.
      Thurston.
       His pride would rather
Plant acorns on Mount Vernon!
       Never waste
Your fruitless arts on him; they will bear fruits
Such as shall well compensate, tried on many
That do surround him. Win but these away,
With Lee, and Arnold, Putnam; and their chief,
Standing alone, not knowing where to turn,
Or whom to trust for service; ceaseless doubts
Shaking his faith in many faithful still;
Abandons, in despair, the fruitless struggle
For the distracted country. Then your power
Closes the strife; France, in disgust, retires
From fields in which her allies flout her aid,
Or fatally turn upon her. The alliance
With France affords to many, as to Arnold,
A fair pretext, renouncing the rebellion,
For their return to loyalty. Seize the juncture,
With all its happy auspices: Arnold won,
And openly in arms against his comrades;
West Point, with England's Red Cross floating o'er it;
And what remains to Washington and Congress?
      Robertson.
  The halter! one of silk for Washington,
For Congress—
      Sir Henry.
   They must be content with hemp

It is perhaps well to state, in this place, at the very opening of the drama, to what degree the conspiracy had advanced between Arnold and the British. The letter referred to in the text, as from Arnold to Beverly Robinson shows him fully a traitor, and that nothing more is wanting, for the completion of the bargain, than that the British commander-in-chief should show himself liberal in his terms. Charles Beverly Robinson was an American by birth, whose property lay within the United States, and who owned a mansion on the Hudson, within the American lines, near West Point: one, in fact, which, as he had directed it, the officers of West Point had converted into Quarters. Robinson was a Colonel in the British army. Arnold thought he should be safe, dealing with him; and wrote to him, as unreservedly as is stated in the text, that the ingratitude of his countrymen had changed his political sentiments; that he wished to render his services to the crown: and, to this and, desired to open a correspondence with Sir Henry Clinton. Clinton caught at the bait, and the correspondence was established. It may surprise the very large number of American readers, who do not keep pace with the progress of historical research, which has been made of late days, in this country, to be told, as they are in the text, of the treason of Charles Lee, and of Israel Putnam—of that of the former there is little doubt among students of history, since the publication, by Mr. George H. Moore, of the New Historical Society, of "Mr. Lee's Plan—March 29, 1777," with the further title of "The Treason of Charles Lee, Major General, second in command in the American army of the Revolution."

This publication affords the complete clues to the conduct of Lee at and before the battle of Monmouth; and accounts for the facilities afforded to his captors when he finally fell into the hands of the British at White Tavern; and for his behavior on that occasion, making a mixed exhibition of frantic rage and miserable fright.*

---

* Published by Charles Scribner, New York. 1859.

For the recent exposes in the career of Putnam, the reader has only to refer to the searching and scorching analysis of his biography by Mr. Henry C. Dawson, of New York; the author of popular "History of the Battles of the United States by land and sea." Mr. Dawson completely strips that crow of all his borrowed plumage; shows him up as the traitor and the coward; and leaves him nothing of that reputation which has been so laboriously manufactured for him by New England writers of fiction, but his gross ignorance; his grosser incompetence, imbecility and cowardice. The whole of his previous biographies seem to be one vast fraud upon the public faith. But let me return to our drama.†

The next scene opens in the city of Philadelphia, at the period when Arnold, disabled by his wounds from active service, is made commandant of that place. Here he soon became unpopular. His arrogance of temper; expensive mode of living; marriage with a lady who brought him within a purely loyal circle; she herself having been a belle at the Meschianza—a famous fete, in emulation of the ancient tournaments of chivalry—given by the British officers when their army was in possession of Philadelphia;—these facts, and Arcold's increasing intimacy with persons of doubtful and suspected character, taken in connection with circumstances of his own conduct, of equivocal nature—lost him not only the popular favor, but the confidence of the local Government.— The latter complained of him to Congress; and, in his efforts to quell a riot, he was stoned by the people. These details will readily enable the reader to understand the scenes which follow.

---

†Printed in quarto, by Dawson, for private circulation. 1860.

SCENE II.

The Bar Room of the Pewter Platter Tavern, corner of Front street and Jones' alley, Philadelphia. Enter Thurston, in the disguise of an old clothes man. He makes a peculiar sign of the hand to the Landlord.

Thurston.
No flies in the liquor here.
    Landlord.
      No! but, 'ware hawk!
The danger's to the poultry. Wherefore come you
At this unlucky hour?
     Thurston.
       Who that serves, can shap
His seasons to his own necessity?
One's luck should still depend upon his will!
     Landlord.
Would you could make it so.
     Thurston.
      I've been pursued
The hounds are on my track.
    Landlord.
      The devil you say!
    Thurston.
A brace of devils, it may be, and more.
They've tracked me from the Highlands of the Hudson.
    Landlord.
What! to the city?
    Thurston.
     Not quite: I've thrown them off,
Baffled them, I think, some twenty miles below.

Landlord.

You'll hardly 'scape in here!

Thurston.

What's now the matter?

Landlord.

Don't stop for questions. To your hiding place,
As quick as may be, and from thence as quickly.
We cannot long conceal you. I am looking
Each moment for the mob. All's in confusion,
And all the town afright. They're gutting houses,
Hunting for such as you. I would not have you
Caught on these premises for all I'm worth!
'Twere my neck's mortgage. They suspect me now,
And you're an outlawed man!

Thurston.

I know it; but I'm hungry;
Faint, feeble, to exhaustion. I must eat;
Must drink; must rest awhile; though every echo
Cries "Gallows" from the streets!

Landlord.

Into your hole!—
We've scarce a moment—'tis no time for eating
Still less for talking! To your cover quickly.

Pushing him through a private room. Ex.

SCENE II.—THE SAME.

Enter Randolph Peyton, Paulding, Williams.

Peyton. Halloo! Who's here?

Re-enter Landlord.

Landlord. At your service, sir!—pray, gentlemen—
Peyton. We come to search your house.
Landlord. And why, sir, please you?
Peyton. For a suspected person—nay, an outlaw,
A traitor—one John Thurston.
Landlord. No such person
Finds harbor in my house.

Peyton. That we must see;—
Your keys;—you, Williams, keep your eye upon him,
While we make search.
Ex. Paulding and Williams within.

SCENE III.

Peyton, Paulding, Williams, Landlord.

Peyton. He has escaped, if he was ever here!
Landlord.—He's not been here, your honor! On my oath.
Peyton. Nay, do not swear! No needless perjury!
You are suspected. He *has* harbored here,
At other seasons.
Landlord. Never, to my knowledge!
Peyton. Ay, to *your* knowledge; so no lying, fellow!
Beware you do not harbor him again!
See to yourself; and if you close your doors,
And take to your prayers, it may be wisdom!
And now for "the Stag," and then the "Hudibras;"
Our warrant will suffice us for the search
Of any premises, for such a traitor!
Ex. Peyton, Paulding, Williams.

SCENE IV —ARCH STREET.

Mob gathering with great clamor and confusion. Men armed with bludgeons. Here and there, a sprinkling of militia men in uniforms, who seem to fraternize with the mob. A group in the foreground.

1 *Mob.* No use in argument! There's but one way;

The men who stand up for Carlyle and Roberts
Must go down with them.
 2 *Mob.* Hurrah, for that! I say!
I'm with you for a scrimmage—so be quick.
 2 *Mob.* We're all agreed. Let's push for "Wilsons's house."
 1 *Mob.* No flinching, fellows.
 4 *Mob.*   Never name it, comrade;
Our blood is up. We've stood it long enough.
They've had their day—a long one—this is ours,
And we must use it boldly.
 1 *Mob.*   Shout it then,
With your free voices. Down with all the tories.
 2 *Mob.* Ay, down with them, and for each rogue we find,
Be ready with your rope.
      Shouts of the mob without.
    Haul him along!
   Enter new mob bringing in Thurston.
 1 *Mob.* Who have you got there?
 5 *Mob.* The Quaker-Tory, Thurston.
 2 *Mob.* Hurrah for that!—he's a most bloody tory,
Was here a 'hail-fellow' with the British Generals,
And did their back door business.
 3 *Mob.*   Bring him along.
 Thurston. Have mercy, friends, I'm not the man you
           think.
 1 *Mob.* Who are you then?
 Thurston. A poor old clothes man only;
My name is Royall.
 2 *Mob.*   That's a tory name,
If ever there was one! He's royal, is he?
 3 *Mob.* I know him for a tory.
 4 *Mob.* So do I.
 Thurston. Mercy, friends!
 3 *Mob.* No mercy for a Tory.
 6 *Mob.* None for him! I tell you, fellows, I seed him
with these same eyes of mine, busy at the Meschianza. He
helped to fix up the flags and shields, for Major Andre and

Oliver Delancy—and was mighty busy with all the officers.
He's great at treasons and discriminations.

5 Mob. What, the devil! does he deal in his discriminations, too? Then, what more proof do you want? I say, hang him right away.

Chorus. "Up with him to the tree, my boys—
　　　　　The tree that never bore
　　　　　Such goodly fruit before.
　　Up with him to the fruitful tree, my boys."

1 Mob. Haul him along—to the first proper tree.

Thurston. Have mercy on me, friends. I'm innocent!
I'm old; a broken down man of seventy years.
Leave me to God, and, in his own good time——

2 Mob. To the Devil, rather; and his time is now,
And your time's come!

3 Mob. 　　　　　No mercy for the rogue!

4 Mob. Haul him along! He innocent, forsooth!
You see it in his face that he's a tory—
A regular sneak and dodge between both parties,
To pocket pay from all. Haul him along.

Thurston. Pray thee, friend.

2 Mob. Don't friend me, Broadbrim.

Thurston. May I not be heard?

1 Mob. Ay, give him time for prayer.

Thurston. Oh! *you* will pray in vain some coming hour,
If thus too greedy for an old man's blood,
You will not hearken mine. My countrymen—

2 Mob. Silence the impudent fellow! Countrymen!
He calls us countrymen; the rascal tory!
Even while he sells his country. Haul him hence.

　　　　[*They drag him along. In the meantime, enter Peyton,
　　　　　　　　　Paulding and Williams.*]

Peyton. (*Aside to Paulding and Williams.*)
They'll hang the wretch outright, and how to save him?

Pauld. Why save him, when the warrant which we carry
Conducts him to the gallows in the end?

Peyton. Through course of law! To do him proper justice,
We need the authorized arm of proper Law.

Wil. They'll never heed your warrant.

Pauld. No, indeed!
Law's not in fashion here. They'll do him justice,
In a rude way and fashion of their own;
And it is just as well!
   Peyton. Not so, my friends.
I'll save him from their clutches if I can.
   Pauld. How will you do it?
   Peyton. Take up the popular cry;
Join with them in their burden, till we have him
In our own clutches; then stand you by to act
As the event shall prompt. But follow me,
With proper firmness, when I give the signal.
They'll soon be led away to "Wilson's House,
Which they're prepared to storm. Keep close to me.
              (*Mob in the meantime grow more clamorous.*)
   1 *Mob.* Silence the fellow's mouthing! Halter him!
Death to the bloody tory.
   2 *Mob.* We waste time!
On with him to the sycamore! We should be
At Wilson's House.
   3 *Mob.* Haul him along.
   4 *Mob.* Give me the rope.
   5 *Mob.* And me. I'll have a finger in that knot!
   7 *Mob.* A fellow full of discriminations—ha! ha!
   6 *Mob.* Hale fellow with George the Third.
   5 *Mob.* If we don't hang *him*,
Who should we hang, I pray?
   Thurston. Oh! hear me friends, awhile.
   All. Never a word. (*They halter him.*)
   Thurston. Oh! do not take my life! These thin gray hairs
Plead for me from the grave! The judgment seat
Implores your mercy, as the throne of God
Prepares for judgment. If you would grow old,
And have your children look to you in honor,
Look reverently on these! (*Touching his hairs.*)
   Peyton, (*advancing.*) Hark you, old man!
These people must have blood. Their blood is up!

The wrongs of years and ages, need, at least,
One day of vengeance! We must purge the city;
And yours is but one life, of many doom'd
This day, to pay the penalties incurr'd
Long ere your hairs grew whiter than your deeds!
  1 *Mob.* That's true—that's right—that justice!
  2 *Mob.* Haul him along.
  Peyton, (*takes him by the rope.*) With me!
                              (*Signs to P. & W.*)
  Thurston. Ha! who is this? You are not one of these?
  Peyton. But they are mine—my people!
  Thurston. Now, I know you.
  Peyton. Perhaps you also know,
That there are some men better left unknown!
You know too much, John Thurston, for your safety.
  Thurston. All is not lost! You cannot so have lost
Your better nature——
  Peyton. 'Tis clear you know me not
Bear him away, my comrades.
           [*To Paulding and Williams, who have
                       also taken hold of him.*]
  1 *Mob.* To the sycamore.
  Chorus. "The tree that never bore
              Such goodly fruit before.
      Up with him to the goodly tree, my boys"
                 [*Peyton, Paulding and Williams
                             haul him forward.*]
  Thurston. Mercy, O! mercy! Spare me, spare me, Peyton.
  1 *Mob.* Whom calls he Peyton here? We have *no* names.
  Peyton. He raves—but let us have him! We'll soon cure
His tongue of idle speaking.
  2 *Mob.* He speaks to you,
As if he knew you.
  Peyton. *We* know *him* better
Than he knows us. He's known our enemy;
The enemy of all who would be free
From foreign bondage;—he's a tory sworn
To crush out the good spirit of the land,
And make us slaves to Britain.

Thurston. Peyton!
Peyton. Hence!
1 *Mob.* Away with him.
Peyton. Ay, let us hence,
And make a finish of him! (*Hauls him along.*)
Thurston. Mercy! mercy!
'Oh! Peyton, can you not forgive the error,
The one sad error, which I still deplore?
Peyton. Too late! too late!
Thurston. Yet save me! You can save!
Peyton. But will not.
Thurston. Will not?
Beware, lest you, like me, shall plead for mercy,
And find as deaf an ear.
Peyton. The risk be mine!
Thurston. But hear me speak.
Peyton. I know you false—as false and treacherous
As the swart tiger, crouching in his jungle,
And looking innocent as the summer flowers
That give him smiling shelter. I know more—
That you are deadly in your leap as he;
As cunning as the snake in the brake;
False to the pledge, that danger nerves you make,
Its penalty withdrawn! Off with him, comrades.
Thurston. Oh! Peyton! Peyton! God, can this be true?
Mob. Death to the bloody tory! To the tree.

[*Drum and trumpet. Enter Arnold, followed by
a few aids and attendants, as Paulding and
Williams, Peyton leading, are dragging
Thurston off.*]

Arnold. Stand!
Peyton. Perdition! Ha!
Arnold. What do you with this man?
Peyton. We bear him hence
To the just judgment he has oft incurred
By frequent treacheries against the State.
He is a traitor known in frequent commerce
With those, in arms, who are our enemies!
Arnold. What warrant have you?

BENEDICT ARNOLD.

Peyton. A sufficient one,
If thousand voices here may speak.
Arnold. I know that voice—
Who is it speaks to me?
Thurston. And you should know him, my Lord. He—
Peyton. He calls him Lord, good people; Oh! good Lord!
The leopard cannot cleanse him from his spots;
And this vile tory, pimp for Lords and Generals,
Must make a nobleman of your own soldiers,
Even with the halter around his neck.
Haul him away, good comrades, to the tree.
Mob. Away with him.
Thurston. Oh! save me, General, save me!
This man who seeks my life——
Peyton. Will he still prate,
And you still listen, commander?
Mob. Away with him.
[*They drag him—he struggles.*]
Arnold. Stay, friends.
Peyton. Why stay?
Arnold. It is *my will!*
Peyton. And mine that they proceed.
Arnold. Insolent! Who are you?
Peyton. A man!
Arnold. What! nothing more?
Peyton. Ay, if you will it so—*your* enemy!
Arnold. Methinks I know you, fellow.
Peyton. If you do,
You know that I am one to bear a will,
As resolute as your own.
Arnold. I am here,
The master, sirrah!
Peyton. Matter still for trial!
Ho! comrades are you patient to behold
The traitor thus the champion for the Tory!
Arnold; Traitor!
Peyton. Here are you in your strength, my comrades!
Look that you suffer not this wretch to 'scape,

Who would betray your liberties. I've warrants,
To apprehend this criminal, for justice!
Gather about me, while I bear him off!
  Arnold. This man misleads you, citizens, to ruin.
  Peyton. His Lordship would be heard; but hear him not;
This is our prey! Gather about me, comrades,
See that there be no rescue!
  Arnold. Have at you traitor!   [*Draws upon Peyton.*]
  Peyton. 'Tis a match between us,
For blows, as well as titles! Come on, Lord?
          [HE DRAWS AND MEETS ARNOLD'S ASSAULT. A
            MELEE FOLLOWS BETWEEN THE MOB AND
            ARNOLD'S ATTENDANTS.]
  Arnold. You're a bold man, of a sudden—strangely bold;
And such as when you were but Randolph Peyton,
The humble suitor of a noble lady,
Who could not see the many virtues in him,
With his own eyes! Is't so?
  PEYTON.   Your wretched taunt
But arms me to new anger? In *her* eye,
Meek, humble, as was ever Randolph Peyton—
It is not thus that he confronts her husband!
No doubts, no sickening feebleness of heart,
Now palsies his resolve, impairs his strength,
Or, by one pang or passion, from his bosom,
Plucks the fierce spirit that inflames my hate.
          [THEY FIGHT. SOLDIERS RUSH IN, PURSUED BY THE
            MOB. STONES FLY ABOUT ARNOLD, AND THEY
            ARE SEPARATED.]
  ARNOLD. Perdition! What is this?
  MOB.   Hurrah! Hurrah!
Down with the Lords and tories!
  PEYTON.   Well done, comrades—
But do not come between me and his Lordship,
'Till I have done with him!
          [TRUMPET SOUNDS AS APPROACHING.]
  ARNOLD. That bugle's ours.

CLARKSON. They come—the cavalry.
MOB (*without.*) The horse—the cavalry!
[CONFUSION AND LOUD CRIES.]
ARNOLD (TO CLARKSON.) Where's Thurston?
CLARKSON. Safe! We've rescued him; and now—
ARNOLD. The guard will soon be here! They come in season!
And now disperse—infatuate citizens,
Ye tamper with sedition! As for this man,
Your ringleader—a traitor—He is mine!
PEYTON. Stand firmly, keep your ground, my gallant comrades,
Even though his Lordship, and his tory allies,
Bring down your own paid hirelings upon ye.
[TRUMPET CLOSE AT HAND.]
MOB, (*rushing across the Stage.*) The cavalry,
They charge us! Fly!
PEYTON. Stand fast, and they will fly!
ARNOLD, (*shouts.*) Charge!
PEYTON. They yield—they fly—at the first sound of danger.
1 MOB. On with us, comrade!
PAULDING. Captain—let's away,
And keep our courage for a brighter day!
[PAULDING, WILLIAMS, WITH THE MOB, HURRY PEYTON ACROSS THE STAGE; THE TRAMPLING OF THE CAVALRY HEARD—ARNOLD, WITH A FEW FOOT SOLDIERS PRESS ON THE RETREATING MOB, BUT ARE ASSAILED BY SHOWERS OF STONES.]

ARNOLD. Why did you let the ruffian 'scape who led
These foolish burghers on? But, for my wounds,
He had not 'scaped my arm! Pursue his steps;
Scatter your band abroad, through all the streets,
And find him at your peril; living or dead—
One hundred pounds to him who brings his head!

The next scene takes place in the dwelling of Arnold—the old mansion house which William Penn inhabited. He has married the beautiful daughter of Mr. Edward Shippen, afterwards Chief Justice of the State of Pennsylvania. Margaret Shippen was one of the *belles* of the "Meschianza," and intimate with the *elite* of the British officers. Among these was Major Andre. Such was her intimacy with him as to lead to a correspondence between them, which was continued after she became a wife. This correspondence furnished a cover to that of Arnold himself, and thus initiated the correspondence between Arnold, as "Gustavus," and Andre, as "Anderson."— Her views, as well as that of all her family, were notoriously with the British. Her associates, in society, were those who favored, if they did not actively contribute to, the cause of the enemy. But I need not anticipate the argument of the Drama. Our present scene is a dimly lighted apartment in Arnold's house—time, evening—Mrs. Arnold speaks, as to a servant, while she enters from an inner chamber.

SCENE V.

MARGARET ARNOLD AND MAID—ANDRE ENTERS TO THEM IN DISGUISE, WITH CLOAK, &C.

MARGARET. To me—a stranger?
ANDRE, (SPEAKING AS ENTERING.) Whose sorrow 'tis to be so.
MARGARET. Andre! here?
ANDRE. Ah! Margaret, where should Andre be,
But where devotion calls him?
    MARG.   You forget,
I am another's right!
    ANDRE.   Alas! the hour
That I should hear such sad intelligence!
You, wherefore thus another's? Did I lose
My right in my misfortune! Was it *my* fault,—
And did it show forgetfulness of thee,—

When, with our armies driven, I sped from hence
To be undone forever!
  Marg.   Speak not thus—
Nor ask, nor wonder, that the fate is such!
The deed is done, and there's no help from Heaven!
  Andre. Yet is there help!
  Marg.   No help! I'm sworn *his* wife.
  Andre. Margaret, an oath as sacred, made you mine.
  Marg. Why tell me now of this?
  Andre.   To bring you back
To pledges still unbroken; which, I'd perish,
Sooner than rupture! Margaret, you *are mine;*
If there be faith in woman;—if her vows,
Sacred as altar offerings, in *my* sight,
Have record anywhere in Earth or Heaven.
  Marg. Away, and leave me, Andre! Should *he* come—
  Andre. I'd brave him with defiance!
  Marg.   You affright me—
Your presence here affrights me.
  Andre.   Let it not!
I come not here without due guaranty!—
Nor to endanger what is sacred still,
The future as the past. Too well thy charms
Are pictured on my heart, for me to lose thee;
And I will be as gentle with thy lord,
As if 'twere him I worshipped.
  Marg.   Do you seek him?
  Andre. Ay, with deliberate purpose.
  Marg.   Wherefore, then?
  Andre. In policy, not hate. But question not!
Better be ignorant of the game we play,
Than err from too much knowledge.
  Marg.   I misgive thee!—
Andre, thou shalt not dream of violence,
If thou hast come with proper guaranty,
Why this disguise?

Andre.   It *is* my guaranty,
'Till we do first adjust some needful terms.
With your great chieftain.
   Marg.   Yet, I fear me much
This secresy—these disguises—and thy presence—
Should *he* surprise thee here!
   Andre.   But this he shall not!
Old Thurston is my surety.
   Marg.   Thurston—he!
Know'st thou that Thurston knit these marriage bonds,
That tied me to another?
   Andre.   Ha!—thou tell'st me—
But he knew nothing of my passion then.
   Marg.   Can'st thou forgive him?
   Andre.   If it pleases thee.
   Marg.   I hate him from my heart! Believe me, Heaven!
That gave thy countenance to his dark intrigues;
Intrigues that, from the very life of love,
And hopeful youth, and all that's dear to woman,
Have cut me off forever.
   Andre.   Think not thus—
There is a remedy—
   Marg.   Hark! Hush! a sound—
Oh! if they find thee here!
   Andre.   Fear it not, Margaret.
Well do I know the secrets of the place,
And wear disguises that no eye can fathom,
Save thine, perchance. But now we separate,
To meet again with better confidence—
This secret passage—See!
               [He disappears through a panel.]
   Marg. (*sinking in a chair and clasping her hands.*)
               I have need to tremble!
I stand above the abyss! Support me, Heaven,
That sees the danger, as my own heart felt it,—
My own soul, that now fails me! Oh! I see

The terrible fate that threatens me, and call
Vainly, on woman's strength, her pride, her virtue,
To succor in the struggle that must follow!
Mother, Oh! mother, from the skies I summon
Thy spirit to my aid. Too soon I lost thee,
And then went erring wide. Let me, no longer,
Thus wander in the maze of self-deceit,
But strengthen me and save! Ah! Who comes there?
ENTER THURSTON.
THURSTON. Thy uncle, Margaret.
MARG. What! Wherefore comest thou?
THURSTON. A very pretty question. I *am* here!
Thou see's me! living—in the flesh I come!
MARG. But wherefore? Is't for mischief, and new troubles?
Why thus encounter peril? What fresh treasons
Prompt thee to risk such dangers as might shake
Even firmer nerves than thine. Thou wast safe,
Safe with thy friends, the British.
THURSTON. They are thine too,
Else thou hast greatly altered in thy favor.
MARG. I am my husband's only, and his people
Are mine, henceforth! Thou madest me wed with him,
And cannot now complain that I am altered.
But wherefore dost thou come? It cannot be
Thou know'st not of the danger. Rescued once
From those who hate thee, here, why risk again
Thy life, endangering others who would vainly
Strive in thy service now? Arnold, already,
Hath saved thee once, but he——
THURSTON. Hath saved me twice—
This day, as on the night which saw thee wedded.
MARG. Oh! hateful night!
THURSTON. What! from saving me?
MARG. Not that! not that! Oh! uncle, 'twas thy work,
Those bitter bonds—those cruel rites, that tore me
From all of hope, and faith, and happiness!
Oh! how I hate thee for it!

Thurston. Foolish child,
It helped us both to power—thee to the joys
For which the damsel barters all of Heaven,
In winning all the sweet delights of Earth;—
The rout, the revel, the festivity,
Gay dance and merry music. These made up
The infinite sum and substance of thy dreams;
Thy days had no object; and thy nights,
Brought every star down from its place to sing thee
Of fresher joys by dawn.
  Marg. No more! no more!
Thou mock'st me with the girlish vanities
Which made thy treacheries easy to achieve.
I am now a woman—changed—how sadly changed,
As conscious of the weaknesses which gave thee
Such power upon my soul—a power which makes me
Feel like a living fraud on him who claims
The affections that were never, and *can* never,
Be rightly mine to give, tho' his to challenge!
I hate thee for it.
  Thurston. Thou'lt grow wise in season!
Girl's loves and hates are just so many fancies,
Sunder'd in a moment, by the passing cloud,
Or as inconstant sunshine. Time will cure them;
And you will find it wisdom, the dispersion
Of the vain dreams of girlhood, by your marriage.
Enough that we have power—we may have wealth,
And surest station, if your head shall tutor
Your heart to proper sense of what should be
The wisdom for your husband.
  Marg. I see it all—
More schemes, more intrigues, more treacheries!
Your coming tells me that your head is busy
With some subtleties, that must endanger
The safety of my husband as your own.
But how did Arnold save thee?
  Thurston. From the mob!
They found and seized me in the market place—

How pierced the shrewd disguises that I wore,
I cannot guess, unless that from the Highlands
They track'd me hither; but they had me tether'd;
The rope about my neck; another minute,
And I had dangled from the sycamore;
But I was rescued.
    MARG.   As before, by Arnold!
    THURSTON. Why, yes—it seems his destiny to save me—
Perhaps 'tis mine to serve him.
    MARG.   Why tempt you Fate?
    THURSTON. My fate do you call it, Margaret—the halter?
    MARG. You've brought me to a worse one!
    THURSTON.   And a noose, too!
    MARG. Forbear this idle jesting at an hour
When all my soul's in terror. Answer me,
Nor mock the terrible doubts that fill my heart,
By wanton jeer at my infirmities.
You found me weak and vain, and you have wreck'd me,
And I must bear the burden of my sorrows
As best I may: the woman's pride to succor,
When hope has fled from fancy; and when Passion
No longer warms with confidence; rebuked
At once by conscience and society.
Thus having done the worst upon my fortunes,
I've right and reason now to claim you leave them,
Even what you've made them—leave me altogether.
    THURSTON. Wherefore this, Margaret?
    MARG.   Why is Andre here?
    THURSTON. Andre here?
    MARG.   Ay, here!
    THURSTON.   I knew it not!
    MARG.   Thou didst.
He says he came upon thy guaranty—
He had not come, had'st thou not counsell'd him.
    THURSTON. I cannot think it, Margaret! Andre here?
    MARG. Here in this city—in this house—this chamber!
How knew he of the secret passage?
But for thy guidance, and thy guaranty!—

How dared, but for thy wantonness of malice,
To fancy that he still kept 'biding place
In this frail woman heart.
  THURSTON, (*sullenly.*) That secret, Margaret,
He better learn'd from speaking eyes of yours,
Than any speech of mine. If Andre's here,
He comes upon no guaranty of mine—
He comes too soon—the fruit's not ripe for him—
  MARG. What fruit?
  THURSTON. That concerns thee nothing.
  MARG.   More intrigue,
More peril—more disaster—O! I see it!
  THURSTON. Blame your own beauty for his coming, Margaret,
Twas with no will of mine.
  MARG.   Get him hence, uncle,
For his own safety speed him.
  THURSTON.   And for *thine?*
  MARG. Oh! bitter malice!—yet thou speak'st the truth—
For mine! For mine!
  THURSTON. 'Tis well! now hear me, Margaret;
'Tis needful that I teach thee that my malice
Hath less of mischief in it than thy arts—
Who think you led the mob to set on me?
  MARG. Who?
  THURSTON. Who, but Randolph Peyton!
  MARG.   He here too?
  THURSTON. Ay, for thy terror and thy punishment,
And it may be for mine! That fine young man,
Whom thy cajoleries, flatteries, cunning arts,
Gay smiles, and pretty practice, hath misled,
To his undoing;—at one moment, sure
Of all thy favors—at the next cast off,
And sinking in thy scorn.
  MARG. In truth, I did him wrong!
  THURSTON. 'Twill ease his heart
To hear thy prompt confession!
  MARG.   Cease thy sneer!
Did Arnold see him?

BENEDICT ARNOLD.

THURSTON. He did!
MARG. And spoke with him?
THURSTON. Ay, fought with him, besides; breast against
breast,
Steel against steel, and the young braggart stood
As fiercely and firmly, as if his spirit
Had caught the fire and force of twenty heroes,
Each powerful 'gainst a host.
MARG. What then? What then?
THURSTON. The billows of the multitude rolled in,
And parted them, ere either had been hurt;
But there were bitter taunts, more sharp than swords,
Between them ere they parted.
MARG. Did he fly?
THURSTON. Who, Peyton?
MARG. Yes; who else?
THURSTON. It might have been thy husband;
But for a sudden charge of cavalry,
That came, at the right moment, he was worsted,
And might--that noise without.
[SOUND OF HORSES IN THE COURT.]
MARG. Arnold comes!
I leave thee, but—
THURSTON. A moment ere thou goest—
Say nothing rashly;—of thy speech beware;—
These secrets in thy keeping are not thine,
And nation's hang upon their utterance!
If Andre's here—
MARG. There, in the secret chamber.
THURSTON. 'Tis well!
MARG. I say 'tis ill! What does he here?
THURSTON. He comes too soon—he was not bade to come;
But his impatience to behold thee, Margaret!—
MARG. Look to it, uncle! I'm a child no longer!
Get that man hence! See to it! I look to thee,
As thou art bound, by all the ties of blood,
To save me! Save me! Leave it not to me,
Weak and uncertain ever, this wild struggle,
Where pride and honor, lost in whirling passions,

Yield in the strife, through fear as much as favor.
  THURSTON. Fear nothing;—but be secret!
  MARG.   Ah! these secrets!
Why dost thou vex me with them? What is now
The mischief that thou bring'st?
  THURSTON.   Away; he comes!
  MARG. (*As she goes out—and pointing to the secret panel.*)
Get that man hence!—in safety, as thou lovest me;
But, get him hence, and speedily.   (*Exit.*)
  THURSTON.   I will!

SCENE VII.—THE SAME APARTMENT.

ARNOLD AND THURSTON.

  ARNOLD. Ha! Thurston, but they had thee in the coils!
That fierce young savage had decreed thy doom,
Short shrift and sudden cord! Why wilt thou risk
These perils? If the game thou hast to play,
Must bring thee to the meshes of thy foes.
Why idly kick against them till thy feet
Grow fastened in the snare.
  THURSTON.   I have not done so.
  ARNOLD. What! made no violent speeches to the mob?
Blabb'd not of loyalty to drunken brawlers,
In orgies of a pothouse? Your gray hairs
Should promise something better.
  THURSTON.   So they should;
And I were well deserving of rebuke,
Had I been erring in this idle fashion.
  ARNOLD. Why, then 'twas Clarkson told me.
  THURSTON.   He has err'd!
My heart and tongue have sins enough to answer.
But this is not among them. It is hard
To hear in silence, and keep down my anger,
These scum and offal mouthings of my sovereign,

In such base terms and foul comparison,
Nor tell them how I loathe them. These gray hairs
Have grown to whiteness in a sort of freedom
That suffer'd tongues to wag. A subject born
To our good king, and England's constitution,
These modern doctrines do not suit me well;
But though it chafes one to hear vulgar voices
Blate of their rights—the people's sovereignty,
Giving us Governors of the Lord knows who,
Making us lieges of the Lords knows what,
And, for our surer and better subjugation,
Making us laws, the Lord defend us from—
Yet, have I still a smack of modest prudence,
That makes me lock up anger, when its freedom
Must only bring its owner into bonds.
 ARNOLD. How came they to find thee?
 THURSTON.   That's the puzzle:
My watch was good—my place of hiding sure,—
Disguise sufficient;—and my apprehension
Is, that I have been tracked even from the Highlands.
 ARNOLD. Ha! tracked? By whom?
 THURSTON. I cannot think; it may be Randolph Peyton.
 ARNOLD. Hardly him! He's not so deep in subtlety—
 THURSTON. He has fierce passions—
 ARNOLD.   You must see to this!
The Heath-hound, once he fastens on your heels,
Will hunt you to the death! Still, I do think,
That, for an old conspirator, old man,
You are too rash—too free of speech—your language—
Even now, is far too bold for ears of mine.
 THURSTON. Forgive me, my good lord, if I go erring;
And change to honest zeal the offence of freedom.
But, speaking of this people—
 ARNOLD.   Whom I govern!
 THURSTON. I do not rank *you with* them.
 ARNOLD.   Yet am I *with them.*
 THURSTON. Not *of* them! I can comprehend the need,—
Not wholly blind, or lacking sense for this,—
Of something striving, striving for a right,

When a great nation's wrong'd. God, in his bounty,
Anon, and ever at sure intervals,
Vouchsafes to men, a MAN!—a monarch born!
Whose mission is to sway! If power perverse,
Or Party, blind and reckless—bitter tongues,
And rival leaders,—baffle his career,—
'Tis right that he arise, prompt and fierce,
To execute the vengeance that is due
When Heaven's great will is outraged! But to see
The wretched herd grow dangerous with the cry
That is the Shepherd's only;—the base swine
Forget their husks to emulate the state
Of him who is their feeder;—and mean spirits
Batten on sacred food, which, as they mouth
Makes their poor wits insane!—This vexes me;—
And thinking of their merits, I forget
That mine is not the strength to scourge the creature
Back to his proper kennel! For this people—
 ARNOLD. And was there *not* a need that Heaven *should*
               send
Some succoring man to *us?*—Some noble Shepherd
To save *us* from the wolf?
 THURSTON. Perchance, I say not nay;—
Though 'twere a difficult thing for honest wisdom,
To find the wolf in Britain's crowned king,
And the meek innocent flock in such as these!
Even were they such at first, it is not now,
When crime runs riot in the land;—the wolf,
Driven back at bay; the herd itself grown wolfish,
And, under leading of the Gallic tiger,
Turning upon the shepherd, though their own!
 ARNOLD. There was a time, most surely, when the nation
Had wrongs that ask'd redress! But not to call
This Gallic tiger, as you fitly phrase it,
To take the herd in keeping! Surely Heaven
Had yielded to this continent a man,
Born to thus sway;—commissioned as you deem it;
Nor made it needful, that we send abroad,

BENEDICT ARNOLD.

For chiefs and allies to our natural foes!
Was there not one?—
    THURSTON.   There was, my lord—one man
I've seen;—whom yet I see!—
    ARNOLD.   Thurston, awhile!
Thrice, in our parley, have you called me Lord.
You did so in the rabble's ears, and heard
The howl that follow'd it! Need I tell you now,
This is no title of mine!
    THURSTON.   It is! It is!
Not granted by your flimsy government,—
Denied by popular vanity; which still
Denies the boon it cannot share itself;—
But yielded by the loyal heart, that feels,
Where the true noble, in his nature regal,
Shows the o'ermastering will, the grand endowment,
And by the glorious nature in his gifts,
Claims loftiest sway and challenges obedience!
This is the very question on which hangs
Whatever of State or safety may belong
To the far future of this wretched people!
I see in Arnold what his people will not,
The man decreed for sway; one who might be
Vice Roy of Britain for this continent!
    ARNOLD. Nay, Thurston, but—
    THURSTON.   Do not check my speech!
I am no flatterer, no adventurous ear wig,
Looking to profit by the wares he brings,
And lauding tinsel, in the vain man's hearing,
Until it grows to gold. I but declare
What still I've felt; and, feeling, ever thought;
And cannot help but think; and still must speak!
What else first brought me to conceive such merit,
In him, my sovereign's enemy, to make me
Come, with reluctant homage—made me bring
The fair young girl, a maid a king might covet—
The image of a sister now in Heaven—
And place her in thy arms? This was my work;

And 'twas because mine eyes beheld in thee
A Lord, endowed by Heaven!—not wholly yet
Denied his right by man!

    ARNOLD.   You phrase it, Thurston,
As if my country had denied me justice!

    THURSTON. And has she not, my Lord? Are you content
With this poor station—with this petty rule—
Here, in a city, which disputes your power,
Strives ever 'gainst your office, and whose people
Hurl spear and stone, seditions, 'gainst your breast,
When you would stay their madness!

    ARNOLD.   A mob! a mob!

    THURSTON. 'Tis all a mob! The mob is everywhere—
Rules in the court, runs riot in the chamber,
Defiles, despoils and everywhere profanes!
The popular rule has ever been a mob!
The standards of appeal, to popular judgment,
Must, on the part of him who would succeed,
Contemplate ever, the most lowly vision,
And square its argument to the basest minds.
Commons take the place of nobles;—vulgar of great;
And the whole moral of the commonwealth,
Must sink in the end to money and to lust!
Then rule resolves itself to appetite;
Appetite to greed; and greed insanity;
That rages in its offal, till it perishes
Of its own foul and self-engendered plague!
This is the fate of this great continent,
If thus the people should subdue their king!

    ARNOLD. A horrid picture, Thurston.

    THURSTON.   Yet, a true one.
But 'tis not only with the common mass,
That failure still awaits you. Follow me:
What says the Governor of this petty State?
Know you that he already makes complaint
To Washington, and Congress?

ARNOLD. Ha! of me?
THURSTON. Your very greatness and integrity,
Are marks for such to strike at! See you here!
Here are the secret charges brought against you;
I have them from sure hands. [*Gives papers.*]
They charge upon you
Illegal acts—oppressive jurisdiction—
Nay, crimes, that might be treated by the Laws;
Though they prefer, with hyprocite profession,
To leave the thing to Congress.
ARNOLD. And, meanwhile,
The slander, borne on every wind of malice,
Speeds through the nation.
THURSTON. You have conjured rightly.
ARNOLD. I must meet these charges.
THURSTON. I have brought them,
That you may do so.
ARNOLD. Many thanks good Thurston;
I owe you much!
THURSTON.
You owe me nothing! 'Tis my pride to serve you;
Still, in the greatness of your gifts, beholding
A natural right to human loyalty!
But, when I counsel you to meet these charges,
I'd rather say—revenge them! There's no answer
That ever stifles slander; which still fastens,
With stain that's ever ineradicable,
Upon the whitest garments.
ARNOLD. Revenge them! Ay!
There yet shall come a time—
THURSTON. Men make occasion,
And *will* can master *opportunity*,
While weakness waits upon the wind's caprice.
I've weighed these people whom you waste your life for—
The people first—this petty province—next.
ARNOLD.
I, too, have weighed them—they are nought to me!
THURSTON. Whither do you turn then?

ARNOLD. To Congress.
THURSTON. Congress!
Turn rather to the vane on yonder house top,
And find the oil to ease its ancient rust.
ARNOLD.
Congress, the nation, North and South, and East,—
The millions in whose service I have bled—
Will do me justice! I have no appeal
To the vile scum that's here.
THURSTON. All scum, alike!
And justice, that, according to their speech,
Is what they mean to yield you; but they add,
'Tis the last thing you pray for!
ARNOLD. Speak they thus?
THURSTON. 'Tis a pet epigram upon the streets!
Such is their hate of you—their doubt—distrust!—
And ask yourself why are you fetter'd here,
Condemn'd to such associates—such a station?—
Put here in trust, where nothing is in danger;
And nothing can assail? What duties, here,
Can give employment meet to Arnold's mind;—
What perils threaten, here, that can give field—
To Arnold's desperate valor?
You forget
The wounds that keep me idle.
THURSTON. You yourself
Forgot those wounds to-day!
ARNOLD. I did! my passion,—
The sudden provocation, and keen impulse—
THURSTON.
Would make you still forget; and you would conquer!
ARNOLD. Congress shall do me justice.
THURSTON, Congress cannot.
ARNOLD. And why not?
THURSTON. It cannot, by its simple resolution,
Take from your cheek the stain of any blow!
The insults and the injuries of to-day!—
Nor, though they do acquit you of these charges,

BENEDICT ARNOLD.

Will they undo the damning imputations
That follow from their making.
    ARNOLD, (*gloomily.*)   True, too true!
    THURSTON. But Congress will not, if it might. The herd
Bands ever, with the hottest sense of self,
'Gainst the superior genius! 'Twill delight them
To see you hunted down; to see your strength
Tapp'd of each good support; and know, the power
That awed them by the shadow of its greatness,
Denied each golden opportunity!
We'rt England now.—we'rt in *her* cause, you bear
The wounds that tell of Saratoga's field;
Of the fierce valor, and the wondrous conduct
That caged Burgoyne, the braggart, with his army—
Methinks, the unconscious tribute of *my* tongue,
That named thee noble, all unwittingly—
Had found its sanction in a Sovereign's accents;
And royal homage, and a glorious peerage,
Had welcomed thee, a Lord, among its Princes!
    ARNOLD, (*in low tones.*) I must not hear thee, Thurston.
    THURSTON.
        Ay, a noble; Peer! and with such ample treasure,
As will suffice for a princely house.
    ARNOLD.   No more! no more!
To Congress—
    THURSTON. Congress still! Then hear me farther!—
The goodly members of that stolid body,
Moved doubtless by the mighty Washington,
Having these weighty documents before them,
Have found them worthy of court martial judgment,
And you—
    ARNOLD.   Court martial!
    THURSTON.   What! you feel it then?
Ha! ha! methought 'twould sting you into feeling!
Quebec's best hero, Burgoyne's conqueror,
Must answer to the Pennsylvania council.
    ARNOLD. Damnation!   (*Strides the room passionately.*)

BENEDICT ARNOLD.

THURSTON, (*approaches him.*)
Let me now show you in what way to triumph.
Hear me, my Lord! I've borne your letter safely—
Seen Robinson—Sir Henry Clinton!—Here—
Read this in secret—burn—and have your answer,
By midnight! I will through your secret chamber,
And hood myself till then. (*Gives a letter.*)
    ARNOLD. Have you seen Margaret?
    THURSTON. She must know nothing!
(*Aside, as he goes out.*)
    He has felt the shaft,
And the wound rankles; but he has the ointment!
[*Exit.*

ARNOLD, (*solus.*)
The whole world sees my wrongs, yet I am silent!
The whole world knows my claims, yet I ask nothing!
The shadow of that man is still upon me—
Chills friends, drives Fortune from my side—denies me
The justice which is mine, and the great merits
Which also had placed the wreath upon my brow,
And fixed all eyes upon me in expectance.
Ha! Washington, thou cold and haughty statesman;
Too much the Hero for the Politician,
Too much the Politician for the Hero;
Yet, blending both, so subtly intermixed,
That each must serve the other on occasion—
Would 'twere upon our swords, which mighty spirit
Should bear the palm and wield this continent:
No subtle web to spin—no plots to manage,—
But a fair field; the wrapt world looking on,
And we the only combatants for judgment!
And it must come to this!—the day approaches:—
I cannot always be denied and baffled!
I feel it here!—a power and will to conquer,
Which will not be subdued;—yet, heart be still
While THOUGHT and subtlest WISDOM tutor WILL!
(*Exit Arnold within.*)

Here ended my first act, with a scene quite too long, even did it possess all other proper attributes, for any dramatic exhibition in our times. But all dramatists understand that cruel surgical process which is called '*cutting*'—a process, by the way, which compels the imagination, in the audience, to supply a great many breaks in the argument. It will be seen, from certain portions of this act, that my aim has been to lift the moral of Arnold, by showing that he labors under the impulse of ambition—that it is not all greed with him, and mere vanity and lust;—but that he is jealous of the overshadowing power of Washington.

The second act opens with the increasing anger and disquiet of Arnold. His accounts have not passed without comment and curtailment. His heavy drafts on the treasury have met with unscrupulous repulse. He is living, much too freely, at the public expense, and terribly at the expense of his own credit. Bad as were the times, and selfish as were many of the public men, in power, the vices and excesses then predominant, were insignificant in compare with those of the United States in *our* day; when no less than thirty members of Congress are found charged at once with corruption;—and when five of them are convicted;—all of them from the very regions in which Arnold obtained all his moral lessons! The same regions now furnish, not only the chief abolitionists to whom the present cruel war is due, but it is kept up by mercenaries from the same quarter, who fatten on its corruptions; who are the contractors and speculators who prey upon their people, having ours no longer to prey upon, through the mixed media of Government and trade. The day which sees the war at an end, will be one of terrible reckoning to both these parties; now playing into each other's hands; and they know it, and dread it accordingly. But this aside. Arnold's mode of life is destructive both of credit and character, in the comparatively simple community upon which he practices.— They might, however, have forgiven his cupidity, but they could not stomach his arrogance. Of haughty and ostentatious habits and carriage, he is exceedingly vain, withal, of the pomps and exhibitions society—fond of balls and gay assemblages. He is a creature of mercurial temper, as well as passions and vanity; and not without moments of generous impulse. His extravagancies some times show like virtues, and help to delude the judgments of men, in respect to his own—to make them even doubt his vices. At this very time, when a diseased ambition, or perhaps a merely morbid vanity, is working evil to his heart and reputation, he was appropriating liberally, from his own funds, for the support and education of the children of General Warren, who fell at Bunker's Hill, and whom the State of Massachusetts had unnaturally and strangely neglected. Congress had determined that the eldest son should be educated at the expense of the United States, but for the three others nothing had been done. It is to Arnold's honor that he resolved to support and educate them himself. But this fact, which is essential to the proper estimation of his character, has nothing to do with the action of this drama.

It will be perceived, in the foregoing scene, that, though Arnold has opened the correspondence with Clinton, Thurston is not yet sure of him. He knows his mercurial temperament too well. Arnold, like Macbeth, is one to falter in decision—to show himself quite capable of conceiving the crime, but to be infirm of purpose, when this crime involves the loss of reputation; which, as a man of great vanity, he values much more than honor. He dreads to think, not of what he may do, but of the public judgment that will follow it. Thurston is not yet willing that he should see Andre; as he dreads the effect upon him, until he has committed himself sufficiently far to cut off retreat. Andre has come prematurely; not so much as a conspirator, as a lover; though there is little doubt that he has no farther passion for Margaret Shippen than belongs to a flirtation, in which the passion is usually hardly strong enough for the plunge from that precipice over which the parties are yet pleased to hover!

In reference to the scene which follows, and which is meant to show the petty influences which contributed to the overthrow of this man, we may mention, as one of the privileges of the poet, in his free use of history, that Col. Jamieson did *not* serve under Arnold while he was Commandant at Philadelphia. His aids, while in this situation, were Majors Franks and Clarkson; but Jamieson is too important an agent, in the subsequent developments of the drama, not to be made use of at the beginning; and we economize, for the necessities of the stage, by condensing, into as small a number as possible, the subordinates of the story. I now proceed to the opening of the

SECOND ACT.—SCENE I.—ARNOLD'S HOUSE.

ARNOLD AND COL. JAMIESON DISCOVERED.

ARNOLD. Another insult, Jamieson! By Heavens!
Each day brings in its new indignities!
What think you hath this commissary done,
To make me loathe this service?
    JAMIESON.   I cannot think.
    ARNOLD. Refused my order for a small increase
Of private stores, when at a time like this,
As well he knows, my doors must needs be wide,
To large official throngs—to visitors
That come on business of the State, and mark
In what our State shall lack of dignity.
    JAMIESON. He hath refused you?
    ARNOLD.   Utterly refused!—
Nor spared his private comments, as I learn;
Bidding me be more moderate and less free
In my demands on Congress, and what not—
For which, be sure, he shall receive my thanks!
Oh! this is to take service from the mass,
Who hate the hand that saves them, and still wrong
The very souls they lack the soul to honor.
    JAMIESON. And you are lacking in your month's supplies?
    ARNOLD. No! I have had the order for the month
Vouchsafed in full;—but then, my mode of life,

The official state which duty forces on me,
Demand increase, and heretofore have had
Some small indulgence from the men in power.
What new caprice now urges them to change,
Is yet behind my ken; but let them pause,
Or I may lesson them in other fashion,
Then now they seem to dream of.
   JAMIESON.   What have you done?
   ARNOLD.
Sent back once more! That I should be reduced
To base practice; and be forced to sue
For that which should be given, with courtly offer,
On the bare intimation of my need!
I've sent to learn by whom I am denied;
And here comes Clarkson back, and in his looks,
I read the offensive answer.
   JAMIESON.   **You are too quick!**
   ARNOLD.
Quick! quick! Methinks the marvel of the world
Will be, I am so slow, and bear so meekly
The gird and sting of these base jacks in office.
But there's a speck of flame that burns with me,
Which yet may fire an edifice.
            (Enter Clarkson.)

   Well, Clarkson, speak!
What hath this man to answer?
   CLARKSON.   But little, sir,
Precise upon the question that I bore.
He spoke too much at large to answer much,
Yet much he prattled of extravagance,
Unseeming living — indiscreet indulgence —
Bearing so straight upon your dignity,
That soon I stay'd his argument, and task'd
His answer briefly to your clear demand.
   ARNOLD. What said he then?
   CLARKSON.   Why, peevishly, it seem'd,
As interruption of a well conn'd speech,
He bade me tell you that his order came

Direct from Congress, where, it seems, report,
Made long ere this, had moved them straiten you.
 ARNOLD. From Congress? Ha! Perdition! a long bolt
Shot by no common hand! But we shall see,
If there be none of answering weight, to tell
Upon that haughty crest!
 JAMIESON.   'Tis very strange.
 ARNOLD.
Strange, do you say! Is't strange that baser spirits
Should chafe at your advantage? Should toil hard
To rob you of your honor? Should grow jealous
Lest you should win the world within your circle,
And leave them in the cold?
 JAMIESON.   Of whom do you speak?
 ARNOLD. No! no! it is not strange. It is as natural
As that the snake should hiss, the owl should hoot,
Dogs bark, and filthy creatures that hate light,
Declare their loathing, in some bestial fashion,
Of each grand orb that grows to central state,
Rising in quiet grace to majesty
Unconscious how they rage!
 JAMIESON.   But you have been—
 ARNOLD.
Denied, you would say!—Denied! You do the work;
Achieve the triumph—turn aside the storm,
And save the State, avert the destroying bolt,
And then are bade, by those whom you have rescued,
To seek the moon and fatten as you may!
I' faith you're right; and still the reason's good,
Would I but see it with submissive eye,
And bear the shame in silence! So I will!
In silence! Oh! in silence! But there's speech—
Volumes of dread significance—in skies,
That have no sound; but droops, as if the death,
Were doubly stretching out his solemn pall,
Well knowing that the bolt, already forged,
Is waiting to be launched.
 JAMIESON.   Congress, methinks,
Errs, in its economy——

ARNOLD.   Economy! you dream,
Good Jamieson. 'Tis Republican, my friend,
To swallow camels, yet to choke at gnats!
To feed some favorite Southern popinjay,
With wanton hands and millions idly spent,
And boast the while of public gratitude.
At the same moment, to the humble plaint
Of some o'ertasked and almost worn-out soldier,
They hurl a rude denial; lecture him,
Through the base pipes of artisans and clerks,
Of his too lavish living. He has notions,
That something to his dignity belongs—
That station calls for state—that office shows
But shame, if stript of its caparisons,
And,—but enough! You smile upon me, friends,
That I should thus be moved, by such as he!
    CLARKSON. The insect fastening on the charger's flanks,
May goad the noble beast to veriest madness;
And proudest spirits, who might face the earthquake,
Sink 'neath the tortures that they never fear!
You cannot know this creature—
    ANOLD.   No, but Congress!
And these *are* men, who may be noble victims,
When wounded honor calls for great revenges.
For Congress! But no matter! Vengeance keeps,
Nor spoils because the winter is a long one.
    JAMIESON. This is the vice of Governments where all
Have equal voices. In a common choice,
The great man never is the favorite;
We fear, too much, to love him; and we loathe
Soon as we learn to fear. The common man,
The temporizing, all subservient, cunning,
Is still most like to be the favorite.
He vexes none with individual thought,
Or individual feeling—has no mood
That's troublesome to yours—will make no quarrel
With any of your tastes and preferences,
But hold your reason good; till you are absent,

And then, perchance, will foul it with his foot,
As if it were your carcass.

CLARKSON.   Such as he,—
A ducking, bowing, sweetly-spoken man,
That walks, without a shadow, still in yours,
Is just the person for the populace.
He does not vex, but lifts, their vanity;
Honest opinion, with his fearless front,
Chafes vulgar self-esteem—will not be schooled
By bold presumption, and a sleek conceit—
Is quite too blunt and sturdy, unfamiliar,—
And rather goes unseen along the highways,
Then shapes his paces for the thing it scorns.

JAMIESON. For this the people find their favorites,
Even in their foes.

ARNOLD.   Well, well,—or Log or Stork,—
What matter who they take, or who they find!—
A MAN, but seldom! Yet a man may be
Their MASTER! He has but to see their need,
And first become their scourge! Oh! I do feel
That there's a spirit brooding in my soul,
That will not brook at this! Prithee, my friends,
Strikes it not full upon my dignity—
The scorn of this denial, and the shame,
That follows on the bruit?

JAMIESON.   Nay, too high
Your anger rates this conduct. With a word,
To Washington, or Congress, you call down
Rebuke on this official—his disgrace.

ARNOLD. Rebuke, disgrace, and on a bird of the dunghill!
And the appeal, most humbly made to Congress
To Washington!

JAMIESON.   Ay; He—

ARNOLD.   Ah! you mistake!
You know *Him* not—you know not *me!* Ha! Ha!
Methinks you spoke of Congress! I could laugh,
To hear you, first discoursing of that body,
So headless, with so many heads.—so heedless
Of every head that might achieve the rule;

Yet hated for this reason;—than to hear
Of justice and redress, from such a body,
For such a head as Arnold's!
  JAMIESON.   Washington!
Will give redress.
  ARNOLD.   You know *him* not, I say.
I tell you this is plann'd— is predetermined—
By Congress, Washington and Pennsylvania,
For Arnold's overthrow and dire disgrace.
  CLARKSON. Not so, I cannot think it.
  JAMIESON.   Impossible!
It is a lower policy of Congress,
And some general rule, and does not aim at you!
Straitened by protracted struggle, and untaught,
By long experience in the cost of war,
Our rulers lack the ready wit to find
Meet entertainment for the vast expense
Growing from the struggle for our independence.
Let but the evil pressure of the day
Pass off, in triumph, as it must at last,
And all will then be well;—the toils of war,
The heats of battle, and each hungry event,—
Will have their pleasant recompense.
  ARNOLD.   This might serve,
For argument of strength to some poor suitor,
Who craves for nightly raid his compensation,
And for the loss of hay, or grain, or beef,
Winds up his plaint with dollars, dimes and cents!
I make no prayer like his, and but demand,—
Serving the State at sacrifice of all,—
That I be spared the strife with creditors,—
The shame of obligations, which are due
To this, the very station that I hold!—
Ask but my day-by-day expenditure,
Proportioned to the exigence of duties,
Such as they force upon me; and, by Heaven,
I hear a sermon from some sodden clerk,
Touching the grace of fast and abstinence!

BENEDICT ARNOLD.

I tell ye, friends, I've never weighed the blood
In battle shed; nor counted wounds I've suffered,
'Gainst any gold in mortal treasury,
'Gainst any jewel in a mortal gift,
Or any prize save honor.
  JAMIESON.   And think you not
The nation knows all this?
  ARNOLD.   Why then this shame?
  JAMIESON. 'Tis their's the shame—the poverty of the land—
The error, doubtless, of some untaught agent,
That lacks discreet direction in his duty.
  ARNOLD. No! no! I know it better! This poor agent
Is but the creature of another's will;
One lurking under the cover of a shadow,
The while he speeds the shaft!
  CLARKSON. What other, General?—
  ARNOLD. I have not won the popular cry;—not heard
The voice of fame, teaching the mountain echoes
The name of Arnold—to and fro rebounding,
From mountain peak to seaboard;—not to rouse
The malice of the selfish, cold ambition,
Which sickens, in its greed of appetite,
To hear another's praise.
  JAMIESON.   I cannot think,
My General, that you suffer from this malice.
Who ranks in popular love with you?—what name,
So dear to all our echoes as your own,—
Save that of Washington;—and *him*, I hold,
Above the angry currents of the strife—
And pure, as he is cold;—free of that envy
That sometimes apes ambition!
  ARNOLD, (*coldly.*) Said I aught
Of Him?
  JAMIESON. I know you honor him too well,
To smile on that hostility which seeks
His ruin as your own. The nation glories
In its twin heroes; and the popular worship
Hath made you heirs of fame, to shine together,
While freedom hath an altar.

ARNOLD.　　　　　　Idlest fancies—
His and my fame!—the popular liberty!—
Alas! I read them all, good Jamieson,
Through *this* denial—in *this* record here,
Of what official violence may dare
In mockery of this worship!—But the hour
Is passing for our toils. Our lady-wife
Bids me entreat your presence, here, to-night,
When she keeps state awhile.
　　JAMIESON AND CLARKSON.　　We shall attend.
　　　　　　　　　　　　　　(*Exit J. & C.*)
　　ARNOLD. That I should chafe with anger at a name!
That, but to hear of *him* should goad me thus!
I strive in vain against him! *He* wins all
Their suffrages and shouts;—their very hearts;—
While Arnold's name grows fainter than an echo!
Who's there?
　　THURSTON. (*Entering from the secret chamber.*) A friend.
　　ARNOLD. Art thou sure of it? For such I need.
　　THURSTON It may be I shall prove so.
　　ARNOLD.　　　　　　　Would you could!
But you lack power to help me.
　　THURSTON.　　　　　　Try me then—
Methinks you have some proofs of it already,
If that you've duly thought upon my mission:
But learn what now is talked of in the city?
　　ARNOLD. What next?
　　THURSTON.　　That Congress *bridles* one for whom
It soon must find a *whip*.
　　ARNOLD.　　　What! this of me?
　　THURSTON. Even thus! 'Tis stated that the commissary,
By Congress ruled, puts limits on our General;—
Measures his absolute need—
　　ARNOLD.　　　I'm patient—speak!
　　THURSTON. Admits you should have rations—
　　ARNOLD.　　　Good! no more?
　　THURSTON. Your pay, at regular periods—
　　ARNOLD.　　　　They are kind!

BENEDICT ARNOLD.

THURSTON. But must be taught that, profligate expense,
Waste, license, use of credit, speculation,
Suits no more with republican resource,
Than with your own good reputation.

ARNOLD. Ah!
Methinks, 'tis very well!

THURSTON. I heard the speech,
And could have smote the cur that cried it loudly,
Throughout the market place, to thousand echoes,
"Who was this Benedict Arnold, ere we made him,
Our General, that he should affect a State,
Becoming a Prince?—a common chapman!"

ARNOLD.
You smote him, did you? On the mouth you smote him?

THURSTON. I had nearly done so, but it would have been
At peril of my neck.

ARNOLD. Your neck? Why, what's a neck
To a man's honor?

THURSTON. Besides, the act had been
Most fatal to concealment.

ARNOLD. You are prudent,—
Most reasonably prudent!—There must be
Some bitter hours for this!

THURSTON. And so there might,
Did these shafts come from any hand but one.

ARNOLD. What hand—what one?

THURSTON. Dost ask? Who governs now
But that Virginian? He is potent here,
As there, in Congress; needs but will, in secret,
And all these creatures, hounds from out the kennel,
Rush at his beckon on their quarry's flanks,
And tear him down for execution.

ARNOLD. Truth—
A goodly pack!—

THURSTON. The excellence that dares
But struggle for the palm, 'gainst him, their champion,
Is crushed to silence.

ARNOLD, (*fiercely.*)　　But they crush not me!
I'm not of this base temper, to succumb
In silence, with no struggle! Oh! methinks,
Before they bring me to the dust, they'll find me,
With teeth and talons, bloody! They may rend,
But they shall feel me, first!
　　　THURSTON.　　　　　　Ay, make them *feel* you!
But, while you nurse the passion, hide the teeth!
I heard you, rashly as I thought, in converse
With these Lieutenants. Beware of whom you trust!
That cold and stately Washington maintains
Strange power upon men's hearts, despite his stern
Unbending carriage! He will triumph still,
In any *open* contest with a rival!—
Be chary of your wrath, and you shall feed
Your great revenges yet! Subdue your rages;
And smile—for smile you can,—even while the venom
Dilates the sack that lurks beneath the fang!
Speak smoothly; and 'tis better you forbear,
Every expression of your discontent,
Until the proper season. Then,—*one* blow,—
Shall bring you your revenges!
　　　ARNOLD.　　　　　　　　Speed the hour,
Ye Deities that wait on mortal Passion,
And stimulate the desperate appetite,
When that the board is spread! That cold, *great* man,—
For such I still must deem him, while I loathe
The policy which wins for him the title,
As still it wins the game—flings his broad shadow
Forever o'er my pathway.
　　　THURSTON.　　　　　　Still must do so,
Unless with wiser policy—
　　　ARNOLD.　　　　　　　　But show me!
　　　THURSTON.
　　　　　　　　He baffled Lee, and Conway; Gates and others;—
Guides Greene and Lafayette;—guides the Senators,—
The very best and ablest of the Congress,—
Simply, by patient waiting on events,

BENEDICT ARNOLD.

And curbing Passion when it would go erring!
He is *not* cold, but fiery as a furnace;
But keeps his valves and vents; and time's his hour,
Prepared for the explosion! When that comes,
No power is idly wasted in the air;
But, to its mark, the missile goes unerring;—
There is a victim—or a victory;—
And he rides on;—the mountain late a volcano,
Once more, all clad in snow! But, in your passion—
 ARNOLD. Well! well! my passion?
 THURSTON. Still robs you of your prize!
Yields up the game to Gates at Saratoga,
And 'stead of being held the conqueror,
By the calm wisdom, as the impetuous valor,
You won the merit simply of a fighter,—
Insanely conquering—raging recklessly,—
O'er the dread field, your *wisdom* could not compass!
On Gates' brows your laurels grew to weeds,
Or Southern willows! That boastful upstart,
Failing to *keep*, what you alone had *won*,
As good as gave it all to Washington,
And raised his fortunes higher by *your* loss!
Mere valiancy may win the moment shout,
But the wise conduct, grasping the whole field,
Alone, secures the fame! Nor is it enough,
To *do* the work of wisdom. You must wear
Her *seeming* also. The unruffled port;—
The calm serene of brow—the ready wit,
To meet the moment summons;—equal mood,
That never suffers change; whether defeat,
Or victory wait the action;—showing, for aye,
The justly balanced mind; the unbending will,
That never shows caprice, and is not moved,
By every rise and fall of fate, to passion!—
To rage because of every small vexation,
Makes men grow doubtful of the hero's greatness!
To rise superior to the petty trial,
Compels their homage; since their consciousness

Tells them that they, condemned to such denial,
Had never leash'd their passions by their pride.
You must subdue your blood beneath your brain,
And curb your fitful passions, but to make them
Do the becoming service; as you train
The wild steed 'neath the yoke; keep racers low,
In flesh, in order that the sinewy limbs,
Should grow to proper vigor. You may yet
Assert your genius. It is not too late!

ARNOLD. What should be done?
THURSTON.   Win *power*, and use it!
ARNOLD. Have I not power?
THURSTON.   Ask yon Commissary's clerk;—
Ask Pennsylvania's Governor;—ask the *mob!*
Your power's a mockery; an idle pageant,
Where you are but the stalking horse of the scene!
Go, ask some *trust* from Congress.
ARNOLD (*eagerly.*)   What trust? What power?
THURSTON. One where the peril opens doors for *deeds*—
One where the greatest fortunes of the nation
May hang upon *your* conduct, or—your *will!*
ARNOLD. Speak! you have more.
THURSTON.   We'll think of it hereafter.
Just now, to something nearer. You have need—
I learn it from the bruit of the highway,
And guess it from the talk with your Lieutenants—
Of succors which your Congress hath withdrawn.
You are my niece's husband—must not be,
Badger'd by hungry creditors!—
ARNOLD.   What mean you?
THURTSON. Take this to meet your present exigency.
                  [*Lays a bag of gold on the table.*]
Nay, 'tis a loan I proffer. You shall pay me
When better station yields you better meed,
And more to your deserving.
ARNOLD.   I need it not.
THURSTON. You do, my Lord.
ARNOLD.   This gold—

THURSTON. Is but a loan!
ARNOLD.
 What, if my scant resource and wretched fortunes,
Deny me in the future as the present.
 THURSTON. It is a *gift*, then, to my relative,
From the old quaker, Thurston! And, to quiet
Your sense of obligation, I must tell you,
My traffic with my kinsman, Anderson,
To which 'Gustavus' lent his friendly name,
Gives promise of the goodliest gain to all—
For you have equal share in each investment!—
He tells me, if the profit shall continue,
As it hath well begun—and he's a tradesman,
Who dreams of nothing better than to make
His sheep breed daily—that our several shares,
May, ere the year be ended—ere another,—
Be thirty thousand pounds!
 ARNOLD. Thirty thousand pounds!
 THURSTON. It may be—guineas!
 ARNOLD. Show me but the way,
To hush these noisy creditors!—
 THURSTON. And, more;
Compass position; State and name; and feed
Your great revenges!
 ARNOLD. Show me but the way!
 THURSTON. Your hand upon it!
 ARNOLD. There!
 THURSTON. Your lady-wife
Throws wide her rooms to-night.
 ARNOLD. Will you be present?
The mask and fancy-dress affords you cover.
 THURSTON. I will; and with your leave, may bring with me
My friend, John Anderson. Shall he be welcome?
 ARNOLD. 'Tis well! I'll look for you.
 THURSTON. 'Till then, my Lord,
Let not this vulgar clamor of a mob,
Goad you to thoughtless passion! Keep you calm;
Not once forgetting that *I* guaranty

Your triumph, and your full revenge, in season!
Though Congress, and the power that governs Congress,
All hate and fear you—you have still a power,
In your own soul, in our own strength and will—
Your Genius, roused to *boldest* purposes,—
To make *them* dread you most, who now despise!
Bring these to bear upon them. Cease the prayer
For old arrears of money, which they have not,
But ask what they *can* give! You seek for glory—
For some high trust—and, wherefore not the navy—
That's a new field;—the ocean waste of highway;
Where triumphs may be won—the noblest triumphs;
Pluck'd from old England's greenest sheaf of laurel,
To keep yours ever bright!

  ARNOLD.   That were a field!
  THURSTON. Yet, there's a threat of Clinton's now abroad,
That his eye covets West Point!

  ARNOLD.   It may well
Covet a fortress most impregnable,—
Well kept, in able hands, 'gainst all the force
That British power may send;—most haply named
The American Gibraltar.

  THURSTON.   To him who dares,
No garden fruits are sacred.

  ARNOLD.   Good Sir Henry
Was never famed for daring.

  THURSTON.   Yet, the prize,
Might well beget a daring in the feeblest,
And works, 'tis thought, in him. The nation's stores,
For future strength and conflict, lock'd within it;
Itself the key of the country;—were it to fall,
'Twere fatal to your Washington!—to all,—
And—

  ARNOLD. 'Twere so, indeed!
  THURSTON.   In worthless hands, even Clinton,
Might dare, methinks, the trial.

  ARNOLD.   Never—he!

BENEDICT ARNOLD.

Thurston. And were Congress wise!—why give they not,
This place of peril to their bravest chieftain?
Why should they fetter such a soul as Arnold's,
In this poor, selfish and ungrateful city,
Where nothing mates his nobleness of nature,
Or needs his eager valor. The marines
Were better in your hands! Upon the seas,
Your banner should defy the jealous breath
That now forbids it flow! West Point in danger,
What valor more than Arnold's could maintain it;
Plucking red trophies from grim-visaged battle,
While raging on its rocky eminence,
None daring to approach! For either of these,
Might Arnold fearless ask; nor would they dare
Deny him the high trust. They might as well
Declare at once that Washington had fears
Of rival genius greater than his own!

Arnold. We'll think of it! You will be here to-night?

Thurston. As surely, as my heart beats anxiously
To see my Lady-niece—my Lady Arnold!

Arnold. What gold is here?

Thurston. A tenth of what is yours,
Should Anderson make his profit as he thinks—
Three thousand guineas only.

Arnold. Three thousand—guineas!

[*Thurston goes through the secret door. Arnold stands musing, with his hand upon the gold, while the scene closes.*]

In this Drama, it has been my policy to elevate the character of Arnold, as much as possible—to pass slightly over his cupidity—his peculation, and petty offences against morals; and to show his vanity only through the higher medium of ambition, and a love of glory. With this object, I have dwelt on his supposed jealousy of the superior eminence occupied by Washington, and have made him, and Thurston, both dwell upon Washington's supposed envy of Arnold himself. It is quite possible, indeed, that Arnold entertained these feelings and opinions. But, in this prose commentary and development, I propose, in some degree, to exercise the privileges of the Historian, and set aside those of the Dramatist. A hundred years hence, were this a successful *acting* play, the correction of its errors would be of no more importance, in the eyes of the audience, than are the historical corrections of the false history in the career of Richard the Third, as pourtrayed in Shakspeare's play. But, as I regard the present as a performance only fit for the closet, the historical narrative may well keep pace with the assumptions of the Drama. Briefly then, and in commenting upon the preceding scene, I beg to state that Washington had no respect for Arnold's morals, only for his courage and soldierly qualities. He appointed him to take charge of Philadelphia, in consequence of his wounds, received at the last battle with Burgoyne, rendering him incapable of any more active service. In this city, Arnold indulged in habits of license and extravagance which were equally inconsistent with his position, his resources, and the condition of the country. He lived sumptuously, entertained numerously, and even lodged the French Minister, and all his suite, in his own dwelling. The better to exhibit his lack of principle, it may be said that he professed a warm attachment to the French, and heartily welcomed the alliance with that nation. Subsequently, he urged this *unnatural* alliance, as one of the reasons which made him abandon his country, and desert to the British. His treatment of the people of Philadelphia was oppressive in the last degree; the shopkeepers were forbade to sell, and, under pretence of the necessities of the army, their goods were impressed by his agents, and subsequently sold at great profit.— He used his authority to enrich his creatures, then quarrelled with them about the division of the spoils. He closed, by his military authority, the courts of justice against the citizens thus abused; and it was only after long and patient waiting, that the Executive authorities of Pennsylvania proceeded to enquire into the subject; finally appealing for redress to Congress.

BENEDICT ARNOLD.

Here, for a time, the interposition of party baffled investigation. At length, however, Congress laid the complaints of Pennsylvania before the Commander-in-chief, and a court martial was ordered. This is the period which has been reached in the progress of the preceding scene. Prior to this period, Arnold had privately become engaged through partners, in *privateering;* but this speculation proved unsuccessful, swallowed up his ill-gotten gains, and increased his embarrassments. In the settlement of his accounts with Congress, that body cut them down considerably. He was thus desperate of fortune, when he was approached, as in the drama, by the tempter! He, at first, made choice of a marine appointment, as suggested in the text—the application for the command at West Point was an after thought. Sir Henry Clinton agreed to give him £30,000 (not guineas) for the surrender of that fortress; and he may, or he may not, have received an instalment of three thousand guineas in advance, as stated in the drama. The Brigadiership was pledged to him; but the base lure of the Peerage was unauthorized; and, we may here mention, that the *full* amount of his £30,000 was *never* paid him; the treason not yielding the anticipated results. Meanwhile, as soon as he had fully opened his correspondence with Clinton, through Thurston, or Robinson, or whatever agent, he was counselled to hush the voice of dissent—to submit placidly to the censures of Washington, Congress, Pennsylvania, and the people;—to dissemble, in every possible way, so as to win sympathy, and, by conciliatory acts, secure the desired appointment to West Point. He was docile as a pupil, smiled away effront, and became, in his language, more zealous than ever in the cause of independence! Though a man of the fiercest passions, he could play the hypocrite successfully, whenever he had a motive of interest to prompt him.

The scene which follows takes place in the apartments destined for *Lady* Arnold's *route*, which was, in fact, a masquerade ball. We call her *Lady* Arnold, for two reasons; though one will suffice. It was something of a custom, in that day, thus to designate the wives of very distinguished persons.—Martha, the wife of Washington, was commonly called Lady Washington; and neither herself, her husband, nor Republicanism, thought the epithet amiss. Parties had not agreed to pacify the vulgar vote by the abolition of rank and caste; it needed that Republicanism should verge upon that moral rottenness which inaugurates an ochlocracy; and this, in turn, needed such an influx of the lowest orders of a foreign population to turn the scale, in all popular conflicts, against the native population. But this is digressive. Amongst the bitter slanders of, and attacks upon Washington, I do not believe that it ever was made a subject of libel upon her husband, that Martha Washington submitted complacently to the title of "My Lady." The word was a good old Saxon word, and simply meant to indicate a woman *lifted* or raised by marriage. It does not seem, originally, to have been restricted to the narrow conventional sense in which it is now employed, as a title of nobility. If the reader is curious on the subject of its etymology, he will find it discussed in the elaborate essay of Horne Tooke.

We must fancy for ourselves what sort of fashionable display was made, in those days, at a route in the city of the Quakers. There was no lack of ambitious effort. We have need to remember two things—first, that America had, by this time, began to lose something of its primitive simplicity of character; and Philadelphia, which had an aristocracy of its own—as much, perhaps, as it possesses to-day, and of a more genuine sort—had only a little while before been in possession of the British army; had witnessed the far-famed glories of the Meschianza; had gazed, with delight, upon the rich uniforms of the *elite* among the British officers; many of whom were sprigs of nobility; and was thus already familiar with scenes of gorgeous and fashionable display; and secondly, and subsequently, they had seen the magnificent reception, and the splendid pageant which Arnold had given to the French Ambassador and his suite. As I have already tried to show, Benedict Arnold, goaded by cupidity, was yet not avaricious. He did not accumulate to hoard. He was far the most ostentatious of all the American Generals, and emulous, seemingly, of outdoing and excelling all that he had heard and seen, of the grand exhibitions of other persons. Unlike Charles Lee, who was frivolous, and a sloven,—Arnold was boldly and honestly fond of state and show and luxury, and forbore no occasion which gave him opportunity for display. In this weakness lay the whole secret of his inferior moral and his final fall! Of the "Meschianza," of which so much has been said already, and which he was evidently anxious to surpass, something perhaps ought to be said here, that our people of to-day may learn something of the pomps and vanities of folly at a period, not unlike our own, and when a bloody war of invasion, seeking the subjugation of the country, was raging in the land.

The word "Meschianza" is Italian, and simply means a *medley* or mixture. The word was, no doubt, provided by Major Andre; whose chief merits seem to have been in getting up scenic displays—in decorating balls of state—and doing clever things for the amusement of his comrades and society.— He could paint cleverly; write clever verses on common things; make an epigram, and play spy, or gallant, with equal dexterity. He does not appear, in any other way, to have distinguished himself. Why he chose the word "Meschianza" or "Medley" to designate this particular festivity, it is perhaps difficult to conjecture. It may be, as the entertainment comprehended equally equestrian an aquatic exercises—feats of rowing and feats of jousting—to say nothing of dancing and supping—that this blending of various sports and exercises, was the true reason for the name; or it may have been chosen to signify the bringing together, on equal terms, of opposite parties—Whigs and loyalists;—indeed, the whole affair may have been meant somewhat to conciliate the former—it being understood that the knights cavalier, who were all necessarily of the Loyalist Party, could scarcely find their partners for the dance, unless by a large attendance of Whig ladies. The attempt at conciliating these, however, if made, was not very successful. The number who attended, was small, and these incurred no small degree of odium from having done so—they were universally regarded as faithless to their political creed—and were doubted, if not despised, forever after. We need enquire no farther. For that matter, *all* such festivities are needless,—'motley's the only wear.'— Enough, that, under the unwonted foreign term, the British nobles reconciled themselves to the policy of mingling, on an equal footing, with 'all sorts of people.' The object of it was two-fold. It was a complimentary festival to Sir Wm. Howe, and designed, at the same time, to commend the royal cause to popularity.

The "Meschianza" was celebrated on the 18th of May, 1778, at Wharton's country seat in Southwark. The occasion was the departure of Sir Wm. Howe for England. Lord Howe and Sir William also, I believe, claimed to have royal blood in their veins—only qualified by the *Bar-sinister*. I have seen original letters of *Lord* Howe which only proved him to be a great blackguard. They were absolutely filthy. But both the men seem to have been amiable, and were popular with their officers and soldiers; though neither of them seems to have been successful as a General.

A splendid "regatta" opened the festivities. Three divisions of boats, each division having its own band of music, darted upon the river at the same moment, issuing from the water edge of Green street, in the "Northern Liberties." These were caparisoned with sails and streamers of the most gaudy and attractive colors. Multitudes of other boats, crowded with spectators, hung about the contestants, while numerous barges were employed to ply about, and restrain them from encroaching upon the precinct assigned to the performers. The wharves, windows, housetops and balconies of the city wherever a point of sight could be found, were also crowded with eager and impatient watchers. The Loyalists were uproarious and triumphant in the display; the poor Whigs, looking on, nevertheless; interested in spite of their politics; but sore and disconsolate! A procession followed on the land—the selected actors in the scene, marching through long avenues of grenadiers, and accompanied by troops of Light Horse.— They all proceeded to a spacious lawn, already environed with troop, the main body of the British army.

This lawn was chosen as a place of tournament. Seven damsels, habited in Turkish costume, were conspicuously placed on a raised *Dais*, faced by balusters. Their habits, by the way, were devised by Major Andre. These damsels were thus chosen, to bestow the prizes upon the successful among the contestants. They were styled fantastically "The Nymphs of the Blended Rose." Their champions, also *seven* in number, were called "The White Knights," and were fancifully habited in white and red silk (the colors of the Blended Rose) and were mounted on *grey* chargers, gayly caparisoned, and in the same colors with their riders. Their Herald proclaimed their challenge of Beauty, declaring that the "Nymphs of the Blended Rose" excelled in Beauty and Wit, in virtue and accomplishment, all other damsels in the world; and in behalf of these claims of their champions proclaimed their challenge against all comers.

This insolent proclamation was answered by the Herald of seven other Knights, habited in black and orange, who styled themselves the "Knights of the Burning Mountain."— Their arms and banner exhibited a mountain sending forth flames, with the motto—"*I burn forever*"—on a scroll. I need not go into close details. It will suffice to say, that, as far as possible, all the ancient practices of chivalry, at joust and touney, were scrupulously observed.

The two bands of knights, respectively, rode around the lists, making their obeisance to the ladies, and winning great admiration for their horsemanship. Then, all things being ready, the warder was thrown down, and the cry "*Laissez allez*," gave the signal for the combat. The trumpets sounded the charge, and the rival knights, each singling out his adversary, rushed into the *melee*.

The first encounter was with lances. These being shivered, resort was had, in the second and third courses, to the pistol— an anomaly in such a scene, and one that could be productive of no effects, unless the battle had been one *a l'outrance*. The pistols, thrice discharged, *en passant*, the combat with swords followed.

From this scene, the company, knights, ladies and favored guests, passed into a spacious hall where refreshments were served—tea and lemonade. Tea, at that time, by the way, was about *one hundred dollars per pound;* a price which may somewhat reconcile us to the present blockade prices, which, I am told, range from ten to twenty dollars, according to qualty, or color of the article, green or black. This pleasant part of the exercise over, the nymphs put themselves in solemn posture, the victorious knights throw themselves at their feet, and, kneeling, received the prizes accorded to their valor.— Adjourning, from this apartment, which is described as singularly splendid, the company passed into a richly decorated saloon, the walls of which were covered with mirrors, candelabra, branches and flowers. Of the former, no less than *eighty-five* were suspended in this one apartment. On the same floor were four withdrawing rooms, filled with refreshments.

Dancing then followed, and this was succeeded by a magnificent display of fireworks, beheld from the opened windows. After these had paled their late 'effectual fires,' at midnight, large folding doors, which had been hitherto concealed by decorations of flowers, at a certain signal, sprang open, as if by magic, and discovered a magnificent saloon, more than 200 feet long and forty wide, with alcoves, covering sideboards, on which a grand supper was displayed. I shall not enter into the details of this gorgeous chamber, nor enumerate the branches of lights, the lustres, the forest of pier glasses, the wax candles, the thousand covers, and twenty thousand dishes. The servants in waiting were all *black servants,* attired in Oriental garments. Enough, perhaps, to quote a single sentence from Andre's written narrative of the affair. He pronounced it "the most splendid entertainment ever given by an army to its General,"

Poor Andre seems to have been the chief architect on this occasion, and something must be allowed for his natural egotism. To him and Captain Delancy are assigned the credit of having painted the scenery and decorations, and of devising the costumes of the Ladies and the Knights. Here, indeed, he seems to have been in his proper sphere. He would probably have made an admirable manager of private theatricals. He was, no doubt, much more fitly employed—more truly in his sphere, and working after his own genius,—in scene painting, and in *festas*, than in politics; better at music and the dance, than meddling with 'treason, stratagems, and spoils.' He has left behind him an elaborate description of the "Meschianza," which he probably regarded as the great event of his life— that, perhaps, excepted, by which it was so ingloriously brought to an end. With a lively fancy for such things, considerable taste and ingenuity, it is certainly a subject of regret that he had not more wisely and blamelessly chosen his occupation, that his peculiar talents should have found employment in an appropriate and peaceful sphere.

In one month after this vain, though gorgeous display, of scenic enchantment, Knights and Nymphs had disappeared, as if by the hateful spell, of such oriental Djinn. The British made a hasty retreat from Philadelphia, and Benedict Arnold succeeded to its Government. But they left the example of luxury behind them—a dangerous example—which the poor Republicans could only emulate at the expense of propriety and honor. That the public mind was vitiated, no less than Arnold's, is hardly to be questioned. The *fetes* that followed, though hardly to be spoken of in the same moment with the Meschianza, were extraordinary attempts, and but too frequently repeated. They largely contributed to Arnold's involvement, and consequently to his dishonor. Still, we should not forget that his character was anomalous, and that there is quite enough in the history itself to justify the assumption, in the drama, of more dignified motives than cupidity and profligacy in bringing about this catastrophe. Arrogance and vanity were there;—but ambition also. He had a just consciousness of services and merits as a military chief, which had been denied reward—and he was impatient of the subordinate position, to which his ill fortune, and not his moral, had reduced him. But I need not anticipate the drama.

In the scene which follows, we find him *alone*, in full costume, in his wife's saloon, awaiting the expected coming of her guests. But he does not look the careless gayety which belongs to the scene. His mind wanders. It broods over troublesome thoughts. His mood is gloomy, if not unamiable; and the soliloquy which he speaks is broken by conflicting suggestions of a vexed and capricious thought.

SCENE.—*Suite of Rooms richly lighted and decorated.*

ARNOLD, (*solus.*)
I have no more stomach for the scenes
That once did so delight me; the high revel,
The joyous music and the glowing pageant,
Gay humors, and the jocund merriment,
Of crowds that banish thought! The thought resists
The blandishment as banishment; and strives
For sole dominion in the fiery brain!
It leads me still away; and much, I fear,
Through paths I should not travel. The disquiet
Breeds ever as I go; and when I pause
Grows mutinous; to the utter overthrow
Of law, and will, and purpose! The outer eye
Forgets its observation; sees things pass,
As floating in a mistlike world of space,
Where the vague shapes go wandering as they will,
Having no aspect; and the sounds that rise,
Challenging the ear's observance, are of like;—
Meaningless, wild! in strange confusion mixed;
That answer to no question, and report
No progress to the mind! All's chaos here,
That suffers no repose, and yet whose waking
Can satisfy no aim!
                But for that man,
Methinks I should sleep sweetly for awhile,
And wake to fortunate action. In my dreams
His image rises to defeat their promise
And fright the coming joys, that hang aloof
As waiting till his aspect shall retire.
He haunts me like a foe. He is *the* foe

BENEDICT ARNOLD.

Of all, and over all, the peacefullest;
As still I feel that every bolt I launch
Goes by him harmless; or but wounds the air.
Innocuous, as shafts that, through a shadow,
Pass with the mind, leaving the hurts to close
Even as they pass! Impregnable he stands,
Cold, statue like, and scornful of the assaults
Whose storms he cannot feel. By day, by night,
In waking and in sleeping hours, he stands
Upright before me; while each look renews
The haunting admonition of his hate,
Which hangs on my horizon like a cloud,
That frowns down all my sunshine.
      Oh! Washington!
Thy name, thy star, is still the bane of mine—
A baleful image ever in the sky,
That's fatal to my hope. In vain I strive!
The fearful spectre of thy happier fame,
Mocks me with grim denial. I but toil
That thou should'st take the prize; but brave the danger,
That thou should'st wear its honors in thy plume,
And mount in my despite. The honor's with thee!
And I, whose daring is beyond thine own,
With skill and courage, whose superior toil
Have won less questioned prizes, bloody spoils;
Triumphant, still, where all besides have fallen;—
I do but serve to swell thy bloated gains,
That grows from all in turn!
      'Twere best not toil,
If still the profit helps mine enemy!
Better 'gainst honor's self to work, than thus
From honest working compass mine own bane!
The Fate's awry, when faithful service stands
A mendicant, and asks for right as favor,
Nor gets the boon it prays for! Better, in evil,
To strive at power, regardless of the faith,
Where faith itself must bring discomfiture
To every hope of Fortune. Why should I—
No boy—no braggart—but a man of deeds,

Play second to this moral Caucasus,
And buckle on his spear! What's 'Washington,'
To better spell the senses of a host,
Than Arnold—both are words of goodly sound—
And for the deeds, that stand for them, whose record
Should better grace the page of history?
Place them together—his and mine—repeat them—
Sound them in popular ears—sing them and shout them—
And those which Fortune, in her own despite,
Links with the name of Arnold, are, methinks,
As glowing, and as grand, in mortal echoes,
As any in *his* record!—Washington!
How cold—how stern—how black—the image rises,
Before my vision, which that name recalls!
Dread aspect—loathsome shadow—get thee hence!
I bid thee down! Hence! Hence! Begone, I say!
Oh! for a weapon which would reach thy heart!
Could but the prayer prevail—or curse or prayer,
To bring thee to the field!—and we alone—
No eye to see—no tongue to shout—no ear
To hearken, of the bloody words we speak,
Or of the clash of those conflicting swords,
That summon Fate to judgment! *(Starts.)*

Enter Lady Arnold.

MARGARET. Moody still!
For shame! Put off your clouds! Your voice in anger,
Heard through the farthest chambers, brings me hither,
To chide you to composure. What's the grief
That darkens thus your sunshine?

ARNOLD. A dread shadow,
That stands for aye between me and the sun!

MARG. But still, a shadow!

ARNOLD. Make for me the sunshine.

MARG. Why so I would, if you would second me.
But 'tis in one's own will and proper humor,
To feel it when 'tis made! Would you tell me
From whence your shadow rises, it were easy
Perhaps to conjure it away from sight;—

But—one thing, Arnold—you will still see shadows,
And very fearful ones; clouds that bear lightnings,
If still John Thurston haunts your house.
  ARNOLD.   Your uncle!
  MARG. Yes, but a dangerous man! I must not ask you
What 'tis that brings him hither; but I tremble
Lest he should work you evil by his presence.
  ARNOLD. An old man, Margaret.
  MARG.   With more than youthful fires,
Perpetual seething in the brain that wears
For crown, the snows of winter! Oh! beware!
  ARNOLD. Your habit is a lovely one.—
  MARG.   Do you like it.
  ARNOLD. I had almost thought, not looking at your face,
'Twere worthy of your beauty.
  MARG.   Ah! you mock me!
You would rebuke me for the thoughts that take
Their color from your countenance—Would teach me
That women have no business in the cares
That vex men's judgments; and I would not trespass:
But, pray you, as you value peace and honor,
Your peace and mine, beware of uncle Thurston—
He's an embodied mischief!
  ARNOLD.   Margaret—
Why vex the natural beauties of that face,
By most unnatural fancies? That old man—
But we'll not talk of him! Let's rather take
The color from the happier world to-night:—
You are very beautiful.
  MARG.   And you, my Lord,
But for that cloud, still lurking in your aspect,
Might stand for an Apollo.
  ARNOLD.   Mars will answer,
If thus we may make free with old Olympus,
And fashion from it shapes for mortal men.
  MARG. Hark! 'tis a carriage.
  ARNOLD.   Our guests are coming.
  MARG. Get in, I pray you—make yourself complete—
And smooth your brow; it is a tell-tale image,

That answers not for Mars, nor for Apollo.
And will not suit these chambers, or your guests.
    ARNOLD, (*going.*) *He's* not a Mars; nor an Apollo—no!
But while he stands between me and the sun,
'Twere vain that I should strive at either aspect.
    MARG. What say you, Arnold?
    ARNOLD, (*musing.*) Yet is my form erect—
My sinews firm—my shadow in the sun,
Might even be graceful, were there any sunlight,
For *me* to walk in!
    MARG. (*overhears and approaches.*)
The shadow's on your *soul;*
Your mind; your thought. and fancy;—and it comes
From Thurston!—From his cunning—O! beware!
    ARNOLD.
You here! Get in with you! No more of Thurston!
'Tis of another and a mightier shadow!
But in with you! They come.   (*Ex. Arnold.*)
    MARG.   It is John Thurston!
'Tis ever thus, whenever he appears!
He has been *my* Fate! And he will be my husband's!

    The scene closes, and the domestic *tete a tete* also. The Host and Hostess retire to re-appear in the saloon of reception. It is still a problem with the Historian in what degree Arnold's wife shared the secrets of her husband. There is no reason to suppose that she was in any way privy to the conspiracy.— Her intimacy with Arnold before marriage, and the correspondence with him afterwards, was, so far as we know, perfectly innocent on her part; at all events, in its relations to the affairs of the country. That her husband used her as a medium, in his communications with Andre, is undoubted; but she appears to have been quite ignorant of what was the occult meaning of his communications.

Mr. Lord, in his drama of Andre, makes Arnold treat his wife brutally. This I hold to be no less an error in history, than a mistake in art. I have seen no proofs of it; nor was it necessary to make the wife at once innocent of offence, and a victim of brutality! It was a mistake in art to lift her still higher at the expense of her husband;—this *must* be the case, under any circumstances; and it does not need Arnold should be degraded any lower than the facts justified. In fact, a proper art requires that he should be *lifted* somewhat in moral, in order that the human interest in his career should be sustained. To strip him of *every* virtue, even that of domestic affection, is to forfeit for him all the sympathies which would make us properly feel his overthrow. I do not suppose that there was any very tender interest for each other in the parties. Margaret Shippen was a fashionable damsel of the time —a *belle*—and possibiy a *fast* young woman. She married, as such persons usually do, not a lover, but an establishment! Arnold, as a man of distinction, one of the great names of the nation, won her fancy. As for the *heart*, the less we say about that, in the possessions of either, the better! Arnold's heart was a mere bundle of selfish appetites, vanities and ambitions; that of his wife, was, no doubt, one of girlish impulses and caprices. I think the probability is that the parties were civil to each other, nothing more; it is probable that there sympathies wrought evenly together, in all cases, where display was to be made; as in the present instance, when there was a *bal masque* on the *tapis*. I assume, also, that the very temperament of Arnold required the support of some human sympathies; and for these it was but natural that he should look to his wife. Besides, she was young, very beautiful, and of good family. He was young enough, and ardent enough to appreciate these qualities. Besides, she was in the way of none of his projects of ambition or cupidity. The natural and unforced reasoning, from the subject, is in conflict with the notion that he subjected her to brutal treatment. He might neglect, but not ill-use her; and her conduct, at the close of the history, was that of a woman neither wanting in love, or veneration of her husband.

While this scene is passing in Arnold's house, another, bearing somewhat upon the event, is in progress in a private apartment in Market street. There we find Randolph Peyton, closeted with Paulding and Williams. Van Wort has just arrived, bearing secret letters to Peyton, from emissaries in and about New York. The perusal of these has inspired Peyton with animation.

"Thurston," he said, "has actually been in New York, and on Governor's island; and he and another person left it together, and went up to the Highlands in company. That is known. From thence, they cut across the Jerseys, and it seems could get a horse whenever they needed one, and find a boat. This shows a free command of money; and, all put together, shows that Thurston has some new scheme afoot, and one of no little importance. The person who left New York with him, seems to have separated from him before he left the Highlands, for he travelled through the Jerseys alone."

"Yes; that's so!" said Paulding, "when I tracked him from the Highlands, he was alone."

"What become of the other? We've lost his trail. But, here, I have a dispatch which shows that an officer of the British army left New York the very day after Thurston, and took the same route, first up to the Highlands, then off, over the Jerseys. Now, I have a shrewd hint who this officer is, and there are good reasons for believing that, like Thurston, he has made his way here also. They pursue the same route, and enjoy the same facilities. This shows that all the arrangements are made for them, and that they are probably working in concert. Now, it is certain that, since Arnold rescued old Thurston from the mob, the subtle old quaker has kept concealed. We cannot find that he has left the city. He is probably harbored somewhere by Arnold's Lady, who is his niece. We have not been able to trace him, after his rescue, to Arnold's house. But there he may be, and probably will be to-night; since her Ladyship has a great ball this evening; one of those foreign fashionable balls where everybody goes in disguise, and wears what dress pleases them. I shall be

BENEDICT ARNOLD.

there, my friends; and shall have my disguise also. If my suspicions be true, and he is there—

"What will you do?" asked Paulding—"arrest him."

"No! I might do so; but of what use? It will be enough if I compel his departure from the city. I have some of his secrets already, of which he little dreams; and can, with a word, I think, compel his departure. If he refuses—but no! he dare not—"

"What do you think he's after?" asked Williams.

"No good, you may be sure; but it is a private matter, comrades;—he is the uncle you know of Lady Arnold, and something must be allowed to natural feelings; but, for the other—and yet—he, too—

"What other, Captain?"

"No matter, comrade! You shall probably know all together. It is mere guess work with me now, and the matter is a delicate one—affecting a lady's honor. To morrow!"

"Shall I see after the boat, and get the hands ready?" asked Paulding.

"They should be all ready at the wharf by twelve to night; and, by the way, how many stout fellows can you muster, besides yourselves?"

"Sailors, do you mean?"

"No! no! soldiers, rather—militiamen off duty, good at pike and pistol! As to the sailors, we shall only need the boat hands."

"I can pick up ten or twenty, or even more."

"Five will be enough! Employ them for the night. Here's money—feed them well, and amuse them as you can till midnight, but see that you keep them sober. Away now to your several duties; while I go to prepare myself with a masquerade dress."

A few more parting words, sufficed to assign sundry detailed duties to each of the men, leaving Peyton alone. He resumed his seat, and sank into a fit of meditation; the words of a broken soliloquy dropping from him as if without his own consciousness.

"What can be Thurston's motive in coming here at so much peril to himself? And wherefore should *he* come—if it be he—that smoothing and smiling, gay Lothario, Sir Henry's Adjutant? Can he be the man? What should bring him hither? He comes, as the fly to the flames; or, is it rather as the bee to the flower? Great God! Can Margaret Shippen be false to all—even to her husband? Can it be thus?— And can it be that Thurston is a pander to the dishonor of his own niece? What else? I'm lost in the confusion of this thought! Oh! Margaret, how I tremble for you *now!* Not for your love—no more of that fond fancy!—All that is past! done!—gone!—lost!—over! 'Tis your honor now! I must save you, Margaret,—save you from him,—yes!—though in your own despite—save you from that wicked, subtle, scheming Thurston,—from that smiling, smooth deceiver!—Yes, though I save you for *that* husband whom I hate and loathe! It shall be done, though, in doing it, Margaret, I risk your hate forever!" [*Scene closes.*]

Let us return to the scene of the *Bal Masque* at Arnold's house. We must suppose it to be a scene of singular splendor: of several suites of rooms, and a great crowd of both sexes, all splendidly costumed in fancy dresses, and most of them wearing visors. Arnold and his wife, however, are both unmasked, he wearing his own costume as Brigadier General of the army, and she habited in the splendid dress which she had worn at the "Meschianza," as one of the "Ladies of the Blended Rose." In those days it was not thought discreditable to wear the same dress on two public occasions; though the economy, as in these blockade periods, was no doubt a matter of necessity. Fortunately, we have had preserved to us a description of this famous dress—from the device of Major Andre; and, for the benefit of our lady readers, we give it here.

"A white silk called a Polonese, or Polonaise (?) forming a flowing robe, and open in front on the waist—the sash pink, six inches wide, and filled with spangles—the shoes and stockings also spangled." This must have been very fine, for aught we know. It was certainly held so, in that unsophisticated period, when George the Third was King. Something more of the costume of the same period. The head dress was enormous—a mountainous structure of successive peaks, or piles—

"Pelion on Ossa throwed, and thrice again,
Heaved upward on Taygetus."

This towering train was made on occasion of the 'Meschianza' to stretch ambitiously above all previous reaches. It was sprinkled, or rather showered, with "a profusion of pearls and jewels. The veil was spangled and edged with silver lace." Such were the leading items of costume on the part of the "Ladies of the Blended Rose." The Rival damsels, "The Ladies of the Knights of the Burning Mountain," (otherwise "The Black Knights") wore white sashes, edged with black, and black trimmings to white silk Polonese." These dresses were all repeated at Lady Arnold's *bal masque*. We are able to state, on good authority, that the return of the Whig ladies to Philadelphia, which soon followed the restoration of that city to the American arms, readily enabled the spectators, at balls and parties, to distinguish between those of the two factions, Whig and Tory—the latter by the tenacity which they held to their mountainous head dresses;—the former by the rustic simplicity with which they allowed the hair, following the example of Nora Creina, "to float as free as nature pleases." In, costuming for Lady Arnold's masque, or for the stage, these facts are of some importance. Neither of the parties failed, at this ball, to habit themselves in their most attractive styles. Nothing was foreborne that might be needful for conquest or attention; and the routes of Lady Arnold were such as to call forth no small expenditure of money and ingenuity. The British Knights and Soldiers had inoculated the Quakers with ideas of taste and fashion which soon made them forgetful of their "skirts and 'tire of moral drab."

We are to suppose the music—the parties dancing, promenading, and broken into groups. The dialogue is to be carried on, without breaking the order of the scene, which is one to yield every several group its sphere without conflict—such a route always implying a most admirable disorder. General Arnold at length advances, brought forward by a masker in Quaker costume. The Quaker is Thurston. But his prudence prompted him to the full use of his privileges, and he wore his mask.

THURSTON. He's here, my friend and partner, Anderson;
ARNOLD. Ah!
THURSTON. Shall I bring him? See him in yon Sultan
Who dances with your Lady.
ARNOLD. A fine graceful fellow,
Who seems more fitted for the gallant's duty,
Than well beseems the trader.
THURSTON. Necessity
Makes traders of us all; gallants and courtiers;
As best may suit the season. Thus we see
The rarest for endowment, take the field,
In conflict with the nature. You, yourself,
Are not yourself, beset by foes and fortune,
And cunning rivals, and sharp enemies,
Who hate you, as you triumph.
ARNOLD. Not to-night,
These sorry themes. Let me forget awhile,
And lose myself in sport.
THURSTON. But, Anderson—
ARNOLD. Anon, we'll speak of him—we'll speak *to* him,
THURSTON. Come hither for awhile—this alcove—hither.

They retire to the rear; and Andre, alias Anderson, in the costume of a Sultan, leads Lady Arnold forward.

MARG. (*reproachfully.*) Still here?
ANDRE. Will you forgive me?
MARG. Will you straight
Begone and leave me. Wherefore are you here?

ANDRE. Forgive me; but I had not strength to fly,
So near to thee and happiness.
MARG. No more!
ANDRE. That happy scene remember'd, that happy hour,
When first I clasp'd this hand.
MARG. I must not hear.
ANDRE. You must!
MARG. Must?
ANDRE. The victim craves but little,
When he demands, that she whose deed hath crushed him,
Shall hear his sorrows plead.
MARG. But thou usurp'st
Another's right to do so. I'm a wife, Sir,—
My husband's claims are first.
ANDRE. *Mine* were the first!—
What husband ever had a right like mine?
Did you not yield to mine that virgin heart,
Ere ever you saw Arnold?
MARG. Andre cease!
Of what avail, is it now,—
ANDRE. Of what avail!
'Tis the worst medicine for a mortal hurt,
To tell the sufferer nothing may avail.
MARG. What else is left?
ANDRE. 'Tis something to have known,
We *have* been on the brink of happiness,
Though toppling from the crag! Say, Margaret,
Was't not——
MARG. 'Twere death to answer.
ANDRE. Life to me!—
The precious right to know how nearly bless'd,
I was, in that sweet season of the heart,
When, newly budding, into green and freshness,
Sprang all the heart's fond hopes—its glorious fancies,
That make a golden halo for the head,
And wing the aspiring shoulders. Doubly dear,
The memory now, when in thy sad caprice
Memory is all that's left me. Tell me, Margaret,
Did you not love me then?

MARG.   And if I did,
It answers not that I should speak it now;
And 'tis not wise in you, nor generous,
To urge me thus, in conflict with my duty:
You wrong me as yourself.

ANDRE.   To be forgiven,
It is my trust, by both! 'Tis not for you
That first made trespass on my right, to murmur
For that I now revenge myself on yours.

MARG. This then is Andre's love?

ANDRE.   Alas! for me!
'Tis Andre's desperation that now makes him
Cruel, where most he dotes! Margaret hear me—

MARG. Hear me, Sir, since your speech can tell me nought
But how your manhood seeks to find in thought
Fit fashions for avenge.

ANDRE.   Not, so Margaret.

MARG. Sir, if you love me—loved me, as you say—
Go hence; and school your passion to remember
I am another's wife! Remain not here,
Where still our mutual presence works in both,
For evil, which must bring due bitterness
In the hereafter. On the instant leave me.
Believe me all your cruel passion deems me
Capricious, heartless—what you please—of evil,—
Save that I'm faithless now! No words; but leave me,
I ask, entreat, implore, command thee, Andre,
Never look on me more.

ANDRE.   'Twere death to go!

MARG. I tell thee, Andre, it is death to stay!
I am no thoughtless, and capricious child,
Such as you knew me late. I am a woman,—
Erring, perchance, and feeble—but determined
With all the will and strength of innocence,
To shape my heart to duty—to my husband—

ANDRE. Where was thy duty, Margaret, in the hour
That gave thee to this man? That made thee forfeit
The vows exchanged with me? What could *he* offer,
This vain, gross braggart Captain—

BENEDICT ARNOLD.

MARG. Sir, be still!
You speak, Sir, of my husband—of a man
That dared defy your Sovereign!
 ANDRE. Yours too, Margaret.
You were most loyal once.
 MARG. And am so yet,
To one who rightly claims my loyalty;
When I merged girlhood into womanhood,
Became a wife, I sought a humbler throne,
Placed my allegiance in a husband's keeping,
And ask'd not who was king.
 ANDRE. Would I could find
The task as easy, from *my* heart to rend
The loyal faith 'twas bred in—to throw off
With such an airy effort, that sweet bondage
That link'd my will and worship to another.
 MARG. Why thus recall——
 ANDRE. Why live—why feel—why suffer?
I am the loser of life's richest treasure,
Have given the whole full substance of my hope,
To one who reeks out of my sacrifice;
Yet must not murmur of my loss——
 MARG. Andre!
 ANDRE. Nay, wherefore speak, if only thus to prove,
How deeply you can wound—you do not feel,—
 MARG. What! do not feel it?
 ANDRE. As a triumph only;
A pleasant boast, when *belles* are in a circle,
Of hearts made captive, and decreed to suffer,
That merry groups may prattle of their conquests.
 MARG. Alas! 'tis vain—
 ANDRE. Faith, 'tis a vanity—
But damsels find it pleasant sport enough.
They deal with hearts as boys with butterflies,
Wing this, pierce that, and prattle all the while,
Howe'er the insect flutters!
 MARG. Why, this is noble!
 ANDRE. Could I deem you feel!
 MARG. I feel it, Andre,
But O! how full of evil even to say it,

When duty stands, with reproachful aspect,
And frowns upon the fond acknowledgment.
  ANDRE. And so you love me still?
  MARG.   Away, Sir,—go!
  ANDRE. One little word?
  MARG.   Away!
  ANDRE.   That look! that tone!
  MARG. Speaks sorrow, Andre—make it not reproach.
  ANDRE. Say—forgiveness!
  MARG. Grief only! I have nothing to forgive,
But much to weep for. Do not linger here,
Lest I forget my sorrow in my anger;
And in the thought of Andre's undesert,
Too soon forget mine own.
  ANDRE. And yet—
  THURSTON, (*coming forward and interposing.*)
                              No more!
His eye is on you;—Arnold's—and another's!
Beware; the Bashaw may be dangerous,
Should he suspect the Sultan.
  ANDRE.   But one word!
  THURSTON, (*taking him off, while Lady Arnold seizes the op-
                  portunity to withdraw also.*)
That word would breed another and another,
'Till you were lost, young man! I tell thee, Andre,
That, in a game like this, to play the Samson,
One needs behold, in every woman's glance,
The snare of some Delilah. Come with me.

  The dancing, meanwhile, has proceeded with due animation, and broken into various groups, those engaged in conversation, have, perhaps, not observed anything very earnest in the action of Andre or Lady Arnold. But the parties have been observed by one of the maskers, and followed with some closeness. He has, by the closeness of his watch, attracted the vigilant eyes of Thurston, who has left Arnold for the

BENEDICT ARNOLD. 413

avowed purpose of bringing "Anderson" (alias Andre) to an interview with him. Randolph Peyton, in the habit of an Italian Bandit, is this close observer. He makes several attempts to approach Lady Arnold, but has been prevented by the interposition of other parties. His soliloquy—unlike any in the speech of Romeo, yet embodies the same passion with which he followed the shining footsteps of the girlish Juliet.

   Peyton, (*aside.*) I must subdue, if not to calm, to silence,
The passion that works in me. It is over—
All the dear hope, the young confiding faith,
The passionate dream and fancy! With the hope
Should end the struggle! Yet, even as the fly,
That circles round his danger in the flame,
I hover near the perilous brightness still,
Each moment nigher to the blaze! Already,
My wing, that once aspired, has been consumed,
And my soul-flight forever maimed! The future,
Yields me no field. No more I wanton free,
In provinces of blue, and bloom, and beauty,
With raptures born of that glad element,
That bore me once in triumph. Love for me
Has taken his purple from the evening sky,
And muffled all his stars! Oh! Margaret, Margaret!
Too heedless, in thy power, of other's pain,
'Twill be for me to teach thee thy true service,
How erring was thy heart! Yes, I will save her,—
Save her, for him, alas! whose happier fortune
Hath been the blight of mine!
                I will be generous,
For her dear sake—still dear—tho' from this hour
I never see her more. I bless this secret
That yields me such a happy privilege!—
To speak to her, to hear her voice, in answer;
Nay, counsel her against the lurking danger.
At last they part! 'Tis Thurston that approaches,
That subtle uncle! He hath sacrificed her—

And wherefore? There's some mystery about it,
Which I shall fathom yet! How beautiful!
Yet 'twas in that unwonted foreign habit,
She toyed and sported with the foreign soldier,
Though even in the moment when he clipt her waist,
He trampled on the altars of her country.
Ah! now I have her! She is near me now.
Lady!—   (*She approaches him.*)

    MARG. Who speaks?
    PEYTON.   One who implores a hearing.
    MARG. What Bandit is it, fresh from the Abruzzi,
Selects me as his prey?
    PEYTON.   As well the hawk
Should ask that question of the trembling dove;
The partridge of the fowler!
    MARG.   Sure, that voice—
    PEYTON. Is one that you should know. No bandit, lady;
To you, I'm still, as once before, the victim.
    MARG. Does Randolph Peyton speak?
    PEYTON.   If yet he may—
If not too base in Lady Arnold's sight.
    MARG. I had not thought it, Randolph, you should set,
In malice, on my husband.
    PEYTON.   In other days,
When woman better loved to heal than hurt,
The world had call'd that malice chivalry.
But not upon the husband did I set.
He drew on me.
    MARG.   To rescue my old uncle.
    PEYTON. It did not need; my effort was to save him,
From those who wove the halter for his neck;
I but assumed a hostile attitude,
To blind the eyes of the infuriate mob,
'Till I could make him safe.
    MARG.   Ah! was this so?
    PEYTON. For your sake, Margaret.
    MARG.   Still generous, Peyton,
As when we pray'd together in our childhood,
And quarrell'd but in fondness.

PEYTON.   Do not stab
My soul with such sweet memories of the past?
Well said the mighty master—"The worst grief
Is to remember, in our hours of wo,
How blest we have been." You deceived me, lady;
Though that, perchance, was only in my fondness,
That saw but as it felt! I loved you, lady,—
Still love you—though my lip shall never wound you,
By word which innocence should blush to hear,
Or true love shame to speak. You treated lightly,
Affections that, grown weightier by your coldness,
Now weigh me down to earth; but do not lessen
The will to serve you with as true a spirit
As if they still had hope.
    MARG.   I cannot answer!
Reproach me as thou wilt, I cannot answer!
You have the right to censure, and the justice,
And I must still submit, too keenly conscious
Of much, not wilful, but still erring in me,
Which may have done you wrong! I but implore you
To think on what is due to *him;* the station,
And name, that now I bear.
    PEYTON.   'Tis that which brings me!
It is because of your high station, Margaret,
Your wedded duties, and the name you bear,
That Randolph Peyton comes within these walls.
I fain would do for him and you a service,
In what I deem your peril.
    MARG.   My peril! Speak!
    PEYTON. Our loyal kinsman—we are cousins, Margaret—
John Thurston walks this chamber unrebuked!
One word but whispered to the populace,
And not even Arnold's station could secure him,
Or save this house from sack.
    MARG.   I know it, Peyton.
I have entreated him to fly this city.
    PEYTON. And still in vain! He will not hearken *you*,
While yet the lurking hope, to hatch new treasons,
Keeps working in his brain.

MARG.   What treasons, Peyton?
PEYTON.   What matter what the shape his treachery takes?
You know him for a dangerous, restless man,
Forever discontent, fanatical,
Still hatching plots—a spider in his snares,
With meshes spread, on every hand, to catch
Each silly fly that wanders.   That he comes
Even now, intent on mischief, well I know,
Though what the particular form his treason takes,
I but conjecture.
MARG.   You affright me, Peyton.
PEYTON.   'Tis well if thus I serve you.   What he means
May work *you* mischief rather than your husband;
And yet the evil may ensue to both.
Him will I serve, but only for *your* sake!
I cannot love the man, whate'er his merits,
Who robb'd my heart of yours.
MARG.   Randolph!—
PEYTON.   I'm hushed!
MARG.   But what of him, my uncle?   Do you know—
PEYTON.   That he is here—a noted Loyalist,—
Skilled in all stratagems—a man of wiles—
Feverish and subtle,—bold,—fanatical—
In danger from the odium of his name,
And still endangering *you*, if not your husband.
MARG.   Why me?
PEYTON.   He does not come *alone!*
MARG.   Ah!—What?
PEYTON.   Yon Sultan!—

          [*Pointing to Andre at a distance.*]
MARG.   Ha! I see! I see!
PEYTON, (*deliberately*)   And know'st him, Margaret?
MARG.   Oh! Randolph, do not search me with those eyes,
As if thou dreadest treachery on my tongue,
And shame within my soul.   Believe me, Randolph,
He comes not with my knowledge—should depart,
Could word of mine have power upon his purpose,
I have implored him—nay, commanded him—

PEYTON. Beware of *him*. (*Solemnly*.)
MARG. I do! I will!
PEYTON. Beware! Beware!—
Oh! Margaret, you are in the frailest barque,
That ever sailed upon the perilous seas,
And knew not of the sun, nor how to steer—
Chartless, and at the mercy of the storm,
That waits but for a whisper to o'erwhelm!
Why comes John Andre here?
MARG. I know not, Randolph
PEYTON. Nay, pardon me—you *do!* You cannot help,
But know it, Margaret. You've a consciousness—
The heart's a rare diviner—that this man
Comes hither, as the mote that seeks the beam,
To feed upon thy smiles.
MARG. He wins no smile
From Margaret Arnold.
PEYTON. Suffered but to seek,
The event is evil!
MARG. I have bade him hence!
PEYTON.
And would you have him gone? Speak, Margaret!
I have a word to send this enemy hence,
Your enemy and my country's!—Bid me utter
This word—say "Speak it Peyton!"—and 'tis spoken;
And he, John Andre, and the man who speaks him,
Shall neither trespass on your house again.
MARG.
Go! Speak it, Peyton! 'Tis my heart entreats you!
And leave behind, at parting, your forgiveness
Of the vain child that mock'd your noble love,
And knew not the folly of her fault,
Until too late for justice.
PEYTON. Should I forgive—
Whose lip hath never vex'd you with a complaint?
MARG. So haughty, Randolph Peyton!
PEYTON. Not haughtiness, but pride!
The pride that suffers, Margaret—still must suffer—
And takes its better lessons of endurance,
From a too often taught humility.

Marg.
Enough! I thank and bless you, Randolph Peyton!—
The woman blesses him, the frivolous girl
Knew only how to forfeit and offend.
    Peyton. I go to send these dangers from your house.
Perchance we shall not meet again. One word—
Beware of *him*—beware the very thought
That whispers Andre's name to Margaret's fancy.
                            [*He leaves her.*]
    Marg. Alas! how vain the counsel!
                    How beware?
Thought *will* rise;—the fancy find its way
To all the founts of feeling! Can I stifle
The bitter memory of the former bliss,
By brooding o'er a present, such as this?
Yet I must do 't; must still of *him,* beware,
Nor see him, lest I fall within his snare!

We are to suppose the usual changes upon the several groups, at such an assemblage, while our more prominent characters engage, at intervals, the ears of the audience in the foreground. The action in the background has been diversified as usual. Arnold has been engaged in conversation with various parties; according some of his attention in all quarters of the saloon. He has been seen with Andre and Thurston together, and with the latter separately. The former, after some by-play with other masks makes several attempts to approach Lady Andre; she studiously avoiding him. At length, when she can avoid him no longer, and he is about to address her, the Italian Bandit interposes, lays his hand upon the arm of Andre, and draws him apart, and into the foreground.

    Peyton. This traffic is too hazardous. The chances
Declare against your purpose. The citadel
Is here too strongly fortified. The virtues
Are all in armor clad, and vigilant!

You can neither sap nor storm; the garrison
Laughs at your efforts! You must raise the seige,
Or you may lose yourself;—you waste your labor!
    ANDRE.
Methinks you miss the white, most worthy archer!
As an Italian Brigand—so your habit
Declares you—your best weapon's the stiletto.
The cloth-yard shaft is a good English measure,
Not proper to your hand.
    PEYTON.   Yet I can wield it.
    ANDRE. I am not him you think me! Once again
You miss the white.
    PEYTON.   'Tis you, me thinks, that miss,
In this most wild adventure of your seeking.
I too well know the mark which I do aim at,
To hunt my innocent neighbor. You are one
To whom, as a friend, though still a foe,
I proffer saving counsel. Get you hence,
With all the speed of fear, and, ere the dawn!
Your boat awaits you! Your companion's danger
Is imminent like your own; 'tis at your peril,
You linger in this town a moment longer.
You are known, Sir.
    ANDRE.   Known?
    PEYTON.   Too well, and not with favor.
'Tis a rare courtesy that prompts me help you,
To flight, from justice; such a courtesy
As one gallant may tender to another,
Having still a lurking sentiment of fancy,
Borrow'd from courts and codes of chivalry!
You err in being here, and most unwisely,
Pursuing, with vain passion, one whose duty
Demands that you depart.
    ANDRE.   For whom, I pray,
Do you conceive me?
    PEYTON.   Something I *know!* Enough
That you are here suspected——
    ANDRE.   I am all ears!—
Good, blundering Brigand!—

PEYTON.   Such a speech as this
Would better grace the pillory.
    ANDRE.   The pillory !—
    PEYTON.   My words shall be the shorter for your ears!
Hark you, a moment! You are here suspected
Of casting eyes of greed upon a treasure,
Too high and precious for your young ambition,
However high it vault. 'Tis thought this treasure,
Even though you reach it not, may sometimes suffer,
As even the polished mirror may be tarnished
By the foul breath—
    ANDRE.   Sir; you are insolent!
    PEYTON.   It may be.   Truth is oftentimes offence;
But must be suffered, even in royal courts,
Where all the moral lies in courtesy.
I say, Sir; your pursuit of this same treasure
May injure good repute; not sully honor;
Which, like the pure white moon glides on through heaven,
Nor notes the envious clouds that crowd between
Her and the unshipping earth.   You must go hence,
And quickly—ere the dawn.
    ANDRE.   At my own pleasure.
    PEYTON.   Hear further. I have told you what's suspected,
Hear what is known.
    ANDRE.   Well, sir, well!
    PEYTON.   *You* are known—
A British soldier—officer;—nay, one
Of rank, and in the favor of Sir Henry.
What do you here?   The fond pursuit which brings you,
Vain in itself, of hope, brings other danger,
And men may find it easier to suspect,
The spy than lover; to assume this habit,
Not so much worn to hide a lover's passion,
As for the baser purpose of the foe;—
May reasonably hold you, in our camp,
Disguised, and dextrous in the espial's practice,
None other than a spy; and hurry you,—
Not suffering plea or shrift to the first halter!

BENEDICT ARNOLD.

ANDRE.   This insolence, this audacity—
PEYTON.   Will answer for itself.
Some fitter season you will find me ready,
To make atonement to you for wounded honor,
In any issue. For the present, please you,
Subdue your anger to this courtly circle;
We'll smile, and look most gracious on each other,
Though every word's a dagger that we speak.
Have I said enough to make you wise and vanish!

ANDRE.   You've said too much for one who knows so little.
Once more, good brigand, waiving your offence,
To some more fitting season, let me tell you,
You lose your labor; I am not your man.

PEYTON.   I would have spared you something.
ANDRE.   Nay, do not spare.
Your ample knowledge somewhat moves my wonder,
But more my scorn—my laughter.

PEYTON.   Well, the laughter
May wait a little ere it grows too hearty.
It seems your ears, whatever be their length,
Need frequent iteration of sore speaking,
Ere they can well take in this useful lesson.

ANDRE.   Would we were out upon some goodly spot,
Of fresh green earth, beneath some forest trees,
With none to see us but the witnessing stars!
Then should I curb this insolence!

PEYTON.   It may be,
That you will find the occasion and the place;—
The man, not wanting! Now, John Andre, hear me.—

ANDRE. Damnation! Ha! (*In momentary consternation.*)

PEYTON.   You see that you *are* known.
You are here, our foe, companioned by a Tory;
And a single word from me, and you're a captive,
And what your doom? You cannot, as a man,
Plead that the passion of a lover brings you;
And who'd believe you, other than a spy,
On treasonable mission.

ANDRE. Ha! *(recovering himself.)* Once again,
I tell that you err! I am not, sir—
    PEYTON. Pshaw!—
Would you play the fool, or make me one?—
See you not that I know you?
    ANDRE. Perchance, and yet
You err as to my purposes.
    PEYTON. The less
You say of them, the better for your safety!
Enough, that I would save you from your error,
Your indiscretion, and perchance save others,
Whom I regard with much more tenderness
Than I do you. I am no friend, John Andre;
Rather a bitter foe! But I would serve you
For reasons not my own. You see my knowledge
Will not admit of parry or evasion—
No, sir, nor much delay; for, tho' I warn you,
And give you counsel and the chance to fly,
Yet must you promptly use it! If, by sunrise,
These city walls enclose you, I denounce you
For ignominious death upon the scaffold!
    ANDRE. This hurry, sir—
    PEYTON. Is your own safety.
    ANDRE. Yet, be generous—
    PEYTON.
Generous! I give you life; the means of freedom,
Escape from death of shame; and you, my foe;
My people's enemy;—and yet you murmur,
And ask for more. What more?—
    ANDRE. Thanks for so much!
But for my purpose here.
    PEYTON. I would not know it.
Enough that you depart.
    ANDRE. I will but speak awhile,
With our good host and hostess.
    PEYTON. Not one word!
    ANDRE. Why this is merest tyranny.
    PEYTON. It is!

BENEDICT ARNOLD.

Your presence here deprives you of the right
To censure or complain. I tell thee, Andre,
Thou shalt this very hour depart this dwelling
Which thou pollutest.

ANDRE. This language shall require
Fit satisfaction!—I am a soldier, sir.

PEYTON. All in good season; and your sword shall claim
Its proper play with mine, in proper time,—
But now, go hence! This is the one condition
On which I close my lips. Refuse,—nay, linger,
And I myself will drag you from this hall!
Yourself will wonder that I now forbear it
When you see this.

(*Showing the continental uniform under the Brigand habit.*)

ANDRE. Another word with *her*.

PEYTON. If thou dars't, thou diest! Another word,
With her, or any other in this chamber,
And I forbear no farther!

ANDRE, (*threateningly and touching his sword.*)
There will come
A time, when I shall thank thee—

PEYTON. As thou wilt!
Hence now!—no pause—no look—no parting word.
Begone!

ANDRE. Hell's curses on thee!

PEYTON. Curse! but hence!

(*Andre goes, Peyton following him to the door.*)

This scene has been watched with anxiety by Lady Arnold. She approaches Peyton, after Andre's departure.

MARG. Thanks, Randolph. thanks.
PEYTON. Now, Margaret, art thou safe!
MARG. Never shall I feel so, till my uncle flies.
PEYTON. Leave me! I see him even now approaching.
He too shall speed as surely! Yet, beware,
Of both, *hereafter*, Margaret, to be safe!
(*She leaves him—Thurston approaches, and Peyton draws him forward.*)

PEYTON.
Your comrade waits you! You have little time
'Twixt this and sunrise.
THURSTON. For what, good Brigand?
PEYTON. For escape, John Thurston.
THURSTON. Ha! Randolph here?
PEYTON.
John Andre waits you. If, at dawn, we find him,
He dies the dog's death.
THURSTON. Well, the respite's something.
PEYTON.
Enough for safety. Hence! I'll see you forth.
THURSTON.
You save me, Randolph. This is kindly of you.
A few days since you were less merciful.
PEYTON. I saved you then, by subterfuge! Opposed,
The mob had torn you piecemeal.
THURSTON. That's a new light!
I thank you, Randolph Peyton.
PEYTON. Thank me not.
I saved you then, and save you now, for *her*—
And not because I love you. But, go hence,—
An hour's delay is fatal—speed at once,
No time for parting speeches—less for treason!
THURSTON. Treason!
PEYTON. An ugly thing, John Thurston, for your ears;
But one that's quite too natural to your tongue.
THURSTON. Your counsel's good, tho' from an enemy,—
And I will use it. (*Going.*)

Yet 'tis hard to fly (*aside*)
Even at the very moment when success
Stands smiling welcome—at the portals stands,—
Throwing open all the doors! But something's done—
The path's made easy for the future-progress,
And the good seed, in good soil set, but asks
The appointed season for the goodly fruit.
How has this boy into our secrets wound,
To know so much: To track us to the burrow?
Yet something still he knows not, or he never
Had suffer'd our escape. He looks on Andre,
Still as a lover, in his eager passion,
Staking life itself in barter for a look.
'Tis well he thinks so—well, his notion of honor
Makes him magnanimous! I must baffle him,
In any future venture. 'Twill be hard,
If that the grey beard shall not match the boy.
(*Ex. Thurston.*)

The scene closes with the dance. Peyton follows close after Thurston; and we shall soon need to follow with him, for he is one to press upon the heels of those whom he suspects, and he is not yet done with the two persons whom he has contrived to expel from Arnold's saloon. He must see that they leave the city. It will be gathered from the preceding scene that Peyton does not suspect the contemplated treason —that he has no suspicion of Arnold whatever; that he looks upon Andre as a criminal only in approaching, with improper sentiments, the wife of Arnold; and though well aware that Thurston is a Loyalist and a man of plots; yet without once entertaining any but a vague notion that he is after evil intents. But his ideas are enlarging. He begins to ask why Thurston comes, and what he meditates; and he broods over the fact that ample provision seems to be made for facilitating his progress between the Headquarters of the enemy and the city of Philadelphia. He reflects that these facilities cannot be afforded simply to accommodate the domestic desires of Thurston, or the amatory feelings of Andre. Meanwhile, his colleagues, or followers, Paulding, Williams and Van Wert, are busy under his directions, and they watch the steps of Andre and Thurston from the moment of their departure from Arnold's house. This has been the plan of Peyton. He was to dislodge the game, and they pursue the trail. Their report is satisfactory, and the next scene finds Thurston and Andre, at an obscure point on the banks of the Schuylkill, without the city limits. A boat waits them, with a full complement of rowers. Andre and Thurston, in no good humor with themselves and one another, have an angry conference at the river side.

"Why have you followed me?" said Thurston.

"Why not?" said the other. "I knew the way."

"But I particularly warned you that you were not to come till everything was ready. We are engaged in no idle play, whether of chivalry or passion. We have too much at stake to trifle now; you have done mischief by coming; have perilled our secret; have suffered yourself to be tracked and housed; and, but for the fanciful magnanimity of that cunning young soldier, your career would have been a short one with a most unromatic finish."

"Yours too, if report speaks truly."

"Ay, indeed; and in all probability I owe my danger to your imprudent coming."

"I don't see *that*—I left New York two days after you, giving you quite time enough. They must have found your track and followed it, and so got the clue to mine. I don't see how my coming has endangered you or our secret."

"Still, you should not have come till I gave you the summons. We have to play warily with such a man as Arnold. He is quick to suspect, and, until fairly limed, must not be startled by seeing how far he is committed. It requires no small skill to bait such a fish, and no slight dexterity to hook him. Here, to-night, but for my timely caution, you would have allowed him to know you without your mask. The time has not come for that. He must meet with Sir Henry's agent, knowing him to be such, only when papers are to be delivered."

"But he has had his money?"

"He has had money, as a loan from me;—such at present is the extent of his obligation. Alarm him, and he flies the track; and is simply *my* debtor for so many guineas, for which you, I, and Sir Henry might whistle in vain."

"Well, d—n these tedious preliminaries; and d—n that impertinent fellow who has spoiled our sport for the present.— Who the devil is he?"

"He was your rival once, a distant cousin of Margaret Shippen, and one of her most devoted lovers. She coquetted with him, as she did with you, and jilted both, as you know."

"Much you know about it! If ever man had Margaret Shippen's heart, I am the man."

"I say nothing about hearts. It is enough that she is the wife of Arnold, and you will beware how you endanger our sovereign's interests by too deep a concern for your own youthful fancies. But for your passion for this practice of flirtation, you would not have risked our objects by too prematurely making your appearance. If this chap, Peyton, does not keep his secret, and it reaches Arnold's ears that he has discovered it, he becomes alarmed, and it will be an even chance that he flies the twig which we are liming for him.— For the present, our game is up. We must lay new plans, and change the scene of action. We must beware how we venture here again. This Peyton knows too much."

"Cannot we silence him?"

"Not that I see. Nothing now remains to us but to heed his counsel and depart with all possible expedition. We shall be blown to-morrow, and the hue and cry after us. The sooner we take to our oars and get down the river the better. Have we all here?"

"Yes, I suppose so. The men seem to be waiting, and a full complement. But I see not why we should fly at the mere warning of this younker."

"You see not! Well, I cannot endow you with the necessary vision. I am not disposed to linger until you shall find the proper sight, and probably be made to feel, as well as see."

"Spare your sneer, I pray you, while I ask if we cannot lie *perdu*, at one or other of the old places,—Mother Seward's for example ?"

"The house was gutted by the mob, searching for me, three nights ago. Hildreth is in gaol, and the house of Peters is watched. No! no! we cannot remain safely, and there is no policy in doing so. You may do as you please; but the march of the stars westward warns me that we have little more night to spare, and I am for giving due heed to the warning of master Randolph Peyton."

And with these words, Thurston strode down to the boat, roused up the oarsmen, and quietly seated himself, taking the tiller into his own hands. Andre still lingered on the banks.

"D—n the fellow and his insolence. The pillory! Would that I had him here!"

Scarcely had he said the words, when, as if in answer to his wish, Randolph Peyton stood before him, still in the costume of the Brigand. Both Andre and Thurston, it may be as well to mention, had resumed their former disguises; Thurston as an old clothesman, and Andre as a Virginia horse trader, or jockey; his long overcoat covering his sword. Andre, it may be well to say, already served Clinton in the capacity of a spy. He exercised his talents, in this province, during the siege of Charleston, where his disguise was that of a Virginia horse trader. For the facts in this connection, and the proofs of it, the reader will refer to Judge Johnson's "Life of General Greene." The facts seemed to be beyond question; and, as showing the habitual practice of the British adjutant, will tend to strip his career and character of something of their romance, and materially qualify the sympathies which were occasioned by his fate. He starts with surprise at the sight of Peyton.

ANDRE. Ha! here again?
PEYTON.   To witness your departure.
ANDRE. But that you may not see too suddenly! Harkee, sir; you have used such speech to-night,

As calls for punishment. Bethink you, sir,
Of your most insolent language, and prepare you
To make atonement.
  PEYTON.   The fool won't learn his lesson!
Get hence, sir, with all possible speed! The dawn
Already steals upon the flitting stars. With day
You die the dog's death.
  ANDRE.   A moment first with you!
But a few minutes will suffice to punish
An hour of insolence. Draw, sirrah, draw!
  THURSTON, (*from the boat.*) What madness are you at?
Leave him alone, and come!
  ANDRE.   He fights me first,
Or tastes the whip! Quick, sirrah, out with you!
Flourish your toaster, ere I flatten mine
Upon your cheek. You wear the rebel colors,
The sword, the epaulette,—and if the tongue
May ever serve to answer for the courage,
Should know to use the weapon and be prompt.
Out with you, ere I smite.
  PEYTON.   Fool! Since you will it,
I shall not baulk you.   (*Draws.*)
  ANDRE.   One, two, three! Fall on!
Ta-la-ta-la-ta-la! la, le, ta!   (*They fight.*)
  PEYTON. I said you had good ears;—
Most musical; and needing, for good uses,
Only a sounding board in open air!
  ANDRE. Ha! (*Assailing furiously.*)
  PEYTON.   The pillory—*al pesco*—but the *pipe*
Somewhat in coventry!
  ANDRE.   Scoundrel! each word
Calls for a mortal stab! (*Presses him.*)
  PEYTON.   And is itself one,
Where there's a mortal consciousness that sees
The far-off coming of the penalty;
And hears the airy voices of the doom,
In the wind's whisper, or the leaflet's fall.
  ANDRE. Ha!—*There!*   (*Thrusts.*)

PEYTON. Foil'd !—and now, sir !—(*presses Andre.*)
ANDRE. Damnation !
Can it be !

Andre is disarmed, his sword flying from his grasp; and Peyton is advancing on him with weapon uplifted, when Thurston rushes between them.

THURSTON.
Strike him not; do not slay him, Randolph Peyton
  PEYTON. No! I will leave him for another fate!
The day may come when he will curse the hour
You came between my weapon and his throat!
Hence now, with all your speed! I tell you, Thurston,
If the sun rises on you, in this river,
You and your silly comrade both will perish!
Even now I spare you most unwillingly,
And 'gainst the public welfare. See how easy
To place you now in bondage.

He whistles, and Paulding, Williams, Van Wert, and six well armed men appear from the thicket, and advance upon the party.

PEYTON.   To your boat!
THURSTON. (*Dragging Andre with him to the boat.*)
Lose not a moment. If his humor changes—
  ANDRE. Curses upon him! But an hour will come!
                (*Ex. Thurston and Andre in boat.*)
  PEYTON.
Now, Williams, take your boat, and down the river,
Follow them at moderate distance. Watch their progress;
Note where they land; with whom they commune;
And all in order, in your memory set,
Whatever may seem curious in their course.
Be back by night. We've stirring toils in hand.

Here the scene closes; the two boats appearing, till lost in the distance from the eyes of the spectators. The next scene, being the first of the *third* act, opens in the camp of Washington. The tents of the army fill the background, a long perspective in the distance, interspersed with the camp fires. The marquee of Washington appears in the centre, the Continental flag flying over it. The sentries at frequent points.— Groups of soldiers pass the stage, and are seen in the background, by the fire-light. A clever manager will of course use every auxiliary likely to produce the most picturesque effects. The time is night.

It may be well to state a few things, in regard to what are supposed important proprieties in the conventional opinions of the Stage. These are important to be known by the Dramatist. A little more knowledge of ART, on the part of the dramatic author, might serve to bring many a good piece forward, or save many a piece from failure. A word sometimes will do it,—as a word will sometimes damn it; a song,—a sudden choice of situation—an impromptu of the actor—will relieve the tediousness of a scene in which there is a deficiency of action. Actors will tell you that it is highly important that you should never bring your hero, or chief person, *abruptly* before the audience, or without a proper introduction. The Hero, unless he suddenly appears, to quell the tumult, and to lay the storm—and these are preliminaries that lead, of themselves, the audience to expect the advent of some hero— must always have a proper introduction. You must be *told* that you are approaching Cæsar, or that Cæsar is approaching you. There must be subordinate parties, and a subordinate scene, devised for this purpose, especially if the said hero is to be seen *in state,* or in any situation of repose. The veneration which the world feels for the character of Washington, makes this proceeding necessary when he is to appear, even though he is not the chief personage of the action. The same veneration for the same character, on the part of the American people, made it very desirable among the actors to bring him on the stage, and attempt his counterfeit presentment.— Should they succeed, in any piece, to make his appearance acceptable, it would make the fortune of the actor who personates him. There are, or were, a few years ago, some three actors (as I have heard) who dressed and *looked* the person of Washington to admiration. One of these I knew, and he sought to persuade me to prepare the present drama for the stage, simply that he might *look* the person of our great hero of civilization. He told me that there were but two other actors in the country who had any pretensions to do so; and he modestly expressed the opinion that he was more successful in the personation than either. But the very extreme of reverence on the part of the people, makes it next to impossible so to delineate the character of Washington as to meet the ideals in the popular mind. Accordingly, the effort to bring him on the stage has been commonly a failure. While there have been hundreds of pieces in which he is made to appear, I know of none which has been even partially successful; and of these attempts, none, I think, keeps possession of the stage. In fact, unless in mere appearance—look, figure and costume—Washington can never be made a stage-hero. You may satisfy an audience by a *lay-figure;* and only a full length portrait would satisfy; but you can scarcely confer upon the character the adequate dignity, the sentiment, and the action, which the popular mind requires. He has no merely personal existence in the people's thought. He is simply their type of liberty and patriotism and sublimer virtues. Such as makes Cato famous in the mind of the reader, but makes him frigid, and something of a bore to the spectator. The result of all these difficulties must be, that Washington, on the stage, must be required to say and do as little as the ghost of Hamlet's father. He must stalk the boards in silent stateliness—under the most solemn aspect, and be content to nod a head, or lift a finger, and so—stalk off; taking care never to unbend for a moment, and above all he must not be seen to smile! The future dramatist and actor will do well to remember these matters; though a hundred years hence these difficulties will be less than now.

The reader will suppose some considerable interval between the last scene of the drama, and those which follow. In this space of time, Arnold has resigned the command which he held in Philadelphia. He had been subjected to trial by court martial, and condemned (Jan. 7, 1779) to a reprimand by the commander-in-chief. The sentence was approved by Congress, and the painful duty was performed by Washington with his accustomed delivery and dignity.

Something might be made of this scene in a drama. Some good and imposing effects could be produced, by a good piece in the hands of good actors, exhibiting lofty dignity, and exquisite propriety of one character, in contrast with the mortified pride and ill-concealed passion of the other. In the hands of a good writer of prose fiction, these effects might be rendered still more impressive.

We may readily conceive that this scene, this sentence, worked in Arnold's brain like madness; that they increased the intensity of his passions, and left him finally unscrupulous in the execution of his meditated crime. His treachery, due perhaps, in the first instance, to his cupidity, was now stimulated by hate and a desire of vengeance.

But he had the art, under the teachings of his British allies, to subdue the expression of his passions. With wonderful exercise of will, he stifled the voice of discontent. He no longer complained, in public, of the injustice to which he had been subjected—affected, indeed, to forget the affronts of his feelings and sensibilities, in the renewed ardor of his patriotism. His policy lay in disarming all suspicion, and in reconciling himself, in every possible way, to that people which still cherished the highest sense of his skill and valor as a hero, and were not unwilling to waive the recollection of his vices and weaknesses as a man.

This policy was essential to his desires of obtaining some renewed expression of the popular confidence in his abilities. He aimed to procure the government of the important military post of West Point. His wounds did not yet allow him to mount on horseback. At all events, this was the sufficient pretext for avoiding any active service; and for justifying his application for a post, held to be impregnable, and requiring only prudence, virtue and the ordinary military qualities for successful defence. Some of the leading politicians of New

York made themselves active in urging his claims and desires, and Washington was prevailed upon to confide West Point to his keeping. This brings us down to the period, the events of which furnish the matter of the scenes which follow.

In the meantime, the under-currents of the Drama have greatly increased the suspicions of Randolph Peyton. These suspicions have taken a definite aspect. He has not been on the trail of John Thurston and other British emissaries for months, without having the sphere of his ideas greatly enlarged, as to the plans and purposes of the several parties.— He can now no longer be persuaded that Thurston seeks Arnold and Philadelphia merely for the purposes of trade, as a cunning Quaker trader seeking only gain from speculation; nor is he now satisfied that the designs of Andre contemplate only illicit meetings with the fair wife of Arnold. He has come with a report of his discoveries—his suspicions rather—and now seeks to make it at Headquarters. This brings us to the camp scene, already described at the opening of these paragraphs. Randolph Peyton enters abruptly, and is hurrying forward to the marquee of the General, when he is confronted by the sentinel on duty, with presented bayonet.

SENT. Who goes there?
PEYTON. A friend.
SENT. Advance! The countersign.
PEYTON. Rochambeau.
SENT. What seek you?
PEYTON. Call me straight
The officer of the night.
LIEUT. Here's my relief.
Enter officer, with guard.
PEYTON. Lieutenant, I must see the General.
LIEUT. To-night! Impossible!
He's busy now in council.
PEYTON. Yet must I see him.
LIEUT. That will be hard to do. 'Twill be some hours
Before they part. There's stirring things afoot,

And every grey beard wags a solemn head,
And every smooth chin brushes up his weapon,
As if he heard the bugle at his ears.
  PEYTON. I tell you, Mercer, I must see the General
This very night.
      LIEUT. What, Randolph, is it you?
  PEYTON. The same, my boy; and now—you know—
  LIEUT.   Oh! sure,—
If any one can be allowed, 'tis you;—
And not awhile yet. You must in with me,
And share my quarters; and, some two hours hence—
  PEYTON. That will be late.
      LIEUT. Yet, better late than never!
Our orders are most strict.—But, in with me,
And o'er our manchet and with pleasant parley,
We'll put to easy death these mortal hours.
                                  (*Scene closes.*)

In the next, the interior of Washington's marquee is discovered, the General seated and Randolph Peyton standing before him. The brow of Washington is clouded, that of Peyton anxious. There are papers before them—to which Peyton still points, while the General examines them. He finally pauses, pushes them from him, looks up and speaks.

  WASHINGTON.
These are grave errors, Randolph. You have used
A wide discretion which conflicts with duty.
You are the nation's servant; with its fortunes,
Resting, perhaps, as heavily on your shoulders,
As on the most distinguished of its chiefs!
To place your personal feelings in the scene,—
To make your selfish passions—your affections—
Run counter to the public interest,—
Were fatal to your claim on confidence!

We have no faith in him whose single eye
Sees not—at sacrifice of every feeling,
That might impair the virtue in his will,—
The lights of country shining over all,
Conducting to the one great goal of Duty—
Howe'ver soiled the path; however stern
The solemn requisition! You have err'd, sir,
And know not yet the evil you have done.
This will I show you. To have cast aside
The garb of your own office—in disguises,
To take the ill-direction of the mob,
And yield your countenance, for a moment only,
To its capricious impulse, was a crime
You rather should have striven against, than seem
To have in aught abetted.

  Peyton.   'Tis felt so, sir.
And hence my own most frank acknowledgment.

  Wash. For this I thank you, Randolph. This, with me,
As man, as father, friend, would still be found
Most ample satisfaction. But not so,
With those we serve—the country!—Not with Arnold—

  Peyton.
He, sir! What should *he* say—of what complain?

  Wash. Did you not tell me you were known to him
'Mongst his assailants? He will let me know it—
Nay, has done so, in these his last dispatches,
Where, writing of a "mob of lawless ruffians,
Who, in the public streets assail'd his life,"
He mentions "those among them who yet hold
Commission under Congress," and "demands
Their proper punishment."

  Peyton.   But I have shown you—

  Wash. Much matter for suspicion—nothing further!—
Much need for watchfulness, and eager caution,
But not for open action. You have shown me
How warier than ever should we be of foes,—

BENEDICT ARNOLD.

How something wary in our faith in friends;—
How great the need of vigilance. Your error
Again declares itself to our misfortune,
Since, acting on the knowledge you have won,
You left me in unhappy ignorance,
That yet may lead to evil! Had you spoken,
And shown us timelily your several clues
When first your fingers touch'd them, I had paused
Ere answering Arnold's wishes. Your delay—

PEYTON. 'Twas in the hope to save, sir,—to prevent—

WASH. A mischievous hope and error, Randolph Peyton!
The assumption of too large a latitude
For your own will, and hostile to your duty!
I gave you a large trust, for I believe you,
Most faithful;—'twas an error to o'erstride it!
You had a secret service, of great import,
And many issues of most vital value,
Hung on the doubtful provinces you watch'd.
It saddens me to find that you can wander,
Beguiled by your own passions. You are now, sir,
One of the trusty Captains in our army—
An army wanting Captains—while the nation
Is every where imperilled;—yet you trifle
Because, forsooth, a damsel who deceived you,
Was yet so potent o'er your boyish feelings,
To lead you at her will!

PEYTON.   Oh! no, sir! no!

WASH. 'Tis this or nothing, Randolph! Lady Arnold
May, or may not be honest;—but her dealing,
By word or letter with a British Captain,
Is matter for suspicion. What though John Thurston,
Be uncle to the lady, and your kinsman,—
Yourself suspected him of evil purpose,
When you dismiss'd him—free for any evil!
A graver error still, the case of Andre,
Set free, when, in the progress of the spy!
A lurking passion for this Lady Arnold,

Made you forbear John Thurston, when you had him
Your prisoner ; and a mis-timed chivalry,
Led to the wondrous magnanimity,
That frees the practised traitor in the spy!
This Andre is the Proteus of the British,
Served as a spy in Charleston, ere it fell ;
Is dextrous in this business, and no other!
He takes no rank in soldiership; has never
Set squadron in the field ; nor won a plaudit,
For any dashing stroke in actual conflict.
Your own blind passion for this Lady Arnold,
Assumes that lady as the soldier's guest!
From what you show me, in these curious papers,
As in our report, I'm bold to tell you,
The visit to the lady masks a purpose,
Of treachery to the country, and John Thurston
Uses his niece, to make his pathway easy
To the most criminal ends.

  Peyton. I dealt with them—

  Wash.
I know what you would say! You had no thought
Of occult purpose;—that a lovely lady
Should be beheld with other eyes that love!—
And Thurston was her kinsman ; and John Andre
A lover like yourself;—and, like yourself,
Too happy to hover near the object
That yet forbade all worship! Like a boy,
You play'd the magnanimous hero in her eyes,
And was repaid with smiles, that soothed the feeling
She could no longer satisfy. How know you
That she herself is free from treachery!

  Peyton. Oh! no, sir—never!

  Wash. She's of a tory brood,
Notorious, and hateful 'mongst the people,
For their most bigoted loyalty. Herself,
Wore British colors; danced to British music:

While British legions trode upon the breast
Of her own city; and her levity,
Marked by capricious humors, found all passions
Sated, when she could gaze about her, and behold
The numbers in her train.
  PEYTON.   Light, sir, and gay,
And thoughtless—and capricious, it may be;
But O! not treacherous!
  WASH.   It may be so:
And yet the levity, the gay caprice,
Masks many a subtle project! As a boy,
It was, perhaps, a virtue to have been
Magnanimous as you were; but, for a soldier,—
And something more than a soldier;—for your trusts
Implied a searching nature in your gift,
Not to be blinded, free of any lures;—
Yours was a weighty error, which deserves
Weighty rebuke;—and you must feel it, Randolph.
Know then, while you were masking with the Lady,
Magnanimously sending off her lover,
The practised spy, John Andre—the old traitor
John Thurston,—both commencing in her household,
And saying nought to me,—I was confiding
To General Arnold's custody, the fortress—
Our country's most important citadel,
West Point—

  PEYTON. Great God! You have not done so?
  WASH. Even so!
  PEYTON. West Point! and—Benedict Arnold!
  WASH. It is done!
  PEYTON. Did he not seek the navy?
  WASH. He did—he rather spoke of it at first,—
But nothing earnestly—his wounded limb—
  PEYTON. You will not leave him in possession now?
  WASH. It must be so!
  PEYTON. What! when I have shown you—

WASH. The causes for *suspicion* you have shown me,
Make not *him* guilty! After all is told
He may be innocent as the child unborn
Of any indiscretion! What you gather,
Touching the course of Thurston and of Andre,
Are clues to follow out;—and, in your sentence,
For I must satisfy the prayer of Arnold,
And punish your most rash assault upon him—
   PEYTON. He drew upon me first, sir,—I have said—
   WASH. Ay, but you were the leader of a mob,
Disguised,—and they were in an attitude
Of trespass, and rebellion 'gainst the laws!
'Tis your misfortune—error—and with patience
You must submit to punishment. It shall be
As light as I can make it; and devised
To give you fullest opportunity
To press your keen inquiries to the utmost,
And bring the issues on. In general orders,
We shall declare you under reprimand,
Suspended for twelve months from *public* duty!—
'Tis with yourself to say, if, in the censure,
You find no proper motive to pursue
Your *private* duty, in a secret service,
Which may detect the treason, if it be
That treason lurks in these intrigues!
   PEYTON.   O! Thanks!
The sting hath lost its smart, sir.
   WASH.   Be it so, then!
You shall have all the needed agencies,
Men for dispatches, secret service money,
And troops, when you shall need them! It is needful
You keep me well advised of every movement;
Of every messenger that plies the Hudson;
Of every wandering skulk along the Highlands;
Of all unwonted circumstance;—every doubt
That finds you unprovided with solution;
Of all that threatens danger! I do not tell you
To hold as objects of suspicion any,

BENEDICT ARNOLD.

Whom now we please to trust; but Thurston, Andre,
Are well known loyalists, all British subjects;
These, as they may devise against our posts,
'Tis fit you watch with such prompt vigilance,
As marks the hawk's flight, or the sailing vulture,
When that you know the partridge cowers beneath.
Haunt not our Generals with your presence, sir;
Presume not on our confidence; Be chary,
Lest innocence suffer hurt! No idle fears
Must lead you to free speaking of your doubts.
Be heedful, Randolph Peyton, of yourself!
My honor rests upon your sense of right,
And on your proper conduct. I have faith,
Most perfect, in your honor; in the truth,
With which you serve your country and your friends;
But much I fear your impulse! In your sphere
You have no room for impulse;—license none—
For the fine magnanimity of spirit,
Which prompts to the suspension of a law,
In deference to a mood! It is my prayer,
That, for *my* sake, and for my *honor*, Randolph,
You keep the beaten paths of simplest duty,
Not suffering personal sentiment or feeling,
To sway you, right or left! I do not sleep
On nightly beds of flowers; but thorny doubts
Still trespass on my pillow; and gaunt Envy,
Howls wolflike, at the portals of this tent,
Which he dare not enter! Let none say
That Washington too quickly hugs the story
That blasts a rival fame! For men, already,
Proclaim me as the form, whose monstrous shadow
Keeps from the sun much nobler than myself,
That else would robe them, with his brighest beams,
And wear his crown alone! No rashness, boy;—
No weakness.—Be but faithful; and recover
The honors you have forfeited.

  PEYTON.   My father—friend!

WASH. No more to-night. We shall provide for you.
To-morrow we shall ask your weapon from you;
Sternly denounce your fault to the whole army,
And send you from the lines. Our conference,
Must henceforth be in secret.
    PEYTON.   'Twill be a pang, sir—
But I must drink as I have brew'd! Enough, sir;
My punishment is grateful, from the trust
You give me; I will labor to deserve it!
Enough, that in the Judge that dooms me, I behold
The father, and the friend.
    WASH.   Your father, Randolph,
Is now before me; is my mental Light;
His noble port, his grand old head, white beard,
Most like a patriarch's, and the speaking face,
Still beaming with that bright intelligence
That takes its glow from virtue! Were he here,
Such still had been his judgment.
    PEYTON.   More severe—
I feel how much you spare me!
    WASH.   Were you mine,
My own son, Randolph Peyton, such had been
My censure on your conduct. But, no more!
Go hence! Take heed of all your steps! Beware!
Be silent in your walks; just in your judgment;
Color no more your object by your passions;
Be slow in the conclusion which o'erthrows
An ancient faith or confidence; but swift,
As lightning, in the action which should follow
The judgment once at rest!—And now, go hence.
    PEYTON. Another word!—There are three soldiers, sir,
Whom I have late employed, and found them faithful.
They have experience on route which needs me,
And I would keep them still!
    WASH.   Send in their names.
    PEYTON. Paulding, Van Wert and Williams.
    WASH.   You shall have them!
And now, good night, my son! Bear patiently;
Time brings the fruits of patience and desert.
                                          (Ex. Peyton.)

WASHINGTON, (*solus.*)
The boy is truth itself! This looks like truth:
All the concurrents to one centre tend,
And argue one conclusion. Why should Arnold—
Skilful, ambitious—one of great resource,
And most confessedly brave—why should he seek
A post that asks no conduct for defence;
Seems threaten'd with no danger;—where no valor
Can well be made conspicious to the world;
Or help the fond ambition which still craves
The vain world's clamorous praises. Such should chafe
At the inaction of a state like this;
Which gives the fiery blood no exercise;—
Nor moves the brain to watchfulness and thought,
Discussing dread anxieties! That he
Should seek such dull position, with such labor,
Argues a secret purpose to attain
That's foreign to his plea! His wounds he says—
Of these he can be eloquent!—Alas!
That one should be a braggart—yet so brave!
If what young Peyton now reports be true,—
And 'tis a most plausible story—in our fears
Lies a most wholesome prudence; with meet cause
For watch and preparation; and must have it!
He must be watched,—be foil'd!—If it be true!—
Who dare believe it?—who but think it now?—
Who whisper of the baseness and the shame,
Mocking the pride of the most noble actions,
With such a downfall and a wreck like this?
That one may challenge commune with the skies,
Yet, at the last, upon a dunghill crouch
And ask no better throne! Yet had this man
Some virtues in his trust;—hath shed his blood
With noblest daring;—first to take the field,
When thousands better honor'd in repute,
Shrank from the peril and the sacrifice!—
Hath skill to shape the agencies of battle;
To plan the attack;—to lead his legions on,

And make the prize his own, when the long doubt
Hangs swaying, like a pondulous thunder cloud,
O'er the opposing hosts;—with matchless valor,
Not once forgetting conduct in his rages,
But shaping them to wisdom by his wits;
Rush at the perilous crisis, to the rescue,
And, standing like a rock against reverse,
Pluck from the fiery cloud, his crimson trophy,
And bear it off triumphant on his sword!
Virtues!—can share his purse's well filled treasure
Even to its own exhaustion, with his foe!—
Yet, for all these, one plague spot in his soul
Corrupts the noble semblance in the rest,
And all the gold pollutes! Mere vanity,—
A pride in little things—poor outward shows,
That cheat the thoughtless into wondering gaze,
Which, like the sudden blazing of the rocket,
Dies; drops while dazzling most! We must deplore,
Though duty sternly summons us to more!

Something should be said here in regard to the characteristics of Washington, as shown in this soliloquy, and in the preceding scene. To the critical reader, I need not say that Washington looms out vaguely, upon the American mind, as a vast myth—a creature of the ideal, of grand proportions—lofty and inscrutable, but indeterminate of aspect; and without such details, as will enable us to enter upon any analysis of his character. Our orators and essayists, in their endeavor to idealize his greatness, have stript him of his humanity. He is represented as superior to human passion—not moved by any ordinary human feeling—a man who never smiled—grave always as a Judge or Senator—a sort of Christian Cato, with all the stoicism of the Roman, blended with the perfect purity of the Christian priest. Recently, this sort of idealization has been much in vogue. The orator, standing in the foreground, has drawn a curtain, showing us in the background a form of vast proportions, surrounded with a glory, but himself in shadow. Meanwhile, there has been kept up a perpetual pyrotechnic play of flashes and fire, designed more to exhibit the orator himself, than the Hero he professed to pourtray. Washington, in fact, was a lay-figure, which the rhetorician sought to clothe in his own fancies; and his ambition seemed to show how fine he could be in *costuming* his subjects, than in analysing it. If Washington was displayed in action, it was only as the *Deus ex Machina,* to descend occasionally from his pedestal, for the extrication of the subordinate personages, who were grouped around him as so many tributaries.

I need not say that all this is wrong; and, tending as it does to relieve Washington from all the attributes of humanity, it had the effect, in the same degree, of removing him from human sympathies. He might, in this aspect, produce the sentiment of awe, in the spectator, but never of affection. To show him lacking in mortal feelings and passions, was to show a monster rather than a man. Now, Washington was, in truth, a man of powerful passions; but he had a mind so admirably balanced, so strong a will, and a training of trial and labor from youth, so exacting, that he was capable of keeping his passions subordinated to his intellect and will; and they served always, as they always should be taught to serve, in compliance with the requisitions of thought, principle and judgment. But it is impossible, at the present time, to unteach our people on this subject, and to disabuse them of impressions which have been produced by the stereotyped teachings of the last fifty years. It will require a century more, before the Dramatist shall be able to delineate him as a MAN, and to assume for him the ordinary feelings, passions, impulses, prejudices and desires of humanity. I have no notion that he lacked in any of these. Far from it. But he was capable of great self-restraint, even as he was capable of great self-sacrifice; and the proof of his vast superiority over all around him, in these and other respects, is to be found in the fact that he rose, at once, to a full sense of the great issues, for the world at large, as well as for his country, which were involved in the American Revolution. This rising to the full appreciation of the work before him, and the destinies involved, sublimed his passions, lifted his aims, strengthened his will, and enlightened his intellect; so that, superior to his passions, he could control and direct the several and superior faculties in others, even where these were possessed in far greater degree than by himself. Briefly, Washington, I have no doubt, had glimpses of that peculiar convenience—that isolated and singular fame,—which was to result from the maintenance of self-abnegation—and the entire surrender of all the properties of his soul, mind and passions, to the grand necessities of his country;—the very respect in which the ordinary hero is apt to fail, in consequence of the instigations of vanity, mere impulse, and the prevalence of vulgar passion. It will be seen that I have preferred to exhibit him, not as wanting in human passions, impulses, sympathies, and even prejudices; but as making them subservient to the great necessities of his situation, and employing them, as agencies, but with great circumspection, and a studious regard to their uses, for the public good. I have shown him willing to use policy, but under the watch of principle; which I take to have been his practice always.

Our scene once more changes to New York, introducing us to the presence of Sir Henry Clinton and others in council. The party grouped around the council table, is not in the best of humors. The events of the past have been far from satisfactory. The prospects of the future are not encouraging. The war has been in progress now nearly five years, and is no nigher to its close than at the beginning. The American people are obstinate. The Congress is firm. There is no whisper of concession—still less of submission. If the States lack a sufficient army, so does Great Britain. She has been compelled to subsidize the troops of the German States. If America is without money, England herself is on the eve of bankruptcy. Her people are discontent—there are mobs which inspire terror in her cities—troubles and commotions on every hand; and, more or less actively, France, Spain and Holland are all in direct or *quasi* alliance with the rebellious colonies.

What is to be done? What can be done? These are questions to perplex Sir Henry Clinton, who is not more profound as a politician than successful as a soldier. To add to his disquiet, at this particular juncture, he is advised that a French fleet and army, under Count Rochambeau, and the Chevelier De Ternay, have just reached Rhode Island, and it is apprehended that they are preparing to co-operate with Washington in a demonstration on New York itself, the Headquarters of the British Generals. Things looks squally, and the face of Sir Henry is troubled. The council is a select one, consisting only of the General himself, Col. Robinson, and one or two other British officers of high rank. Let us listen to their conference.

Sir Henry.
This business needs despatch. If it be true
That Rochambeau and De Ternay are at hand,
It follows we must look to Washington
For other movements.
 Robinson.   Thurston sends report
To the same purpose. Washington, he thinks,
Will move on Kingsbridge, with a strong division,
While threatening Staten Island with another:
At the same moment we may look to see
Rochambeau and De Ternay on Long Island,
Both seeking us from thence.
 Sir Henry.   Says he nought
Of his mysterious ally, Gustavus?
 Robinson.   Nothing farther.
 Sir Henry. Could *that* business ripen!
But we must look to *this*, the present danger,
And—What now?
     Enter Andre.
 Andre. Despatches from old Thurston,
Which bear a deeper meaning than they show;—
These——— (*handing letter.*)
 Sir Henry, (*reads.*)
Ha! there is here significance indeed!—

Arnold is made Commandant at West Point;—
Already in possession;—and—Gustavus—
Sends his last letter thence!
    ROBINSON.   Has it no more?
    SIR HENRY. Yes, he demands a meeting—asks that one
Of personal worth, and high official station;
Empower'd to make all necessary terms
Be sent with due authority to do so!
    B. OFFICER. A troublesome requisition.
    ROBINSON.   Gustavus
Will chaffer with no prentice.
    SIR HENRY.   He requires
A master like himself. He doubts old Thurston,
And plainly names the person he would see.
    ROBINSON. Andre?
    ANDRE, (*eagerly.*) 'Twill pleasure me to serve his majesty.
    SIR HENRY, (*smiling.*)
So eager, Andre? But I do remember—
The wife of Arnold is a lovely lady.
    ROBINSON. And gracious too, methinks.
    SIR HENRY.   Our adjutant
Hath all the luck! His fortunes smile upon him—
There was the glory of the Meschianza!
    ROBINSON. Its profits too, if Rumor deals not falsely!
Smiles in the gay saloon—and, in the gardens,
The stolen kiss, the sly embrace, the fond——
    ANDRE. Oh! Gentlemen———
    ROBINSON.   He hath no blushes.
    SIR HENRY.   Spare him!
They will not fail in presence of the Lady,
If still he wills to seek her Lord and Master.
A bright young creature was she, I remember,—
And thought too lovely for a camp's contagion,
Unless with that grim Dragon at her side
Whom sober men call Prudence.
    ROBINSON.   She is lovely!—
And would she fail in her fidelity,

Can safely challenge, in her Lord's despite,
His own example.
  SIR HENRY.   That should silence him.
But hearken, adjutant, how well he argues
For sins which youth may fancy. You may trespass,
Safely, in such a case; with but one duty,
To make it certain that *his* pliancy
Shall furnish rule for her.
  ANDRE.   If zeal can do it,
His Majesty shall win the prize he seeks,
Though Andre meets with none.
  SIR HENRY.   Loyally said;
And were but Rodney here, to check De Ternay,
Your mission should go on. But, with the French,
Looking to dart upon us through Long Island,
And Washington, with stern and stealthy watch,
Fix'd upon Kingsbridge;—'tis not in our power
To make the due diversion in your favor,
And send the requisite amount of troops,
Along, and up the Hudson.
     (*Enter Aide-de-Camp.*)
  AIDE. Despatches, sir,
From Sir George Rodney.
  SIR HENRY.   Auspicious! Where is he?
  AIDE. His fleet but waits the wind at Sandy Hook.
He will be up by dawn.
  SIR HENRY.   Enough, sir.   [*Ex. Aid.*
This,
Gives us our wings again! Now, adjutant,
'Tis with yourself to go down upon this mission.
The nature of this business, and its dangers,
Are equally unfolded to your eyes.
I plead not, urge not, argue not, command not;
The law of duty calls not;—and the peril,
Is death and degradation!
  ANDRE.   But the triumph?
  SIR HENRY.
Brings swift promotion, and the royal favor,
Ensured to you through life!

ANDRE. Hold the work done!
  SIR HENRY. Nay, be not rash! Be cool and vigilant!
The duty is no easy one; its dangers.
Should school the eagerness of youthful zeal,
Nor suffer it to wanton. In with me,
For your instructions; and, before the dawn,
You leave us, in the Vulture. Robinson,
We need your help and counsel.
                                           (*Exeunt Sir Henry, &c.*)
                 Manent Andre.
  ANDRE.   Now Margaret,
We meet again once more! Once more, once more:
Let but the unwilling Fortune smile upon me,
And not in vain we meet! Speed me this quarry,
Which now I aim to strike, and make it mine;
Then let the Fate perverse, take its own progress,
As the wind wills! The present fortune mine,—
Love as the lip, triumphant in embrace,
While the gay fortunes fill the ambitious sail,
Spread for the conquest; and what more remains?—
Then Fortune as thou wilt! Love's treacheries,
Are precious still, they say, in Fortune's eyes!

Our scene again changes, and this time, to West Point.— Arnold, as we see, has attained one of his objects, and that one of vital importance to all the rest. He has not suffered the grass to grow beneath the feet of his ambition. He has renewed his correspondence with the British;—Gustavus through Anderson, and, in his own character, Arnold through Thurston and Robinson. The arrival of Sir George Rodney has strengthened the hands of Sir Henry Clinton; and, prepared thus to encounter the French fleet, he thinks himself able to cope with any land force that Washington can bring against him. The Vulture man-of-war is to take Andre up the Hudson, approaching the defences of West Point as nearly as possible; and he is then to seek the interview with Arnold; and the parties are then to exchange their mutual guaranties. Arnold is already bought and sold. The question is how far he can make sale of the resources and independence of the Confederacy. The prospect is encouraging. Thus far he seems to have succeeded in his strategies. He has a strong party in his support. He has persuaded the Northern people, not only that he is their greatest general, but that he is something of a martyr, and this to the jealousies of ambitious rivals; he has hoodwinked Washington; (as he thinks)—has in keeping the only fortress of the nation, supposed to be impregnable; and this contains the entire stock of material supplies, ordnance, arms and ammunition which is to provide the whole army of the continent! Verily, he has reason to congratulate himself upon the realization, almost complete, of all the promise of his crime, if not all the hopes of his ambition. The rest seems easy. A few days, perhaps hours, and his projects will be matured, and his triumph certain. He will be a British Brigadier, instead of an American; will be free of all his debts, and with thirty thousand guineas in his pocket; and, if as a British Brigadier, he shall achieve any striking successes, a coronet of the British peerage looms up before his eyes, borne conspicuous (at least) on the promise of John Thurston. With these pleasant prospects and assurances before him, Arnold ought to be exultant, or, at all events, in the best of humors. But this is not the case. He is not satisfied with himself, as how should he be, with his conflicting passions and ambitions? And the recent events, in State and Congress, still rankle in his heart, to the mortification of its pride. That Court Martial which sat upon his alleged offences can never be forgiven. His vanity is stung to the quick—his passions are all outraged. Congress has seconded—which he did not anticipate—the charges made by the President and Council of Pennsylvania. Of these charges, we have already heard something;—enough to show their character. Arnold condescended to defend himself in an elaborate paper; but his defence was only partially successful. It is but justice to state that so only were the charges; and he seems to have had some reason for complaint and resentment, though not such as to justify the revenges he proposed to take. The proofs against him did not entirely sustain any of the allegations;

but two of them were thought by the court sufficiently well grounded to authorize a reprimand from the commander-in-chief. The scene in which this reprimand is administered must have been galling in the last degree, to the pride and passions of Arnold; however mildly and gently it may have been administered. Under this reprimand, delivered by one whom he did not love;—one of whom, according to our dramatic construction of his case, he had long held himself an injured rival—he was smarting at the very moment when our scene opens at West Point. His present companion is Col. Jamieson; a person of whom we have already been permitted to make the acquaintance;—a very good and honorable person, but, perhaps, a somewhat dull one; who, in one stage of the affair, at least, exhibited such a singular degree of obtuseness, as might have justified suspicion that he himself was privy to the conspiracy. Such, however, does not seem to have been the case, and he escapes the rebuke of treason, in the milder judgment which left his obtuseness beyond dispute. In this scene (which is only designed to delineate character and suggest motive, and which does not promote the action, or embody incident, and is therefore measurably undramatic) Arnold seems preparing those arguments which are to justify his treason. He speaks for his wrongs and provocations—rights denied, honors withheld, and injustice wantonly inflicted. He also exhibits his jealousy of Washington; though, to the dull mind of Jamieson, this is not made sufficiently apparent. We may assume, also, that much of which Arnold says is designed to *sound* his companion, and see how far he may hope to make him an accomplice. The virtues of the worthy Colonel are, however, some degrees superior to his intellect.

ARNOLD.
Nay, argue not for him! I tell you, Jamieson,
Had he not wink'd at this conspiracy,
There never had been trial of my conduct,
On such poor grounds as these.
  JAMIESON.   You do him wrong!

BENEDICT ARNOLD.

ARNOLD.
He does *me* wrong!—Has always done me wrong!
George Washington is still mine enemy;
Beholds me with an eye of evil seeming,
And sees no worth in any deed that's mine.
JAMIESON.
On my life—
ARNOLD.
Ay, but I know it, Jamieson.
JAMIESON.
Nay, I could swear that, right in all besides,
You still are wrong in this!—For him I know—
A pure, proud soul, superior to the goad
Of self and personal yearning—still devotee,
To the one passion, over all the purest,
His fond, proud love of country! O! mistake not,
I pray, the strong necessity which sways him,
For any will or passion of his own!
ARNOLD.
And yet you hold these charges frivolous!
JAMIESON. The proofs are so.
ARNOLD. Yet am I reprimanded!
Set in the pillory of this chief's rebuke,
Before the eyes of the armies I have tutor'd
To pluck the eagles from their enemies,
When others skulk'd the conflict! Were he noble,
Having the power which he still holds o'er Congress,
He had cried out,—"There is no cause for censure—
This man is outraged—these are jealous foes,
That seek to hurl him from that eminence,
They cannot reach themselves!" But, no! it pleased him
Rather to see the warrior overthrown,
Whose better fortune, in the field of battle,
Hath cast a shadow, hurtful to his own,
O'er the great height, while still his cold ambition
Had hope to reign supreme. But he shall feel,
I have a spirit to be matched with him—
And power of which he dreams not! Speak not for him!

JAMIESON.
For *him* I speak not, General; but for *you*,
That, by this timeless anger, urged at random,
May do yourself great hurt among your people,
And lose their favor. Let one soldier see
His General, in his passions, mailless thus,
And mark me, but he scorns you.
    ARNOLD.   You are right!—
But who hath power, when passion shakes the soul,
To crush it down to silence?—hush the tongue?—
Subdue the blood to meekness?—make the face,
Put on the smoothness of untroubled waters;
Or, in the eye, that let's great secrets out,
Veil every tell-tale glance of that emotion,
Which, swift as lightning, to the gazer's sight,
Betrays the storm that rages wild beneath?
  JAMIESON.
The very man your angry thought would censure;
George Washington!—
    ARNOLD.   I deem it then no virtue;
JAMIESON.
Yet, doth it prove a wondrous property,
Of will and self-command, that speak for greatness,
And make its pathways sure to power, for good!
We see, and must admire; and, in our awe,
Even love; if that there be a human feeling,
Within that soul whose bearing is a God's!
I have been nigh him, where the hostile waves
Of Fortune hath beset him;—when his barque
Was of the frailest; and the angry wave,
Lash'd by the fiercest storms,—had gulph'd it quite,
The roaring billows waring all around,
As certain of their prey; while every heart,
Made its half choking prayer; and he alone,
Was calm; with mind serene, and judgment clear,
And will as firm; with eye as placid bright,
As shines the moon serene, half way in Heaven,
While the whole Earth below, convulsed in storm,
Groans in the abyss as lost!

BENEDICT ARNOLD.

ARNOLD.   I count it not,
Manhood, but stoicism: a cold virtue;
Strong, as it lacks insensibility:
Which braves the danger, as it does not see;
And bears the bolt because it doth not feel!
He lacks the consciousness which makes acute
The suffering; is superior to the shame,
The blow, the pain; from thickness of the skin!
Knows neither holiest love, nor honest hate;
Glows not with indignation; never burns
With the magnanimous motive; never feels
The generous triumph, the rejoicing fervor,
That circumstance still makes in healthful tides,
Compelling all the soul to overflow,
Respectless of the argument and rule.
    JAMIESON.
Oh! what great wrong your Passion does this man!
The power to keep the passions in subjugation,
Proves not their lack. 'Tis only in degree
Men differ in possessions of the soul,
The feelings or the passion. Washington,
Lacks nothing of the wealth in other men,
But holds besides, in more than wonted measure,
The sovereign will for sway. Upon himself
He places first restraint; then follows sure
His sway o'er those who fail to rule themselves,
And thus demand a master.
    ARNOLD.   None of mine!
    JAMIESON.
How should he else thus conquer in this struggle,
With the responsible weight of all this people,
And their unprivileged freedom to sustain!—
Still curbing faction and still baffling foes,
With such resolved purpose and calm method,
Undaunted by the danger, as undazzled
In the full flush of each delusive sunbeam,
That wasted all its gold upon the cloud,
Whose bosom holds new storms. It wonders me,

His noble courage, self-restraining spirit
Such placid calm, such stern, yet modest manhood,
Such patience mid disaster, and such faith
Forever rising to a bow of promise,
Even while the sky is blackest fraught with dread!
His eye forever seems to pierce the cloud,
And finds the bright beyond! And, then it is,
He neither doubts nor fears; assured within!
So sees he nought but hope; feels nought but duty,
And with his own, so blends his country's honor,
That, striving in her cause, he makes his own,
This self-forgetfulness,—
   ARNOLD.   No more, I pray you.
   JAMIESON. Is Washington's great secret.
   ARNOLD.   No more! no more!
You're eloquent; but I do not like your theme;
It may be true; but suits not with my mood.
Your Washington! It is his very name
That, in the hours when other men find sleep,
Expels her from my pillow—fills my thoughts
With memories of denial and defeat,
And hopes that, born of the most lovely promise,
He would not suffer ripen! His rebuke
Makes your theme irksome. Be the truth confess'd,
I love not to hear of him.

After this very broad hint, one would suppose that Arnold had quieted the warm eulogist of Washington; but his Colonel, as we have said, is a dull person—one of those who, like Polonius, lack in wisdom, but speaks usually oracular morals. He expresses his wonder, that a theme so grateful to himself, should be anything but agreeable to his superior. His real wonder is that Arnold is not pleased to listen to his well rounded periods. He, accordingly, declares his wonder.

   JAMIESON. This is strange!
I know no marvel in the soldier's keeping,
So fit to rouse the sleepy sentinel,

And make him heedless of the midnight air,
As this of Washington. You'll hear them say—
The army that serves under him—that he
Can draw more profit from his own defeat,
Then other Generals from victory.
  ARNOLD.
A silly speech,—a very silly speech!
This rabble still will prate! What are his profits—
Where are the famous—the successful deeds,
That justify this homage?—Many a boor
Now lost amid the mass, in lengthening files,
Unmark'd among his fellows;—graced, perchance,
By some wild freak of fortune, would become
In a brief space, his equal! Greene, his copy,
Who apes his solemn state, and haughty carriage,
Of the same build and school, as cold and cautious,
Is, to the full, as good an officer :—
Give him the knowledge and the dashing of Lee,
A better! His prudence in excess—his wit—
Valor and strategy—too lean for action,—
What's left him but that policy which keeps,
His army safely—safe, but—in the cold.
  JAMIESON.
And war, my General, is a mingled game
Where valor plays but part. If Washington
Can win his game by strategy and skill,
Then is his policy what more we need
Than Lee's or Conway's valor.
  ARNOLD.   Still, I scorn
The temporizing method—tedious watch—
That would wear out the enemy, not fight!
It shames and starves achievement—chills the soul
That dreams of glory, and the embattled heights
Where eagles soar that eagles may o'ercome,—
And will not sleep again! The terrible hum
That makes the battle's element and music,—
Tramp of advancing legions—desperate sport,
That breaks with joint and double utterance

From warrior thousands when their hearts are high,
And the blood boils in earnest of the strife;—
These, in the thought of Arnold, are more precious,
Than any drowsy game of hide and seek,
Your warrior-politicians ever play.
   JAMIESON.
And yet Humanity may well deplore,
This preference, and give ear to policy—
   ARNOLD. Humanity, forsooth! What's she, I pray,
When men are set to fight, with fearful mood,
The fruit of other and as fearful moods,
Which War is meant to tutor and subdue?
War is Humanity's necessity—
Her refuge, when Humanity grows dumb.
It is not Peace—it is not pleasantness—
'Tis dire attempt, and dreadful circumstance;
And the more dread and dire the circumstance,
The swifter rescue for Humanity!
When Policy has play'd her subtlest game,
She hoods herself; and with her folded arms,
Sits by, while War and Valor take the field,
To try their fortunes at another table!
I do not love this policy!—my humor
Prefers to hark the dogs to the affray,
Rather than sit, purring over petty schemes,
Of caution, prudence, watch and circumspection;
Nice questions of how much may we gain,
And, nicer still, the how much may we lose?
Councils of War, which Generals, skulking War,
Propose for sanction of their kindred skulks.
All these are shifts of feebleness, that tell you
How little is the generalship at work;
A mockery to the human, as the nation's hope!
When War hath yoked his steeds, and whet his scythes,
And glory with her bloodshot eyes, and hair
Dishevelled, in the wild delight she feels,
Have led where harness'd legions are at bay,
Thick as the grass that waits the mower's stroke;—

BENEDICT ARNOLD.

All parley, and all policy, must amend,
And leave the Hero to repair, in blood,
The wrongs of men and nations! So, Amen!
  JAMIESON.
Oh! these are fiery metors to ambition;—
Brave words, bright fancies, that inflame the courage,
Lifting the mounting spirit into madness,
Which few have yet withstood! The savage nature,
Still lurks in Christian bosoms. Few have risen,
Above the instincts, to the laws of nature;
Or look with proper loathing on the glories,
That prompt most human wars! That fierce delight,
Which made the great delirium of the Hun,
Still nursed by frail Humanity, too fondly,
Makes us but too forgetful of the woes
That waits on victory; the blood and tears,
Warm from a people's eyes, that long must flow,
When the grim savage dreams of the triumph,
No longer spell the fancy with its dreams!
The rarer virtue, and the true ambition,
Is that of Washington. Among the few
Of glory still regardless, he but seeks
How best to save his people, shield the State,—
Protect the right from evil, and establish
The perfect guaranties of peace and justice.
He uses War but as the means to this,
Great end of every conflict. He is one,
Who seeks no man's applause—who does not heed
The giddy rabble's shout—nor fears their hiss.
And glory still resolves itself to this—
A passionate people's clamor—a long shout
Of exultation,—or a howl of hate;—
Some sorry pageant and a holiday;
Plumes, and gay weapons glittering in the sun,
And then—a vault of marble, which a season
Buries in weeds, forgotten! Washington,
But yields him to a dire necessity;
And fights for home and altar—home as sacred,

As any altar;—and for future times!
Not for himself, or for one single honor,
That any fortunate stroke of War may bring him.
And so, still struggling only for success,
And conquest of our purpose, he will fight
Or fly, or league in wily stratagem,
As policy—that practice you despise,
And most unwisely—may declare the best,
For the one object! And thus, unmoved by taunt,
Untempted by the spoil, uncaring fame,
Unvext, and scorning all, he soars supreme.
 ARNOLD.
You phrase it Colonel, in devotion's blindness,
And make this man your idol!
 JAMIESON.   And he is!
Nor mine alone. Our armies idolize him.
 ARNOLD. It were a secret to be bribed of Fortune—
—If vulgar homage were of any value—
To catch his popular art of winning worship.
Whence hath he this success? More stern than brave,
Far from adventurous; with no eager impulse;
And wearing in his breast, in place of heart,
A globe of perfect ice; his would not seem
The soul to penetrate the soldier's nature,
And shape it to his own! I do misdoubt me,
Your judgment follows only *your* regard,
And does not speak for theirs. He knows them not,
And never seeks them with that open grace
Which wins the confidence. He hath no smiles
Suited to catch them in their pliant moods;
And shapes no conduct to beguile their hearts
To a like beat with his.—No, Jamieson,
'Tis your own favor that reports him thus,
Successful with the troops as with yourself—
He wins *your* tribute only.
 JAMIESON.   Wins from all!—
His parts are so made up, and so complete,
His virtues are so many, and so noble,

His character so elevate and pure,
His ingredients all so ample and proportioned,
That he compels, what other men solicit,
With arts which he disdains! It needs no art,
To prompt the admiration which cries out,—
Scarce conscious, as it looks upon his aspect—
This is a man, a hero, a great master,
To sway the souls of men! He does not smile,
Or rarely; but in such a sort he smiles,
That men see beauty in the unwonted sunshine,
And feel the glow as healthful and as true!
Nor is the absence of the smile a leak
In his most perfect gaze. He hath no arts.
To conquer, say you? Wherefore should he have?
For none is needful where the end is won,
By natural seeming and sincerity,
And 'tis the happy temper of his mind,
His visage, his look, expression, and the tones,
Of his clear, simple, and unstudied speech,
That suffers none to doubt that his heart feels
What his head counsels, and his visage looks,
And all the natural sentiment he shows
In face or voice! Most bountiful,
Have been the gifts of Nature to this man;—
The finer elements so ample in him,
So blended with the coarser traits which make
Our mixed existence; yet superior still;
They elevate to majesty his form,
And make its action fitting. These, they crown,
With a magnanimous virtue that sublimes
Each feature; so that on his front would seem,
Enstamp'd the very signet-seal of Heaven,
Set on it by the Godhead!—So we worship!
'Tis still my wonder, General, that your bosom.—
Yourself so well endowed for noblest station,—
Hath never felt his greatness.

    ARNOLD, (*vehemently, yet huskily.*)
            'Tis this! 'Tis this!—

It is *because* I've felt—*still feel* this greatness,
Which still retards mine own, and lets my progress,
That I can never worship. He keeps from me
That glorious sun, which, but for his vast shadow,
Had circled my brows in light.
    JAMIESON.   Yet, do you share
His fame, though standing on a humbler height.
    ARNOLD.
I tell thee, Jamieson—talk of humbler heights!—
That I would struggle to unsphere the sun,
And seize his eminence, if it were given
The mortal to attempt immortal crowns,
By any desperate challenge of the Fates.
No middle height for me—no meaner aim,—
While there is yet one eminence beyond,
That daring flight may reach. Fame beckons not
From meaner height, to him whose eagle eye
May spread the eagle's wing. The upper skies,
Where clouds grow into canopies of blue,
And the Lark carols, seeing nought beyond,
But noonday, and celestial brightness ever!
These make the realm I covet, and will dare,
Let who will soar besides!—Enough, my friend;
Your eye hath seen my weakness, and your ear
Hath heard my soul's impatience. Washington,
But chafes my emulation, as thou seest,
And moves no other feeling.—It grows late;—
'Tis time you spread your parties for the night.
There's one John Anderson, who comes to me,
In secret from the city.—Give him progress,
Unstay'd, when he shall offer you his name.
'Tis needful we should gather all we can
Of good Sir Henry's doings and designs.
He keeps close counsel; but we'll sound his depths!
    JAMIESON.
De Ternay's coming prompts his watchfulness!
May we not look for certain movements now?
Washington—

ARNOLD.
Had bid his trumpets bellow long ere this,
Had Arnold been the chieftain!—But—no more!
Our wings are clipt and fetter'd! We must wait,
'Till Fortune bids them grow, and soar in State.

Here the scene closes—one of those scenes which, as I have already said, do not sufficiently advance the action—and not sufficient, in action, for stage effects—and can only serve for declamatory purposes. It is possible that some of the speeches might be employed in schools. The speeches of Jamieson, descriptive of Washington's character, career and influence, are *ad captandum*, designed only to give voice to popular sympathy. They might tell, to an American audience, even as the declamation about Liberty and Virtue, in Addison's "Cato," were found effective by a British audience. But the young play-wright, who aims at Dramatic success, will do well to eschew them. It is very certain that the actors will cut them out; and that, where any piece succeeds before an audience, which contains such passages, it must succeed in spite, and not in consequence, of *them*. The only *business* matter which this scene contains, is that in which Arnold seeks to make a case for himself—to suggest the motives for, and provocations to, his treason; his jealousies of Washington, as well as the sense of injustice at his hands; and his own extravagant ambition. Were the piece to be played, the actors would probably cut out the whole of the scene with the exception of that brief passage, at the close, which hints to Jamieson the probable coming of Anderson, and suggests a false motive for his coming. As most writers for the stage fail, because of the mistake which confounds lofty declamation with stage effect, I am thus particular in speaking of this scene. Declamation is for the rostrum. It rarely produces any, but a tedious effect, upon the stage. Occasionally, a brilliant passage, which, in effect, will allow of a classic and passionate action—will allow of picturesque effects—is permitted to be spoken; but, generally, writing for the stage, the young Dramatist cannot do better, than, when he thinks that he has written a particularly fine passage, to strike it out. It will do, perhaps, to restore it when he prints, and may be as successful as he desires, in the calm reading of the closet. As in this essay, I am dissecting myself, for the benefit of future writers, I do not scruple at these hints and suggestions, which are the result of equal experience and thought. I do not doubt that there will be play-wrights coming after me, in long future years, who will take up this subject of Arnold. If so, this Drama, in an essay, may serve at once as guide and beacon.

The action of the Drama will, henceforth, be confined wholly to the range of mountains along the Hudson. There is the pretty and picturesque precinct of Haverstraw; there, crowning the scene, stretches away the impregnable peaks of West Point. The Hudson spreads away below. The British sloop-of-war, the Vulture, lies at anchor in the narrow gorge between Teller's Point, and the opposite landing. The season, approaching the close of September, is one in which the scene appears to most advantage. The foliage, in which the Northern forests are most deficient to a Southern eye, has yet all the fulness of summer's fruitfulness; while autumn is beginning to tinge the tree tops with that brightness of tint and hue, with which she would conceal her decay. The time is early morning, when the following scene opens. On a point of rock, overlooking a well known gorge, called, in the dialect of the country, "the Clove," (cleft from cloven,) the figure of a man suddenly appears, clad from head to foot in a dark gray cloak. This is Randolph Peyton. He stands, half in shadow of the foliage, gazing down intently upon the river, from which his eye ranges anxiously along the opposite shore.

RANDOLPH PEYTON, (*solus*.)
Thus, then, our labor lightens! We have toil'd,
In devious passages, by night and day,
Following the reptile in his sinuous route,
Impatient of the finish to our task,

BENEDICT ARNOLD.

Yet with each several faculty in use!
Impatient, yet not blind! Thus have we track'd
The wolf and serpent to his several den;
And, at the last, we find them housed together!
We reach our consummation. Ere the night,
Shall Andre, gliding to this traitor's ear,
Whisper his bland seductions. Ere the dawn
Will he steal off, his treacherous office done,
To meet fit recompense. Our snares are set,
For both these reptiles! Neither can escape,
If those now set to watch them, do but keep
The vigilant eye and the unshrinking faith,
Which have not failed as yet. The wanton spy,—
The ambitious traitor—both of whom have sped
Triumphant, in *my* overthrow of hope,—
Spoiling my garden of its treasured wealth—
That flower which now, within my bosom shrined,
Had raised me high in loftiness of heart,
As now its loss brings low—they both shall feel
Love finds its own avenger!—Yet, my soul
Speak not, in voice of dread rebuke within,
That I have toil'd for this! My country, ho!
Thy safety, thy security, thy fame,
Have found one full commission for the toils,
That feed my own revenges. Had this Arnold
Been true to thee, I had not track'd him thus:
Should not exult that I have compass'd him,
With snares that bring him to the fearfullest doom,
That ever fell on head of infamy!
My wrong had slept unchallenged! I had spared him,
Though every hour of life, and every honor,
Had made him dearer in the eyes I love—
Had added to that bitterness of thought,
Which still must vex my life! (*Whistle heard.*)
    The messenger!—
He comes from Washington!—He must be at hand,
Prompt as the Fates, at my intelligence—
Still questioning, still watchful o'er my passions,

As the o'er jealous movers of my fears,
And these most terrible suspicions—born,
He fancies, of the hatred in my heart,
He'll do this poor heart justice. He shall see,
I have not toil'd in vain, nor idly taught,
The wolf-cry to the shepherd.
                    (*Enter Officer.*)
    OFFICER.   Randolph Peyton.
    PEYTON.   The same.
    OFFICER.   There's one who sends one to you.
    PEYTON.   Well!—
Sends me no token.
    OFFICER, (*showing a peeled wand of willow.*)
This.
    PEYTON.   No word?
    OFFICER.   But one!—
    PEYTON.   Declare the speaking syllable at once,
Even tho' it still reproach me with a doubt,
Mix'd with a warning. It is meet it should,
Coming from him, the perfect one, to me,—
All passion, as he deems me! Speak the word!
    OFFICER.   Beware!
    PEYTON.
Enough! I thank that solemn monitor!—
Beware of danger—treachery beware—
Beware of thine own heart—For that he means!
Well, he shall see 't—as firm, as true of faith,
As he hath ever known it. He shall know
It hath not falter'd in its trust, nor yielded
Though Passion, with its all prevailing accents,
Hath sorely vex'd and tempted. Lead me to him.
                            (*Exeunt.*)

The scene changes to a hollow—a deep recess in the mountain range, several miles from the river. There we find Washington and Lafayette in close consultation.

BENEDICT ARNOLD.

WASHINGTON.
The youth is full of nobleness and truth;
With never a taint of meanness in his soul;
Is free from indirection, as from falsehood;
Has judgment; is keen sighted, fearless, firm;
May sometimes err 'neath the wild goad of passion;
But never, with deliberate will and malice,
Unjustly deal in censure. Yet, I dare not
Accord a faith to this most dread report,
Which summons us hither now Yet is he clear,
As confident of speech; and still renews
His former tale of treachery, now urgent,
In presence of a danger pressing close.

 LAFAYETTE. You have no choice but hear him.

 WASHINGTON.   Yet, suspicion
Too often conjures up from innocent action
The shadow which deforms it. The best virtue
Lies open to this danger. We, at least,
Have need to fence our ears, with sternest questions,
Against that censure, which, assuming substance
Claims credence without proof. No shows, no signs,—
No mere equivocal aspect in the action,
Must move us to a sad celerity,
In stamping it as foul. The fame of greatness,
Hath such a need of angel purity,
To keep its proper potency 'mongst men,
That we should shrink, as from a mortal sin,
To link it in our faith, or in our fears,
With any form of baseness.

 LAFAYETTE.   So the need
With him who would be great, to have stern heed,
To his least action and most innocent deed,
Lest he give food, and furnish to suspicion,
Occasion for its question. The wife of Cæsar,—
Though innocent, still meets with punishment,
When she but prompts suspicion. In degree,

Still, as we highly, we must purely aim,
And with meet caution, that our idle footsteps,
Stray not one moment into doubtful paths.

WASHINGTON.
A stern and perilous truth! Exacting thus,
Men still avenge upon the ambitious mortal,
Their hurts of self-esteem; glad to discover
The weak place in the armor of the chief,
The base spot in his nature; the one weakness
Which brings him toppling from that eminence,
Whereon they lifted him an hour before!
The humbling consciousness of a lowlier state,
Makes them forever watchful to discern,
The shame in the superior; and it shows
Sadly conspicuous, in the shining object
As doth the blot upon the sun's great disk,
Which had not stain'd the earth.

LAFAYETTE. And yet, suspicion,
In proper season, meetly entertain'd,
Might save a nation.

WASHINGTON. We are here for this!—
Not that we hold it probable, this tale;
But that,'tis possible, and our high trust,
The nation's fate, a people's liberties,
At stake, makes that, which is a possible danger,
Become with us a care. But, hark! he comes.

Enter Randolph Peyton.

PEYTON. **My General!**
WASHINGTON. Randolph! Welcome; but beware!
The warning, in the single word I sent you,
Was not, I trust, forgotten when you wrote me,
I come upon your summons—resolute
To deal with strength and prompt severity,
However high the station of the victim,
If that your tale be sooth. And yet, beware!

PEYTON.
Sir, your have been my father, and my friend
And the wise parting counsel of your lips,
Hath never left my sense. My heart has felt,
Still feels, what virtue lies in that "beware!"—
And sure the passions which I know are mine,
And quite too frequently the masters o'er me,
Have not despised its schooling. I am ready
To answer, with that warning still before me,—
Seen in your aspect, stern in all your accents,
And speaking to my conscience, fresh from you.
  LAFAYETTE. Pardie! Well answer'd!
  WASHINGTON. Now, sir, speak.
  PEYTON.   A moment, sir,
First let the signal from yon bark, the Vulture,
Carry to the boats below, a swift dispatch
That all is ready here, as late agreed on,
And the whole army of Sir Henry——
  WASHINGTON.   That, sir,
Has been prepared for.—We are ready for him,
Or will be in due season. But, to answer;—
Where is old Thurston?
  PEYTON.   Safe in bonds below,
In Col. Campbell's keeping.
  WASHINGTON. Andre?
  PEYTON.   Above!
  WASHINGTON. Art sure of it?
  PEYTON. Was sure of it last night!
Beheld him on his way.
  WASHINGTON. Why let him pass?
  PEYTON. That he might furnish, to his own conviction,
Proofs of his dirty labor!
  LAFAYETTE.   That was right.
  WASHINGTON.
Peyton, beware! It is your passion speaks.
  PEYTON. But speaks truth, sir. It may be my heart,
Moved by some worthless feelings of its own,
Exults in this detection; but it suffers

No blinding impulse to deceive its justice,
And every revelation from these lips,
Is fortified by proof.
    WASHINGTON.   'Tis well! and yet,
'Twould better have rejoiced me, had these traitors
Been frighted from their game, by timely action;—
To scare them were to save!
    LAFAYETTE.   Your mercy errs!—
The youth was right, I think. Unwind the snake,
From the victim's neck, and let him go;
He still remains a snake—will seek his prey,
As full of spite and venom as before,
In the next moment! Treachery is ever
Of this sly serpent nature. Scared away,
It but waits the newer opportunity,
For stealing on the slumbers of its victim.
Best watch and suffer it to feel secure,
'Till the last moment, when, upon his head,
You set the heavy heel and crush it quite.
    WASHINGTON. Perhaps, 'twas right—and yet—
    PEYTON.   Oh! sir, what proof,
Short of the absolute, would content your eyes,
Dealing with one so high in rank and favor?
All evidence short of absolute conviction,
Had been rejected, as a slanderous fable,
Meant for a rival's overthrow. 'Tis needful,
I bring the charges home to him, and show
The criminal naked, in the fact;—denial,
Doubt, question, all impossible! The truth,
Apparent, with no help of argument;—
The victim left without a cover, refuge,
Bare to the world's wide eyes.
    WASHINGTON.   Be it so!
And this man—so rich in high renown,
So full of high ambition—with endowment
To rise in spite of Fortune, and to sway
The heads and hearts of men, and grow in stature,
With every day increase of fame and power;—

That he should foul the glory in his hope,
And sink to shame like this! Can it be true?
Speak Peyton,—to your proofs.
    PEYTON, (*giving papers.*)   These letters, sir—
Signed—
    WASHINGTON. Gustavus; but not written in *his* hand.
    LAFAYETTE. A hand disguised.
    PEYTON. They come from him, at least.
    WASHINGTON. How know you that?
    PEYTON. Old Thurston's messenger,
Betray'd him to our gold: His letters brought,
Were copied, and the copies sent to Clinton;
The genuine are here.
    WASHINGTON.   Yet these say nought,
That can be held of treasonable nature—
They speak of trade and barter,—merchandize—
    PEYTON. But do not name the article of trade.
    WASHINGTON. Can you?
    PEYTON. By nightfall I will do it.
    WASHINGTON.   Enough!
You have your watches set?
    PEYTON. They line the river,
Both sides, from Teller's Point to Tarrytown:
'Twere easy to arrest the English spy,
At any mile of his progress.
    WASHINGTON.   Why not do it?
    PEYTON. For the reasons that I gave already—
To make it sure, once separate from Arnold,
That all his papers will be ratified;—
The seals affixed;—the guaranties exchanged;—
The terms of trade declared;—the merchandize
Defined—whate'er prime commodity;—
Its price;—the when and manner of delivery;—
All matters very needful we should know,
But which we should *not* know, if, seizing Andre,
We frightened his associate from the perch.
Arnold may keep him company awhile—
May see him, to some distance, on his way,

And keep his papers 'til the parting moment.
To arrest either now, were premature:
Their caution, sometimes better than our own,
Might spoil our snares forever.

LAFAYETTE.   Right again;—
Our friend's a politician.

WASHINGTON.   You assume
That Andre takes the road on his return:
Why not the river?

PEYTON.   Doubtless he would do so,
But, at my signal, will our batteries open
Upon the Vulture, driving her below.
I have had heed to this.

WASHINGTON.   Our signal then?

PEYTON. Shall be sure news of the arrest of Andre,
Arnold's should follow fast upon the tidings.

WASHINGTON.
And will! Now, Peyton, once again I trust,
Your virtue, as your vigilance and skill;—
Take all the needful steps, and make all sure,
Within the narrow limit I have set you!
Beware how you shed blood! Secure your captive
That he may answer—with his life, if need be,—
But under rigid judgment of the Law.
Be sure of tangible proofs to make him traitor,
And justify your action, as mine own.

PEYTON. Your warning weighs upon me, sir.—

WASHINGTON.   Remember,
That you have motives for hostility,
To both these parties, in defeated passions,
That make very life in youthful hearts.
This feeds misgivings and suspicion still
To your own great disquiet. Keep good watch,
Upon yourself; and, jealously to judge
Upon your share in the events which aim
To bring such victims to disgraceful judgment,
Must be, with me, a peremptory duty,
Which suffers no evasion. Randolph Peyton,

BENEDICT ARNOLD.

Though you were precious to me as the son,
First born of my affections, and their hope—
A hope I may not have;—yet, as I live,
These lips shall speak, nor falter in the speech,
The sternest doom of judgment on your head,
If you do err in this! No plausible plea,
Shall save you; no mistake of fact, or the fancy;
Thought or opinion, or mistakes of others,
By which you were misled. Once more, beware!
Be sure you rightly do, before you dare!
(Exeunt Washington and Lafayette.)

PEYTON, (*manent.*)
Sharp and hard judgment! Sternest requisition!
How is it, O! my soul? Doth this "beware,"
Disarm thy resolute purpose? Is thy will
Subdued, which yet, in the pursuit of Justice,
May happen on Revenge? 'Tis so much gain
To my heart's passion, with no loss to virtue,
If thus, my foe, of his own head and purpose,
Becomes the foe of Fate, and 'gainst his country,
Lifts parricidal hand! It is the Fate,
That summons me to this! They bring me succor;
And sanction, by success, that appetite,
Which in my heart cries evermore—'revenge!'
Why should I doubt, when that the very blow
Which strikes my insolent enemy to the earth,
Avenges all our people, and secures
Our country's liberties? No, Arnold, no!
I must not shrink to strike the fatal blow.

And now, for a brief period, the Essayist must here take the place of the play-wright. The plot between Arnold and Sir Henry Clinton has ripened into a perfect understanding between the two parties. In the drama, we have shown that the clues to the conspiracy, were, however, in other hands than their own; that Washington, if not actually assured of its progress, has had his suspicions aroused; and that a highly trusted young officer is secretly engaged in ferreting out the conspirators and preparing to foil their enterprise. History tells us nothing of this; on the contrary, it teaches us that no suspicion was entertained, and that the discovery of the plot was purely accidental. But the drama leaves nothing to accident! The Fate is present in every stage of the action, though the chorus may be silent. *Everything, in dramatic performance, demands the agency of design.* In this narrative, there is nothing improbable in the case, as reported by the dramatist. He does not really conflict with the Historian. He only knows *more* than the historian has been suffered to find in the written records. Treachery and conspiracy use very few written records; and, if possible, leave no tracks behind them in their progress. Washington may very well have had, in his own hands, all the clues to the conspiracy, even as the Dramatist has shown it; yet be silent. He prefers not to be seen in the connection. He prefers that the detection of the treason may seem providential; that the American people may be made to believe that the Lord of Hosts is fighting their battles, watching parentally over their cause, and guarding it against treachery as 'against open foes. We repeat that there is nothing inherently improbable in the case as it is reported by the playwright; and the gain is great, for dramatic purposes, from the assumptions that have thus been made. The characters of the *dramatis personæ* are lifted by the proof shown by them, of an ever-frequent design. It is not blind chance which is at work. The great master-minds at work are exhibiting thought, foresight, circumspection, and the necessary degree of intellect, or genius, which is required to contend with a vague and monstrous danger. This is the proof of highest heroism, and, **just in the degree as the audience sympathises with the hero, and follows the progress of his mind, and passions, in just that degree will the drama be successful.** So far the Essayist. We now make the necessary summary of the Historian.

The terms of the conspiracy being agreed on between the British and American Generals, and the immediate object being understood, viz. the delivery of West Point, and the sacrifice of the army having the post in keeping—Clinton urges Arnold to the immediate performance of his contract. Clinton is urgent, 'or it is now understood that a second division of the French army had sailed from Europe; and, thus reinforced, there is no doubt that Washington, upon its arrival, will begin the leaguer of New York. The Marshal de Castries, the French Minister of Marine, has advised Washington of the approaching departure of this second army, and the fact has been verified to Clinton beyond all question. It is necessary that what he does shall be done quickly. The possession of the forts at West Point; the surrender of that division of the army which holds the forts; and the treason of Arnold and his junction with the British, will be such a blow, moral and physical, to the American cause, that Washington must be too much dismayed to do anything; too distrustful of his own troops and officers to attempt anything; while the French must be encountered before landing, by the British fleet of Sir George Rodney; and should they escape the fleet, they will find too little to encourage them, at landing, from their American allies; and, denied their support, may be safely encountered at Newport, or elsewhere, by the concentrated forces of the British. At all events, the loss of West Point and its garrisons, and the defection of Arnold, it is fairly concluded, will utterly prevent any attempt of the allies upon New York.— To precipitate the performance of his contract, by Arnold, is now the urgent necessity of Clinton. He accordingly notified him that it is time to act; and that he must fix the day for the surrender of the forts. He also required that plans of the forts be sent him, with all the necessary instructions, by which the British troops snall obtain possession, as by a grand *coup de main.*

But the urgency of Clinton only embarrassed Arnold. It found him temporarily under *surveillance.* Washington was unexpectedly at West Point, and he had to be circumspect.— Now, Washington's presence, at this juncture, would seem to correspond with the action of Randolph Peyton,—and, so far, it supports the case of the Dramatist. It is not accidental.— Arnold writes to Clinton, in the mysterious style, and in the character of Anderson, that "the Master is there, but will depart on the 17th—(Sept.) that he will be absent five or six days. In this interval, we will arrange our business. Come immediately, meet me at the lines, and we will settle the risks and profits of the copartnership. This interval is indispensable, and must precede the sailing of our ship." The approaching departure of Washington was then announced to Clinton. The former had appointed to meet the French Admiral and General at Hartford. But here Arnold was deceived, whether purposely, by Washington, himself, (and we are at liberty to assume it) or by accident, does not matter. It is enough that his mistake had serious results. The 17th Sept. passed, and Washington still lingered at West Point. Why? Was it design of Providence, or man? The 17th was Sunday. Washington would not travel on that day. Arnold then appointed the 19th as the day on which Andre should leave New York; reaching West Point on the 20th. Accordingly, on the night of that day, Andre did embark in the Vulture. He was accompanied by the Loyalist Colonel, Beverley Robinson, through whom he had just began his correspondence with Clinton.— Robinson's superior discretion was meant to temper the eagerness of Andre; and as Arnold occupied Robinson's house, his coming, as a refugee, on private business, was a good cover for other proceedings. On the 20th the Vulture appeared in sight; five miles below West Point, and nearly opposite Fort Montgomery. Here she anchored beyond the reach of the American artillery; and here, at low water, she grounded.— Colonel Livingston, commanding at Verplanck's Point, thought she might be reached and sunk by heavy cannon. He applied for them to Arnold—and was refused. Livingston was surprised at the refusal, but silently submitted. Two days more elapsed, the 19th had passed, and to Arnold's great annoyance, Washington still lingered at West Point. The dramatist has suggested a reason for this delay, while the historian is at a loss. Arnold became uneasy; but he feared to excite suspicion, by communicating the fact to Clinton. But the latter was informed through other agents, and he became uneasy also. He began to apprehend a double treachery in Arnold: as yet, Andre and Robinson kept within the Vulture, making no effort to reach the shore. They naturally awaited the communications from Arnold. At length, growing impatient, they sent a letter, under a flag of truce, addressed to Putnam, designing, through an indirect channel, to ascertain whether Washington had or had not departed. At that very hour Washington, in the barge of Arnold, was preparing to cross the river on his route to Hartford. With his spy glass, he examined the Vulture, and, in low tones, which Arnold could not hear, he gave an order to an officer near him. This alarmed the traitor, who, apprehending that Washington knew of the flag of truce and letters which he had just received, thought to anticipate the consequences by frankly telling him of them. Washington, with much earnestness, advised him to have no communication with Robinson; hinting to him that any *private* affairs of the refugee must be referred wholly to the *civil* authorities. After this, Washington pursued his way to Hartford. His absence opened the way to the conspirators. But the solemn and imperative words of Washington, at the moment of departure, impressed Arnold with new caution. He could not now venture to receive Robinson, on private affairs, through a flag of truce; and their interviews must be in secret. For this Arnold had to arrange. He employed a Loyalist named Smith, who was permitted to live within the American forts, to go on board the Vulture, carrying two passports, one for Andre, under the name of Anderson, the other for Robinson in his own name. His letters required the parties to meet him on shore. Andre and Robinson were disappointed, that Arnold did not come himself, and refused to go on shore. Andre, young and zealous, ardent and eager through a variety of motives, mostly personal, no doubt, complied with the requisiton in spite of Robinson's counsels to the contrary. Covering his uniform with a great surtout, he accompanied Smith and found Arnold awaiting him at the river's edge.—Here, they discussed the conspiracy for sometime, and finally adjourned to Smith's house, where Arnold laid before Andre the plans of the several forts, including a memoir, by the French Engineer Duportail, which exhibited all the detailed means by which they were to be attacked or defended. The instructions furnished to the British Adjutant, were such as would enable the British army successfully to surprise and possess the forts, for the doing which, Arnold was so to dispose of the American troops, as to render the operation easy and strip it of all its dangers. Briefly, the troops under his command, were to be sacrificed with the post. The best passes were to be left unguarded, while his men were to be scattered and entangled among the mountain gorges, in such a manner as to be compelled to surrender at summons, or be cut to pieces. From the chain across the river, he had detached a link, so that it offered no impediment to shipping; and he was to fire certain beacons on the neighboring heights, which should signal the enemy when to advance. Briefly, the plan was matured in all its parts, and nothing remained but the safe return of Andre to his superior. They agreed upon a countersign, to be given on the 24th and 25th, and for the first time, all *the draughts, instructions and necessary papers, in Arnold's own handwriting, were suffered to go out of his hands.* They were now in those of Andre; and all danger seemed at an end. Andre had only to return to the Vulture, and be safe. But the Fates were hostile to this simple arrangement, as we shall show hereafter. We now return to the drama. Our scene changes to Arnold's dwelling—The Robinson House—*where we find* Lady Arnold, seated, and in a musing attitude.

MARGARET, (*solus.*)
This passion grows upon him, and he broods
In a strange humor of forgetfulness;
Still absent in his moods, and without purpose,
He leaves the present purpose all undone,
As foreign to his thought. He takes no food,
And with a mind still wandering from its object,
Achieves it with no living consciousness,
Then stares to find it done! His cheek grows pale,
His eye glares wild yet earnest. With a start,
He leaves the table ere the food is touched,

BENEDICT ARNOLD.

And hurries to the shore. And, when I speak,
Though but in answer to his own remark,
He wonders that I've spoken—wonders more
That he himself had furnished theme for speech,
In that I answer him. And, night by night,
He wanders in that forest, dense and dark,
Or through the mountain gorges, o'er their heights,
Without companion; and at morning comes
Pale, wearied to his couch, and snatches sleep
Such as requites not; troubled still with dreams
Of terror, that awake him with a cry,
Such as his manhood, resolute and bold,
Would never show by day. Some evil broods
Over his head and house. My prescient soul,
Grows conscious of a danger—
     Who is there?
    (*Enter Andre, disguised.*)
 ANDRE, (*his face half covered.*)
'Tis courage still that conquers in the field,
And Fortune yields her favors to the bold!
He merits not to win who cannot dare,
The hazards of his hope; nor can he strike
The white, which is the all within his aim,
Unless the soul, as eager as the sight,
Gives spur to resolution! The great bird
Would never know the power within his wing
But for the will, within his breast, to soar.
'Tis not in strength, but in audacity,
We climb the mountain, stride beyond the cloud,
And pluck our blisses from the bright-eyed stars.
So thus—
 MARGARET. What spirit is it soars so high,
That seems not natural here? And, so abrupt,
Makes challenge of a greatness, with an aim,
Which, lacking favor from all other tongues,
But show the braggart's his! That voice, methinks—
 ANDRE.
Not know me, Margaret? Can this mean disguise,

So shut me from thy memory, as thy heart,
That still needs the open voice to say,
Behold, 'tis Andre. *(Throwing off his disguise.)*
 MARGARET. Wherefore art thou here?
 ANDRE.
Canst thou ask, Margaret! Wonder that the Bee
Should seek the richest flower? The wanton moth,
Still singe his gaudy vestments in the flame,
Which binds him, by its beauty, to the fate.
 MARGARET. Oh! fate indeed, to come!
 ANDRE.   —or, that the Bird
Should from the common tribe, still seek the wood
Where sits in sweetest solitude, that mate
Whom most his soul affects?
 MARGARET.   I'm not thy mate!
 ANDRE.
But should have been, had Fortune not been niggard,
Nor meet with frowns, and a denying aspect,
The passion that true love made dutiful,
And slaved, without requital, in her worship.
 MARGARET.
Enough that Fortune frown'd—that Fate decreed!
Submissive, let us learn another lesson,
And find in self-denial, and new duties,
The peace that comes from virtue. Go hence, Andre,—
This moment! Leave me, nor distress my ears,
With words, not fit for thee to speak,—unmeet,
For ears of mine to hear, or me to pardon.
 ANDRE.
Nay, this is prudery, Margaret! You are frigid,—
And take too soon the dreary tone of years;
Mock youth with lessons age alone can learn,
And dull the joys of beauty and of love,
By much too sad a burden for such shoulders.
 MARGARET. Now, leave me, Andre.
 ANDRE.   Hear me, Margaret:
I have a joyous hope that speaks for both,
In the fast-growing future. There will come,

An hour of love for thee, for both of us,
When, from this bondage freed, and cold restraint,
Thy heart shall flourish in a happier clime,
Where youth may sport her plumage, nor find challenge
For any flight her roving wing may take.
   MARGARET.
Hear me a moment, Andre,—then go hence!
My soul misgives me that your purpose here
Is evil—full of danger to my husband,—
His peace and honor, if not mine—
   ANDRE.   What fancy—
   MARGARET.
It is a terror that oppresses me!
It shook me ere you came, with shapeless phantoms,
That, in your coming, grow to form and substance,
That fancy cannot conjure. Get thee hence,
With all dispatch, with all the secrecy,
With which thou camest. Get thee hence, I say,
And never seek me more; my house or me!
I know not what thou mean'st, and cannot think—
I will not—dare not! Should my husband know—
   ANDRE. He knows—he knows.
   MARGARET.   Thy presence bodes him ill—
But shall not compass mischief to his wife.
   ANDRE. Wherefore this fright?
   MARGARET.   Thy safety, Arnold's—mine.
   ANDRE.   What danger?
   MARGARET.   Washington is here.
   ANDRE.   Is gone!
That vulture hath flown northward, and his shadow
Makes all our sunshine free, and gives our birds,
All liberty of song.
   MARGARET.   But not of flight!
And he will soon return; and—Arnold knows,
You tell me, of your presence?
   ANDRE.   We are safe!
And now, my own, my beautiful———

MARGARET.　　　　God help me!
Or I shall go distraught. Hear me, Andre,
This sort of speech is madness. You mistake me,
And have no proper right;—I was a child—
That loved a graceful knight and gallant soldier,
And thought of life, but as a summer progress,
Through realms of flowers—still attended
By troops of gallant suitors. In that season,
How much I err'd with thee, in thoughtlessness,
That reck'd not reason——
　　ANDRE.　　Ha! dost thou repent?
　　MARGARET. I will not err again.
　　ANDRE.　　This is cold welcome,
For him, it pleased thee once to lure with hope,
And torture with denial.
　　MARGARET.　　Thy reproach,
Is something true; it is my grief——
　　ANDRE.　　It is all true!
What of *thy* grief,—and how shall grief of thine,
Repair *my* hurts of heart and loss of hope.
　　MARGARET. Alas! alas!
　　ANDRE. Art thou, indeed, the maid
Whose Virgin feeling woke at once to mine
With warm and natural instinct? And thou forgett'st—
　　MARGARET.
Andre, I am no more the thoughtless child
Thou knew'st me in that season of my error—
And being thus changed, am nothing now to thee.
　　ANDRE.
The all thou ever was't, as in my heart,
Assured, I find myself still all to thee!
I cannot suffer thee to trample thus,
The fires thou'st kindled, which must ever burn,
'Till this heart perish!
　　MARGARET.　　　　Go!—
　　ANDRE.　　Shalt thou woo
The worship, but to drive it from thy shrine?
Provoke the passion till it maddens me,

Nor stay to soothe its rage? No, Margaret, no!
Thus guilty of the wrong that leaves me wretched,
Thou shalt not leave me too! I will not lose thee!
By this sweet hand———
     (*Seizing her **hand and conveying** it to his lips.*)
 MARGARET. Unband me, Major Andre!
 ANDRE. But one fond moment.
 MARGARET. Rouse me not to anger.
Off, sir! (*Flinging him off.*) Thou dost mistake.
 ANDRE. I'll not believe it.
 MARGARET.
Thou shalt! I tell thee, I'm no more the child,
That suffer'd idle gallantries, nor thought,
In my own ignorance and innocence,
Whither they could tend!
 ANDRE, (*bitterly.*)
   And so, at my poor cost,
Your have grown wiser.
 MARGARET.   If to know my fault,
And resolutely to resolve against it,
Be to be wiser, I have wiser grown.
Deceive thyself no more. When I became
The wife of General Arnold, suddenly,
I grew to conscious womanhood, I trust,
With all the wife's best consciousness of a duty,—
And setting up his station in mine eyes,
Grew into woman's stature, and became,
So far as it is yielded to my keeping,
The guardian of his honor as mine own.
 ANDRE. His honor! Ha! Ha! Ha!
 MARGARET. What may this mean?
That sneer—that laugh?
 ANDRE. Was nothing—nothing.
 MARGARET.   Well, sir—
The guardian of *his* honor—of the trust,
Most proud as it was precious: eager still,
In his pure fame, and high integrity,
To be the chief participant; and thus, sir,

Made myself free at once from all toils,
That girlish fancy wove about my heart.
  ANDRE.
T'would seem, an easy task. But if these toils,
Haply, enmesh'd another's.
  MARGARET.   For you, John Andre,
I sorrow, if perchance, my heart inspired
A profitless flame in thine. I sorrow still—
And it is pity—'tis no longer passion—
That hearkens to thy speech—thy erring language:
Not that it glides with favor to my senses,
But that I would not chide, though erring still,
The heart that mine has wrong'd. Now, thou know'st all,—
Go hence, and in more fortunate pursuit,
Forget that I beguiled thee of a glance,
Which other hearts had better recompensed.
  ANDRE. I cannot take thy pity for thy love,
Nor, having won the first fruits of thy heart,
Content me with its fallen yellow leaves.
Still must I love thee, Margaret—still must dream
That the dear love thy lips had promised first,
Thy heart must treasure yet. (*Takes her hand.*)
  MARGARET.   Forego this folly—
This grasp upon my hand! Thou know'st me not—
'Tis clear thou know'st me not!
  ANDRE.   This precious hand—
  MARGARET. Is sacred, from thy touch.
  ANDRE. On my knees, Margaret.
  MARGARET.
Rise, sir: you wrong my husband as myself,
And him you shall not wrong. And let me say,
You wrong him by your presence in this place.
  ANDRE. 'Tis by his will, I came.
  MARGARET.   If that be true,
Thou speak'st a mortal dagger to my soul,
And fill'st my fever'd brain with dreariest doubts!
For what com'st thou? What mission—what design?
Thou dar'st not say he knows. What thou would'st say—

BENEDICT ARNOLD.

Hast said, of passion's madness! Speak! But, no!
Him will I question of thy presence here!
From thee, I ask no question. But, go hence—
Release me from thy grasp.

   ANDRE.   I cannot think,
Thou speak'st a resolute wish, when thou command'st,
Thus, hopeless, I depart!

   MARGARET.   I do! I do!
I pity, and I sorrow for thy sorrows,
If, with exulting speech, and daring front,
Thou hast a sorrow worthy of the name!
I can no more; and now, command thee, leave me.

   ANDRE. My faith is stronger in thy virgin heart,
Than in thy woman words! I better trust
The angel sweetness lurking in thine eyes
Than the cold practised accents of thy tongue.
I cannot leave thee, Margaret—dare not thus,
Unless, with sweet assurance of the future,
You justify the past.

   MARGARET.   Then know me, sir,
Superior to those weaknesses of girlhood,
On which you still presume. Another moment,
And, from within, I summon to my succor,
A will more apt to be obey'd than mine.

   ANDRE. Cruel!

   MARGARET. (*Noise without.*)
No! Him!—Rise, sir!—My husband's footstep!
Let him not see you thus! For my sake, Andre,
Spare me this shame!

   ANDRE. (*Arising—aside.*)
         Damnation! But for this!

   MARGARET.
'Tis well! Depart! No words! No more!

   ANDRE.   But one!

       Enter Arnold, hastily.

   ARNOLD.
What! Not away; and the disguise thrown off!—
What madness moves to this?

ANDRE. What danger here?
ARNOLD.
Danger is everywhere, for him who wears
A habit not his own; and when the mask,
Thrown off, reveals a fatal garb like this,
Then peril follows fast at heels of peril,
Dogging it like a Heath hound to its doom.
MARGARET.
Why came he here,—and thus?
ARNOLD. You hear the question?—
Make answer, as you only can,—by flight!
Why do you linger?
ANDRE. Still the danger, where?
Methinks that treachery takes no shape like this;
And had I thousand lives, I'd peril all
Upon the sweet security and faith,
I hold in woman's heart.
ARNOLD. Pshaw, get thee hence!
Waste not in gallantries these precious moments,
And peril not thy charge by vain delays!
'Tis not thy life alone—nor thousand lives,—
That thou dost put to hazard.
ANDRE. Thou remind'st me!
(*Cannon heard.*)
ARNOLD. Hark!
ANDRE. 'Tis cannon!
ARNOLD. Ay, 'tis a knell! Away!
Our batteries open on the Vulture now!
That pestilent Livingston! To your boat at once,
Or you will lose the passage by the river!
Away! Away!
ANDRE. (*Aside to Margaret.*)
Am I forgiven, Margaret?
MARGARET. Ay, if thou straightway fly'st.
ANDRE. I go!
ARNOLD. (*Impatiently.*) Away!
Stay not for idle carpet courtesies,
That may defraud our purposes and safety,

Life hangs upon these moments—life!—a nation!
(*Aside to Andre.*) Thy sovereign favor, Andre.
 ANDRE.   Farewell, lady,—
I go,—not hopeless quite—and think of thee.
 MARGARET.
Think of me nothing—think of us no more.
Hence! Hence!
 ARNOLD. (*Cannon heard.*)
Hark!—and again! I fear 'twill be too late,
With me!—our chances rest upon our speed.—
 ANDRE. (*Waves a kiss to Margaret.*)
Farewell, lady!—I had hope to———
 ARNOLD.   Oh! hence!

 Here, the scene closes. The history supplies us with a few details which need interpolation here. When Andre returned to the beach, to go on board the Vulture, she was gone. Col. Livingston had brought a cannon to bear upon her, where she lay grounded. She had already sustained some damage from this piece, when the rising of the tide enabled her to float. Col. Robinson immediately had her anchor weighed and she was removed several miles lower down, and quite beyond the reach of this gun. When Andre repaired to the beach, the rowers, who were Americans, refused to row to such a distance. Andre returned to Arnold, to get him to assert his authority over them; but the latter, already anxious and alarmed, was still more so at the reappearance of his colleague; —he feared to coerce the rowers, or to show himself, openly, in communication with the spy. It was then arranged that Andre should return to New York *by land*, having Arnold's pass to White Plains, or lower, "on public business." It was made out in the name of Anderson. Another dress was procured for him, and he was put under the guidance of the loyalist, Smith. Arnold, whose fears had become greatly excited by these repeated embarrassments, was anxious to repossess himself of all the papers he had given to Andre; but the latter made light of the danger, and positively refused to part with those proofs of his successful enterprise, which were to secure him the highest distinctions of his superior officers, and his King. And thus they parted; Andre, eager with the hopes and vanities of youth; Arnold, trembling with the vague terrors which must be natural enough in the bosom of a traitor, on so large a scale of crime! When, after finally getting Andre off, he returns to his own dwelling, where, according to the Dramatist, a scene occurs with his wife, which exhibits her prescient anxieties also. They do not serve to lesson the volume and burdens of his own. It is midnight:

ARNOLD.
What! watching, Margaret? Wherefore not abed?
MARGARET.
I cannot sleep! A terror weighs me down.
ARNOLD,
What terror, woman? What's the danger now,
And why these idle fancies?
MARGARET.
          Are they idle?
Can you look up to me, and face me, Arnold,
With the old honest smile upon thy visage,
And say "thou dreamest, my wife—thy fears are idle."
ARNOLD.   And wherefore not?
MARGARET.
Well! But thou dost not look!
ARNOLD.   Pshaw!
MARGARET.
There were some words of thine—don't heatken me?
ARNOLD.   Proceed!
MARGARET.
"Thy safety and thy purpose!" Arnold—
These were thy words, and to an enemy;
One wrapt in strange disguises, and yet wearing,

BENEDICT ARNOLD.

Beneath his cloak, the scarlet coat of Britain:
And he beneath this roof! Why were these words,
And why the apprehension in thy face,
The paleness on thy cheek and in thine eyes,
The wild uncertain gaze, as if thou look'dst,
Each moment for the enemy's assault,
At that last parting? Why dost look so, now?
Look, speech and action so unlike thyself.
   ARNOLD.
What wilderness of fears thy speech betrays—
What nonsense! 'Tis a nightmare, Margaret,
Has troubled thee in sleep.
   MARGARET.   I have not slept.
   ARNOLD.
Well, stir in waking, then! We have waking dreams,
As potent on the senses as in sleep.
Get thee to rest. There's nothing to alarm.
Perchance, I do look haggard with night-watching,
And surely feel more badly than I look!
No more of this—you trouble me.
   MARGARET.   'Twere well I should!
Why was John Andre here?
   ARNOLD.   Why should'st thou ask?
He brings despatches from the enemy—
Such as still seek us each returning day,
As ours seek him, a thousand businesses,
Thus bring together, peacefully, the foes
Who, at another season, come in wrath,
With pomp of drums and cannon. We have need,
Even in our strifes, of gentlest offices:
Exchange of prisoners, overture of terms,
Treaty, or armistice; when war lays down
His mace and bloody ensigns, and in smiles,
Clothes his late terrible visage!
   MARGARET.
                  False to me!
Oh! Arnold, know I not these offices,
Of amnesty in war? But these, which come

With the occasion, daily, and have grown
Familiar to performance, wake no stir,
Of passion or of fear, in gallant souls;
Pale no proud cheeks, and lend no fearless eye,
To commerce with the ground, in sudden dread,
As conscience sings of danger! Arnold, Arnold!
My lord and husband, censure not my doubt,
Unless to still it, with a single word,
Which says 'all's well' with you; that guilty thoughts
Vex not your bosom with that nightly strife,
Which makes your sleep the terror of mine own,
As still it seems of yours;—makes all your moods
Those of a man, not conscious of his steps,
Yet all too painfully conscious. Makes you move,
Look, speak, as if the creature of a will,
That, not an innocent native of thy breast,
Still rules it to its ruin.
    ARNOLD.
                         You but vex me—
And wherefore, woman?
    MARGARET.
                         Yes, I am a woman,
And so, a thing of conscience! Hear me, Arnold—
My prayer is that you speak, if but a word,
Yet, with frank brow, and all unclouded visage,
Assurance to me of a conscience free,
A soul aroused, and with a natural loathing,
Spurning reproach of guilt—spurning all question,
That casts a shadow on your pride and honor.
    ARNOLD, (*groans.*)
Great God! this torment—Hell!
    MARGARET.
                         Do not blaspheme!
Pray, rather, Arnold! Nothing do I seek,
But the one sweet conviction—that the heart
On which I fling myself with hope and homage,
Is faithful to that visage in my soul,
That seemed to me its likeness.

ARNOLD, (*in a hollow voice.*)
                    I know not why—
But thou hast chafed a sore place in that heart,
And it were easier for my lips to move,
Than chide thee with my answer.
   MARGARET.
                    Chide O! chide me,
With any angry answer, if thou wilt,
Or canst;—and I will gladden at reproof,
Which takes suspicion from my heart.
   ARNOLD.
                    Suspicion!
And what dost thou suspect?
   MARGARET.
                    That which I dare not
Name to myself or thee.
   ARNOLD.
                    Woman thou pain'st me,
As one who tears a shattered limb away,
And asks—'where art thou wounded?'
   MARGARET.
                    'Tis a good heart,
If all the rest of the body be but whole!
Where are thy wounds, I ask thee—where thy heart,—
My question is the probe to reach thy hurt,
For healing; and, but suffer me to seek,
We may find cure for it. Have I thought lightly,
In the vague terrors that distress my soul,
Lest that this man, so specious and persuasive,—
John Andre, and that subtler still, John Thurston,
Have led your mind astray—aside from duty—
Forgetful of your country——
   ARNOLD
                    No more! no more!
This is mere midsummer madness, on my soul,
The silliest woman's fancy.
   MARGARET.
                    On thy soul!
A terrible adjuration! Arnold, Arnold,

My husband, look to me the words thou speakest,
But lift thine eyes to mine—but rest thy hand
Upon my shoulder, as thou speak'st those accents,
And I will bless thee—ay, wilt bless and thank thee,
Nor vex thine ears with my suspicions more.

   ARNOLD.
Suspicions! what hast thou
To do with treasons and suspicions?

   MARGARET.   Treasons? Ah!
   ARNOLD.   Margaret—
   MARGARET.   Well!
   ARNOLD.   Go to your child!
   MARGARET.   Arnold—
Will you command me bring him?—If I do,
Will you look on him—scan his innocent face,
And think of the brave name that he will bear.

   ARNOLD—(*turns away.*)
Leave me! You vex—you chafe me.

   MARGARET.   You will not look on him,
Nor yet on me! Oh! Arnold! O! my husband,
You leave my soul to terrible surmizings!
I knew thee discontent—that, in thy heart,
Rankled the strongest hate to Washington—
But had no fear—

   ARNOLD.   No more! That single name,
Conjures the impatient devil from his depths,
And makes all rage again within my soul!
I will not hear thee, woman! What am I,
Or thou, that thou should'st dare to school me thus,
To my disquiet? To thy room, and hide thee;
And learn the proper duty of the wife,
To see, submit in silence, and believe
Her Lord, in spite of all that meets her eye,
Is law, authority and right! In this
Allegiance, stands her honor.

   MARGARET.   I obey thee!
Yet, O! if there be reason in my fears,
I but remind thee of the name thou bears,
The glory that enskies it—thy brave deeds—

The future of thyself and of thy child,
That child thou dar'st not look upon—O! Arnold,
His little voice, imploring through mine own,
Begs for his goodly heritage of honor,
Unstain'd—begs for his mother's pride—thy wife's—
Thy wife! (*Exit Margaret.*)
  ARNOLD. (*Manent.*)
It is not yet too late! The damned deed,
That blackens me forever; wife and child;
Friends, country, honor'd name and ancient valor;—
Is not beyond recall! I will recall it!—
My horses!—Andre is not out of reach!
I will not forfeit the renown made certain,
Nor risk the fair report of the far future,
For any chance of fortune. Better far,
Yield the vain struggle, with the goal in sight;—
Forego the wreath so desperately challenged,
And like the gamester, by success made prudent,
Forego the contest with the dice unthrown!
Ay, yield the sway, the prize to Washington—
That hated minion of Fortune, whose existence,
Hath been the bane of mine!
                 What! yield to him,
And suffer still the mock of his French minion,
And all the servile parasites around him,
That puff his sails with praises, night and morning,
'Till in his fancy he becomes a God!—
When I can hurl him downward from his tripod,
And ride upon his neck!—forego the prospect,
Nor feed, to surfeit, the dear bought revenge,
That whelms the nation headlong with its idol!—
Shall I forbear, and suffer men to cry
That my heart falter'd, with my hands enwreathed,
With the strong reins of power. Hear them cry,
The name of Washington, for thousand echoes,
To seize, and still reduplicate in triumph,
While mine is hiss'd with scorn? No! I will pluck
The glory from his grasp: will tame his Eagle,

And still denied occasions, as his rival,
Will conquer as his foe—the nation's foe—
That sanctioned his rebuke!—Those damned deeds—
I cannot now recall them. 'Tis too late,
And I must force occasion out of Fate!

Our scene changes to another point of the Highlands of the Hudson. John Thurston appears, emerging through a rugged pass, and about to ascend the rocky heights beyond. He is breathless, but presses forward eagerly for awhile, then pauses for rest. He stoops and drinks from a rill that ripples from the hill and forms a stream across the road. Having slaked his thirst, he seats himself upon a boulder, and soliloquizes as follows:

THURSTON—(*Solus.*)
Thanks for that draught! I feel another man,
Yet still am weary. But I should be thankful!
I've 'scaped the ruffians—I am free once more!
So much for gold with the King's Picture on it.
These freemen of Conneticut forswear
Their monarch yet crouch humbly to his image!
Will part with rights, laws, loves and liberties,
For the bright metal, glistening from the mint,
Though Satan's self, in his most hellish aspect,
Glared from its face, the sovereign. 'Twill not need,
That he should challenge loyalty or homage,
Or prove his rights divine. They find them so,
And need no argument when the gold, once tried,
Sticks to the patriot fingers, proved of weight!
Ha! Ha! these virtuous sons of liberty,
These pious pilgrims, working to salvation,
By pick and sleight of hand. The wretched curs
That yelp of Constitution, Congress,
Charters and Bills of Right; yet wrest all law
To cover up their infamies; and make,
Even while they blate in nasal psalmodies,
Idols of each worst appetite of man,

BENEDICT ARNOLD.

Each christen'd from a virtue; grovelling still
In bonds to all bad passions—all of these
Summ'd up in vanities and greed of gain!
Oh! how I loathe them, as of monstrous things,
Foulest and worst; morally so deformed,
That, in their thoughts as in their souls, all things
Promiscuous grow confounded; and they know not,
To separate the pure and virgin truth,
Though to all eyes legitimate of Heaven,
From the most hideous hell-engendered sin,
That ever wormed its snaky way 'mongst men,
And foul'd with leprosies where'er it wrought.
I've 'scaped them, Grace o' God! and in my freedom,
Have left them fettered fast beneath their own
Self—valued at five guineas! One more day,
And Britain's legions, trampling on their throats,
Will find them stronger bonds—it may be halters,
It better fits their felon throats to wear!
But I must on; nor shout till free of the woods;
Must, ere the night, see Arnold—ay, and Andre,
If that he be not gone with his dispatches.
There's danger on his track as well as mine!
This boy, this Randolph Peyton—curse on him!
Like an inveterate Heath hound, dogs our heels!
How came he to the knowledge of our clues?
There's treachery somewhere! Can it be that Butler,
Or Seward, has betray'd us? These wretched rogues
Would sell a mother, a mother's grave,
To make a cabbage garden! This the danger,—
The curse that waits upon the use of gold,
To buy the thing that never should be sold.

He ascends the mountain, and passes from sight. Meanwhile, but a mile distant, a group of scouts, armed, are assembled, apparently in doubt and deliberation, at the foot of the mountain. Randolph Peyton suddenly joins them.

1 Scout. Ho! stand!
Peyton. A friend! Hold!
2 Scout. 'Tis the captain.
Peyton. Why here, good fellows—were you not—
1 Scout. He's gone, sir.
Peyton. Who's gone?
2 Scout. The tory Quaker!
Peyton. What, Thurston?
You do not tell me Thurston has escaped.
1 Scout. It's true, sir. But we're on his track.
Peyton.
On his track, are you? Wherefore do you stop?
2 Scout.
We only wait the hound, to take the mountain.
He's on it now.
Peyton. Thurston? Art thou sure of that?
1 Scout. As that we're here.
Peyton. 'Tis lucky that I too am here.
I know the tory's burrow. Follow him,
With all your speed and vigilance. I'll take
Another pathway,—meet you on the summit,
And see that he escapes not t'other side.
On, with your hound and hallor! I will steer,
More silently, my way. We must secure him,
At every hazard. If you come upon him,
Let him destroy no papers. They are precious,
Worth all our lives. Secure him, or you answer
For his escape. (*Ex. Peyton.*)
1 Scout. Hark! 'tis the hound.
2 Scout. I hear it.
He's on the scent.
1 Scout. Put out, and scatter all,
Shoot, ere you lose the rascal—give him ball!

The scene changes, midway up the mountain, Thurston is discovered pressing forward. He suddenly stops to listen, and stoops with ear to the ground.

THURSTON.
It is the deep bay of the savage hound,
Traveling the mountain. They are at my heels,
And I grow faint—faint, but not spiritless!
There shall be some to bite the dust in blood,
Ere they shall have these treasures.
                    (*Feels in his bosom.*)
             They are all safe:
How shall I keep them so? I have it! Hark!
The cries come ringing sharply to mine ears:
I have no time to lose! I'll hide them here.
            (*He conceals the papers under a rock.*)
'Tis done; and now away;—even as the Bird
Who cunningly flies her nest, when that she hears
The fowler in the wood.
                Me, they may take!
What care I, if it keep them from my nest?
What will it profit them, an old man's life?
What my offence?—A fugitive from bonds?
That's not a crime to need that blood be shed.
Ah! but to have been loyal to my king;
That's my perdition, when the power to judge
Lies with the rebel who denies his king.
What matter how they judge me? Let them slay;
If so they will it! I shall never pray,
For love or mercy! They shall hear me sing,
In the last spasm of death, 'God save the King!'

But John Thurston approaches the end of his loyal career. He has not been so fortunate as he fancied himself. Even while he is engaged in the concealment of his papers, Randolph Peyton, having reached the summit of the mountain, appears on one of its spurs, for a single moment, and sees what he is about. The next moment Peyton disappears, but only for a brief interval, and he suddenly re-appears, before the audience, but not immediately seen by Thurston, who is leaving the place behind him as rapidly as he can. As Peyton is winding down the ledges of the rocks, the sudden barking of the blood hound, and the hallooing of the scouts, confounds the senses of Thurston; he stops, and involuntarily turns about him, and looks back. At that moment he sees Peyton rapidly advancing to the very rock where the papers are concealed. All this scene may be picturesquely brought before the audience. At the sight of Peyton, approaching the rock, Thurston, with a wild scream of apprehension, rushes towards him, drawing, at the same time, a pistol from his bosom and cocking it.

THURSTON.   Touch, and thou diest!
PEYTON.   Not for twenty deaths,
Can I forbear!   I have them—they are mine!
               (*Turning over the rock, seizing the papers and
                            waving them aloft.*)
THURSTON.
Thou doom'st thyself! Thy blood upon thy head!
A thousand lives, more precious far than thine,
Were better lost than these.
                         (*Rushes on Peyton and fires.*)
   PEYTON.
Better for thee, old man—thy sleep o' nights,
Thy heart—thy conscience—that thy erring aim
Hath kept thy hands from blood.
    THURSTON. (*Rushes upon him.*)
               I must have them!
The papers, Randolph Peyton! I must have them,
Or slay thee, boy!—An Empire's destiny
Hangs on those papers!—What's thy wretched life,
Thy blood, though it may course from mine own heart,
To the great destinies of States and people!
         (*Thurston grapples with Peyton, who flings him off
                staggering. He recovers, draws another pistol,
                                          and advances.*)
   THURSTON.
There's still another moment!. The papers, boy!
Or—Ah!—the earth—it's reeling round—

He falls forward in the confused speech and cry. He has been shot by the scouts from below, and is mortally wounded. After a rapid succession of groans, the dying man recovers himself and speaks.

THURSTON.
'Tis over, and the hope of years is gone!
The toils—the unwaving faith and loyalty,
Are lost! The rabble rules—the reign is done,
Ah! why hath thou deserted me, Oh! God!
Why given this wretched boy to set at nought
And baffle these great schemes and purposes,
That, let to ripen, had restored to peace,
And safety, all these nations!
    Randolph Peyton,
An old man's blood upon a young man's head,
Is never a blessing! Be my curse upon thee,
Thou robber of my labors and my hopes,
As of my life! My latest curse upon thee!
God and thy people curse thee! Thy success,
In this, that thou dost baffle me and mine,
Will be their curse in seasons yet to come,
When they shall drink in fullness from that cup,
Of bitter overflow—license for liberty,
Which thou and thine have helped them to compound.
My blood upon thy head! An old man's blood,
That never yet much nourish'd a young growth;
Thy people's curse and mine; be both upon thee!
 PEYTON.
Alas! old man, I pity thee! Thy curse
Affects not me; and for thy blood now spilt,
In thy own great insanity of aim,
It rests not on my hands, nor on my head!
I raised no weapon 'gainst thy aged breast,
Have saved thee once, and spared thee more than once.
 THURSTON.
No weapon of thine!—thy blood hounds on my track,
Thy curs of Liberty, with venomous bark,
Worse than their bite!—Ah! God, be merciful!   (*Dies.*)

By this time the scouts have come in, and group themselves around the parties.

PEYTON.
'Tis over with him! All his stratagems,
His subtle schemes that would not let him rest,
Nor suffer rest to others, now have rest!
Give him sufficient burial where he lies;
He needs no further!—And, this duty done,
Betake you to your posts. The hunt is up;
You'll find fresh game within your nets by noon,
To-morrow,—and all foxes! This one's fate,
Hath a sufficient warning—be not late!

One word to the reader, or rather to the writer, of art in fiction, and especially in dramatic fiction. A few words also to the student of history, and to him first. Having disposed of John Thurston, it is well to inquire who and what he was. In the historical narratives such a person does not appear.— He may have been, or may not—may, or may not, have acted the part here assigned him. That Arnold and Andre must have had such agents and participants, in their long protracted schemes of treachery, is beyond all question. It was quite proper, and even necessary, for the development of the action, that they should appear and be employed; and the name of John Thurston answers the purpose just as well as that of Joshua Smith, whom we know to have been one of the fraternity. But it was better to use Thurston than Smith, simply because the dramatist is less fettered by the ordinary facts; and we can dispose of Thurston summarily, while we can take no liberties with history, in the final disposition of Smith, who must be left to the ordinary processes of law, as a suspected traitor. Having employed Thurston from the beginning of the action, and having assigned him an important role among the *dramatis personæ*, it was essential that he should be disposed of in a manner commensurate with the importance of his agency in previous scenes. It was necessary that he should be employed to the last, and in services upon the issue of which would seem to hang the destinies of the superior parties. We are to suppose, accordingly, that the papers which he carried, and for the safety and recovery of which he lost his life, were essential to the completion of that large event, for which Andre encountered the perils of the spy, and Arnold those of the traitor. It matters not to say what these papers were. All that we have need to do, in dramatic art, is to suggest to the reader, or spectator, an adequate motive for the action; an adequate action, itself, by which the result is to be justified; and a sufficient degree of earnestness, in the performer, to show that he himself attaches a vital importance to that which he is doing, or is about to do. The imagination of the audience supplies the rest. The details should involve anxiety, activity, and the degree of passion, which shall become the character of the agent, and be consistent with the nature of the event displayed. A series of small events, mere hints in fact, afford the material out of which the highest interest may be extracted; provided, these details, or hints, shall bring out the character of the party, or animate his passions. Whenever this effect is produced, the emotions of an audience will be sufficiently awakened. It is a law in dramatic writing that no important agent shall be introduced at a *late* hour in the story; for this would argue that the new agent is thus brought in, as a mere *fetch*—a sort of *"Deus ex Machina"*—to enable the dramatist to escape from a difficulty for which his own invention cannot provide legitimately. The persons of the drama, who figure importantly in bringing about the catastrophe, should appear at an early period upon the scene, and there should be an evident *design* in the arrangement of the events, which shall leave nothing to *accident*. Fate, not accident, gives the impressive lessons, of power, passion, grief, terror or sympathy, through the regular growth of events, to the souls of the spectators. In John Thurston you have a study in the *fanaticism of loyalty;* and this character of mind is a proper sort of foil, to such a character as that of Andre; who has, with the cleverness, all the habitual *looseness* of the mere soldier—a quickness at subterfuge, the glibness of the courtier,—and the unscrupulousness of the adventurer. So, also, it contrasts with the anomalous character of Arnold; whose vanity looks like ambition; who is mercurial, capricious, passionate, and, in morals, dissolute according to the usual training of his people. John Thurston nurses a leading idea with intense solicitude—allows himself to be diverted by no other object—sacrifices everything for this idea, and, to his mind, a servile loyalty is sublimed to patriotism, until it becomes his only surviving passion. He opposes *will*, and all his human faculties, to *Fate*; and it is the struggle between this Human will, and the mind, and the Fate, or Fortune, which seeks to enthrall and to overthrow the man, which constitutes the great charm in the Magic Drama, and, in great degree, of all art in fiction. In degree as the man exhibits will, courage, endurance, design and power, in contending with the fate which grows out of hostile events, does he rise into the attitude of the Hero, and compels the admiration of mankind. The exquisite art in Shakspeare's Hamlet, which chooses a subject out of which a hero *cannot* be made, is found in his being able to raise the sympathy and pity of the audience, in behalf of one who must fail to excite their admiration. But we must proceed with our drama. We are approaching the general catastrophe.

Our scene changes to the highlands near Tarrytown. Time, 10 o'clock of the morning on the 23d September, 1780, Andre, on horseback, appears upon the scene. Were the piece designed for performance, the horse would be omitted from the scene, and his presence, in the contiguous woods, would be accounted for by some brief passage in Andre's soliloquy. There would also be some change necessary in the manner of his arrest. These alterations would require only a small degree of art in their management. Andre has now passed all the American lines—all the regular posts of our military—the last outpost. He is upon the neutral ground, or rather upon ground which is traversed usually by the British parties. His course, according to the historical facts, may be given in a few words. Accompanied by the Loyalist, Smith, (who, by the way, has left a volume of narrative on

BENEDICT ARNOLD.

the subject, designed chiefly for his own excuse or justification,) he has reached Crompond. Here they meet an American militia officer, who is easily satisfied with their passes, but who tells them it is too late in the day to reach other quarters for the night. To escape suspicion, though anxious to proceed, Andre consents to remain there. On the next day, the 23d, they cross the Hudson to King's Ferry. They reach, at length, without interruption, the village of Pine's bridge, upon Croton river. Here, almost in sight of the British videttes, his farther progress is deemed secure from danger, and here Smith takes leave of him. Andre, so soon as he receives this assurance, and is left alone, dismisses all his previous precaution, and claps spurs to his horse. Four leagues farther did he make his way in safety—the Hudson once more opens before him, and he approaches the border village of Tarrytown; his heart full of confidence—his brow elevated—all his prospects favorable—and the triumphant issue of his mission no longer a subject of question in his mind. His spirits are exultant.— He is about to win the "well done" of his commander, and the honors of his Sovereign; when—but let the dramatist report the rest in his own manner.

ANDRE. (*Solus.*)
Now grow my wings! The cloud is off my spirit,
And I could dance or sing—or do any folly
In token of the freedom that excites me!
That dreary, doubtful progress, o'er these plains—
Those keen suspicious sentinels that watch'd me,
Still mumbling over, with rare show of reading
Our Arnold's pass for Johnny Anderson!
Most worthy Johnny Anderson! A good one,—
John Andre turn'd to Johnny Anderson!—
But not without his guerdon. Yet, by Heaven!
I would not suffer such another trial,
For all in his Majesty's coffers. A cold sweat,
Comes o'er me to recall it! I could fancy
That still some vigilant Captain Boyd pursued me,

With—"I would mumble o'er the pass again"—
Or—"By your leave, where said you, you are going?"
Thank Heaven, that danger's done! And for the rest,
The path lies smooth and clear; the prize awaits me;
His Majesty's favor—that betokens knighthood;—
And meet reward!—Why, that is told in guineas,
Sufficient for the state and post of knighthood!
And love! Ah! there's a brighter boon and blessing;
Delicious lips and raptures that find Heaven,
Even in a cottage; where the rosy treasures,
Make state forgotten, or soothe down its grandeur,
Till we heed little of the wealth of Egypt,
While Cleopatra times for us the billows,
With the quick pulses beating in her viens,
While the white arms enclasp the panting bosom!
Yet, stay! 'Twere something of a question,
If Margaret truly holds that foreign temper,
She late has shown me. Can it be, her passion,
Hath found abatement, which she once confess'd;
That no more power abides in lover's pleading
To make his pleadings potent; that her fancy,
Ranges to him from *me!* I'll not believe it!
She's mine as ever still! A prudish humor,—
Perchance, a sudden fear, hath made her captious,—
Or the caprices of the sex, made active,
By something overbold in my approach,
No matter what it be. She cannot 'scape me,
When once the absolute spell of British power,
Secure by this most happy operation,
Shall once more sway the land. Love, station; fortune;
Shine out, ye stars; the wings are at my shoulders
And my soul leaps exulting in its triumph,
Which nothing now may baffle!

    A Voice from the wood.

Stand!
 ANDRE.   Ha! Stand!
    [*Paulding, Williams and Van Wert suddenly
     emerge from the wood. The former lays
      hand upon his bridle.*]

BENEDICT ARNOLD.

PAULDING.
Stand, when I bid you, sir.
  ANDRE. (*Attempts to urge his steed.*)
    Get from my path, good fellow;
Lest that you make me angry.
  PAULDING.
      That's a good one.
You are our prisoner. Aim, to urge your steed,
You perish on the instant.
  ANDRE.
      Who are you, sir?
  PAULDING.
Alight! 'Tis ours, not yours, to ask that question.
  ANRDE.
I will alight; but why should you detain me.
You are, if I mistake not, of our party.
  PAULDING.
Why, that is to be seen? Where are you going?
  ANDRE.
Below! You, too, are of the Lower Party?
  PAULDING.
We are; but how much lower is the question.
  ANDRE.
Then let me go at once. My need is urgent,
You've but to know that I'm a British officer,
To speed me on my way.
  PAULDING.
      We are urgent too.
  ANDRE.
What mean you, sir.
  PAULDING.
      That we suspect you.
  ANDRE. Ah!
  PAULDING.
You have mistaken us, sir. We are no Britons
Nor Loyalists, nor Cow Boys, but true men,
In arms for Congress.
  ANDRE. *Handing Passport.*)

BENEDICT ARNOLD.

Then read this paper.
PAULDING. (*Reads.*)
True, no doubt.
ANDRE.
Ay, that is clear enough.
PAULDING.
And yet no pass for us,—no pass for you!
Sir: we suspect you. You're a British officer,
This pass was probably stolen. We must search you.
Be pleased to draw that boot.—
ANDRE
My God! You cannot——
PAULDING.
Empty your pockets—draw your boots, my friend,
Or we shall do it for you.
ANDRE.
But, Gentlemen—
You cannot mean it—this indignity.
I pray you, for your sakes, let me go.
Here is authority from General Arnold—
Obey it, or you bring yourselves to peril.
PAULDING.
Obey *us*, or *you* bring yourself to peril.
We know the risks we run, but we will teach you,
That yours is something greater. Sir, *we know you.*
ANDRE.
Ha!—to be sure—my name is Anderson.
PAULDING.
Well, have it what you will, but doff your boots,
The left one first, as 't please you.
ANDRE. Hark ye, friends,
I am a Gentleman—an officer—this affront—
PAULDING. Must be endured.
ANDRE.
Will money Gentlemen,
Persuade you to respect my person?—gold—
Here is gold!

WILLIAMS.
    Wilt give us gold?
 ANDRE. All that I have:—
My purse—(*offering it.*)
 VAN WERT.
Rather a light one, friend.
 ANDRE. (*Eagerly.*)
      You shall have more.
But here's my watch, my horse, and, my word for it,
Say where the money shall be left, I'll send you
One hundred guineas!
 PAULDING. (*Sternly.*)
      Did you say ten thousand,
'Twould help you just as little. We are freemen,
Not to be purchased. Set here by our people,
For an especial duty; and we'll do it,
Even though your name, in place of Anderson,
Were written Major Andre.
 ANDRE.   God have mercy!
All's lost! Do with me as you will!
 PAULDING. With us.
 ANDRE. Whither?
 PAULDING. To the first post.
 ANDRE. And that?
 PAULDING. North Castle.
 ANDRE. Who commands there?
 PAULDING. Colonel Jamieson.
 ANDRE. (*Recovering himself.*)
'Tis well. Lead on. He will respect my pass.
 PAULDING.
Will see! He'll hear from us your proper title.
 ANDRE. (*Aside.*)
Was ever fate like mine. This hour with wings,
Exulting in the mountain's prospect won,
And now in the abyss,—and all undone.
        (*Exeunt omnes.*)

According to the historians, Andre blundered inconceivably. Taken by surprise, he lost his head, and instead of showing his pass, and asking no questions, he used such language as roused the suspicions of the militiamen, and when deceived by their equivocal answers, he told them he was a British officer, their suspicions were necessarily increased. The simple showing of his pass, whether to a party of Americans or British, would have secured his safety. The former would have dismissed him, the latter might have sent him to Head-Quarters as a prisoner, and he could have desired nothing better. The preceding scene very closely adheres to the history in all its facts. The captors conducted their prisoner to Col. Jamieson, by whom the outposts were commanded. Before Jamieson, Andre recovered his composure, insisted upon his passport and the name of Anderson, and requested Jamieson to send notice to Arnold of his detention. With intolerable stupidity, Jamieson determined to send Andre himself to Arnold, and had actually forwarded him under a guard; when, re-examining the papers, which he had retained, he sent an express after him, and had him conducted, under proper guard, to another post at Old Salem. At the same time, he prepared dispatches for Washington, narrating all the circumstances.—Here, having satisfied the Historian, we let the Dramatist resume.

The scene changes to the post at North Castle, held by Col. Jamieson. Randolph Peyton enters to him suddenly at his quarters.

PEYTON.
Paulding, and others, whom I set to watch,
Have brought you Anderson, a British spy,
Otherwise Andre.
 JAMIESON. They did!
 PEYTON. His papers, too, they brought you?
 JAMIESON. They did.
 PEYTON.
Then give them me at once.

JAMIESON. (*Giving papers.*)
                    Here are they.
A pretty tale of treachery they tell,
If we could but believe them.
    PEYTON.   How believe them?
Can any mortal doubt, if once he reads?—(*reads*)
Ay, as I thought! 'Tis Arnold's own handwriting.
Without the small precaution of disguise!
What blindness! Madness—rare stupidity,
As well as guilt and treason. Let us see!
Ah! here are all the pretty plans of cunning—
Artillery how disposed to meet attack;
The force at West Point and dependencies,—
The requisite strength of soldiers for the works—
The works themselves—the ordnance of the forts—
Where strong—where weak—where easy of access—
And where access made easy of assault—
How all, in brief, arranged for sacrifice,—
And further yet—a plan of the next campaign!—
Ah! matchless traitor;—but we foil him now,
Where is the prisoner? Deliver him up to me.
    JAMIESON.
Him have I sent to Arnold!
    PEYTON.
            What! Sent to Arnold?
The very party to his treachery?
Impossible. You could not do this folly!
    JAMIESON.
In truth, I know not why,—I see it now,
The folly; but when first the prisoner came,
In the surprise and wonder of my mind,
I never thought how much of it was truth,
That lay within these papers, and—
    PEYTON.   You sent him?
Oh! monstrous madness—sent the spy to Arnold!
    JAMIESON. I'm sorry now—but did!
    PEYTON. Shall they escape us?
The spy and traitor!—after all my toils,

Escape us?—Swiftly, Colonel, man a troop,—
Speed after them like lightning! Ho! my horse,—
Without there, troopers! We must mend this botching,
Though death be on our speed! By Heavens! Jamieson,
This act of thine makes shame of all thy judgment!
But we shall mend it still.
    JAMIESON. I wrote to Arnold—
    PEYTON.
Well, wrote to him?
    JAMIESON.
          The purport of the papers!
    PEYTON.
Oh! worse and worse! Great God, what lack of wit,
At the right season, mocks the best of judgments,
And baffles the best plans! To horse, to horse!
Send forth your troopers, Colonel, with all speed!
Methinks, already, do the British drums
Strike on the ear of eager apprehension,
That knows what danger waits. Dispatch to Sheldon
To keep his cannon pointed on the Vulture,
And sink each boat that seeks her from the shore,
We'll take the sting from out this prickle, Folly,
And zeal shall make repair, by desperate spur,
Of what this Dullard, Drowse-in-Duty, mars us.
To horse! to horse! it needs that winged feet,
And desperate will, shall make our work complete.

The scene changes to a secluded spot, among the Highlands, a few miles from West Point. There is a group present, consisting of Washington, Lafayette, Count Luzerne, &c., with *aides-de-camp*, seen in the back ground. Washington has returned from Hartford, taking a different route on his return from that which he pursued in going. This fact secured the escape of Arnold. The messenger of Jamieson failed to find the commander-in-chief, on the old route, had to retrace his steps, and the delay, in the meantime, enabled Arnold to receive the communication which Jamieson had written him, announcing the arrest of Andre. Never had good Colonel a head so muddled. While recalling Andre, on his route to Arnold, because of his newly awakened suspicions, he yet deems it due to a person so high of rank, to advise him of the whole tenor of his discoveries; and Arnold received this dispatch before Washington could reach West Point. But to the scene before us.

LAFAYETTE.
Our youth o'ershoots his time.
    WASHINGTON.
               Nay, patiently.—
Here were we bade to wait: and we must do it;
Though the delay would seem to prove it needless.
God grant it be so! 'Twere a cruel fortune
To find this dreadful tale of Arnold, true!
Yet such the worth of Peyton—such his honor—
His quick judicial mind, his vigilance,
'Tis quite as strange that he should err so wildly,
In this suspicion, as that he, the other,
Should swerve thus madly from the paths of duty!
Peyton may be the victim of some practice,
Which we must heedfully search. Some enemy
May, by the subtlest agencies, implant
Suspicion in the hearts of wisest statesman,
To the discredit of our bravest soldiers;
And we should sit beside them, at our councils,
Yet hold in loathing their most precious virtues!
This were to ruin all! We must be wary—
Must tant, with keenest surmise and suspicion,
The very proofs that make us most suspect.
    LAFAYETTE.
We should be perjured else! And yet, I hold
No faith, like yours, in Arnold. Brave, he may be,
And somewhat skilful, and a daring soldier.
But bravery in the man must be a virtue,
Superior to the courage of the brute,
That rushes, blindly, 'gainst the obstacle,
In total ignorance of the relative force,

Of that which he encounters, with his own!
To one he seems as one who lacks some virtues
That most beseem the soldier. His vanity,
Scarce rises to ambition; and is jealous,
Of the acknowledged virtues in another!
He lacks the magnanimous feeling, which applauds
A rival's triumph; and, with feverish malice,
Turns loathing from each favorite of his people!—
As one, himself denied, that should be honor'd,
He frets and chafes for station far beyond
The virtue in his wing. Now, this young Peyton,
Seems a bold and generous youth, as frank as fearless;
His modesty still mating with his merit,
In a most nice propriety and grace.
If, as you think, there's something in his passion,
At conflict with his judgment, in this matter,
It does not serve to blunt his sense of justice,
Nor shake his loyalty, to truth and country!
I like the youth.
    WASHINGTON.
              He'll grow upon your liking,
When that you know him better.
    LAFAYETTE.
              Would he were come;
For I am something hungry and athirst;
And, deeming, with yourself, that this suspicion,
Grows from a business, which, when clues are furnish'd,
Will take away all stain of treachery,—
I do confess that General Arnold's dinner,
Is somewhat in my thought.
    WASHINGTON.
              Say, Lady Arnold's;
For she's the Queen of the feast, and you, young soldiers,
Are all enamor'd of her charms and graces.
But for this present duty, we should ride,
And warn her of our coming. But—
    LUZERNE. (*Advancing.*)
           Some one comes.

LAFAYETTE.
'Tis He !
                    Enter Randolph Peyton.
WASHINGTON.   Randolph!
PEYTON. (*Giving papers.*)
            And now, "beware" who will !—
My work is ended! Here, behold these proofs !
    WASHINGTON. (*Reads.*)
It is all true! The damnable proof is here !
Whom shall we trust!
    PEYTON.
            Not now to think of trusts,
Or anything save prompt and present action,
If you would keep the traitor from escape,
And face him with the spy ! For, by a blunder,—
To stamp the business with no harsher name,—
Jamieson has forwarded dispatch to Arnold,
Declaring all that's done—the arrest of Andre,
The seizure of his papers, and—
    WASHINGTON. (*Impetuously.*)
                To horse! We must ride on !
It may not be too late!—Come, Gentlemen,
Draw swords, and put your coursers to their speed;
We must be resolute now.—Where go you, Peyton ?
    PEYTON.
I take a shorter route than you can take—
Which I've already traversed. As *he* knows it,
He may attempt escape—
    WASHINGTON.
                Then hurry forward—
We'll let no grass grow 'neath our horses heels !
Make ready, gentlemen !—Great God ! to barter,
A name so goodly for a traitor's shame,
And blight for aye the laurels of his Fame !
                            (*Exeunt.*)

Our scene now changes to the battlements of West Point,
Arnold, in great agitation paces his chamber alone. As yet,

he knows nothing of the arrest of Andre, or the detection of
the plot. Jamieson's dispatch has yet to reach him. But the
conflict, in his mind is not less agitating, in character; for, to
his credit be it said, he is not insensible to that perdition, and
utter ruin of his previous reputation, and future character,
which caused the pathetic ejaculations of Washington, in the
previous scene. He speaks in soliloquy.

ARNOLD. (*Alone.*)
There's not a minute in the glass of Time,
But now becomes so precious to my fate,
That, in its progress, every hurrying second
Seems like a passing knell! Would it were over!
Or ne'er had been begun! The knell, how fearful,
That speaks my treachery to the nation's ear;—
And this impregnable post, its troops, its treasures,
Delivered to the foe!—Methinks, I see,
The cities trembling; populace aghast;—
I hear the trumpets sounding the alarm;
At midnight; and behold their thousands flying,
Women and children, naked, and affright,
Yet staggering wildly, heedless where they fly,
And rushing headlong to the throat of doom!
Then flames the city, and its lurid fires
Proclaim the Fate at work, with serpent tongues
That feed while they destroy! And that proud man,
Whose stern, cold soul, and still elastic spirit,
No danger yet could daunt, or loss subdue,
For once confounded;—witless where to turn,
And blasted by the rival he has wrong'd!
Yet, though I triumph in this great revenge,
And heal my hurts of soul and wounded honor,
And soothe the angry passions that have been
The restless counsellors that, night and day,
Have kept me sleepless;—though the British Lion,
Borne by these hands, shall wave above the heights,
And from the billows of the Atlantic sea,
To the vast wild's of Apalachia's summits.

BENEDICT ARNOLD.

The stars and stripes go down;—the shame is mine,
Not less than his I conquer! With a stroke,
I blot the giant star of Washington,
From out the sky; yet, even defeat *to him*,
And dire catastrophe, and dreadest fate,
Brings no such shame and blight as light on *me!*—
Mine only,—deeply stamp'd upon my brow,—
My name, and fame, and memory;—all the past,
Of honor, and pride, obliterate; while obloquy,
With all her thousand curs, shall yelp behind me,
As at a thief o' the highway!—Is it then so?—
Are these the dark and damnable penalties,
That follow on the heels of my dread vengeance,
And is there no escape?—Have I cut off
My own retreat, and dug the gulf behind me,
Fearfully deep and wide,—impassable;—
While the dread fate looms up, a mighty shadow,
Spectrally vast; without a form and void;
Eyeless and headless.—but, with tongue of fire,
Most like a hissing serpent, that shoots out,
And, ever and anon, uncoils itself,
And stretches forth towards me, circling high,
And wide, the airy space about my head;
Narrowing and momently contracting, till
I feel the pestilent heat that from it flows,
Threatening my brow as with a ring of fire,
And mocking me with likeness of a wreath,—
A crown—whose terrible circlet speaks but doom!
And may I not escape? Is it too late,
To baffle this dread gorgon?—Ah!—I have it!—
I have made terms with the enemy; but who
Shall make me *keep* them? He who works by treason,
May not complain if treachery baffles him;—
Invites him to the prize; and, as he grasps it,
Foils him with perilous hurt? That *were* to conquer!
Why yield the post! Why not do battle bravely,—
And having lured the enemy to the snare,
Close its great jaws upon him! It is but.

To *will* the proper use of mine own power,
To crush the power of Britain on our soil,
By admirable strategy! Should it be,
That, by this cunning, Clinton is o'erthrown,
Then do I triumph in the popular eye,
Beyond the dreams of rival! Even now,
The British Legions march—already gain
The Highlands—they are hovering on our skirts!
Methinks I hear their drum! And, 'tis with me,
To welcome them to ruin or triumph,—
Captivity or conquest!—In *my* will,
Lies the great issue! It is not too late;
And I may win, if I but will it so,
A bloodier triumph, here, o'er British columns,
Than made my wreath on Saratoga's plains!
Then 'twas for Gates, I triumph'd! Shall I now,
Achieve this newer triumph for another—
Strengthen the arm of Washington, and see,
My honors 'twine his brows? How I could loathe,
The weakness that but fattens with such prospects!
No! it must be! Be stern, be strong, my soul!—
Too long have I been weak! I must not change,
And lose, through weakness, all my great revenge!
     Enter Lady Arnold.
Margaret!—
 MARGARET.
    What! still with cloudy forehead?
 ARNOLD.
Can'st smoothe its furrows!—I am as a man
That sees a spectre ever at his side
That will not down, even tho' he stamps his foot!
Who hears one terrible whisper in his ears,
"Thus shall it be forever!"
  MARGARET.
     Oh! my husband!
Wherefore this voice, this look of agony,—
These terrible presentiments of ill?
It is your wound that troubles you!—

ARNOLD.
                My wound!
My wound!—Ay, one more deep than ought you know,
Or dream of; in my *heart!* My *bodily* wound
Is my least trouble;—gives no pain at all,
But rather something of a pleasure, since,
It tells me of most honorable deeds;
My country's homage, and my people's love,
In days when I grew proud!
MARGARET.
                Arnold,—wherefore—
ARNOLD.
I am proud no more!
MARGARET.
                And wherefore not, I pray?
Let me not vex you with my woman fancies,
But O! my husband, if, in the strange mission,
That brought John Andre here——
ARNOLD.
        Peace, Woman, Peace!
MARGARET.
If you can tell me, Arnold, it *is* peace,
And not a terror!—Ever since his coming
I've mark'd that you have been a wretched man;
Most wayward, restless, with capricious moods;
Impatient, with a mind that wander'd strangely,
Still erring wide of purpose.
ARNOLD.
        Would it were!
I tell thee, woman, I have *kept* my purpose!
MARGARET.
What purpose?
ARNOLD.
        I prithee, do not question me!
I tell thee, I am haunted by a fiend,
That's ever at my elbow;—day and night—
Still hangs upon my footstep;—dogs my thought;
With a perpetual whisper of his presence;—

Now flatters me with glorious dreams and fancies,
Now tortures with reproach and cutting sneer;
Suspicions dark and wild;—entreaties foul;—
Incitements high, and dangerous designs;—
Distracts me with division in myself,
And lures at once and threatens;—till I grow,
More feeble than the infant, from the terrors,
That make his midnight strife.

MARGARET.
     My husband, this
Borders on madness! It is very strange!

ARNOLD.
No! No! it is not strange! 'Tis natural!
This devil is a common one, that haunts
The audacious spirit most! To some, a God;
That brings no evil mood—chafes with no sneer;
Moves to no hatred;—with no jealousy,
Sets the blear eye of Passion on the watch
To see the thing which is not;—but, still bent,
As kitchen maids declare the Lubber-fiend,
To do kind office for his favorite,
Converts his evil power to honest use,
And, at the struggles of the simple virtue,
Gives succor without charge.

MARGARET.
     An honest fiend!—
And now I guess the secret of your riddle;
And yet, in my poor thought, it is *no* fiend,
That moves the brave to action;—prompts great deeds,
That saves one's country, and—

ARNOLD.
     No more of that!
It is a fiend, I tell thee, unto *me*,
This thing of which I speak; and rather prompts
My spirit with a passion to *destroy*,
Than save, or spare, or succor! Hear me, wife—
Methinks you must have heard—nay, thought—

MARGARET.
Of what? Why pause Arnold, in your question?
ARNOLD.
Ambition!—That fierce devil which drew down
The Heavenly Host to ruin!—Which, at seasons,
Lifts earthly spirits up to seize their thrones,
And crowns with a glory, such as never
Honor'd the erring legions! Which, at others,
And, with proud spirits whom it does not love,
Impels the infuriate passions into madness—
Heedless of right or reason; pride or virtue;
Making the victim, with self-daz'ed vision,
Still covet and strive, all reckless of the cost,
At the one prize;—the high sovereign station,
To which the eye, as with a natural bent,
Turns only; nor, in progress to its goal,
Dreams that beneath the still alluring vision,
The yawning hell lies bare! It is the fiend,
That travels, with my spirit, to this goal,
Which yet I know awaits, but do not see!
MARGARET.
Nay, Heaven forefend, my husband! 'Tis not so!
Your mind is sick with fancies, that pervert
Your reason from its method, as its calm!
We must expel this devil from your mood!
Will exorcise it with most loving prayers,
That fix our hopes on virtue; fill our hearts
With strength, as from the angels, caught by night
When God's own spirit the whole earth sublimes,
Subduing Life's wild waters with his love!
Oh! Arnold, yield thy soul to this sweet sway,
Be less impatient of thy hour and state
The time will soon be yours—
ARNOLD. (*Fiercely.*)
    Is mine already!
I soon shall be triumphant!—
MARGARET.
   Are so now.

Else, what may mean these honors?—this high trust,
Which lifts you next to Washington?—
    ARNOLD.
            That name!—
I prithee speak it in mine ears no more;
Lest I grow savage! Look on me as one,
Who chafes at power supérior to his own!—
One whom a Fate has doom'd;—whom fiends beset;—
A wreck'd but striving mariner, who sees
With open eye, the rock before his prow,
Yet drives the keel upon it! Such is the will,
To brave all danger but to gain that height,
The last and great'st of all; and, still denied,
Will rather topple the tower in the gulph,
Even though he whelm himself! That I should stand
But next 'neath any man, and not supreme,
Makes me to feel that nothing hath been won;—
Is my perdition! 'Tis the fiend at night,
When thou, unconscious of its secret throes,
Dream'st on my bosom of thy innocent child—
That tortures all within with fires of hell,
And keeps me still, a miserable watcher,
To see its aspects rise! And, still by day,
Not even secure in daylight and the sun,
That jibes me ever with a rival's fortunes,
Which shroud mine in the shade! And thus I struggle!
And then am I o'erthrown!
    MARGARET.
            Oh! not o'erthrown!
    ARNOLD.
Not quite! Not quite! Another hour's at hand,
When you shall see me rise! Cities shall burn,
And sacrifice of human hecatombs,
Shall bleed to make my triumph!
    MARGARET.
What dreadful pictures are these your passions paint!
Oh! yield not to the malice of this fiend;
But, looking on your child—I hear him calling—

Forget not, that his best inheritance,
Must be his father's glory!
  ARNOLD.
                There's a pang
In every word you utter! (*Bell rings.*)
  MARGARET.
                Hark! within,
They summon us to dinner. Smooth your aspect;
Let not your aides-du-camps see these fearful passions,
That still deform your visage.
  ARNOLD.
                Let us to 't!—
Though still it seems, as if the meats before me,
Were bright with serpent eyes; and, in the goblet
But freshly fill'd with wine, great gouts of blood,
Stand thick and clammy red!
  MARGARET.
                Oh! horrible!
  ARNOLD.
And yet you bid me eat; and bid me drink:
And say, with pleasant smiles, "the wine is bright,
The viands rare—come, husband, eat and drink!"

The scene changes to the dining room. Arnold has improved his toilet and subdued the wild expression of his countenance to something like calm. He is grave, however, and he and his wife take their seats in silence.

  MARGARET.
Shall we await your aides?
  ARNOLD.
                No! they had leave,
And, if I rightly guess, have cross'd the river.
  MARGARET.
Will you not eat, my husband?
  ARNOLD.
                Said I not?—
The very question!—yet, behold the wine,

The blood yet bubbling, frothing on the top;
And, for the meats—
  MARGARET.
              Oh! God, forbear! forbear!
This wayward mood, seems near akin to madness.
  ARNOLD.
'Tis very like it! Hark! do you hear nothing?
  MARGARET.
No! nothing.
  ARNOLD.
A drum! Methinks I hear a drum!
  MARGARET. (*Seeming to listen.*)
The murmur of the river, or the wind.
But, truly, I hear nothing.
  ARNOLD.
          'Twas like a drum!
And now it seems to me, the measured tramp,
Of marching regiments!
  MARGARET.
          'Tis but the wind.
  ARNOLD.
That surely is a horse at fullest speed,
And he comes hither in hot haste, and—stay!
  MARGARET.
I hear no horse! 'Tis nothing but the wind!
  ARNOLD. (*With a deep sigh.*)
It is the wind and ocean of wild thoughts,
In sleepless strifes, that make of the poor brain,
A field of perilous conflicts; hopes and fears,
In desperate issue o'er some game of life,
Not worth the breath that names it! Thus we struggle,
To our pernicious conquests; as the infant,
That sees a glory in the burning candle,
And grasps it to his bane! Would I could sleep!
  MARGARET.
You are fever'd, Arnold! Better lose some blood!
  ARNOLD.
Ha! Ha! lose blood! 'Twere better for to shed

The blood of others! I need all my own!
I've grown, through very weakness, into childhood:
Frighted by silly fancies and blear shadows;
That only need that 1 should lift a weapon,
And they all flee! Yet, can I lift a weapon?
'Twas never thus before! Even when a boy,
Nay, since I've grown to manhood—'till this season,
Fear was, of all things, strangest to my heart!
The shadow as the substance still I scorn'd,
And, with a jibe, as resolute as its own,
I've met the grinning spectre of my schoolmate,
'Till he forgot his part; and, in *my* aspect,
Beheld a terror greater than he play'd!
And in my manhood? But, I dare not boast,
Feeling such wretched feebleness as now!
Hark! some one, Margaret. Who is there? A step—
    Enter Major Franks.

Ah? (*With a deep sigh of relief.*) Major, welcome,
You are just in season—we had but sat down.

MAJOR FRANKS. (*Handing letter.*)
This letter, General.

ARNOLD. (*Taking the letter.*)
Sit Franks! The meats are cooling.
Whence is this letter? Jamieson; methinks.

FRANKS.
It is, Sir,—brought in haste for quick dispatch.

ARNOLD. (*To his wife.*)
Said I not, 'twas a horse? I heard a horse!—

The letter is the important one from Jamieson, announcing the capture and arrest of Andre, and the discovery and retention of his papers. It is the moment of crisis in the fate of Arnold; yet he opens and reads the letter, and with the exception of an involuntarily start, which escapes the notice of Franks, though not that of Lady Arnold,—who is watching him,—he conceals every show of anxiety or emotion. Having possessed himself fully of the contents of the dispatch, he deliberately folds and puts it into his pocket;—for a moment he eyes Franks keenly; then, as he meets the glance of the other, he fills his own glass with wine, and pushes the decanter to Franks.

ARNOLD.
Some wine with you, Major.
  FRANKS.
          With all pleasure, Sir.
ARNOLD.
You cross'd the river, I think?
  FRANKS.
          I purposed it,
As you remember—I advised you of it—
But—
ARNOLD.
Truly you did.—And Varick?—
  FRANKS.
          He has gone.
ARNOLD.
And so this letter came to you but now?
Your health, Sir. (*Lifts, but puts the glass down untasted.*)
  FRANKS.
          The instant ere I came.
  ARNOLD.   Well!—
And him, the messenger?
  FRANKS.   He waits.
  ARNOLD.   Waits, say you?—
'Twill need dispatch.
  FRANKS.
          Matter of moment, General?
  ARNOLD.
Of moment, do you say? Ay, Sir, of moment!
(*Aside.*) Of precious moment every moment now,
To mine own safety! Be but firm, my soul.

FRANKS.
Pray, make me useful General!
ARNOLD.
Thanks, for I know you are ready—I will do so—
And yet this business,—Ha! Varick, here?
Enter Major Varick hurriedly.
VARICK.   You see, Sir!
I've made my day a short one in the hope
That we shall have another, I've come to bid you,
Prepare for noblest guests—George Washington—
ARNOLD. Ha! Ha!
VARICK.
The Marquis Lafayette, the Count Luzerne—
The Colonels Hamilton and Livingston,
With twenty others—they are close at hand.
ARNOLD. (*Feebly and hoarsely.*)
At hand?
VARICK.
    A mile or more perhaps—yet scarcely that.
ARNOLD. (*Recovering himself with effort.*)
Then is there time—(*pause*) to give them meet reception,
Fly, gentlemen, to meet them and beguile them,
To slow approach, and passing observation,
So that our Lady-wife may shape her household,
To give due honor to such noble guests.
Away, my friends, and do your devoir **bravely**:
We must look trim and stately, for *their* greatness,
If heedless of our own. No form; but hasten,
    Exeunt Franks and Varick.

Arnold listens, and when he hears the sounds of their retreating footsteps, he thus addresses his wife.

ARNOLD.
Now, Margaret, all your strength—for you will need it;
This hour I leave you! It may be forever!
It is with peril of my life, I fly;
Its certain loss to linger. Look upon me,
A false and perjured man—false to my country,—
Beguiled from honor by that wily agent,
John Andre, succor'd by that wilier villain,
Your subtle uncle, Thurston. Yet, I blame not
These creatures of the occasion, and my temper,
That sought the fatal poison which they brought;
The fiend was in my heart! This made my passion,—
Has made me what I am—a thrice-dyed traitor,
Henceforth, the mark and by-word of the nation,
That yielded me its trust.

MARGARET.
              What have you done?
This is but madness!

ARNOLD.
              Would it were; but no!
The madness leaves me when the deed is done!
The fiend deserts the temple overthrown,
And the high roof in ruins! I have barter'd,
Or striven to barter, with the enemy,
The treasure in my trust—this citadel—
My country's liberties—its strength and valor,
With my own name and honor!—

MARGARET.
              Mock me not!
These are but idle fancies.

ARNOLD.
              Truths, not fancies!
Terrible truths! The citadel is safe—
The country;—all but Arnold and his honor!
The scheme is nought—the creature, Andre, taken;
And I am lost forever to myself,
And, it may be, to thee! Forgive,—forgive me!

MARGARET.
Can this be true, Oh! God?—And Andre taken?
ARNOLD.
Yes, and I share his dread captivity,
And his most terrible fate, unless by flight,
I 'scape these toils.
MARGARET.
Have mercy on me, Heaven!
ARNOLD.
'Tis this that brings the exulting Washington;—
His cold imperious soul rejoices now,
In triumph over mine!—My wife—my child!
MARGARET.
Oh! kiss *him*, ere you fly!
ARNOLD.
I dare not! Hell,
Would stare me into madness from his face;
And every innocent smile, would seem a terror,
Speaking to my soul of guilt!—No more! no more!
One last embrace!

(*He clasps her in his arms, then pushes her from him, and departs.*)

MARGARET.
And I am desolate!
She falls forward upon the sofa, and here the scene closes. Arnold seeks his chamber for a moment, arms himself with sword and pistols, and retires, by a back door, from the dwelling. Here a horse stands ready saddled beneath a tree. He approaches the horse, when he is confronted by Randolph Peyton, with sword drawn.
PEYTON.
Thou can'st not 'scape! All avenues are closed,
Even as the one before thee. I give thee chance,
For honorable death! Draw, traitor, draw!
ARNOLD.
I cannot stay for such a let as thou!

Saying this, he suddenly draws a pistol, and shoots down his assailant.

PEYTON. (*Falling.*)
I should have known it! I have made a waste,
Of magnanimity, and been repaid,
By murder! I was warned of this before!
I should have known the coward in the traitor!
    ARNOLD.
Ha! coward! But I pray thee spare thy rage!
'Twere less for thy revenge, if, on my sword,
Thy blood were streaming now;—thy blood or mine,—
The same! I carry with me, Randolph Peyton,
A torture worse than death—than loss of life,
With all its sweet possessions! But, for coward—
Thou know'st not Arnold.

    PEYTON.
                Yet thou fly'st from death?
    ARNOLD.
I would not have mine enemy mock my fate,
Nor that cold rival, whom I still must loathe,
Look on me in my overthrow! We've stood,
Match'd evenly together in men's eyes—
    PEYTON.
Thou match'd with Washington!
    ARNOLD.
                I waive thy sneer!
Enough, he shall not see it, when my star,
Goes toppling from its summit! As for thee,—
I would not have thy blood upon my hands—
I would thy boyish rage had spared me this—
But it was written with the rest;—and still,
In vain we shun the inexorable will!

                                Exeunt Arnold.

BENEDICT ARNOLD.

PEYTON.
God's curse upon thy dark philosophy,
As upon thee!—He has slain me, as I think;
I feel as if 'twere spoken—thou must die,—
By this same bullet!—We'l, the work is done!
Would Washington were come; though not again,
To waste his warnings on my boyish passion;—
That may be spared me now! Yet, should he linger.
This traitor may escape!—He seeks the river!—
Yet will they turn their cannon on his galley,
Ere she can reach the "Vulture!" Cruel Fortune,
That shuts mine eyes upon the game, the moment
That tells me it is won! Yet, at such moment,
'Twould soothe, could I but look on *her* once more—
The Margaret that was mine—now lost forever!

The scene changes once more to the dwelling. Washington, attended by Luzerne, Hamilton, Livingston, Varick, Franks and others, enter the house, and at once scatter themselves over the apartments. Washington passes into the dining room. Shot heard without.

WASHINGTON.
He has escaped! That shot! Pursue him quickly.

Clamors are heard above, and in the chamber; voices and hurrying footsteps. Suddenly, Margaret rushes into the room, and places herself between Washington and the entrance.

MARGARET.
You shall not?

WASHINGTON.
              Where is your husband, Lady?

MARGARET.
In my heart!

WASHINGTON.
           We cannot pluck him thence!

MARGARET.
You shall not! He is gone—gone hence—far gone;

WASHINGTON.
We must seek him, Lady.

MARGARET.
        And wherefore would you seek him?
Ah! I know! But I'm his wife, Sir—

WASHINGTON.
        Be but calm, dear Lady.

MARGARET.
Oh! you are very merciful! You would spare
The husband whom you have not;—yet will slay
The woman through her terrors!—He is fled,
By this, in safety.

WASHINGTON.
        Suffer me to pass.

MARGARET.
What! will your bitter hatred stick at nothing?
Would'st kill the father in the child? Go forward,
With arm'd heel, above the infant's cradle,
And, flinging down these barrier arms of woman,
Which even the murderous savage would forbear,
Show to the world how merciless you are,
When jealous rage and measureless ambition,
Urge you to crime? I know you, Washington,
My husband's life-long enemy and rival.

WASHINGTON.
Nay, Lady, but 'tis plain you know me not!—
Let me go forward.
MARGARET.
Only o'er my corse!
WASHINGTON. (*Seeks to put her aside.*)
Each moment lost!
MARGARET.
(*Aside.*) Is a life-gain to Arnold! (*Struggling.*)
Is this your manhood? To assault a woman?
This is no gentleness—no courtesy!—
It is not noble of you! Oh! Sir, think,—
What matters it to you this life you seek,
That never more will cross your path to power,
Or rival you in fame!
WASHINGTON.
      You wrong me, Lady;
I'm not the man you think me—know no rival—
Contend with none for fame!—But do my duty!
I pity you, madam, this sorrow.
MARGARET.
      Spare *him* then;
Pursue not!
WASHINGTON.
    I should be guilty as I dare not be,
To listen to your pleadings. (*Ex. Washington.*)
MARGARET.
     Stern, cold man!—
But I will follow in this fell pursuit,
And share the peril which they threaten him!
I have delayed them something! I can more!
Oh! Arnold, wherefore hast thou set at hazard
The dearest gifts of life—the holiest treasures,—
Thy fame—thy child—thy wife! Oh! Why? why? why?

The scene which follows is the same as in the encounter between Arnold and Randolph Peyton, in the rear of the building, and on the edge of the grounds and wood. Washington and his companions are grouped about the dying man. Peyton is mortally wounded. Washington supports his head tenderly.

WASHINGTON.
Dost know me, Randolph?
PEYTON.
    As the great, good man,
To whom my youth owes all I know of worth,
My manhood of performance. Father, friend,
I feel that I am dying! My young life,
Is ebbing fast, and whatsoe'er my hopes,
Of struggle and achievement, are at end!
Not vainly, as I trust, my toils were taken,
For thee and for our country! I have err'd,
Or this had never happ'd! But, for *her* sake
I strove to slay the fugitive, her husband;
To save him from the life-dishonoring fate.
He lack'd the nobleness of soul to meet me,
And to my sword opposed the sudden bullet.
I should have known him better.
  WASHINGTON.
     Sad mistake!
Yet can I not reproach you. It was noble
And worthy of a heart, that, generous still,
Deserved more generous fortune. Oh! my son,
Your moments now are brief—and nicely measured,
By the assured and visible hand of Death.
Commend yourself to God!
  PEYTON.
    I am in his hands;
Hopeless, but from his mercy!—Yet, one word—
Have I done well, my father, and my friend?—
  WASHINGTON.
Well hast thou done, my son!

BENEDICT ARNOLD.

PEYTON.
        I'm satisfied!
Thy words of approbation—Ha! I hear!
It is *her* voice.
  MARGARET. (*Without, and entering.*)
     Where is he? My husband!
Ye have not slain him! Tell me—where is he?

The circle opens as she appears. She rushes in, and suddenly recoils, clasping her hands.

MARGARET.
Peyton! Thou!
PEYTON.
    I am dying, Margaret!
MARGARET.
My God! Have mercy!
PEYTON.
      In a few moments,
And I will pass into thy memory,
In passing from thy sight. Go to thy child—
Thou hast one, it is told me. I bequeath it,
The dying kiss of one who would have been—

He falters: a slight convulsion passes over his features. She falls on her knees beside him.

MARGARET.
Oh! Peyton, look on me! Unclose those eyes!—
Speak, tell me, sirs:—Oh! surely, 'tis not death!
                    (*Cannon heard.*)
  PEYTON. (*Starts from his swoon.*)
Hark! 'tis the cannon!—If they train it well,
He cannot reach the 'Vulture.' Hark! again! (*Cannon.*)
How—silent—and how sudden—grows the night!
Friend—father—Margaret; do not let me lose you!

He makes an effort to rise to Margaret—lifts his arms, as if to embrace her, falls back and dies in the effort.

WASHINGTON. (*Fervently,*)
To the good God, my son!
MARGARET.
He sleeps, Sir, now.
WASHINGTON.
Lady, it is the awful sleep of Death!
MARGARET. (*Shrieks.*)
Oh! do not say it in that terrible voice,
Or I must think it true! 'Tis only sleep,
   if we straight remove him to the house,
And send for—
WASHINGTON.
It is death, Lady!
MARGARET.
Have mercy, heaven!
WASHINGTON.
Amen!—My brave and noble boy! My son! my son!

Washington turns away and covers his eyes. Margaret takes Peyton's hands tremblingly into her own and hangs over the body. Cannon again heard,—and, suddenly, a voice from without cries aloud—

Voices without.
He has escaped! The boat has gained the 'Vulture.'
LAFAYETTE.
What men are these who come?
VARICK.
It is the guard—
They bring with them the spy.
WASHINGTON.
John Andre.
ANDRE. (*Entering with guard.*)
Here!
MARGARET. (*Starting up with a shriek.*)
Ha! take him hence! Let me not look upon him!

'Tis he hath done all this;—orphan'd my child,
And made the mother widow'd and distraught!
MARGARET.
Thou dost not say he dies?
WASHINGTON.
     Within the hour!
The flight of his accomplice seals his doom!
ANDRE.
Hear you that, Margaret! Should not this atone
The error, which, amid the ruin it makes,
Lays down the actor's life!
 MARGARET. (*Wildly.*)
   Oh! spare him! Spare him!
 WASHINGTON.
I may not, Lady!—Bear him to the tree. (*To guard.*)
'Tis need that crime so bold, and Treachery,
Reckless alike of penalty and Faith,
Should meet prompt doom and terrible infliction;
So that the virtue, halting on the threshhold,
May gain new strength, in keeping honest purpose,
By timely sense of fear!—Away with him!
 ANDRE.
I am prepared for this—prepared for Death,
And trust to meet its terrors like a man,
But it should be a man's death, not a dog's!
Oh! Sir, I pray you, be magnanimous;—
Let not the accurs'd rope defile this neck,
But, be the stroke that severs me from being,
Such as becomes the soldier—sword or shot—
It matters little—I'll confront them bravely,
With open brow and breast;—but I should falter,
To face the dishonoring gibbet.
 WASHINGTON.
     It must be so!—
The soldier's death is due the soldier's action;—
The gibbet for the spy! Your death is nothing;

But the example of your punishment,
To those who seek a nation's desolation,
By stealth, by serpent-like intrigue and cunning,
Is due, as a becoming spectacle,
With all its hideous aspects, made as fearful,
As, in just limits of humanity,
Humanity can make them!
   ANDRE.
          I am answered!
   MARGARET.
Have mercy, Sir; have mercy!
   WASHINGTON.
          I could weep
Over this wretched, dark necessity,
But, with this cruel spectacle before me,
The brave man murdered in his country's service,—
The great man taught to stain his former greatness,—
The babe dishonor'd and the wife deserted,
And all by base and traitor subtlety,—
The tears of pity freeze upon my cheek,
And justice claims her victim! Hence with him!
   ANDRE.
Margaret!
   MARGARET.
Who speaks?
   ANDRE.
      'Tis Andre!—One last word!
   MARGARET.
I know not if mine ears can hear your voice;
Or my brain take the sense of what you speak—
Yet speak!
   ANDRE.
      Am I forgiven?
   MARGARET.
         As surely as my trust,
Looks to Heaven for mercy for myself.
   ANDRE.
Farewell.   *(Soldiers lead him out.)*

BENEDICT ARNOLD.

Margaret.
   He goes to death! Oh! God! oh! God!
Will no one lead me where I may lie down,
And rest, and sleep? I am so very weary!
    She sinks down upon Peyton's body.

Washington.
Assist her gently from the ground—she swoons;
Far happier in this deep unconsciousness,
Than in to-morrow's waking. For this boy,
The noble son of a most noble sire,—
The best friend of my youth and happiest manhood—
Bear him without, that proper funeral rites,
May consecrate his burial to his people.
This is a mournful tragedy, my friends—
This goodly household wreck'd—a noble fame,
Polluted with such utter infamy;
And for the other, now beneath our doom,
The ignominous rope, and mocking scaffold!
'Tis something we may meditate with profit,
With due misgivings of ourselves and strength,
To make us question our security,
Whatever be our state! The issue here,
Hath one redeemng virtue in its evils,
In that it saves the country—gives us courage.
To prosecute our struggle to the last!
This baffled treason shows the British power,
Unequal to the conflict—shows the knowledge
Of its own weakness; which, by base devices,
Would make repair of what it lacks in might!
Thus may our griefs, upon this mournful threshhold,
Still find some healing in this fond conviction,
That, through the storm, triumphant like our Eagle,
Untouch'd by mortal shaft, our country goes,
Sailing supreme, serene, 'neath skies serene,
With a great destiny of good before her!

 The body of Randolph Peyton is borne out, by the soldiers on a litter, Washington and the rest following in a march, to slow and solemn music.

And here ends our rough hewn tragedy. It is perhaps proper to remind the reader that, while the absolute and vital facts of history have been altered, the events have been greatly condensed in the drama. For example: Andre had a regular trial before a court of general officers. The deliberations of law were made to operate so as to occasion much delay— one object of this delay being to allow of certain negotiations by which the Americans proposed to save Andre by recovering Arnold. They would cheerfully have spared the one, could the other have been made to take his place upon the scaffold. During this delay, a secret and audacious effort was made to capture Arnold, before the execution of Andre, the attempt resulting in the romantic episode of Lt. Champe, of Lee's Legion. But, for this narrative, the reader must look elsewhere. In ignoring this court and its decision, and conferring upon Washington the powers of a Dictator, who decrees, according to his own will, the Dramatist makes a great gain, in affecting the rapid progress of events before the eyes of the spectator. The interest might be heightened in this place, and at the close of the scene, by the tolling of a bell, by the roll of muffled drums without, and the final discharge of a heavy cannon, when Washington, or some other of the parties upon the stage, might be made to utter some simple ejaculation of solemn import, implying that the execution of Andre was over; at the same time, to heighten the effect, the scream, or cry of a woman, or of women, might be heard within—a sudden, piercing shriek, which the audience would ascribe to Margaret. All these things might be devised by the manager of a theatre, with regard to stage effects. If the author has any theatrical experience, he will conceive them. But a manager ought to be able to suggest them. Snakspeare's experience, as actor and manager, gave him great advantages as a dramatist. They taught him the secret of scenic effects. Goethe, at Weimar, was equally fortunate, in the situation of manager. Indeed, one of the greatest secrets of success, in theatrical management, would be the possession of a Poet, who is at once capable of the picturesque, and is a man of experience and sound common sense. Unfortunately, most.

managers in this country—that I have known—have been singularly illiterate, conceited and obstinate. The late Mr. Burton, an Englishman, who was very successful as a manager, was a well-educated man, a good actor, a man of letters; and hence his successful management. Such a manager, as in the case of Shakspeare, can, by a little judicious attention, make a piece successful, which, as originally written, has proved a failure. That Shakspeare thus employed himself upon old pieces, is beyond doubt or question. Even the piece which I have here concluded, might, I think, be adapted for the stage, by judicious abridgments, here and there; by the interposition of minor scenes, possessing briskness of movement; and, possibly, by the *graffing* upon it, of some secondary, or minor plot, which will introduce new characters.— Had I not been anxious to concentrate all the interest upon the chief persons of the drama, I should have brought in one or more females, keeping them subordinates, but working in an episode, or minor story, to run, *pari passu*, with the chief story, and occasionally to affect, in some degree, its progress. The last act of this drama possesses action enough for the stage, and needs little in the way of abridgment, or from the lack of accessories.

Having already sufficiently premised my design, and the perhaps erroneous judgment under which the plot was first conceived—having also avowed the purpose of the present publication, for the benefit of future playwrights, and that the piece may become a beacon, rather than a guide,—I shall need to make no farther apologies. What is said in our chronicles, of the treachery of Arnold and the proposed surrender of West Point and the army, is as closely adhered to in this drama, as dramatic writing will admit. The variations are such only as were needed to ennoble the subject into tragic dignity, and, somewhat, though not in the alteration of any final facts, to increase its dramatic efforts. Something, indeed, has been here and there suppressed, but not to such an extent as to impair the value of the record, or to place it beyond the judgment of the reader; and, in the original *graffings* made upon the record, in no instance, do I think, have I exceeded the privileges of dramatic art.

With regard to Andre, it has been seen, in the *proem* to the drama, that I have been disposed to take a very different view of his career and character, than it has been the habit of the critic and historian hitherto to do. He has, in all previous histories, and works of fiction, been employed as the *foil* of Arnold; and, in proportion as the latter has been made infamous, so the virtues of the former have been exaggerated, while every effort of art has been employed to work upon the popular sympathies in his behalf. In this way, a great deal of mawkish sentiment has been expended upon his memory, and the sentiment has been as much misapplied as it was mawkish. Arnold, surrendered as a victim, to the unmitigated scorn and loathing of the world, seems to have absorbed all its censures; yet none now will venture to deny that Andre perished justly, as a participator in his crimes. That Arnold did not share his fate, was not in consequence of human partiality or injustice. His fate reserved him for a worse penalty in the stereotyped infamy of his name, and the perpetual record of his treason. The moral of Andre, as a gentleman, may be better than that of Arnold, but he merits our sympathy just as little. It is enough that he shared in the crime of Arnold; that he contributed to his temptation, and, in this aspect, was a still greater criminal. It will not be necessary to remind the reader of hints previously given, in this essay, that the offence of Andre, in the case of Arnold, was not the first. The proof goes to show that he had been employed as a spy of Clinton on previous occasions. These proofs I have published elsewhere.

— In relation to his alleged passion for Mrs. Arnold, I have but to say that the hint is drawn partly from the popular scandal of the time, and partly from her intimacy with him before, and after marriage—an intimacy distinguished by a private correspondence between the parties, under which it seems that Arnold sheltered his first treasonable approaches to the enemy. I have endeavored, however, while acknowledging her attachment to Andre, to relieve it from all censure, and to lift it into respect, by the purity of her sentiment and the propriety of her course. A severe and scrutinizing judgment, however, would probably decide that she was a young woman of much levity—light and frivolous—of not much character anyway—doubtless, sympathizing with the British along with her family, and most likely to have been privy to the treacheries of her husband. In our times, she would probably be rated as a *'fast woman'*—one of those smart young creatures, with just cleverness enough to be audacious, and to pride themselves upon their mental and social independence, at the frequent sacrifice of the proprieties of both.

The character of Randolph Peyton is, of course, pure fiction; so, indeed, is that of Thurston. These, indeed, are the only ideals drawn in the piece; both are types; the one of youthful chivalry; the other of habitual and tenacious loyalty—grown, from habit, into doggedness, which forbids the exercise of any faculty except in slavish obedience to the prevailing will; and thus becomes monomania—though not of an exaggerated type.

For the plan and conduct of the piece, I shall say no more. It is yielded to its fate. I probably see, quite as clearly as any other critic, the objections that may be urged against it. Were I to choose the subject *anew*, I should make many changes; and under the *present* aspect of affairs—with the Revolutionary History grown so much more distant than when this was written, nearly forty years ago—with the present trying and terrible issues tending to make the old chronicles still more obscure,—I should take greater liberties with the subject, and become more bold in the introduction of incidents, which would tend to a great increase of dramatical situations and effects. But, on this head the reader is referred to the earlier portions of this essay.

But, if this skeleton drama fails in this department of art, it seems to me to be quite suggestive of the general susceptibilities of the subject for *prose fiction*. The privileges of the Novelist are far greater than those of the Dramatist. The action is not addressed to the eye, and those portions which can make no show upon the stage, may be yet made singularly attractive in the closet. The drama admits of little narrative. The novel requires considerable narrrative; details of history, and nice questions may be discussed through this medium, and the greater space allowed to the novelist, will enable him to compass greater numbers of persons, and varieties of character. How finely, in this greater space, could the anomalous character of Arnold be elaborated. How easily, and with what interesting exhibitions of the moods and passions, could his gradual progresses, to crime and treason, be made to appear under the seductions of some wily tempter like John Thurston. What a touching history of caprice on the one hand, and disappointment and defeated love on the other, might be developed in the intercourse of Margaret Shippen and Randolph Peyton—she, the *belle*, the coquette, with a generous and true heart, but with vanities awakened, and judgment perverted, under the flattering ministeries of the accomplished John Andre, and a crowd of gallant gay Lotharios in the British army. What excellent matter for gorgeous chapters, are to be found in the scenes of the far-famed *Meschianza*;—and, in the delineation of individual portraits, in addition to those of Andre,—are those of Washington, Lee, Lafayette, Greene, Hamilton, Steuben, De Kalb, and others, of the American side, with those of Howe, Clinton, Cornwallis, Rawdon, and others, of the British. Nor would there be any lack of scenes of great vivacity and striking event. The invasion of Canada; the battle of Saratoga; the approaches of the British to Philadelphia; their expulsion from it; the affair of Germantown; the several exploits of the rival legions of Lee and Simco, the interesting episode of Lt. Champe; the occasional popular outbreaks in Philadelphia;—these constitute a body of available material, in using which, the artist in Prose Fiction would only need to select and discriminate. Then, if his attributes include the descriptive faculty, there is the scenery of the Schuylkill and the Hudson; the picturesque beauties of West Point and other places, which the progresses of the parties must cover. The very flight of Andre, from West Point towards New York—the fluctuations of his fears and feelings; the caprices of his fate;—his tremour, as he traverses the neutral ground;—its dreary wastes, crowded by imagination with visions of cowboys and skunies, rebels and rumagates, that haunt his footsteps, and admonish him momently of his fate. We see the admirable uses made, of the very sort of material, by Mr. Cooper in his admirable romance of "The Spy." It is matter of surprise to me that this powerful writer never chose the subject of Andre for his theme. He probably would have done so, had his success been greater in "Lionel Lincoln." The, subject was properly his own, and with his equal knowledge of the scenery and events, I have no doubt that he would have have succeeded, in his mature years, not only in redeeming his failure in "Lionel Lincoln," but in achieving one of those masterpieces of fiction which the world would not willingly let die. Nor could any writer have done better than himself, in the *moral* delineations of such a subject—the biographical as well as the passionate—those great self-struggles in Arnold's own bosom—assuming him to have possessed the most ordinary human sensibilities,—before and while yielding to the tempter—the touching scene—mixed madness and tenderness—in which he reveals his treachery to his wife—the panic in which he flies—the melancholy bonds of Andre—the attempts to retake the fugitive, and the terrible catastrophe. The body of material thus suggested, all suited to the use of *prose fiction*, is as various, ample and admirable, as is ever found in the pages of Romance.

www.ingramcontent.com/pod-product-compliance
Lightning Source LLC
Chambersburg PA
CBHW022102290426
44112CB00008B/515